P9-DJK-977

WITHOUT RESERVATION

WITHOUT RESERVATION

■

THE MAKING OF AMERICA'S MOST POWERFUL INDIAN TRIBE AND FOXWOODS, THE WORLD'S LARGEST CASINO

JEFF BENEDICT

HarperCollins*Publishers*

HarperCollins books may be purchased for educational, business, or sales promotional use. For information please write: Special Markets Department, HarperCollins Publishers Inc., 10 East 53rd Street, New York, NY 10022.

FIRST EDITION

Printed on acid-free paper

Designed by Jackie McKee

Library of Congress Cataloging-in-Publication Data

Benedict, Jeff.

Without reservation : the making of America's most powerful Indian tribe and Foxwoods, the world's largest casino / Jeff Benedict.—1st ed.

p. cm.

Includes index.

ISBN 0-06-019367-0 (alk. paper)

1. Pequot Indians—Gambling. 2. Gambling on Indian reservations—Connecticut. 3. Casinos—Connecticut. 4. Pequot Indians—Government relations. 5. Pequot Indians—Economic conditions. I. Title.

E99.P53 B45 2000
338.4'7795'09746—dc21 00-024479

00 01 02 03 04 ❖/RRD 10 9 8 7 6 5 4 3 2

To Merle, whose courage I desire,
and Josephine, whose inner beauty I adore,
and Harriet, who never forgot me,
and Newt, whom I will never forget—
this one's for you

CONTENTS

1

OATHS AND VOWS

TOWN HALL

JUNE 13, 1969
GROTON, CONNECTICUT

"THE FIRST THING YOU NEED TO DO IS FILL OUT THIS WORKSHEET," SAID town clerk Sally Sawyer, handing a blank form across the counter. "After completing it, you give it back to me and I'll type up your marriage license."

Twenty-one-year-old Richard "Skip" Hayward coolly wrote his biographical information under the column labeled "Groom." Looking over his arm, seventeen-year-old fiancée Aline Champoux twirled one of her pigtails. Her long strands of brunette hair dangled over the front of her shoulders and sprawled over her chest. Her thin, nicely shaped legs beneath her miniskirt showed off her early summer tan, her sleeveless halter top drawing attention to her youthful, 108-pound figure.

"You are Aline's mother?" Sawyer asked, turning to fifty-year-old Betty Champoux, who stood behind Aline wearing a conservative red-and-white-checked summer blouse.

"Yes," said Mrs. Champoux, her mind preoccupied. Days earlier her husband, Leo, a lifelong smoker, had been admitted to a Veterans Hospital in Rhode Island where he was diagnosed with lung cancer. His life expectancy was less than one year.

"When they're finished filling out their portion of the form," Sawyer continued, struggling to make eye contact with Betty, "you'll need to sign the back, granting your permission for your daughter to marry as a minor."

Betty affirmatively nodded her head in silence. Both she and Leo had complained to Aline that she was too young and Hayward too financially undisciplined for marriage. But the onset of terminal cancer had sapped any strength they possessed to fight Aline over her choice for a husband. Nor would it have done any good. She had fallen hard for Hayward the moment she met him, while on a blind date during her sophomore year.

It was early in 1967 when Champoux, then fifteen, told her parents that she and her best friend, Debbie Sherwood, were going to the Friday night basketball game at their high school in Coventry, Rhode Island. Instead, they sneaked off to Ledyard, Connecticut, nearly a forty-five-minute drive away, to meet Sherwood's boyfriend, Fran Pyle. When they arrived at Fran's house, he introduced Sherwood and Champoux to his best friend, Skip Hayward, a strapping, six-foot two-inch nineteen-year-old with broad shoulders. Aline immediately noticed his brown eyes and wavy black hair that hung over the collar of his button-down red shirt with yellow polka dots. His blue jeans were held up by a black leather belt, the buckle situated off to the side of his thin waist. Aline thought he looked like Jim Morrison.

When Pyle and Hayward invited the girls dancing, they eagerly accepted. By the end of the night, Champoux had agreed to be Hayward's girlfriend. For a young Champoux, he had the qualities she responded to. He was a great dancer. He loved rock and roll, although his favorite singer was Johnny Cash. He owned a Honda motorcycle and his own horse.

"Here, Aline," Hayward said, handing her the worksheet. "You need to complete your half."

Smirking, Champoux filled in the column under the word "Bride" and handed it back to Sawyer, who reviewed it for completeness.

Groom's Name: Richard Arthur Hayward.

Date of Birth: 11–28–47.

Age: 21.

Race: White.

Occupation: Pipefitter.

Birthplace: New London, Conn.

Residence: North Stonington, Conn.

"Everything looks good there," Sawyer said, reading on.

Bride's Name: Aline Aurore Champoux.

Date of Birth: 11–22–51.

Age: 17.

Race: White.

"Oh, Ms. Champoux, you forgot to fill in line 14," Sawyer said, pointing to the heading "occupation."

"I don't work yet," she said sheepishly. "I just graduated from high school yesterday."

"Oh, well, I'll just put 'student' there," Sawyer said. "Now if you'll wait just a minute, I'll be back with your license."

Hayward reached for Champoux's right hand, smiling confidently as he clenched it tightly while waiting for Sawyer to return. Resting her head against his arm, Aline stared down at the engagement ring on her other hand. Hayward had never formally asked her to marry him. Instead, one day he took her on the back of his motorcycle to Zales, a department store that sold jewelry, and paid $100 for a tiny diamond. It was all that he could afford on his meager salary as an apprentice at the Electric Boat division of General Dynamics. He had not attended college and had no career plans. To cut down on wedding costs, Aline sewed her own dress by hand. No wedding announcements were ordered. Instead of a reception, they planned a breakfast with their immediate family.

"Look over the license and make sure that everything is correct as typed," Sawyer said, handing it to Hayward.

Saying nothing, he scanned it, then gave it back.

"Everything is correct?" Sawyer asked.

Hayward nodded.

"OK. Each of you raise your right hand," Sawyer instructed.

Tentative, Aline looked up at Skip, whose eyes were focused on Sawyer's. Wide-eyed, Aline faintly raised her hand, her fingertips barely reaching Skip's shoulder.

"Do you both solemnly swear that the information contained in this license is true and correct to the best of your knowledge, so help you God?"

"Yes," Skip said, his raspy voice drowning out Aline's soft whisper.

"Now, you both need to sign the license right here," said Sawyer, pointing to blank lines beneath their typed names.

Betty looked on in stone silence as Aline signed her name below Skip's. She was too numb to cry. She was losing her husband to a disease with no cure and her teenage daughter to a man with seemingly no future.

Sawyer signed the license and stamped it with the town seal. Folding it, she placed it into a white self-addressed envelope and handed it to Skip. "You give this to the person who is going to be performing the ceremony. And it is that person's responsibility to return the license to us after the wedding."

DAYS LATER
CALAIS, MAINE

It had been a long drive from Washington, D.C., but Tom Tureen felt exhilaration, not weariness. With the Beatles' *Sergeant Pepper* playing on his eight-track tape deck, twenty-five-year-old Tureen, fresh out of law school, edged his green Volvo station wagon along Main Street. He passed stores, banks, and bars until finally, across from the Mobil gas station, he found building number 173. At street level was the Halfway Outlet, a discount clothing store, and upstairs would be the office for the Indian Legal Services Unit. He would be opening his practice here, in the unlikely town of Calais, Maine.

Located at the northeast tip of the United States, across the St. Croix River from Canada, Calais had just four thousand residents. They lived in the second poorest county east of the Mississippi, putting bread on the table by fishing and logging. Then there were the Indians, over fifteen hundred of them from the Passamaquoddy tribe, who wallowed in extreme poverty on a vast wilderness reservation outside town.

Tureen always figured his career as an attorney would begin in a place like this. All through law school Tureen had his sights set on one overriding goal: helping impoverished Native Americans. There was no poorer Indian tribe in the country in 1969 than the Passamaquoddy of Maine, whose per-capita income was $400 annually. Seventy-five percent of the tribe was unemployed and more than half were on welfare. Tureen was determined to change that.

Many well-intentioned legal careers begin like Tureen's. Law school teaches students how justice may not be so impartial when it comes to the poor and the disenfranchised. Some law students vow to right society's wrongs and champion the downtrodden. Eventually, though, these high ideals are eclipsed by cold practicality: There's a lot more money to be made representing clients who have it than those who do not.

Tureen, however, was not led to law school by ideals but by the voices of children—Indian children. Before his senior year of college at Princeton, he took a summer job teaching at a boarding school in South Dakota run by the federal government's Bureau of Indian Affairs. All two hundred students were Indian children, predominantly Sioux, between ages eight and fifteen.

Shortly after arriving, Tureen observed one ten-year-old boy say to another boy who was sneaking extra food from the cafeteria lunch line, "Don't do that. You'll get cracks."

Puzzled, Tureen stepped toward the two boys. "What does 'cracks' mean?" Tureen asked.

The boys nervously looked away and scurried off silently, the tattered bottoms on their secondhand pants dragging under the soles of their worn-out leather shoes.

Over the course of the next couple weeks Tureen would hear the expression "cracks" time and again, but none of the children would tell him what it meant. Tureen ultimately figured it out for himself. One of the school's physical education instructors, an intimidating man in his thirties, carried a small wooden baton on his belt. Although he never witnessed the man use the baton, he observed how the children became fearfully quiet and still whenever he was around. Tureen was eventually told by the other instructors at the school that children would be beaten with the baton for any number of reasons, including taking extra food from the lunch line, failing to follow instructions, or speaking in their native tongue. Tribal languages were strictly forbidden. The rule that bothered Tureen most was the government's policy that the children, once placed at the school, could not return home for visits. Their families, too poor to travel to the school, were deemed dysfunctional by the government.

"This is more like a detainment center than a school," thought Tureen.

Tureen abruptly came face-to-face with brutal social injustice. It was a face he did not recognize, having been raised in a prestigious St. Louis suburb, where he attended private schools and tagged along with his mother to the country club.

He left South Dakota determined to change what he saw. Upon returning to Princeton in September, Tureen abandoned his plans to become a college professor specializing in the romantic poets. He decided instead to become a lawyer. "The Indian problem is basically political, and therefore legal," he reasoned. "It is one of rights and relationships. And I'm going to do something to change the way Indians are treated in this country."

Tureen completed his degree in English at Princeton and entered George Washington University Law School in the fall of 1966. Shortly after enrolling, he accepted a forty-hour-per-week job working at Edgar Cahn's Citizens' Advocate Center, a Washington-based welfare-rights advocacy group that represented the interests of poor people receiving federal assistance. Through lobbying and public-awareness campaigns, the center was a major force behind the enactment of the Food Stamp Act. Tureen also did some volunteer work for Ralph Nader assisting Native Americans.

During law school, Tureen married Susan Albright, a college student studying to become an elementary-school teacher. They had met while he was at Princeton, and she was attending Sarah Lawrence, a private school in New York. Their honeymoon was spent doing field research for a book Tureen was helping Edgar Cahn write, entitled *Our Brother's Keeper: The Indian in White America*, an exposé on the Bureau of Indian Affairs. Tureen and Albright spent a summer driving across the country on a whirlwind trip visiting Indian reservations. Unable to afford a motel, they spent their nights sleeping in the back of Tureen's Volvo. By the end of the summer they had set foot on dozens of the reservations throughout the United States.

Tureen also spent one summer during law school clerking in Maine for a lawyer whose clients included the Passamaquoddy Indians. Tureen became a friend to tribal governor John Stevens. Unlike many of the members of his tribe, Stevens had spent time off of the reservation; he had availed himself of educational and employment opportunities and had served in Korea for the U.S. Army. He became active politically, the state of Maine appointing him state commissioner of Indian Affairs.

Before the summer was over, Tureen was working almost exclusively for the Passamaquoddy. For Tureen the work was gratifying. For Stevens, he had never seen a non-Indian work so hard for Indians, and do it for free.

When Tureen's volunteer legal work was done, Stevens appealed to Tureen to come work for his tribe full-time after law school. Given the right opportunity, Tureen knew he would return. And sure enough, before the end of his third year of law school Tureen received a call from Pine Tree Legal Assistance. It was a state-run agency in Maine that provided legal counsel for poor people. On Stevens's recommendation, the agency offered Tureen $9,000 a year to take over the Indian Legal Services Unit in Calais. He accepted the agency's offer immediately and left D.C. as soon as he completed final exams, even forgoing the graduation ceremony.

A steep, dilapidated staircase led to the second floor above the Halfway Outlet. The law office was cavernous and sparsely furnished. There were four old IBM electric typewriters, some mismatched tables and chairs that had been donated, and one large metal desk with a swivel chair behind it. During winter, the one working radiator behind the desk rattled so badly that the front casing often came loose. But Tureen wasn't complaining—at least there was running water in the office bathroom. That was more than could be said for the small apartment he and his wife rented. The kitchen had a wood stove, but no hot water. And the bathroom held only a toilet. They had to bathe and wash their clothes in the lake that bordered the property. On weekends they drove across the Canadian border to a hotel in St. Andrews for hot showers.

The first thing Tureen did when he got to Calais was raise nearly $10,000 in grant money to buy the hundreds of law books sitting on the shelves of his new office. They belonged to his predecessor, who had left the post after his arrest and subsequent conviction for possession of marijuana. The books would be invaluable tools in achieving Tureen's objectives. Rather than travel to the federal law library in Portland, Tureen needed simply to take a few strides to research federal codes, state statutes, and Supreme Court decisions.

Tureen did not necessarily require the expensive law books to perform his duties. The state had only asked him to represent the tribe in civil cases—divorce proceedings, satisfying outstanding debts, and minor misdemeanors. But Tureen did not relocate to one of the poorest parts of the country to work on divorces and petty crimes. He went to make the Passamaquoddy a sovereign Indian nation with the power to control its own affairs on the reservation. Unlike the tribes Tureen had visited in the West, the Passamaquoddy did not govern their own land—the state did. Maine even imposed its state game laws, restricting the tribe's ability to hunt and fish on the reservation. In Tureen's view, these laws designed to regulate big-game hunters and sport fishermen infringed on the tribe's culture and severely limited its ability to sustain itself. Hunting and fishing were the only sources of income on the reservation. Further, the state was doing little to deter area residents from trespassing on tribal land, allowing recreational use and even the logging of the tribe's rich forest land.

Tureen not only wanted to reverse these problems, he wanted to help the tribe become financially wealthy. But the suggestion that the poorest Indians in North America could become rich sounded so absurd that even Stevens laughed. Tureen was not joking, however. The Passamaquoddy already possessed the surest ticket to wealth in America—real estate, and lots of it. The tribe lived on seventeen thousand acres. Better still, federal Indian land—even in the late 1960s—was typically free of local environmental regulations and zoning laws, as well as from state sales tax and local property taxes. It was a capitalist's dream come true—large, undeveloped tracts of land that were exempt from government regulation. A business enterprise could thrive under these conditions. The only problem was that the Passamaquoddy reservation was under state regulation, a situation Tureen knew he had to try and change.

JUNE 25, 1969

Aline's long hair flowed out from under her white veil; her handmade wedding dress, which hugged her tiny waist, did not have a wrinkle. Fresh out of the box, her white shoes with narrow straps showed off her tanned bare feet. Giddy, she stood beside Skip at the front of the Church of God, a Pentecostal church that he had convinced her to join four months earlier.

Wearing the same Hush Puppies shoes and gray suit with a white shirt and blue tie that he had worn to Aline's graduation, Skip looked over his shoulder. The chapel pews were empty except for the first row. Aline's father, who had managed to get out of the hospital to be present for his daughter's wedding, sat next to Betty on one side of the aisle. Across from them sat Skip's mother, Theresa, his aunt Libby, and his two little brothers, six-year-old Rodney and five-year-old Robert. Skip's father, Richard Hayward Sr., and Skip's six younger sisters did not attend. The family had just moved to Maryland, where Skip's father was from, and they did not make the trip back for the wedding. Skip did not care; he and his father were not particularly close.

No other relatives were invited. There was no organist, no flowers, and no rice waiting to be thrown when the newlyweds emerged from the chapel. His best friend, Fran Pyle, and Aline's best friend, Debbie, had eloped and moved to Montana. Skip's only other friends were people he knew from church, and they were more like acquaintances. He asked church pastor Earle Cushman to be his best man. He asked his co-worker Kingdon Collins, also a licensed minister, to perform the marriage.

Skip had always been a social outsider. His father, a career navy man, was transferred so often that none of Skip's eight siblings shared the same birthplace. They were born in navy towns across the country, from Camp LeJeune, North Carolina, to New London, Connecticut; from Newport Beach to Long Beach, California; from Long Island, New York, back to North Carolina, this time Cherry Point; and then, finally, North Kingston, Rhode Island.

Skip never lived anywhere long enough to develop lasting friendships. By his senior year of high school in North Kingston, Rhode Island, he had become a cipher, managing to get through the first three years of high school without his name or picture appearing in the yearbook. The caption under his senior photo read simply, " 'Skipper'—Plans to attend Naval Training School."

But he was not sincere about following in his dad's footsteps. Skip was much closer to his mother and siblings. They bonded during their almost annual change in neighborhoods and school systems, often seeing little of their father when he had sea duty. In his father's absence, Skip was a surrogate father to the family, earning their admiration and respect.

Aline did not mind that Skip had virtually no friends. She had few friends too, having ignored her high school classmates since her sophomore year when she met Skip. From that time forward she wanted one thing: a large family and nice home that she and Skip could raise them in. Her favorite picture was one of Skip's family that she carried in her purse. It was taken during one of the first visits she made to Skip's parents' house. In the photo, Skip's younger brothers, one wearing a cowboy hat and the other a cardigan sweater that matched his dusty blond hair, are kneeling down and laughing. Next to them, Aline is huddled with Skip's sisters, their broad smiles displaying their straight, shiny white teeth. The Haywards' tidy, comfortable family room provided the background. And the ideal.

"Richard Hayward," Reverend Collins said, a large, wooden cross mounted to the wall behind him, "in taking this woman you hold by your right hand to be your lawful and wedded wife, before God and these witnesses present, you must promise to love her, to honor and cherish her in that relation, and leaving all others cleave only unto her."

Proud, Skip grinned at Aline.

"Do you promise to be to her in all things a true and faithful husband so long as you both shall live?"

"I do," he said.

Collins turned to Aline and began reading the words of the vow to her. Her eyes never left Skip's. Her mind never focused on Collins's words.

"I do," she said at the appropriate time.

Skip calmly slid the size four-and-a-half wedding band over Aline's ring finger.

"I pronounce you husband and wife," Collins said. "You may now kiss the bride."

Skip's mother and Aline's mother took turns taking pictures. Skip placed his hand around Aline's waist, pulling her hips close to his. His suit jacket buttoned across his slender torso, Skip quickly patted his neatly parted hair, cut short above his ears and collar.

While they smiled, neither Aline nor Skip wanted to spend much time posing for pictures. They were eager to get home and pack for their honeymoon. They planned a cross-country trip in a 1962 mobile camper to visit their friends Fran and Debbie for three and a half weeks in Kalispell, Montana. Having never been west of New York, Aline could hardly wait, viewing the trip as the first episode in an adventure in which she would forever be known as Mrs. Hayward.

Tom Tureen had decided that his first priority was to help the Passamaquoddy get the bare necessities: food, suitable housing, and health and dental care. Familiar with the welfare subsidies available to Indian tribes through the federal government, Tureen looked there first. He helped Stevens apply for some of the funds that Congress annually appropriated to assist more than five hundred of the nation's Indian tribes. But Stevens's application was promptly denied. Congress, he was told, appropriated funds only for those tribes identified on the Bureau of Indian Affairs' list of federally recognized tribes. Despite being the poorest tribe in the country, the Passamaquoddy were not on the BIA's list.

"Why not?" Tureen wondered. "It's not as if they don't exist. It's not as if they're not a tribe. They have their own separate language. They have a very high quantum of Indian blood. And they have a real Indian culture."

Tureen turned to his law books. The answer, he soon discovered, was directly related to why the state of Maine was able to get away with imposing state regulations on the Passamaquoddy's reservation.

At the end of the Revolutionary War in 1781, tribes within the thirteen colonies—such as the Passamaquoddy—entered into treaties directly with the states that grew out of those colonies. With their reservations established on state lands, any financial assistance paid to a tribe came from its respective state. These tribes had no treaty relationship with the federal government and they did not live on federal land, thereby classifying them as "independent" or "state" tribes.

In contrast, when President Thomas Jefferson completed the Louisiana Purchase in 1803, the tribes residing in the vast unsettled West began entering into treaties directly with the federal government. Tribes such as the Sioux, the Cheyenne, the Navajo, and countless others became recognized as "federal" tribes, with their reservations being established on federal territory that had yet to be carved into states. The responsibility for these tribes' welfare fell to the federal government.

The result was a two-tier system of Indian tribes—"federal" tribes in the territory west of the thirteen colonies and "state" tribes within the thirteen colonies. Under federal law, the western tribes enjoy sovereign status on their reservations. The only powers they do not have are those specifically taken away from them by Congress. For state tribes in the East, the opposite is true. They enjoy no sovereign powers on their reservations except for those specifically granted them by the states.

Stevens was beside himself when Tureen explained to him why the federal government felt it had no obligations to his tribe. After all, the Passamaquoddy had fought under General George Washington in the Revolutionary War and played a crucial role in holding off the British Navy along what is now the northern coast of Maine. Stevens told Tureen that Washington had personally signed a treaty in 1777 that promised the federal government's "perpetual protection" of the tribe in exchange for the Passamaquoddy's help against the British. The parched paper with Washington's faded signature affixed to it was in a shoebox, along with other important documents saved by the tribe. It had been passed down through generations of tribal leaders.

Encouraged by Washington's promise of federal protection, Tureen began researching Indian laws passed around the time Washington was president. And then he came across the Nonintercourse Act.

It read:

> *That no sale of lands made by any Indians, or any nation or tribe of Indians within the United States, shall be valid to any person or persons, or to any state, whether having the right of pre-emption to such lands or not, unless the same shall be made and duly executed at some public treaty, held under the authority of the United States.*

Tureen studied it carefully. "The statute says that any land sales involving Indian land are invalid unless preapproved by the federal government," Tureen thought. "Wait a minute. What about all the land the Passamaquoddy gave up?"

He knew that much of the Maine territory once belonged to the Indians. But in 1796, the state of Massachusetts, which at that time included the territory of Maine, had acquired millions of acres of tribal land in a treaty with the Passamaquoddy. But the state of Massachusetts never got approval from the federal government to purchase the Passamaquoddy's land. If the Nonintercourse Act was in effect in 1796, Massachusetts was in violation of federal law, and that meant the state of Maine was illegally in possession of millions of acres of Passamaquoddy land.

"When was this statute adopted?" Tureen said to himself as he scanned down the page with his index finger toward the small print at the bottom. There, under the heading "Legislative History," was the date of passage for the Nonintercourse Act. Too nervous to look, he covered the date with his finger before reading it. He knew the four digits under his index finger could hold the key to a jackpot.

Quickly, he pulled his finger back. "Holy shit!" he shouted, leaping up out of his chair.

The act was passed in 1790, *four years before* the Passamaquoddy treaty was signed. "I can't believe it." In rapid, short strides, he paced across his empty office, desperate to share his discovery with someone, anyone. But he was alone.

Still not believing, he read the law once more.

". . . No sale of lands made by *any* Indians . . . within the United

States shall be valid" unless approved by the federal government. The Nonintercourse Act was one of the very first laws drafted by the First Congress and signed by George Washington. The president supported the law because he believed it was the federal government's duty to protect Indians from being taken advantage of in bad real estate deals.

Tureen knew that the federal government had hardly proven to be a reliable protector of Indians' land interests. It often stripped land from the Indians and reneged on its treaties. Nonetheless, the law required states to seek federal authorization before entering into land deals with tribes. And Massachusetts had failed to do so before buying land from the Passamaquoddy. The wording of the law was plain and contained no distinction between federal and state tribes. "If this law means what it says," Tureen said out loud, as if he were arguing before a judge, "it applies to *any* nation or tribe of Indians. The federal government should have policed *all* land sales—including the Passamaquoddy land sale to Massachusetts."

That evening, as soon as he got home, he told his wife what he had found. "Well, that's interesting, Tom," she finally responded, unsure of what it all meant. "But what are you going to do about it?"

"I don't know," Tom replied.

Susan knew little about the law. But she had hit on a very fundamental truth. Some of the most brilliant legal theories have no practical application. Tureen's discovery may just have been better suited for debate in a law school classroom than it was for application in real life. Even if a federal law was violated, that violation took place when George Washington was still president. And it was the state of Massachusetts that violated the law by taking Indian land without federal approval. But all the land Massachusetts had taken from the Indians was now part of the state of Maine. So who would be liable, the state of Massachusetts or the state of Maine? In either case, thousands of residents now lived on that land, with deed and title to their property. Was it fair to hold those people responsible for a state's failure to comply with federal law over two hundred years ago? And if so, what would be the remedy? Ejecting thousands of families from their homes and returning the land to the Indians?

It was obvious to Tureen that a lawsuit aimed at returning one-third of Maine's land base to an Indian tribe would not only raise perplexing legal questions but also public outrage. That was the beauty of it—there were no easy answers. Tureen figured that when push came to shove, the state politicians would do everything in their power to avoid the risk of having a federal judge come up with solutions. A court might find that indeed the law was violated and that the Indians have a legitimate case. As unthinkable as it sounded, the fear of the unthinkable—thousands of Maine landowners having the titles to their property thrown into question—was precisely what Tureen wanted. He had learned from his association with Cahn and Nader that lawsuits are powerful devices for shaking up the status quo and forcing changes in social policy. Tureen's true target was putting the Passamaquoddy on equal footing with western tribes and entitling them to federal assistance—not taking away people's homes. But the threat of taking homes could secure the bargaining chip he needed to get the federal government to the negotiation table. And as the party with the least to lose by filing such a big lawsuit, Tureen and the tribe would have the most leverage when it sat down to negotiate a settlement. Tureen's initial investment would be limited to the court fee for filing a lawsuit: $20.

It all sounded absurd, suing to take away one-third of Maine's property. But to Tureen, it was no more absurd than European settlers driving millions of Native Americans from their homes—homes that they maintained for far more than two hundred years—and placing them on reservations.

"You're actually going to go through with this?" Susan asked.

"I was raised to believe I could do anything, that there are no limits," Tom said. "I was taught, 'Don't be afraid to think big.'"

2

QUICKSILVER

SEPTEMBER 1969
NORTH STONINGTON, CONNECTICUT

TOO TIRED TO STAND, ALINE SAT ON THE METAL MILK-BOTTLE BOX outside the doorstep to the aqua-colored, two-bedroom house she and Skip had rented. Hunched forward, she untied her laces and removed her shoes, providing instant relief to her aching feet. Days earlier she had started her first full-time job working at a nearby farm that raised chickens for research purposes. None of the eggs produced at the farm were sold, but instead were analyzed by scientists. Aline performed clerical tasks in the research office and collected eggs by the hundreds from the coops, tasks that required her to be on her feet eight hours straight. Her feet had yet to adjust.

Looking forward to some down time, she opened the screen door and entered the house. The collection of documents she found scattered across the kitchen table puzzled her: Skip's high school transcript, his federal income tax return from the previous year, his Social Security card, and a handwritten résumé.

"Skip," she called into the living room, "what are you doing with all these papers?"

"Sending them to a guy that I'm applying for a job with."

"But you've already got a job at EB."

"I've decided we're moving to Montana, to Kalispell," Skip said.

"Moving?" Aline said, stunned by Skip's matter-of-fact tone.

"Yeah. I wanna go there."

"But—"

"Fran and Debbie are there," Skip continued, cutting Aline off. "There's a lot of open land there. We should settle out there."

"Skip?"

"What?"

"Skip, we can't . . . we can't just *move* to Montana."

"Why not?" Skip snapped, raising his voice.

"Well, what will you do for work?"

"I told you—that's what those papers are for. I'm going to work at the plant where Fran works. He can get me a job."

Silent, Aline looked away from Skip.

"Don't turn your back on me, Aline," he demanded, agitated at her reluctance.

He placed his hands firmly on her shoulders and forcefully spun her around. "Well, say something," he shouted.

"We can't go," she said, tears welling up in her eyes. "We can't go . . . now."

"Why not?"

"Because my father's so sick," she said, her voice fading. "How can I just leave my mother when my father is dying? What about my father?" Sniffling, Aline wiped her nose. "He doesn't have much time left," she said, her upper lip trembling. "I can't move out there. I need to be here."

"Sue the state of Maine?" John Stevens asked cynically. "Tom, are you nuts?"

"Why not?" Tureen grinned dubiously, his hands clasped behind his head.

Smiling, Stevens shook his head. The sunlight pouring into Tureen's law office illuminated Stevens's shiny, jet-black hair. The wrinkles in the dark leathery skin around his eyes rumpled up as he tried to conceal his skepticism.

"You don't believe me, do you, John?" Tureen said, reveling in Stevens's reaction.

Tureen's confidence came from his father, whose parents were poor European immigrants. After his drugstore business failed during the Depression, Tom's father opened a hotel in St. Louis. Following World War II, he bought three more. In an era that preceded hotel chains, Tom's father owned four prosperous hotels in St. Louis, employed over a thousand people, and became one of the city's most successful businessmen. Yet when he started he was so poor that he was on the verge of bankruptcy. He had a keen sense for recognizing business opportunities and seizing them. He taught young Tom all the basic concepts of capitalism during the process.

Tureen's childhood mirrored that of other affluent children living in the suburbs in the postwar boom. He grew up in a two-car family, one of which was a pink Cadillac belonging to his mother. While his father worked excessive hours and earned a handsome salary, Tom's mother belonged to a country club and golfed daily. Tom attended private school, and his sister went to finishing school. But unlike most privileged children, Tom spent every free moment working. When Tom turned eight, his father put him to work nights and weekends in his hotels. At thirteen, Tom was working over twenty-five hours per week. By the time he was eighteen, he had held every job in the hotel business, including manager.

Tureen knew, however, that it was going to take more than confidence and hard work to sustain the lawsuit he was contemplating. Nothing gets people up in arms more than threats against their property, and Tureen anticipated tremendous public opposition to the suit. So he went looking for allies. First, he placed a call to the Native Americans Rights Fund (NARF), a special-interest law firm in Colorado that exclusively represented Indian tribes. Eager to help, NARF offered to provide whatever Tureen needed. He asked for lawyers and money. In short order, NARF attorneys from other states showed up in Maine and began working out of Tureen's office. And Tureen was put on NARF's payroll, which instantly doubled his salary to $18,000.

Tureen also looked for some political clout. Although the tribe was capable of suing the state on its own, Tureen thought the tribe's chances of success would greatly increase if the Justice Department filed the suit on the tribe's behalf.

"The law really says that we have a right to recover that land?" Stevens asked.

"John, that's exactly what it says. The statute is clear."

"Well, the court will never rule in our favor," Stevens said. "And the Justice Department's never going to help us."

"John," Tureen said, "this is about recognizing an opportunity and not being afraid to seize it."

DECEMBER 1969

All ready for church, Skip leaned back on the badly worn sofa covered by a bright red blanket. He propped his legs up on the brown coffee table, his sock-clad feet nearly touching the glass ashtray. "Come here, boy," he called, inviting Kimo, his and Aline's new Alaskan malamute puppy, to join him on the couch. Contemplating a cigarette, Skip waited for Aline to emerge from the bedroom. He hoped to make it to church in time to attend Sunday school.

Suddenly, Aline entered the room, wearing for the first time a white dress she had made specifically for Sundays—the only day she had occasion to dress up. She had sewn it on the sewing machine her father purchased for her. The modestly cut neckline revealed just enough of her white skin below the neck to provide a contrast to her silky smooth brown hair, elegantly draped over her shoulders.

Eager for a compliment, she stood before Skip, nervously waiting.

"Why do you want to look like a Jezebel," Skip snapped.

"What's a Jezebel?" she asked.

"You're no Christian, Aline," Skip complained. "You don't know the Bible. Jezebel's a harlot in the Old Testament."

Humiliated, Aline took a step back toward the bedroom.

"You look like a harlot in that dress. Wear something over it."

"What's the big deal?" she complained, looking down at her chest.

"You can't go dressed like that to church. Go fix it!"

Moments later Aline reappeared, dutifully wearing a jacket. Cloaking her shoulders, it obscured the dress's beautiful design and Aline's petite, attractive figure. Resentfully, she stared at Skip, who seemed to be considering the Christmas tree. Bulky and disfigured, the tree was consumed by silver tinsel, which made up for the scarcity of bulbs and other ornaments. No presents were under the tree. Behind in their rent, they were unable to afford gifts. Yet the room was cluttered with items Skip had purchased: a 30-30 Marlin shotgun, a .22 Ithaca rifle, a new acoustic guitar, and two velvet paintings hanging on the wall—one of wild horses, the other of Christ.

"Skip, what are we going to do about our rent?" Aline asked, not bothering to ask if the jacket was acceptable.

"Aline, I'm thinking about Bible study right now. That's what ought to be on your mind."

"It's just that we don't even have anything for Christmas."

"When we move to Montana we won't have to worry about money."

"Skip, I told you I'm not moving away while my father's alive."

"Then don't bother me with talk about bills."

"You've been badgering me about Montana since we got off our honeymoon. Do you want my father to hurry up and die so we can move? Is that what you want?"

Skip sprung to his feet and clenched Aline's skinny arm.

"Ouch, you're hurting me, Skip," she said, wincing.

"Don't you ever argue with me," he shouted, raising his open hand.

Cowering, Aline ducked before the palm of Skip's hand slammed down on top of her head, knocking off her white hair ornament and dropping her to her knees.

Leaving her on the ground, Skip headed out the door toward the car. "Let's go," he said.

Aline reached for her hair ornament before slowly standing up. Afraid he would only get angrier if she did not get in the car, she quietly walked outside, her head throbbing.

By the time they completed the thirty-minute drive to church, Aline had stopped crying and tidied up her smeared makeup and disheveled hair. Trailing Skip, she watched with wonder as he entered the church and greeted members of the congregation with grace before flawlessly delivering a spiritual message about the Bible to members of his Sunday school class. Discovering his violent side after marriage was shocking enough. But Aline was more amazed by Skip's ability to go from private tyrant to public Good Samaritan in an instant.

JANUARY 30, 1970

It was dark outside when Skip picked Aline up after work, late in the afternoon. Having argued that morning on the way to work, the ride home was silent. As they pulled into their driveway, they both noticed their landlord's wife standing outside, as if she were waiting to tell them something. Sullen, she approached Aline's side of the car.

"Your father is real bad," she said, offering few details. "Your brother-in-law called about an hour ago, said your mother and sister were already at the hospital. He wants you to call him right away."

Aline looked at Skip. "Maybe Dad's just having another bad bout."

"I've fixed you both some dinner," the landlady said, motioning toward her house. It was located on the same lot as Skip and Aline's house. "You kids will need something in your stomachs before you drive to Rhode Island."

Too nervous to eat, Aline called her brother-in-law while Skip polished off a plate of food kept warm by tinfoil. Aline's brother-in-law asked her and Skip to drop by and pick him up en route to the hospital.

When they arrived at his home in Hope Valley, Rhode Island, Skip ran inside, leaving Aline in the car. Ten minutes later Skip returned to the car alone.

"He's dead," Aline thought. "That's it."

Skip would not look at Aline as he opened the driver's-side door.

"Don't even tell me," Aline said, starting to sob hysterically. "I know. My God, he's gone."

Watching Aline shake like a brittle autumn leaf as she recoiled against the inside of the passenger-side door, Skip sat frozen in the driver's seat, unsure how to comfort her, incapable of reaching out. When hurt as a child, Skip did not experience much in the way of embraces or compassion from his father. Crying was deemed a weakness. Rather than talking about pain, Skip had learned to internalize it.

"Even when he was sick, at least he was here," Aline whimpered. "At least he was here."

Skip could only look away from her.

3

WALL STREET CAN WAIT

FALL 1970
CALAIS, MAINE

FROM HIS LAW OFFICE WINDOW, TUREEN COULD SEE JOHN STEVENS approaching with his fiancée, Susan MacCulloch, an attractive white woman in her twenties with shoulder-length hair. Months after Tureen got to Calais, MacCulloch arrived from California, where she had just finished her Ph.D. program in anthropology at Cal-Berkeley. She had come to Maine to observe life on the Passamaquoddy reservation, in part to further research she had been conducting on eastern Indian tribes. Her cotton-polyester pantsuits and academic vocabulary immediately distinguished her as an outsider on the Passamaquoddy reservation. Stevens, however, agreed to participate in a series of one-on-one interviews with her. During these private sessions, he found MacCulloch's soothing voice to be a welcome reprieve from the drumbeat of complaints and frustrations constantly being brought to him by tribal members who were struggling in extreme poverty. And she found him both intellectually stimulating and physically attractive. Ultimately, Stevens asked her to marry him, despite complaints from some tribal members who were concerned that their leader was marrying a non-Indian.

"Well, hi, Susan," Tureen said, ushering her and Stevens toward chairs placed around a table.

"Hi, Tom," she said.

"I've been telling Susan about your plan to sue the state of Maine on our behalf," Stevens said. "And it has occurred to us that there might be a lot of other tribes that could use your help."

"Tom, there are Indian tribes up and down the East Coast that are not recognized by the federal government," MacCulloch said. "Like the Passamaquoddy, these tribes lived in the original thirteen colonies and never entered into treaties with the federal government. Instead, they signed treaties with the states."

"How many tribes are we talking about?" Tureen asked.

MacCulloch pushed a document across the table. On it were the names and locations of dozens of eastern Indian tribes that once occupied land within the states that now stretch from Maine to Florida. None of them were known to the federal government.

"Susan put that list together herself," Stevens said. "She knows more about these tribes than anybody in America."

Tureen did not need to be convinced of MacCulloch's credentials. She was probably the only person in Calais with more education than he had. And she had been researching Indian tribes from the original thirteen colonies for more than a decade.

Born September 13, 1934, MacCulloch discovered her first Indian arrowhead in the soil on the farm where she grew up in Sudbury, Massachusetts. Her father was a farmer and let her ride alongside him as he plowed the fields. Whenever the plow turned up arrowheads or other Indian artifacts, Susan would jump down from the tractor and pick them up. Her father, a history buff, would tell her stories of the Indians who used to populate the area before the arrival of the Pilgrims.

Enchanted by the relics and the history associated with them, Susan began collecting the arrowheads in her farmhouse bedroom. She checked out books at the library and began reading about Indians. The illustrations of their peculiar dress, colorful headdress, and darker skin tones only fueled her curiosity more. They looked like nobody she had ever seen in her rural town located thirty minutes outside Boston.

By high school she was doing research papers on Indians and had decided to major in anthropology at the University of Connecticut. Throughout her four years of college and later as a graduate student working toward a master's degree in anthropology at the University of Massachusetts, she began compiling an index of every Indian tribe that had inhabited the New England states. The list grew out of extensive research and interviews, and it took over five years to compile. Even her professors had not heard of most of the tribes MacCulloch identified.

From her list, she selected one tribe—the Nipmuck of western Massachusetts—to search out and do a written documentary on. She went looking for any remnant of the small tribe long believed to be extinct. Joined by her father, she spent her weekends hiking the woods in western Massachusetts searching for a small twelve-acre reservation she had noticed on an old map. She finally located it in Grafton, Massachusetts. It was deserted except for a small hut. But MacCulloch discovered that an old Indian woman, Zara Cisco Brough, lived alone in the hut. Under her bed she had a box with documents, some of which were over a hundred years old, that revealed the Nipmuck's history. As the last living descendant of the tribe, Brough was the caretaker of the records.

MacCulloch's discovery helped her get accepted into a Ph.D. program at Cal-Berkeley, where she furthered her Indian studies and expanded upon her list of eastern Indian tribes. In Tureen's hands, her list was a potential Rolodex of plaintiffs.

"We need to find out how many of these tribes still exist," Tureen said.

"In order to do that, every one of the sites on my list needs to be visited," MacCulloch said. "It is the only way to determine if any Indians are still occupying these lands."

"That's how Susan found the Nipmuck in Massachusetts," Stevens added.

Tureen noticed that in addition to the New England states, MacCulloch's list included tribes that once lived in Kentucky, Virginia, Maryland, North Carolina, and a host of states stretching all the way to Louisiana. "We don't have the money to hire people to travel to all of these states searching for remnants of lost Indian tribes," Tureen said.

"You're always good at finding money somewhere," MacCulloch said, smiling. "You raise enough money for gas and food, and I'll take the trip to search for these tribes." MacCulloch had always dreamed of taking a journey in search of the tribes that she had begun identifying back when she was in college. "I'll sleep in my car if I have to."

"And I'll go too, Tom," said Stevens. "I'll take a leave of absence from my tribal duties."

APRIL 1971

Thanks to the donation of a wealthy friend, Tureen had secured just enough money to finance MacCulloch and Stevens's expedition to search for tribes. He handed Stevens $3,000 in cash, and gave MacCulloch a set of written questions designed to determine whether tribes would qualify as plaintiffs.

"You have three things to look for," Tureen told them before they climbed into their car, its backseat stuffed with sleeping bags, clothes, and food. "First, you have to find tribes that still exist. Second, the tribe must not have abandoned its territory. And third, the territory had to have been taken away from the tribe after 1790, without federal approval. These are our basic prerequisites to making a claim."

MacCulloch and Stevens left Maine and drove until they reached their first destination, a tiny reservation located twenty miles outside Richmond, Virginia. Since most of the New England states were close enough to Maine to visit on short weekend trips, they decided to forgo them until a later date and dedicate their extended road trip to searching for tribes that once lived in states south of New York.

By summer's end they had toured from Virginia to Louisiana. Relying on maps and historical sources MacCulloch had compiled, they stopped to search for tribes in every state in between. They slept in their car, ate what tribes would feed them, and seldom showered. When they returned to Calais, MacCulloch handed Tureen a day-by-day journal account of their travels and promised to spend the next few months typing up a comprehensive report that included information on all the tribes along the Atlantic seaboard.

"This is legal entrepreneurism," said Tureen, delighted at the prospects before him. It reminded Tureen of the scene in *Titanic* when the crewman returned to rescue people, calling out, "Is anybody out there? Anybody still alive?" They were going back. And there were some tribes barely hanging on.

• • •

NOVEMBER 1971

"Shit," Tureen said, staring down at a memo his law clerk had typed up for him. It indicated that on July 18, 1966, Congress had imposed a six-year statute of limitations on any lawsuits brought by the United States that were intended to recover damages for wrongs suffered by Indians. After July 18, 1972, it would be too late for the Justice Department to file a civil action on behalf of the Passamaquoddy. Tureen could still file the suit on his own after the deadline, but without the government's help he felt he had no chance of winning.

For over a year he and his new law associates from NARF had been conducting legal research, formulating arguments, and meeting with other experts capable of guiding them in how to approach a lawsuit of the magnitude Tureen wanted to file. Now a statute of limitations law threatened to kill Tureen's potentially blockbuster case before it ever got filed. He was sure that all the work MacCulloch and Stevens had done to locate additional plaintiffs had all been for naught. There would never be enough time to contact them, much less file a complaint on their behalf, before the deadline.

Tureen met with Stevens and explained that it was time to try and convince Louis R. Bruce, a Mohawk Indian who was commissioner of the Bureau of Indian Affairs (BIA), to lobby the Justice Department to sue on the Passamaquoddy's behalf. Under federal law, Indian tribes are treated as wards of the nation, with Congress having power over their affairs and responsibility for their protection. To assist in meeting its responsibility, Congress delegated its authority over Indian affairs to the secretary of interior. To aid the Interior secretary, Congress also created the BIA and placed it under the direction of the Interior Department. Bruce, as commissioner of the BIA, reported directly to the Interior secretary and so was in a strategically crucial position to help Tureen's cause.

Stevens knew Bruce personally and wrote him a letter under Tureen's direction. The letter explained Tureen's legal theory that entitled the tribe to compensation and asked Bruce to try and convince his boss, Secretary of Interior Rogers Morton, to seek intervention from the Justice Department. For symbolic reasons, Tureen dated Stevens's letter February 22, 1972—George Washington's birthday.

Bruce was sympathetic to Stevens's letter and enthusiastically forwarded a memo to Morton, recommending that the Justice Department consider the case. Word of a potential lawsuit quickly spread through the BIA and made its way back to many Indian tribes. Within weeks, the leadership of another Maine Indian tribe, the Penobscot Nation, approached Tureen. It too had entered into a treaty with Massachusetts after 1790 (in 1796, two years after the Passamaquoddy) and was interested in recovering their lands. When Tureen studied the maps he realized that if the Penobscots' land claim was combined with that of the Passamaquoddy, the two would be claiming a right to a combined twelve million acres, or just over two-thirds of the state of Maine. This included enormous tracts of land owned by the Scott Paper Company, the Georgia-Pacific Corporation, the St. Regis Paper Company, the International Paper Company, and the Great Northern Nekoosa Corporation—the largest landowner of all, with over two million acres within the Indians' claim area.

While Tureen awaited a response from Secretary Morton at Interior, he added the Penobscot to his short list of clients. Meanwhile, lawyers from NARF and other tribes around the country mounted a rigorous lobbying effort to have Congress extend the six-year statute of limitations for filing Indian claims. MacCulloch's list suggested there were potentially many other land transactions involving eastern Indian tribes that went unapproved by the federal government over the years. But it would take an act of Congress to extend the deadline for filing suits of this type. Optimism flourished on March 20 when legislation was introduced in Congress to extend the deadline. But by mid-May Congress had recessed for the Democratic National Convention without voting on the legislation.

The news got worse when Tureen started getting signals from Washington that Interior Secretary Morton and the Justice Department were intent on letting the clock run out on the Maine tribes' case. Morton's office told Tureen that the Justice Department needed more time to study the matter because it was so complicated. To Tureen, this was a diplomatic way of saying, "Don't ask the federal government to try and take away two-thirds of Maine's land base."

• • •

JUNE 2, 1972

Over the previous forty-eight hours, Tureen had barely slept. With less than two months before the statute of limitations expired, he had done the unthinkable. He sued Morton and the Department of Interior over their refusal to take up the Maine Indians' case. He knew of no other way to beat the deadline. Tureen asked the court for an emergency hearing and a preliminary injunction ordering the federal government to file the lawsuit on the Indians' behalf before the statute expired. The request was extraordinary given that the judiciary branch of government does not have the authority to tell the executive branch which cases to file. To prepare, he spent his days committing the necessary laws and his oral arguements to memory. At night he paced the floor, rehearsing what he would say to the judge and how he would refute the opposing lawyers.

Running on pure adrenaline, Tureen bounded up the steps outside the federal courthouse in Portland, Maine, skipping every other step. Gripping his overstuffed briefcase tightly in one hand, he wiped a drop of sweat from his clean-shaven face. He then ran his hand over his neatly combed short hair, making sure the part was straight.

Entering the main courtroom, Tureen stopped and stared at Judge Edward Ginoux's empty seat at the head of the courtroom. At twenty-eight years old and three years removed from law school, Tureen had never appeared in a federal courthouse in his life. Suddenly, he found himself moments away from arguing before one of the most revered judges in America. Tureen looked around the gallery. John Stevens and dozens of tribal members packed the courtroom. Across the aisle were the Justice Department lawyers, his opponents, who were intimately familiar with the workings of federal court. And Tureen had to rouse them if he had any chance of getting the Indians' case into court.

Judge Gignoux, a tall, imposing man who had been appointed by President Eisenhower, emerged from his chambers. He held a copy of Tureen's injunction petition in his hand, a bold request that was very susceptible to dismissal. All the government had to do was tell Judge Gignoux that it had considered the Maine Indians' complaint and decided against filing a case on grounds that it was not in the federal government's best interest to attempt to right wrongs that allegedly took place some two hundred years ago. Maine, at that time, was not even a state.

Tureen knew this simple explanation would leave Judge Gignoux little wiggle room to tell the government how to exercise its discretion. On the other hand, judges do have authority in disputes involving interpretation of laws. Tureen's strategy was to bait the Justice Department attorneys into an argument over the meaning of the Nonintercourse Act.

After some preliminary comments, Judge Gignoux invited Tureen to speak. His conservative tie already snug under the starched collar of his white shirt, Tureen tightened the knot more. His knees nearly gave way as he rose to his feet to present his argument. Not only was two-thirds of the state of Maine at stake, but Tureen's entire legal theory was on trial. There was no more time for dress rehearsals.

"The government is delaying," Tureen insisted to the judge, after explaining the theory behind the Nonintercourse Act. "Not because they are exercising prosecutorial discretion, but because they are not correctly interpreting the law. The government thinks the Nonintercourse Act does not apply in the original thirteen states. That's why they're not acting. Your Honor, you've got the power under the Administrative Procedure Act to give us a declaratory judgment to set these guys straight so they decide with a proper understanding of the law whether they should proceed."

The request was clever. It called for Gignoux to order the government to file the case before the statute of limitations expired in order to preserve his authority to decide whether the Nonintercourse Act applied to the Passamaquoddy. Tureen justified the request by insisting that by misinterpreting a federal law, the government was cheating the Indians out of their day in court.

Enticed by Tureen's challenge, Justice Department lawyer Dennis Wittman argued that Tureen was the one who had the law wrong. Wittman insisted that the Nonintercourse Act applied only to federally recognized tribes. Since the Passamaquoddy were not on the government's list of federal tribes, the statute did not protect them.

The Justice Department lawyers had taken the bait. That was all Tureen wanted, a debate. As the argument dragged on over whether the Nonintercourse Act applied to the Maine Indians, the clearer it became to Judge Gignoux that there was a legitimate dispute over the interpretation of a federal law. And since judges have authority to make rulings on interpretations of law, Tureen seized the opportunity.

"Your Honor, you've got infinite power to protect your jurisdiction,"

Tureen said breathlessly. "This issue is going to become moot if they don't file this lawsuit. The only way to protect your jurisdiction is to order them as a protective matter to file suit."

Gignoux did just that. On June 23 he ordered the Justice Department to file the lawsuit on the Indians' behalf by July 1. He would then hear oral arguments on whether the Nonintercourse Act applied to the Maine Indians.

Tureen and Stevens received word of Gignoux's order back at Tureen's law office.

"You did it, Tom," Stevens said. "I don't know how. But you did it."

"Well, sometimes you get real good judges," Tureen said. "And other times you get stupid judges. With Gignoux we got a real good one."

"Now I really believe in the system," Stevens said. "This makes me feel good to be an American."

The Justice Department immediately appealed Gignoux's ruling. But while awaiting the appeal, it complied with his order. At the end of June the Justice Department reluctantly sued the state of Maine, seeking $150 million in damages on behalf of the Passamaquoddy. Two weeks later, the government filed a separate suit against Maine on behalf of the Penobscot Nation, even though Tureen had argued on behalf of only the Passamaquoddy. The Penobscot suit also sought $150 million in damages.

Stevens called a meeting of the tribal leaders so Tureen could announce his tactical legal victory over the Justice Department. "It was the first time in the history of the American judiciary that a federal court has ordered the federal government to file a lawsuit," Tureen boasted. "Judge Gignoux loved it."

Tureen loved it too. His initial hope in filing the lawsuit was to ask for something big—millions of acres of land—and settle for something less—the federal government's willingness to bestow federal tribal status on the Passamaquoddy. But now there were two tribes involved. And Gignoux's unprecedented ruling suddenly put the Maine tribes in a position to do more than merely achieve equal footing with western tribes. The Passamaquoddy and Penobscot stood to recover a combined $300 million, more than enough to accomplish the other objective Tureen had when he first arrived in town: generate capital to finance tax-free business enterprises on the tribe's massive land base.

No one was more elated by Tureen's tactical victory than John Stevens. As tribal governor of the Passamaquoddy, he rarely had opportunity to announce good news. But just days after telling the tribe that Judge Gignoux was giving them their day in court on the land claim, Stevens received more good news from Tureen. On July 17, 1972—one day before the deadline passed for filing trespass claims on behalf of Indian tribes—Congress passed an amendment extending the deadline. Beginning October 13, 1972, Indian tribes had an additional five years to file lawsuits to recover land. The extensive lobbying by Tureen's NARF colleagues had paid off.

From a personal standpoint, Stevens did not benefit from the extension. Both his tribe and the Penobscot Indians had already filed their cases. But now all the other qualified tribes that he and MacCulloch had located would get their day in court.

"Congress wasn't really paying much attention," Tureen thought, eager to follow through on all the effort MacCulloch and Stevens had invested locating other eastern tribes. "That extension of the statute of limitations has left the door open for countless other tribes to file land-claim lawsuits."

Since the federal government historically did not recognize the eastern tribes, there was no need for an official list of state tribes. Hence Congress had no idea how many potential Indian tribe plaintiffs qualified under Tureen's Nonintercourse Act theory. Even the Bureau of Indian Affairs maintained no official list of "state" tribes. The only such list in existence had been produced by MacCulloch, with the help of Stevens. The list had not been published and was not publicly available. It had not even been photocopied. Only an original existed, and Tureen had it.

Titled "Atlantic Seaboard Indians," MacCulloch's list was seventeen pages long and contained the names of two hundred eastern tribes, most of which had been contacted by MacCulloch and Stevens over the previous twelve months. Only the New England tribes on the list had not yet been visited. Now that the statute of limitations for filing lawsuits had been extended, MacCulloch and Stevens were primed to finish what they had started and search out the tribes in New England.

"I want to find out all the places where my legal theory might apply," Tureen told Stevens. Armed with MacCulloch's list and an extended deadline to work under, Tureen saw the potential for his legal theory to do for eastern Indians what the hamburger did for the McDonald brothers, the suburban housing development did for Bill Levitt, and chain hotels did for Kemmons Wilson and Holiday Inn. A chain of disruptive land-claim lawsuits seeking millions of acres and millions of dollars could potentially be filed in every one of the original thirteen states. The strategy in every instance would be the same: agree to drop the lawsuits in exchange for the state tribes' receiving a cash settlement and federal tribal status. That way Tureen could help the tribes devise business plans to put their money to work for them, setting up businesses on tribal lands that would be newly exempt from all state and federal regulations and taxes.

"When I first graduated from law school and moved to Maine," Tureen thought, "I figured I would work with the Indians for a few years and then eventually end up on Wall Street doing corporate law. But now I don't think I'll ever leave."

4

THE IRON LADY

FEBRUARY 1973
MYSTIC, CONNECTICUT

DONNING NAVY BLUE COVERALLS, SKIP CLIMBED INTO THE BROWN-AND-white milk delivery truck parked in his driveway. The red lettering painted on the side of the truck read MAPLE SHADE FARMS INC. DAIRY PRODUCTS. He and Aline had been married less than four years and Skip was already on his fifth different full-time job. And they were living in their fifth residence. For the first time, however, they were earning enough money to live comfortably. In addition to having his own early-morning milk delivery route, Skip had been offered an opportunity to run a fast-food takeout restaurant. The Sea Mist Haven, located one block from the historic Mystic Seaport, southeastern Connecticut's biggest tourist attraction, served hamburgers, hot dogs, grinders, and

French fries on paper plates. During the summer months business was superb, with thousands of customers exiting the Seaport in search of a quick bite to eat. Skip had signed a one-year contract with the owner to manage and operate the business, predicting to Aline, "I'm gonna be rich, you wait and see."

Less than one mile from the Sea Mist Haven, Skip and Aline rented a small two-bedroom waterfront home along the coast where the Mystic River dumps into the Atlantic Ocean. Skip bought Aline a bicycle to get herself back and forth to the restaurant, where he put her in charge of dishwashing, busing tables, and running the cash register. Skip bought himself a used boat, which he anchored just offshore from their home. Aline tried to talk him out of making the purchase, pointing out that they really could not afford it. But Skip was taking money out of the restaurant business to purchase things that they had always gone without.

Consumed by trying to become wealthy in his first attempt at being a businessman, Skip's interest in religion waned. Nor did he have time to take his seventy-eight-year-old grandmother, Elizabeth George, up on an offer she put to him right after he started running the Sea Mist Haven. George, who lived in Ledyard, the next town over from Mystic, wanted Skip to move into her homestead and take over her land—all 214 acres of it. Her health was declining and she was looking for someone to entrust her property to. Skip was her eldest grandson. He had also lived with her briefly after he got out of high school. She figured he was the most qualified, and deserving, of the offer.

Without consulting Aline, Hayward turned his grandmother down, convinced he was on the verge of a lucrative business career in the tourism industry. In his mind the Sea Mist Haven was only the first step toward ownership of a larger restaurant business. Despite not being asked, Aline supported Hayward's decision to turn down his grandmother. She loved Hayward's grandmother and thoroughly enjoyed visiting her, as they often did on weekends. But she too saw no future in taking over Grandmother Elizabeth's land. For starters, they could never own it, since the land belonged to the Pequot Indian tribe. Scattered around the boundaries to the 214-acre reservation where Hayward's grandmother resided were wooden signs. WESTERN PEQUOT INDIAN RESERVATION ESTABLISHED 1667, they read, their painted yellow letters fading. The tribe had died out generations ago, decimated by European colonists and rival tribes. But the state of Connecticut had never dismantled the reservation, instead permitting various individuals, who claimed genealogical ties to the old tribe, to reside there.

George, one of the last known living descendants of the old tribe, was the only person left on the reservation. One of the reasons George decided to live out her life in isolation on the reservation was her fear that the state of Connecticut would convert the land into a state park for tourists if no one resided there. The reservation looked nothing like the western reservations typically featured in history books or movies. No barren wasteland. No arid dust swirls. No clusters of desolate run-down shanties. Instead, the reservation rested on an undulating New England landscape in Ledyard, thick with maple, white birch, and oak trees. Their lush green treetops obscured the rock ledges and dirt footpaths that ran through the reservation's forestland.

So despite the absence of indoor plumbing or adequate heat, she stayed. To residents of Ledyard, George was the last remnant of the Pequots and was known as "the iron lady." Stories of her gritty defense of the Indian land over the years were legendary. Once a state health inspector appeared, pursuing a complaint by neighbors that George's dogs were wandering off the reservation. Angry that the health inspector was more concerned about stray dogs off the reservation than the inadequate living conditions on it, George refused to chain her dogs and, armed with a shotgun, chased the agent away. She had also once used her gun to chase off a photographer from *Life* magazine.

If Skip did not change his mind, however, and move into her homestead, she feared her years of perseverance would be for naught.

MAY 1973
CALAIS, MAINE

The checklist was nearly complete. MacCulloch and Stevens had investigated ten leads on potential Indian tribe clients in Massachusetts. After visiting the ten sites around the state, two tribes appeared to satisfy Tureen's criteria for filing a land claim: the Waupanoag Indians at the Gay Head Indian Village on Martha's Vineyard and another branch of the Waupanoag Indians that claimed to have an Indian village in the town of Mashpee on Cape Cod. Both groups wanted Tureen to sue on their behalf.

In Rhode Island, MacCulloch and Stevens confirmed that one tribe still existed, the Narragansett Indians in Charleston. They too agreed to have Tureen represent them, as did the Oneida Indians in upstate New York. The state of Vermont turned up no potential clients. Neither did New Hampshire. Connecticut was the one remaining state they had yet to visit. According to MacCulloch's research, Connecticut was once home to six Indian tribes.

Looking under the heading "Connecticut" on MacCulloch's New England states' list, Stevens recognized some of the contact persons and Indian reservations they were due to visit, such as the Schaghticoke Indian Reservation, the Golden Hill Pequot Reservation, and Courtland Fowler, Sr., of the Mohegan Indian Village.

The last entry on the short list was the one that caught his eye, however. It read, "Eliza George, Western Pequot Reserve, Ledyard, Connecticut 06339." A triangular symbol in the margin next to this entry indicated that a state Indian reservation existed in Ledyard.

"Susan, there's supposed to be a tribe in *Ledyard, Connecticut?*" asked Stevens, who had never heard of Ledyard.

"I don't know if the *tribe* is still there," MacCulloch said. "But there should be a reservation there."

MacCulloch had never visited Ledyard. But while attending the University of Connecticut in the early 1960s, she had a classmate from Ledyard who told MacCulloch that there was an Indian reservation in her hometown. MacCulloch researched state records and confirmed that a reservation existed in Ledyard and that an Indian woman named Eliza George resided on it. "I beat the bushes to find an address for her," said MacCulloch. "I don't remember exactly how I came across her address. But somehow I confirmed that George had a post office box at the Ledyard post office."

"Well, if she's still there," said Stevens, "I'll find her."

Stevens agreed to go to Ledyard without MacCulloch, who had just given birth to their first child. Carrying a copy of MacCulloch's list and a map of southeastern Connecticut, Stevens set out on the ten-hour drive to Ledyard.

• • •

ONE DAY LATER
LEDYARD, CONNECTICUT

"I guess Susan was right," Stevens thought, passing a road sign on Route 214 in Ledyard that indicated he had just entered the Pequot reservation. Taking the first dirt road he saw after the sign, he followed its winding curves until coasting his cream-colored rental car to a stop at the road's end. In the distance he saw a home. The brown paint was peeling and faded. The gray-shingled roof sagged in the middle and seemed to be held up by the brick chimney on the far side of the house. Some of the windows were boarded up with rough sheets of plywood; dilapidated casings that hung at odd angles framed others. The front door, cracked and split, was rotted out at the bottom. Bookending the house were rusty propane gas tanks on the left and an outhouse on the right. The house seemed a complete anomaly in the beautiful setting. Yet it was much nicer than what many of Stevens's tribal members lived in on the Passamaquoddy reservation.

Stepping from his car, Stevens was surprised to see two white people, a man and a woman, walking toward him through a small field. Skip and Aline were working on the house for Skip's grandmother when they heard the sound of Stevens's car.

"Kimo, come here, boy," Aline said, trying to calm the dog, who was aroused by the presence of a stranger. "It's OK. It's OK."

Skip hesitated, not recognizing the short, slender man with glossy black hair standing less than fifty feet from his grandmother's homestead.

"Do either of you know Eliza George?" Stevens called out in a friendly tone.

"Yeah, she's my grandmother," Skip said. "Who are you?"

"My name is John Stevens. I'm from Maine. I'm the commissioner of Indian Affairs and a member of the Passamaquoddy tribe. I'm working with other tribes around New England, helping them organize themselves. I'm helping them set up tribal government structures. And I'm working with a lawyer that is helping us and other nonfederally recognized tribes to reclaim their land. I'm looking for Eliza George because she is the only name I had that was connected to the Pequot reservation." He extended his hand.

"I'm Skip Hayward," Hayward said, grasping Stevens's hand and shaking it firmly.

"I've been trying to find out if there are any Pequots in Ledyard," Stevens continued. "But I can't find any sign of anybody who belongs to that tribe. This is the tribe's home turf. But there doesn't seem to be any tribal members left."

"I'm a member of the tribe," Skip claimed.

Stevens tried not to appear suspicious. "*This* guy is Native American?" Stevens wondered. He had seen his share of Indians with fair complexions, yet his doubts about Hayward went beyond skin color. He was not sure just what exactly, besides his appearance, caused him to question Skip's claim. He just sensed something different from what he experienced in his previous visits to dozens of reservations around the East Coast. But Stevens had been taught to take a man's word at face value, and he was not comfortable questioning Hayward's professed identity.

"Are there are any other tribal members here?" Stevens asked, unsure of what else to say.

"Only about four or five of us—me, my mother and grandmother, and my sister and my aunt. We're the only ones here."

"Hi," Stevens said cordially, noticing that Aline had been silently staring at him from the moment he began talking to Skip.

"Hi, I'm Aline, Skip's wife."

"She's a white woman," Skip said. "She's not a member of the tribe."

Sensing there was no tribal structure in place on the reservation, Stevens described the form of government his tribe had in place, as well as the effort Tureen had made to help them apply for federal grant money to improve their reservation. "Tom has done a lot for us," Stevens said. "He helped us learn about a lot of programs out there that tribes are not aware of, programs that can improve the quality of life on reservations."

"How would we find out more about these programs?" Skip asked.

"Well, first you have to set up your tribal government. You're welcome to come to Maine. I've been inviting tribes that are not organized to come to Maine and look at our tribal government. That way you could see how our tribal administration is set up and how it functions and how we contact with the Bureau of Indian Affairs."

Stevens had been there only ten minutes when he started walking back toward his car. He wanted to ask Skip for his phone number in order to contact him again. Under the impression that Skip lived in the homestead, however, he decided not to bother asking. "I don't even see any phone lines or telephone poles on this reservation," Stevens thought. "The man is probably so poor that he doesn't have a telephone."

Stevens removed a pencil from his car and quickly scribbled something on a piece of paper and handed it to Skip.

"207-796-2301. JOHN STEVENS, PASSAMAQUODDY TRIBAL OFFICE," it read.

"That's my number in Maine," Stevens said. "Call me."

Skip folded it in half and placed it in his wallet, volunteering no information about his home telephone number in Mystic or his business telephone number at the Sea Mist Haven.

MAY 1973
PEQUOT INDIAN RESERVATION

As the engine died, Curtis Moussie removed the key from the ignition of his cream-colored Lincoln hardtop convertible. His brown corduroy pants slid smoothly over the leather seat as he stepped out onto the dirt road. Slowly approaching Elizabeth George's homestead, he saw the front door slowly open.

"Oh, Curtis," called out George. "Are you coming up to have a cup of tea?"

Moussie paused and smiled, pleased that Elizabeth's usual greeting had not changed. "Sure," he replied.

Moussie, a forty-six-year-old freelance photographer who had grown up within walking distance of the reservation, had been stopping by unannounced to check on George's welfare for years.

Inside, George offered him the same chair as always. Then, as she had done in each of Moussie's past visits, she brought out a plate of cookies. He would never dare to ask, but Moussie wondered how a woman with so few resources and even fewer visitors managed to have fresh cookies on hand.

George put the teakettle on the stove, which was about as worn down as the house. The floor was warped and badly in need of repair. The lighting was dim, and the meager furnishings did little to brighten the place. But it was clean, and the hospitality was more than anyone could expect.

George was the poorest person in Ledyard. She could not even afford a used car. Her only source of income was a monthly Social Security check and she had no savings. Moussie, on the other hand, was a professional photographer whose work appeared in such high-end magazines as *National Geographic, Town and Country,* and *Connecticut.* He had also taken portraits for the most famous families in America. His subjects included the Rockefellers, the Vanderbilts, the Brewsters, and the Harknesses, heirs of the Standard Oil Company. Many of these portraits were eventually featured in a magazine series he published called "Lifestyles of the Rich and Famous."

Long before the visits to the opulent homes of the wealthy and the black-tie dinner parties, Moussie had befriended George. He began visiting her when he was a young man. His mother, who built and owned the Dew Drop Inn, a café in North Stonington, Connecticut, was a friend to George. Since its opening in 1918, it was famous for homemade coconut-cream pies. George regularly walked the five miles from the reservation to enjoy a slice of her favorite pie along with a warm cup of tea. Moussie's mother knew that George could scarcely afford the nickel that it cost for a cup of tea alone and so would often send her home with a complimentary pie.

One day as George left the restaurant, she said to Curtis, who was then a young teenager helping his mother behind the counter, "Son, if you're ever up my way, stop in." Most folks were never up her way. The reservation, created by colonists even before the town of Ledyard was formed, was in a remote area purposely to keep Indians out of sight. Isolated from her Ledyard neighbors, George was easy to neglect. But Moussie took George up on the offer and made the three-mile trek to see her when he was fifteen.

By the early 1970s, Moussie had been calling on her for over forty years. Whenever he had a day off, he drove by and checked on her. His visits gave her something to look forward to, something to interrupt the loneliness of being the only person on two-hundred-plus acres. Too, she was getting on in years and Moussie felt she needed the attention.

"Curtis, here's your tea," Elizabeth said, handing him a cup and saucer.

"Thank you, Liza," he said, taking it from her and placing it gingerly on the table.

As they sat sipping tea and catching up on the recent news in each other's lives, Elizabeth abruptly changed the subject.

"Curtis, you've always wanted to photograph me," she reminded him. "Would you still like to?"

Moussie slowly pulled his teacup away from his lips. "You bet," he said softly. He could hardly help recalling the old cliché: *Photographers take their best pictures on their days off.* Moussie, however, had left his camera equipment home. His dilemma suited Elizabeth just fine. She wanted time to prepare.

"You be back here at four-thirty and I'll be ready," she said.

Perplexed, yet pleased, by her sudden eagerness to be photographed, Moussie did not ask any questions. All the way back to his house he marveled over her request. Shortly after his photography career had taken off, Moussie had asked to take Elizabeth's portrait. She refused, but occasionally Moussie would revisit the request. Each time, however, her polite response was the same. "I'm sorry, but I don't let anybody take my picture." Eventually, he stopped asking. He did not want to violate what she claimed was an old Indian superstition—that being photographed was like capturing a person's soul.

It was a superstition that Moussie hardly understood but fully respected. Elizabeth's loyalty to preserving the reservation had inspired her not to follow her siblings off the reservation and into a more comfortable home and all the conveniences that come with living in a town. She felt it was her duty to sacrifice all that to maintain the lifeline of what was once one of New England's most powerful tribes.

When Moussie returned to the reservation at four-thirty, Elizabeth was waiting for him outside with her twenty-one-year-old granddaughter, Theresa, who was Skip's younger sister and who worked part-time for him at the Sea Mist Haven. Moussie drove them to nearby Lantern Hill Pond. During the Revolutionary War, the colonists lit lanterns on the hilltop to signal the imminent arrival of the British. The hill also had historical significance to the Indians. It held an Indian council seat made out of stone, where three or four of the area's old Indian tribes used to meet.

He positioned George and her granddaughter, whom George wanted in the picture. Through his lens, Moussie brought them into focus. George's longhair braids ran over her shoulders. Thick colorful beads graced her neck. Her face was perfectly straight and her eyes seemed lost in the distance. "She looks very stately, very beautiful," Moussie thought.

Flash.

After seventy-eight years, George had been captured on film for the first time.

Moussie could hardly wait to process the film and prepare her portrait. He had already decided he would deliver it to her gift-wrapped as a token of their forty-year friendship.

JUNE 11, 1973
MYSTIC, CONNECTICUT

One by one, customers coming to and from the Mystic Seaport approached the Sea Mist Haven only to find its front door locked, a handmade sign taped sloppily to the inside of the window. CLOSED DUE TO DEATH IN THE FAMILY, it read.

Four days earlier, at 10:20 P.M. on June 7, Elizabeth George suffered a heart attack and died at her homestead. Following a private funeral, George was buried in the old Pequot burial ground, located near the reservation.

Curtis Moussie was not invited. He learned of his dear friend's death only after reading her obituary in the local newspaper. The brief ten-sentence tribute described her as having been "the oldest living Pequot Indian."

Standing in his den, Moussie slowly uncovered George's gift-wrapped portrait. He gingerly slid it into an oversized envelope and tied its flap. Then he slid the proofs into a yellow manila file for storage. "She must have had a premonition that she was going," Moussie thought. "That's why she decided to let me take her photograph."

After seventy-eight years, only death could take Elizabeth George from her homestead. For the first time since 1683 the reservation was completely unoccupied.

SEPTEMBER 1973
CALAIS, MAINE

It had been months since Stevens submitted his handwritten report indicating that he had found the Pequot reservation and that indeed

Elizabeth George was alive and residing on it. Tureen finally found the time to read it.

"Nothing but woods," the report began. "No permanent housing." The only structures Stevens reported seeing were a small homestead, a shack, and an outhouse.

As Tureen read along, he learned that one of George's grandchildren was with her on the reservation. "I explained that it was important for them to get together and make an impression on the federal government to get their claim in," reported Stevens, who informed Tureen that he explained to George's grandson how they could receive federal aid while suing to recover ancestral land.

"The old woman was not interested in working with lawyers," Stevens reported. "Skip Hayward was the only one who really talked with me. He appears to be the leader of the group."

Tureen was not surprised to read that Stevens struck up a conversation with Hayward. Stevens's genuine interest in helping absolute strangers enabled him to immediately put people at ease.

"Skip Hayward is living there, I think," reported Stevens. "I told him there was a lot of federal funds available and a lot of Indians didn't realize it."

Tureen noticed a roughly drawn map that accompanied Stevens's report. It depicted a square piece of land located at the outer edge of Ledyard. A key in the corner of the map identified the square parcel as the Western Pequot Reservation, being 204 acres in size. A sliver shaped, nine-acre detached piece of land was also shown on the map and identified as the Pequot cemetery.

After reading Stevens's report, Tureen placed it at the bottom of a pile of reports he had yet to act on. The acreage involved was minuscule compared to the Maine tribes' claims and those he was contemplating filing on behalf of tribes in Massachusetts, Rhode Island, and New York. More importantly, however, was the apparent lack of enthusiasm on the part of the Pequots.

5

SAFE SECRETS

MARCH 11, 1974
MYSTIC, CONNECTICUT

THE REAR OF SKIP'S FORD PICKUP TRUCK WAS WEIGHED DOWN BY AN eleven-foot by six-foot white camper with green trim that was mounted to the truck's bed. Armload by armload, Skip and Aline carried clothes, food, and blankets from their house, cramming as much as they could into the camper. Skip's one-year lease with the owner of the Sea Mist Haven had expired, during which time Skip's mismanagement of the business and his personal spending habits had plunged him and Aline into debt. He had been buying things he could not afford, including the camper and the used boat. Shortly before his business went under, the boat, which he'd never bothered to insure, was stolen. Still owing payments on the boat and suddenly out of work, Skip fell behind on his rent. With his landlord threatening to evict him and creditors pursuing him with past-due notices, Skip accepted an offer from a group of local families in the Church of God who were relocating to Maryland. They invited him and Aline to join them in Maryland, promising to let them park their camper on church property until they were able to find jobs and a rental home.

FOUR MONTHS LATER
LAUREL, MARYLAND

In a field outside a rural town located nearly halfway between Baltimore and Washington, D.C., the Haywards' camper rested less than one hundred feet from the home of Bruce Truitt, the pastor of the Church of God's local congregation. Unemployed since leaving Connecticut, Skip spent his days inside the trailer engrossed in Bible study. He had decided to become a pastor, hoping to one day lead his own congregation. To minimize expenses, Skip and Aline lived in their camper rather than rent a home. Skip drew electricity and water from the pastor's home to the camper with extension cords and hoses. He and Aline went without a telephone and ate many of their meals with church members.

Aline provided the only income. She had secured a clerk's position at the Goddard Space Flight Center in nearby Greenbelt. She was thrilled to have some place to go forty hours a week, even if she did not get to keep the money she earned. Skip made her turn over her paycheck to him each Friday. But she was just glad to be out of the trailer, which Skip had converted to his private pulpit, practicing his sermons on Aline. Possessing a rare ability to remember Scripture passages, he would make her sit down while he recited verses verbatim without looking at the Bible.

Church members in Maryland who listened to him discuss the Bible in Sunday school were convinced he had a promising future as a preacher. Besides his captivating oral delivery and command of the Scriptures, Skip impressed parishioners with his strict observance of the church's rigid moral code, which forbids smoking, drinking, dancing, listening to popular music, watching popular movies, and playing cards. Skip denounced card playing as the devil's tool to entice people into gambling, which, according to the church, was one of the most egregious sins of all.

Aline marveled at Skip's ability to abstain from dancing, music, and movies. When she married him, he thoroughly enjoyed all three. He even installed a jukebox in the Sea Mist Haven, stocked with records from the Rolling Stones, the Beatles, Janis Joplin, the Doors, and Bob Dylan. But now he forbade anything other than gospel music. And he refused to view films other than those produced by Christian organizations.

His changes in lifestyle were as unpredictable as they were extreme, convincing Aline she did not know the man she had married. With the ease of a chameleon, Skip put up fronts that allowed him to go from a charming boyfriend to a violent husband almost overnight. Similarly, he changed from a wealth-seeking entrepreneurial restaurant manager to a Bible-toting preacher content to live in extreme poverty.

The personality under the facade only became more bizarre.

"Skip, where are we going?"

"Just c'mon," he said, leading her from the camper to the passenger side of the pickup truck.

"Where are you taking me?" Aline persisted.

Saying nothing, he drove a few miles out of town until reaching a four-way intersection. Nervously, Skip turned his head side to side. No cars were coming in either direction, yet he hesitated.

"Skip, what are you doing?"

Skip sped around the corner and down a road that was unfamiliar to Aline. Remaining silent, his eyes nervously shifted between the rear- and side-view mirrors. In the distance, Aline noticed a massive outdoor movie screen erected in a field. "I didn't know there was a drive-in out here," she said.

Shifting uncomfortably in his seat, Skip turned the wheel, downshifting as he guided the pickup truck toward the admission booth. A rusted, unlit neon sign above the booth said, ADULT MOVIES.

Shielding his eyes with his left hand, Skip handed some money out the window with his right hand. "Skip, I'm not going in there," Aline said, suddenly realizing the drive-in offered XXX-rated movies.

"We're going," he said.

"I don't want to go."

Ignoring her, Skip proceeded toward a remote and empty corner of the drive-in lot and parked the truck.

THE NEXT MORNING

Late for work, Aline started the truck engine before rushing back into the camper to grab her wallet and driver's license. Surprised, she noticed Skip was out of bed. He had gotten up to use the bathroom.

"Aline," he said, stopping her before she could get out the door.

"What?"

"You look like a slut, wearing all that seductive makeup," Skip said, never missing an opportunity to remind her that the church discouraged women from wearing makeup.

"Skip, it's *mascara*."

"I know you want other men."

Unable to erase from her mind the pornographic images she had seen on the screen the previous night and the way she had been asked to emulate them after they returned to the camper later in the evening, Aline said nothing, feeling too cheap to respond. Her silence fueled Skip's jealousy.

"Who have you been seeing behind my back?" he demanded.

"Nobody, Skip."

"I know what you are. I know what you're like."

"No!" she complained. "No. No. No. I've never cheated on you, Skip. Never."

"Don't lie to me, Aline. I see how you look at other men."

"No matter what I say, you won't believe me, so I may as well say nothing." Turning to exit the camper, she was yanked backward.

"Don't turn your back on me when I'm speaking, you liar," Skip said, clenching her arms.

"Stop, Skip. You're hurting me."

"You are lower than the ground I walk on, Aline. You're a nothing."

Black streaks of mascara ran down Aline's cheeks to the front of her shirt.

"I'm too much of a Christian for you," he continued. "The people in the church think I'm a great Christian."

"The people at church don't see your bad side," Aline wept, throwing her hands up in front of her face. "You're no Christian."

Skip's open hand struck Aline upside the head, sending her hurling into the cushions on the trailer's built-in couch. Screaming hysterically, she flailed her arms in an attempt to escape as Skip grabbed her from behind. He quickly subdued her with his powerful arms, threw her down, and applied all of his weight on her back. Taking a fistful of hair, he yanked her head back before grabbing a pillow with his free hand and forcing it over her face. Releasing her hair, he pushed her head down into the pillow, muffling her screams until she gasped and begged for air. Finally, he climbed off, leaving her curled up in the fetal position as she struggled to catch her breath.

ONE WEEK LATER

Anxious, Aline peeked out from behind the skimpy curtain hanging from the camper window. A shiny red Ford Maverick drove across the sun-scorched brown field, stopping feet from the camper's side door.

"Hi, Ma," Aline said as she stepped from the camper.

"Aline," Betty said, throwing her arms tightly around Aline's shoulders before kissing her on the cheek.

"How'd the trip go?"

"It was fine," Betty said, following Aline inside the camper.

"I figured you'd hit a lot of traffic."

"It wasn't too bad," she said, setting her purse down on the table. Having viewed the camper shortly after they bought it, Betty could hardly believe it had become her daughter's home. "So where's Skip?"

"Oh, he's around somewhere."

Offering her mother a seat at the snug four-by-four pull-down table that doubled as an eating space and desk, Aline poured some cold water into two plastic cups. "The heat down here is brutal," she said.

When Aline turned her head, Betty immediately noticed a black-and-blue bruise on Aline's cheek, just below her eye.

"Ooh! Where did you get the bruise on your face, Aline?"

"I don't know."

"Well, how did you get it?"

"Ma, it's nothing."

Sensing defensiveness in Aline's tone, Betty backed off.

"How's Lorraine doing?" Aline asked.

"Your sister is just fine. She misses you, though. Wants to know when you're moving back to Connecticut."

"I don't know, Ma. That's up to Skip. He's already talking about moving to Missouri."

"Missouri? You guys barely got here. Now he's talking about Missouri?"

"Yeah. Debbie and Fran are there. They moved there from Montana. And they have a big ranch. They said we could park our camper there."

"The last time you called me I thought you said Skip wanted to be a pastor or something like that."

"He still does."

"How's he gonna do that if he's living on a ranch in Missouri?"

"He's always changing his mind. I guess he wants to be near Fran. He's practically the only friend Skip has."

"How do you feel about moving to Missouri?"

"At least I'll be with Debbie. I hate it here, except for my job. This is the first time I've had a real good job. And I like the people I work with. They treat me good. But I hate everything else about this place, especially the church people Skip hangs around with. Anyplace would be better than here. Besides, maybe Skip could get a job in Missouri."

• • •

FALL 1974
CALAIS, MAINE

"What do you think our chances are, Tom?" Stevens asked.

"Gignoux is a very smart judge," Tureen said. "And I think he likes our argument."

At Judge Gignoux's request, Tureen had submitted a brief in support of his position that the Nonintercourse Act applied to the Passamaquoddy Indians. In it, Tureen argued that the Nonintercourse Act makes no distinction between federally recognized tribes and state tribes. Rather, Tureen pointed out, the federal law pertains to all Indians. Hence, Congress should have policed the Passamaquoddy's land sale to Massachusetts, and its failure to do so entitled the tribe to a remedy.

The government countered in its brief that it had no obligation to help the Passamaquoddy obtain restitution under the Nonintercourse Act, because the Passamaquoddy were not federally recognized. The government argued that its trust responsibility to advocate for Indian tribes extended only to federal tribes.

Since the argument over whether the Nonintercourse Act applied to the Passamaquoddy was a pretrial dispute that had to be resolved solely by Judge Gignoux, the process toward reaching a resolution went on largely outside public view. The correspondence between Gignoux and Tureen and the Justice Department was limited almost exclusively to briefs, memoranda, and written orders. Tureen viewed this as a big advantage to the tribe. He was confident that if the process received the same public exposure as a trial, landowners and politicians alike would mount an opposition campaign aimed at defeating Tureen's novel legal approach.

"When do you think the judge will make his ruling," Stevens asked.

"I suspect he'll reach a decision early next year," Tureen said.

"By then Susan and I will have met with many of these other tribes," Stevens said.

Tureen understood that if Gignoux ruled that the Nonintercourse Act applied to the Passamaquoddy, it would also apply to other nonfederally recognized tribes on the East Coast. While awaiting Gignoux's ruling, Tureen worked with MacCulloch and Stevens to organize meetings with the Indian tribes they had contacted in their travels. The meetings were informative in nature, designed to educate Indians on the legal remedies that were potentially available to them in the event that Gignoux ruled that nonrecognized federal tribes were entitled to sue for recovery of ancestral lands under the Nonintercourse Act.

DECEMBER 1974
SPARTA, MISSOURI

Frigid air whistled through the poorly sealed doorway to Skip and Aline's camper. Icicles clung to the windows. The green garden hose stretching from the camper to Fran and Debbie's house was frozen solid. Propped up on concrete cinder blocks and situated in the middle of a snow-covered field, the trailer was a virtual tin icebox.

Suddenly, the flimsy door flung open and Aline bolted out of the camper. Wearing no coat, she sprinted toward the pickup truck, hopped in, and turned on the ignition. Trailing her, Skip emerged from the trailer. Both out of work and wallowing in poverty, the fighting between them had become nearly a daily occurrence, enhanced by the fact that they were cooped up in the trailer all day alone. The temperature outside was too cold for outdoor activities, and their friends Fran and Debbie were both away at work all day.

Grinding the gears in her attempt to escape, Aline careened toward the metal gate that separated the field from the main part of the ranch property. Reaching the gate, she shifted the truck back into park and darted out to open the gate. Struggling with the gate's combination lock, she looked over her shoulder. "Oh, God," she said, letting go of the lock and lunging back into the truck.

Unable to unlock the gate in time, she grabbed the steering wheel. In the rearview mirror, Skip was closing in on her. Reversing direction, Aline recklessly spun the truck around. Skip was now running right toward the truck's front bumper.

"Do it," she thought, frantically revving the engine. "Do it. Run him over."

Through the windshield, Skip looked blurry as she cried.

"Run him over before it's too late," she told herself.

Frozen at the wheel, Aline finally flinched when the driver's-side door was flung open.

"Get out here, you whore," Skip yelled, pulling her from the truck. In between delivering blows to her body, Skip dragged her toward the camper, her feet bouncing over the snow-covered frozen ground.

Finally reaching the camper, Skip tried forcing Aline back inside.

"Let go of me," she screamed, kicking at his legs. "Let go."

"No one can hear you," he reminded her. Fran, Debbie, and Debbie's father were all at work. The closest residence was a half mile away.

Wrestling her to the ground, Skip tore her shoe off without untying it, then started beating her over the head and back with it. The hard rubber sole made a thumping sound each time he clubbed her.

"Stop, stop!" screamed a familiar voice coming from the direction of Fran and Debbie's ranch house.

Shocked, Skip looked up and saw Debbie racing toward him. "Skip, stop," yelled Debbie, a horrified expression on her face. She had unexpectedly come home early from her milk delivery route.

Flinging Aline's shoe inside the camper, Skip quickly hooked his hands under Aline's armpits and dragged her up into the camper.

"No," Debbie shouted, reaching the door just as Skip dropped Aline on the floor. "Stop it."

"Let go of the door," Skip yelled, beating Debbie's hands from the doorknob.

"Skip, stop. Let me in," Debbie cried. "Let me in."

Slamming the door in Debbie's face, Skip quickly locked it from the inside.

"Dear God, help me," Debbie prayed, leaning against the camper door, sobbing uncontrollably.

Inside, Skip panicked. No one had ever witnessed him beat Aline. And no one would believe he was capable of such violence without seeing it firsthand. Now their friend had seen what he was capable of doing.

"Get up, get up," he ordered Aline impatiently, hustling her toward the kitchen area. "Go sit at the table. Just sit there."

Aline crawled toward the table.

"Don't cry. Nothing happened here. Just sit there and act normal."

Desperately trying to preserve the image he wanted his friends to see—that of a God-fearing Christian who would never mistreat his wife—

Skip waited impatiently for Aline to wipe the tears away from her face and put her shoe back on.

"Stop crying," he commanded in a hushed voice. "Hurry up."

"Skip, open this door," Debbie continued shouting, her fist pounding on the cold aluminum siding.

Finally, Skip unlocked the door, hoping that Aline would preserve his secret by lying for him and that Debbie would be gullible enough to believe it.

"What . . . are you . . . doing?" Debbie asked, panting for breath as she stepped into the camper slowly. Skip stood in silence, glancing toward Aline, who sat motionless at the table. Her tears had stopped flowing. Her feet, one of them still shoeless, twitched, and her hands shook uncontrollably.

Debbie tried unsuccessfully to make eye contact with her. The two of them had been girlfriends since grammar school, sharing the most intimate secrets. But Aline seemed more distant and detached than ever.

"Aline, are you all right?"

"Oh, yeah, it's nothin'," said Aline, her voice soft and tired.

"Are you sure?"

"Yeah. I'm OK. It's all right."

JANUARY 20, 1975
CALAIS, MAINE

Judge Gignoux's long-awaited decision had been handed down. Exuberant, Tureen clenched the judge's written orders as if he were holding a winning lottery ticket: the Nonintercourse Act applied to the Passamaquoddy Indians, despite the fact that the federal government did not officially recognize them as a tribe. Gignoux decided that it applied to all tribes, both state and federal. He rejected the Justice Department's argument that the act did not apply to tribes originating from the thirteen colonies.

The reports compiled for Tureen by MacCulloch and Stevens suddenly became extremely valuable. Any eastern Indian tribes that remained in existence and had land that was sold after 1790 without federal authorization were eligible to sue to recover it. Almost every group MacCulloch and Stevens contacted had once been in possession of land that had been bought up by states in violation of the Nonintercourse Act.

For the next two months, Tureen weeded out many of the two hundred tribes contained on MacCulloch's list, primarily because they lacked one fundamental requirement: They did not currently possess or live on a reservation. In addition to the Passamaquoddy and the Penobscot, the only tribes he was confident he could represent successfully were the Waupanoag Indians on Cape Cod, the Narragansett Indians in Rhode Island, the Schaghticoke and Golden Hill Paugussetts in Connecticut, and fewer than a dozen tribes in states south of New York. The others lacked a reservation, which implied the existence of a tribe. And tribal status was needed to establish standing to sue.

Before long, Tureen found himself again reviewing Stevens's report on the Pequots. The tribe had a state reservation, though only 214 acres in size. "So Connecticut still considers the Pequots a tribe," he thought. "The Pequots are down to so little land that they seem to be a sort of curio of Connecticut, as if the state is proud of its little Indian reservation. That, however, says to me that legally Connecticut is going to be unable to deny the Pequots' existence."

"John," Tureen said, "we need to make contact with the Pequots again. See if you can get ahold of Skip."

"I left him my phone number," Stevens said. "But I haven't heard from him since I visited him."

"Well, see if you can find him," Tureen said. "Get him on the phone so we can talk to him."

MARCH 1975
SPARTA, MISSOURI

"Stop!" Aline shouted.

"You're a whore," Skip said.

"I've been a good wife."

"I know you, Aline. I know what you're like."

"No."

"Don't lie to me. Don't try and hide it. Tell me. Tell the truth."

"All right!" she blurted out. "I did it."

Skip froze, his voice halting as if he were suddenly mute.

"I did it," Aline repeated in a hushed tone, her voice trailing off to a faint whisper. She was even surprised by her admission. She had been a virgin when she met Skip as a fifteen-year-old and remained one until their wedding night. In marriage she had remained faithful, despite the rapid deterioration of their relationship. But in Maryland, she had become involved with a co-worker during her brief employment stint at the Goddard Space Flight Center. She had slept with him three times, then lost contact with him when Skip took her to Missouri.

Hesitantly, Aline walked toward the camper door. Skip made no attempt to stop her. Instead, he stared into space, saying nothing.

Stepping outside, Aline spotted Fran.

"Fran," she called out, stopping him before he climbed into his truck.

Observing the tears running down Aline's face, Fran's typically stoic expression turned to solemn concern. "Aline," he said, softly. "What's happened?"

"Fran, I hurt Skip."

"Hurt Skip?"

"I hurt him real bad."

Fran lunged toward the camper door.

"No," Aline called out. "No, it is not that kind of hurt. I hurt him, but not that way."

Puzzled, Fran carefully turned the doorknob to the camper door. "It's locked," he said. "Is Skip in there?"

"Yeah, he's in there."

"Well, he's got the door locked," he said, looking over his shoulder at Aline. "Skip, it's me, Fran," he shouted toward the door. "Are you OK in there?"

Minutes passed without a response from Skip.

"I knew it would hurt him," Aline said, crying. "I thought if I finally admitted to it maybe he would stop. I thought if I finally told him what he wanted to hear, then maybe he would stop."

For the next three days, Skip refused to come out of the camper. Nor did he allow anyone to enter. Aline slept inside Fran and Debbie's house, the three of them wondering what it would take to get Skip to come out. Finally, Skip agreed to let Fran's mother come inside. He had been close to her since his teenage years and viewed her as the most spiritual person he knew. She prayed with him and finally coaxed him into coming out. He spent much of the next two days talking on Fran's telephone, in isolation from Aline. She finally got the courage to approach him when she noticed him mounting the camper to the bed of the pickup truck.

"What are you doing?" she asked.

"We're going back to Connecticut."

"Thank God," she thought, making sure not to let Skip see her enthusiasm. She could see that he still appeared depressed.

"I'm going back to work on the reservation," he continued.

"Oh," Aline said. She had heard him talk vaguely about moving onto the reservation numerous times ever since John Stevens had mysteriously shown up there. But she had always dismissed Skip's talk as just that—talk. Until now.

Stunned by Aline's admission that she had been involved with another man, Skip finally assessed where his marriage and his personal life were headed. He had been in and out of work since 1969 and steadily unemployed since leaving Connecticut. For more than a year they had lived in a tiny camper, moving from place to place. They slept till noon most days, scrounged off friends for food, and their marital problems, while escalating out of control, were creeping into public view. He had even come to grips with the absurdity of aspirations to become a pastor. He had neither the discipline nor motivation to sustain a lifelong commitment to the ministry. And he knew it.

"Aline, I'm going to rebuild the reservation," Skip said.

THREE WEEKS LATER
CALAIS, MAINE

"Telephone's for you, John," Stevens's secretary said.

"Who is it?"

"Some guy named Skip. I think he said his last name was Haywood or Hayward."

"Skip?" Stevens paused. He had not heard from Hayward since meeting him nearly two years earlier. "Oh, Skip." Stevens eagerly put the receiver to his ear.

"Hello."

"This is Skip."

"Hi, Skip."

"I want to come up and see your operation. I want to see how you administer programs there."

"Well, I'd be happy to show you. When do you want to come up?"

"As soon as possible."

"OK. Let me tell you the best way to get here. The easiest thing is to fly into Bangor. Then I can pick you up at the airport."

"I can't afford to fly."

"Well, I could send you the money to get a ticket."

Within minutes, Stevens and Hayward had firmed up plans to meet at the Bangor Airport one week later.

6

FIERCE ADVOCATES

APRIL 4, 1975
STONINGTON, CONNECTICUT

AFTER SPENDING A WEEKEND WITH STEVENS IN MAINE, SKIP COULD NOT wait to have his first meeting with Tureen, who agreed to go to Skip's home, a run-down house he and Aline had rented after returning from Missouri. Tureen, who had purchased a small twin-engine plane in order to travel around New England to do business with his growing list of Indian tribe clients, flew to Connecticut.

With only a couple of family members waiting inside, Skip escorted Tureen inside his home and introduced everyone. "This is Tom Tureen," Skip said, looking at his family.

"Hi," Tureen said, smiling cordially and looking each of them in the eye.

"This is my sister, Theresa," Skip said, going around the room. "This is my mother. This is Aline, my wife."

"Nice to meet you," Tureen said, extending his hand.

"And this is my . . . "

As Skip named two other family members present, Tureen had already forgotten the names Skip had just said. His mind was preoccupied with sizing up whether Skip was capable of leading his tiny group through the rigors of a lawsuit, and whether he and Skip would work well together in an attorney-client relationship. The outward differences between them were already apparent. Short and slender, Tureen looked miniature standing next to Skip, husky, broad-shouldered, and fending off a pouch starting to form around his waistline. His hair cut short above the ears, Tureen stood with a pressed white shirt and tie, dress slacks, and neatly polished wingtip shoes. Hayward's hair was messy and long, and his worn-out T-shirt was untucked over his blue jeans. His hands were dry and chapped, rugged and thick from years of working with industrial tools. Tureen's fingers were silky smooth, having handled nothing but papers and books since leaving home after high school.

Other differences were not so discernible. Tureen was punctual and detail oriented. Skip was notoriously late and disorganized. Although not afraid to take risks, Tureen never did anything without a practical plan and carefully mapped-out objectives. Hayward was a grand dreamer with no sense of how to achieve his goals. Tureen, who came from wealth, was thrifty. Hayward, whose family always scrimped to get by, was wasteful.

"Have a seat," Skip said, extending a hand toward an orange sofa. Walking across a multicolored throw rug in the middle of the floor, Tureen sat down next to Theresa and set his briefcase on a beat-up coffee table. Two lamps with the plastic still over the lampshades sat on end tables at opposite ends of the room.

Before getting into the nuts and bolts of the lawsuit, Tureen discussed the history of the Pequot tribe with Hayward, whose knowledge was limited to the stories his grandmother had told him before passing away. He knew a great deal about what his grandmother said had transpired on the reservation over the past century. But he was not as familiar with the origins of the ancient Pequot tribe's dealings with Europeans, an area MacCulloch had collected information on and shared with Tureen.

Shortly before the first Dutch traders made their way into the Connecticut region in 1614, the Pequots crossed the Hudson River and invaded the Connecticut River valley region. Facing steep opposition from two tribes—the Podunks and the Nipmuck—the Pequots were driven southeastward until they finally settled in the area presently comprising the towns of Ledyard, North Stonington, and Mystic.

When the Dutch began trading and settling along the Connecticut coast in the early 1630s, they too had disputes with the Pequots. By 1634, both the Dutch and their chief trading partners, the Narragansett Indians, were preparing for war against the Pequots. Apparently tired of the Pequots' attempts to frustrate their trade with the Narragansett, the Dutch along the Connecticut coast killed a Pequot tribal chief and some of his men. The Pequots, in turn, killed some Narragansett Indians who were allies with the Dutch and had come to trade with them.

By November of 1634, the Pequots had invited the English from John Winthrop's Massachusetts Bay Company to establish a colony in southeastern Connecticut. "The reason why the Pequots desired so much our friendship," wrote Winthrop in his journal, "was because they were now in war with the Narragansett . . . and likewise with the Dutch who had killed their old sachem [chief]. They [the Pequots] offered us . . . what they could if we would settle a plantation there."

But by 1637, relations had soured between the Pequots and the English to a point where on May 12, 1637, the Massachusetts Bay Company received word that the Pequots had attacked one of their settlements in Weathersfield, Connecticut. Six men, three women, and a number of farm animals had been killed. In addition, two English girls were taken hostage.

The English formed an alliance with the Narragansett tribe and the Mohegan tribe—a group that had splintered off from the Pequots in a power struggle over tribal leadership. And under the direction of Captains John Mason and John Underhill, eighty English soldiers and more than a hundred Indians began marching toward the Pequot village under the cover of night on May 25, 1637. The soldiers arrived at the Mystic River in southeastern Connecticut just as the sun was rising on May 26. The Pequots were still asleep in their wigwams. Before the ambush began, the Narragansett and Mohegan Indians placed a distinguishing mark on themselves so the English would not confuse them with the Pequots once the fighting began.

When the English and the Indians quietly set fire to the Pequot village, men, women, and children burned in their sleep. Those who did not die sleeping emerged from their wigwams unarmed and disoriented, face-to-face with armed Indians and English soldiers standing ready with swords. "Down fell men, women, and children," wrote Captain Underhill in his journal. "Those that [e]scaped us fell into the hands of the [Mohegan] Indians that were in the rear of us. Great and doleful was the bloody sight to the view of young soldiers that never had been in war, to see so many souls lie gasping on the ground, so thick, in some places, that you could hardly pass along."

The bloody massacre lasted less than two hours. When the dust and smoke settled, the English had lost just two men, and no one from the Mohegan or Narragansett tribe had been killed. The casualties were almost exclusively on the Pequot side. It quickly became apparent that virtually no Pequot warriors had been in the village at the time of the attack. The dead consisted of 150 elderly men, women, and children. "Sometimes the Scripture declareth women and children must perish with their parents," wrote Underhill. "Sometimes the case alters; but we will not dispute it now. We had sufficient light from the word of God for our proceedings."

The event signaled the beginning of the end of the Pequot War that had been ongoing in the Connecticut area. Over the next few weeks, the English and their Indian allies pursued, killed, and captured Pequots throughout the Long Island Sound region and the Connecticut valley. The Pequot tribe was nearly wiped out altogether. The few survivors were divided up as slaves, with most of the women and children going to the Narragansett tribe and some to the English. Still others were sold as slaves and shipped to a Caribbean island off the coast of Nicaragua, which had been colonized by English Puritans.

In 1666, nearly thirty years after the Pequot War, the General Court of the Colony of Connecticut began establishing small regional reservations for those enslaved Pequots who remained alive. The reservation carved out in Groton was two thousand acres in size and called the Western Pequot Indian reservation.

By 1725, all Indian tribes in Connecticut were put under the jurisdiction of the governor and council of Connecticut. Although the Pequots were small in number, they were included.

Then in 1761, Connecticut's general assembly reduced the size of the Western Pequots' reservation, giving them title to roughly a thousand acres. Following the Revolutionary War, Congress passed and George Washington signed the Nonintercourse Act, requiring that any further land transactions involving Indians be preapproved by the federal government. This federal law, Tureen explained to the Haywards, entitled the Pequot tribe to recover eight hundred acres of Ledyard real estate that was once part of the existing reservation. In 1855, Connecticut reduced the Pequot reservation to just over two hundred acres when it sold to white settlers the other eight hundred acres. The federal government never approved the sales. As a result, according to Tureen, all the present landowners holding title to those eight hundred acres were illegally in possession of Pequot land.

Skip was completely unaware of the legal implications of the reservation's history. The prospect of acquiring real estate intrigued him. He had never owned land, much less eight hundred acres. And his chances of affording that much property were remote. Despite getting his old job back at Electric Boat and pulling in $229 per week, he had no savings. Worse still, he and Aline had a terrible credit history. But suddenly he saw opportunity. His lineage provided the potential to inherit old Indian land.

As a child Skip had always respected his grandmother's Native American culture. As a boy he had listened with interest to her renditions of the reservation's oral history and the tribe's ancient struggle to survive. Now, as a twenty-six-year-old adult, there was more reason than ever to claim that culture as his own. Tureen was offering a once-in-a-lifetime opportunity. "This is about restitution," said Tureen, explaining his approach in filing the suits. "Our objective is a little grander—to put our clients in the position that they would have been in if the laws had been obeyed and the Indians had been treated fairly all along. If that had happened, almost all of the Indians would be rich and powerful."

Rich and powerful was what Hayward wanted. It would be an antidote to his nightmarish financial situation.

"I have friends who are Rockefellers," Tureen said. "And nobody questions their wealth. Well, their wealth is fairly recent, a hundred years old. But nobody questions their entitlement. Certainly nobody ought to question the entitlement of any Indian tribe to be rich and powerful."

As eager as Skip was to retain Tureen, he knew he and his family were first going to have to undergo some significant lifestyle changes before they could file a lawsuit. Tureen's other clients had avoided assimilation into America's mainstream culture. They were minorities living on reservations where they remained isolated and maintained their own languages, rituals, and systems of tribal government. Unlike immigrants who willingly came to the United States to join America's great "melting pot," Indian tribes had historically not adapted their culture. In order for Skip and his family to sue as members of the Pequot tribe, they were going to have to behave more like immigrants, willing to suppress some of their American cultural habits in favor of the Pequot culture. For starters, they would have to stop referring to themselves as "white" on all government documents and job and license applications. And they would have to move onto the Indian reservation and claim membership in arguably the country's most neglected class of minorities.

When Tureen left Skip's house to return to Maine, he knew he had another client. But all the way home, a thought kept crossing his mind. He tried to ignore it. Yet it was persistently tugging at his conscience, like an eager toddler pulling at the pant leg of a preoccupied father. He had to admit, at least to himself, that Skip and his family were not like the Passamaquoddy and the Penobscot. The Haywards were Caucasian, did not speak a word of Pequot, were extremely few in number, and lacked the basic knowledge of the very tribe they claimed to belong to. None of them lived on the reservation. They were without a chief or tribal government, yet Skip had agreed to have Tureen sue on their behalf.

Now that Tureen had met Skip in person and conducted a preliminary meeting, he had to do what every other lawyer does at this stage—decide whether he could represent the client. The typical factors to consider—whether the case has merit, what the prospects of winning are, and whether the client has the means to afford legal fees—were not issues. Property records confirmed with certainty that Connecticut had sold off eight hundred acres of Pequot land without federal approval, giving the claim merit. And finances were irrelevant because Tureen was being paid by NARF, not the Haywards. The decision whether to take Skip on as a client turned on competing ethical rules. Lawyers have a sworn duty not to file lawsuits that they know to be frivolous. If Skip Hayward and his family were not true tribal members, then filing a lawsuit aimed at returning the tribe's land to them was frivolous. On the other hand, lawyers are advocates, not judges. Their responsibility is to zealously represent clients. Hayward was certainly a descendant of Elizabeth George. His bloodline to the Pequots was tissue thin, but, Tureen reasoned, it nonetheless existed. And Hayward claimed to belong to her tribe.

Tureen knew, however, that an ethical mistake at this stage could jeopardize all the other tribes he represented. "Our credibility is everything in these cases," thought Tureen. "They are theoretically so difficult to start with. And we are approaching all of these Indian land claims as a family of lawsuits. If we go down on one, we could lose them all."

Since helping the Maine tribes file hundred-million-dollar suits that were seeking millions of acres, Tureen had been approached by a number of individuals and groups that were not legitimate Indian tribes yet saw an opportunity for instant wealth. Native Americans referred to them as "wanna-bes," impostors trying to claim a distant relationship to an Indian in hopes of cashing in on new laws and legal theories designed to help economically depressed Indian tribes. Tureen had rejected six cases that he decided were without merit. "But this is certainly a legitimate claim," Tureen thought. He was intrigued by the complexity presented by the Pequots' case. "It just raises a very hard question as to tribal existence."

And he projected that the Haywards' credibility as a tribe could become a thorny issue if he filed a suit on their behalf. In 1901, the United States Supreme Court decided the issue of tribal existence in *Montoya v. United States*. Estanislao Montoya and his partners were in the livestock business in San Antonio, Texas. Approximately $3,000 worth of their horses and livestock was stolen by a group of marauding Apache Indians that had broken away from their reservation in Arizona. Montoya sued the federal government for compensation under the Indian Depredation Act, a law that enabled citizens whose property was taken or destroyed by Indian tribes to recover the value from the government. The question in the case turned on whether this group of roaming Apaches constituted a tribe. It forced the court to define for the first time what constituted a tribe. "By a 'tribe,'" the court wrote, "we understand a body of Indians of the same or a similar race, united in a community under one leadership or government, and inhabiting a particular though sometimes ill-defined territory." Montoya lost his case because the roaming Apaches did not satisfy the definition.

If he filed a suit on behalf of the Pequots, Tureen anticipated that defense lawyers would use the Montoya case to challenge his clients' tribal status. "The Pequots are all Haywards," Tureen thought. "That's all the tribe is."

In contrast, another one of his newest clients—the Waupanoag Indians—resembled a more traditional tribe like the Passamaquoddy and Penobscot. "In Mashpee there is a much more real Indian community and certainly much more of a tribe," Tureen thought. "But the state of Massachusetts no longer recognizes them as a tribe. The intriguing thing is that Connecticut still recognizes the Pequots as a tribe.

"That ices it," he thought. "If the state of Connecticut treats the Pequots as a tribe, then it will be prevented from denying the tribe exists."

From a legal standpoint, Tureen's analysis was sound. But Tureen knew he was pushing the envelope. "With Pequot, we get to the theoretical limits of what a tribe is," Tureen thought.

But, as a plaintiff's attorney, he was obligated to advocate for his clients, not question their legitimacy. That was the government's job. "I'm not a judge," he insisted. "I'm their advocate. Our job is to do as much as we can for federally nonrecognized tribes. That's the way our legal system works. We are representing the Haywards. We are not the federal government or the state of Connecticut. We are advocates, fierce advocates for our clients. Our approach is to never exaggerate, overstate, or puff acreage but to bring every claim that can possibly be brought."

7

JOINING THE CLUB

AUGUST 10, 1975
WESTERN PEQUOT RESERVATION

MUGGY AIR AND CLOUDY SKIES BLANKETED SOUTHEASTERN CONNECTICUT as more than twenty individuals parked their cars near the old Elizabeth George homestead. They had traveled from nearby towns, eager to find out why Skip Hayward had so enthusiastically invited them there. His mother and siblings had already been clued in to his meeting with Tureen. Other distant cousins, aunts, and uncles did not know him personally but came on the recommendation of relatives who did. For some, it marked the first time they had ever stepped foot on the reservation, and they required directions on how to get there. All of them, however, shared one thing: They were somehow related to Elizabeth George.

This diverse group of distant cousins, half sisters and brothers, and in-laws arrived just after noon. An old wooden stove assembled outside the Elizabeth George homestead was lit. On it, a pot of succotash—an Indian dish comprising a mixture of cooked corn, lima beans, and tomatoes—was stewing for them to eat.

Once everyone was seated outside the small house, Skip stood up, and with passion and conviction, he began by sharing his grandmother's hopes, and her struggle to maintain the reservation to avoid the very real possibility that the state would seize it and convert it into parklands. He had plans, he said, to preserve the reservation and enlarge it to nearly five times its current size. Using federal subsidies, they could finance some start-up businesses on the reservation. And, as a federally recognized tribe, any revenue generated by these businesses would be tax-exempt and subject to few government regulations. It was a great opportunity, a chance to take a spin at the wheel of fortune and come up big.

Reading the skepticism—about him, about his plan—Hayward told them they had a powerful ally. A week earlier, a lawyer from Maine named Tom Tureen had visited his home and agreed to be the family's attorney. Tureen offered to file a lawsuit against a host of Ledyard residents living on the land directly adjacent to the reservation. According to a federal law, all that land was illegally taken from the tribe in the 1850s and rightfully belonged to them.

What did it have to do with them? As descendants and relatives of Elizabeth George, they were eligible to join their names to the lawsuit as plaintiffs. "It would be better if it was more than just the Hayward family," Skip said. "The more people that could get involved, or the more people that could claim lineage from the reservation would give us a stronger case." Still, they could work with what they had.

To join the litigation, family members first had to join the Pequot tribe and start identifying themselves as American Indians. They needed to come together and start acting like a tribe. That meant a tribal constitution had to be drafted, leaders had to be elected, and membership rolls had to be created, in order to show that the tribe was populated. Most importantly, the group had to establish residency on the reservation.

All of these steps were aimed at satisfying the legal definition of a tribe, as described by Tureen. If accomplished, the group would undergo a sort of cultural assimilation through civil litigation.

The requirement to start identifying themselves as "American Indian" rather than "Caucasian" was more formality than substance. It was not as if the sudden change in title was going to instantly transform their cultural makeup from white Americans to Native Americans. Yet it still caused some in the group to pause. For them, it was a completely foreign way of viewing themselves. Until then, they had never seen themselves as anything other than what they were raised to be: ordinary citizens who got up every day and went to work or school, lived in residential neighborhoods, paid taxes, and hoped to achieve financial security. The concept of tribal membership was completely foreign. They knew little or nothing about the Pequot history and culture, or what it meant to belong to a tribe. To that point being an Indian in American society was more of a burden than a benefit.

That very thing had caused some individuals to avoid the meeting on the reservation altogether. One Ledyard resident distantly related to Skip vehemently brushed off his invitation to come to the reservation. "I ain't no damn Indian," the relative said.

"Skip had to get tribal membership numbers up, so he was looking around for members," said another relative, who was familiar with the incident. "But the individual Skip approached, as well as his family, were getting along just fine financially. He didn't want to get involved in something that was going to subject his kids to being slurred and the stigma of being an Indian."

A noted absentee at the meeting was Skip's father. Although Skip's mother and siblings were eager to go along, Skip's father wanted no association with the Pequot tribe. He had moved his family back to Ledyard from Maryland, but stayed clear of the family's talk of preserving their grandmother's legacy. Skip's father never got along with her to begin with.

Rather than deter him, though, his father's criticism only motivated Skip further. Yet he seemed the most unlikely person to lead a group of people to a successful verdict in a civil lawsuit. He had trouble holding down a steady job. He had never gone to college. And he was terrible with managing money.

"It was hard to imagine," said Bruce Kirchner, a twenty-five-year-old professional with a degree in business administration who listened to Hayward's proposal. "But Skip had a way of keeping people interested, motivated." Kirchner was a distant cousin of Hayward's, and like some of the other relatives he had never met Hayward until the reunion on the reservation. He reluctantly attended at the urging of his grandmother, an elderly half-sister of Elizabeth George. Kirchner's grandmother thought that his business background would be useful to Hayward in his plans to reestablish a tribal presence on the reservation.

Prior to hearing Skip, Kirchner had heard almost nothing about the Pequots. He grew up in nearby Norwich, and like any other grade-school child in southeastern Connecticut he learned of Indian history through field trips to a makeshift Indian museum operated by the nearby Mohegan Indians. But he had never experienced the Indian culture, or even been to the reservation, much less lived on it. His only childhood recollection was his grandmother's occasional stories about having been born on the reservation. "The tone of the talk was, 'This is ancient history,'" recalled Kirchner. "There was no talk about who's left." Yet he was intrigued by the possibilities of Hayward's plan.

He saw something in him, as did the others who attended the meeting, and was taken by Hayward's charisma and natural leadership qualities. Too, his pitch to unite as a tribe was almost evangelical.

Watching Skip's performance in front of his relatives, Aline was impressed but not surprised. Fluidly, he was reinventing himself into a tribal leader. Using the same captivating speech qualities she had seen him use to excite and motivate people in the church, Skip spoke to his family as if he were in the pulpit. His enthusiasm was contagious.

By the end of the day, every person who had attended the meeting had pledged their support to Skip's effort to establish a tribal government and a set of guidelines and qualifications for adding individuals to the Pequot tribe. Skip introduced a constitution, which Tureen had drafted for them. Article I of the document stated: "The name of this organization shall be the 'Mashantucket (Western) Pequot Tribe' being the same organization as that referred to in Connecticut State Legislation as the 'Western Pequot Tribe' of Connecticut."

The document also hinted at the tribe's intention to expand its present reservation. Article II of the Constitution identified the tribe's jurisdiction as extending to the present reservation "and to such other lands as may hereafter be added thereto under any law of the State of Connecticut and of the United States."

The six-page constitution was ratified and signed by Skip, Bruce Kirchner, three of Skip's sisters, one of Elizabeth George's surviving daughters, and four other individuals. After ratifying the document, the group held its first election, unanimously selecting Skip as the newly organized tribe's first chief. His formal title was "tribal chairman."

Since Connecticut law had no fixed eligibility requirements for tribal membership, the group drew up a set of by-laws of their own, patterned after the ones John Stevens had shown Skip on his visit to Maine. It allowed them to determine wholly independently who would qualify as a Pequot. That was not always the case, however. In 1961, the state legislature passed a law requiring that persons identifying themselves as Indians possess a minimum one-eighth quantum of Indian blood. The blood-quantum requirement was established to reduce fraud and abuse, and it was widely supported by Indians across the state. Non-Indians, some of whom were jobless and others of whom were just exploitative, had been moving onto state Indian reservations to take advantage of the free land. Some of these trespassers even held down jobs off the reservation while receiving state welfare benefits that were earmarked for bona fide Native Americans.

The law eliminated the fraud and by the early 1970s was seen by the Indians as no longer necessary. On April 19, 1974, just months before Tureen met Hayward, the state legislature amended the old law and did away with the one-eighth blood-quantum requirement. Connecticut's Indian Affairs Council, which was established in 1973 by Governor Meskill and consisted of three state-appointed attorneys and a representative from each state tribe, recommended the change.

Bob Nicola, an attorney who was appointed to the council by the governor, thought it was necessary for the survival of the state's tribe. Widespread intermarriage was diluting bloodlines quickly. "This statute would have virtually eradicated Native Americans in the state. One of the first things that we did was pass an internal resolution to pass onto the legislature saying that each tribe had the ability and authority to determine who qualified as a member of their tribe. We eliminated the blood quota."

At the urging of the Indian Council, the state legislature amended the 1961 law. "Membership determination shall be made in accordance with the practice and usage of the tribe in which membership is claimed," read the amendment. Without this change, Hayward and his relatives would have been unable to qualify as Indians under the old state law. Their bloodline was simply too diluted. But under the new law, Skip and his relatives set a standard that admitted individuals who were "genealogically recorded as a Western Pequot by the State of Connecticut." Anyone who could trace his or her genealogy to an individual who was identified as a Pequot Indian on the 1910 census was eligible to pay a small fee and join the tribe. Elizabeth George, although dead, was the last living person who lived on the reservation in 1910.

One year after Connecticut changed its law on tribal admission policies, Irving Harris, the chairman of the state's Indian Affairs Council that recommended the change, expressed concerns over what was resulting from the law. "People want to be instant Indians and it has to stop," said Harris, a member of the Schaghticoke Indian tribe. "We have to make sure that things that are meant for Indians, go to Indians. People have been crawling out of the woodwork and saying they belong to different tribes."

MARCH 1976

John Stevens was hardly surprised when his secretary told him Skip was on the line. Since deciding to retain Tureen, Skip had been telephoning Stevens on almost a weekly basis. He had already taken numerous trips to Maine to observe the new homes the Passamaquoddy were constructing with loans and grants that Tureen helped them secure. And he had been leaning on Stevens for advice on ways to govern his small but growing tribal community in Ledyard.

"I'm glad you called," Stevens said. "I need to tell you about an important hearing that is coming up in Boston next month."

Due in large part to the efforts of the Native American Rights Fund and activists interested in improving conditions for Native Americans, Congress had formed the American Indian Policy Review Commission. Its task was to conduct a comprehensive study on how to improve the government's ability to better service all Native Americans.

The commission, which was made up of congressmen and Indian leaders, formed eleven task forces and assigned each one a particular area of Indian policy to review. "The Task Force of Nonfederally Recognized Indians" (Task Force No. 10) was asked to make policy suggestions on what to do about state tribes like the Passamaquoddy that did not appear on the federal government's list of tribes. Given the legal developments in Maine, the commission nominated John Stevens to serve on that task force. George Tomer, a member of the Penobscot Nation—one of Tureen's other clients—was named as a task force specialist.

Using Susan MacCulloch's list as a reference, Task Force No. 10 invited every state tribe in New England to Boston for two days of hearings. Since members of Congress had pledged to attend the hearings, the task force wanted to show the government just how many Indians it had been neglecting.

"It's very important that your tribe be represented at this meeting," Stevens told Hayward. "This hearing is to help eastern tribes get federally recognized. And I want you to take part in the process. It's important for you to make an impression on the federal government in order to get your land claim into court."

Hayward explained that he was out of work and could not afford the gas it would take to drive there, much less the cost of one night in a Boston hotel.

"Don't worry about the expenses. I'll pay your way."

Skip paused before offering to bring it up with his family and see whether they thought he should go.

"I'm putting your name on the witness list. I want you to testify at the hearing."

"I'll see what my people say," Skip said before hanging up, unsure if he wanted to stand up in front of government officials and hundreds of other Indians.

APRIL 1976
JFK FEDERAL BUILDING IN BOSTON

Seated in the middle of the cramped room, Susan MacCulloch put a checkmark alongside the last Indian name on her agenda of witnesses scheduled to testify. She looked up at the clock on the wall. It was 2:30. In thirty minutes, the second and final day of testimony before the task force would be over. When she had put together the mailing list for the hearings months earlier, she never imagined that so many Indians would actually show up in Boston. There were not enough seats to accommodate them all, forcing many to stand against the wall or sit on the floor.

Her husband's expectations had been exceeded. Stevens wanted nothing more than to show the government that the tribes in Maine were not alone. There were dozens of New England tribes that had been denied federal funds and sovereign status on their reservations. MacCulloch could not help feeling proud as she stared at her husband sitting on the platform at the head of the room alongside Ada Deer, one of the commissioners on the Indian Policy Review Commission. MacCulloch's only disappointment in the hearings was the absence of Skip Hayward. Her husband had placed him on the agenda to testify. And she was looking forward to meeting him for the first time after hearing so much about him from Stevens and Tureen. She, more than anyone, was responsible for Tureen and Hayward linking up.

As the last witness was concluding his remarks, a disturbance in the back of the room distracted the audience's attention. Heads turned. A husky white man wearing a black leather jacket stood in the rear of the room. Three white women flanked him, their shabby clothes and disheveled hair causing eyes to shift from the leather-clad man to them.

Not recognizing them, MacCulloch was sure they were uninvited.

As the four individuals approached the stage area, John Stevens scurried to his feet and whispered something in the ear of the person chairing the hearing.

The chair suddenly rose to his feet and addressed the audience. "The task force would be pleased to hear from Pequot tribal chairman Richard Hayward."

Stunned, MacCulloch craned her neck to see who Hayward was.

It was the white man in the black leather jacket. "He doesn't look particularly Indian," she thought to herself, noting his light-skinned complexion.

"I understand the purpose of being here today is to prove to the federal government that we are a tribe of Indians that might receive recognition as such," Hayward began, his voice edged with defiance. "You asked us how large we are and I say that we wouldn't be so small if you had not killed us all off and tried to destroy us from the earth, even our name. Is this how you finally try to put an end to us, by denying us services that would allow us to return to our reservation and survive as an Indian community so that we might flourish and prosper or have such luxuries permitted by other races?"

Hayward had immediate command of his audience. MacCulloch noticed that he was not relying on notes or a written text. "He speaks pretty well," she thought to herself. "He seems a little better educated than some Indians." But MacCulloch could not escape the thought that Hayward looked Caucasian. Yet he spoke with the conviction of a Native American.

"The policy of dealing only with so-called recognized tribes is totally arbitrary," Hayward continued. "In the Passamaquoddy case, the courts have said the United States can't deny protection of federal law to tribes on the grounds that it is not recognized, so why does this committee come here and address us as unrecognized tribes? And I resent the implication that I am a second-class Indian."

Task force member George Tomer from the Penobscot tribe listened to Skip, intrigued. "Who are the Pequots?" he thought. "The Western Pequots were the least documented group of all the ones that testified. We have some very learned people among the New England tribes, people who did a lot of research and presented very well documented cases of who they were and what they were. The Pequots, except for Skip's knowledge of the history, had nothing in document form to show us who they were." Yet Tomer was captivated by Skip's speech.

Hayward went into a graphic description of the Pequot War and the brutal massacre of women and children at the hands of white colonists. Two of the women with him—his mother and sister—began sobbing. Aline expressed no emotion, her eyes never looking up from her lap.

"I felt compelled to come here today to testify out of a promise I made to my grandmother to continue this tribe," Skip said before stepping down.

Tears welled up in the eyes of Tomer. Looking across the audience, he observed that he was not alone. Virtually all in the room were emotional. Hayward had delivered the most gripping testimony in the entire two days of hearings. "The committee had seen some extreme forms of poverty throughout the United States," Tomer thought. "But the Pequots were poor. Skip's description of the tribe's conquest and defeat at Pequot, the death of warriors, and the death of the elders, women, and children was very compelling."

Finding himself instantly surrounded by strangers, Skip, always uncomfortable in a crowd, searched desperately for a familiar face.

"Skip," Stevens called out, working his way through the crowd.

Sweating, Skip reached out to him.

"Skip, I'm so glad you made it. That was a great presentation. I think you really made an impression on the group."

8

ADVERSE POSSESSION

May 10, 1976
Ledyard, Connecticut

School buses were lined up outside Ledyard Center School. Grammar-school children trying to beat the 8:30 bell rushed inside the one-story redbrick schoolhouse that was surrounded by a chain-link fence. Across the street, the doors to the town hall had just been unlocked. A tall, slender man with long sideburns and wavy hair, twenty-eight-year-old David Holdridge, who had just dropped off his seven-year-old son at school, parked his green Chevrolet Impala between the town hall and the firehouse next door. Dressed in jeans and a sweatshirt, Holdridge, a member of the town council, entered through the front door and passed by the plaque in the entryway that bore the name of his father, Paul Holdridge, who was on the Ledyard board of selectmen when the town hall was built in 1956. After retrieving some paperwork, Holdridge exited the building and got in his car to head home. Before pulling out of the parking lot onto Route 117, Holdridge sat patiently while cars and pickup trucks drove through the center of town dutifully abiding by the twenty-mile-per-hour speed limit that was posted around the school. Looking to his right past the firehouse, he saw the pharmacy and the local diner. On the opposite side of the street, alongside the schoolyard, was the largest building in town—the Congregational Church where Holdridge attended. Turning left onto Route 117, he drove past Holdridge's tree nursery—a garden store owned by his family—and the bakery and the post office before stopping at the town's only traffic light. Less than two minutes later he pulled into his driveway at the corner of Church Hill Road and Spicer Hill Road, streets named after families that settled the area hundreds of years earlier.

A recently hired political science instructor at nearby Mohegan Community College, Holdridge could hardly wait to get inside his modest ranch-style home and prepare the lecture he had to deliver that night to the freshmen in his American government class. It was his first teaching job since finishing graduate school, and it allowed him to do what he loved most—talk about politics. His passion for politics developed in his early teens when his father, Paul Holdridge Sr., a loyal Democrat, was serving as one of Ledyard's first selectmen. While attending the University of Connecticut in the 1960s, David joined the Democratic Party and led antiwar protests. In 1968, the year after he graduated, he was drafted and sent to Vietnam and Laos. After being discharged, Holdridge campaigned for presidential candidate George McGovern in 1972. That same year, Holdridge convinced the Ledyard Congregational Church to establish a refugee placement program. Under his leadership, families from war-torn Laos were brought to Ledyard from refugee camps and provided with housing. Before his twenty-eighth birthday, Holdridge was elected chairman of the Democratic Party in the town of Ledyard and won his seat on the town council.

Besides his own political aspirations, Holdridge's enthusiasm for teaching American government was fueled by Ledyard's rich history. Holdridge's ancestors were among the first English Puritans to settle in the Ledyard area, not too long after the Pilgrims landed at Plymouth Rock in 1620. In the mid-1600s, John Winthrop Jr. left the Massachusetts Bay Company to become governor of the Connecticut Colony. He sailed from Massachusetts to Long Island Sound before heading up the Thames River, where he docked and named the territory Groton, after his home in England, Groton Manor. In 1705, Groton became its own town.

Groton Heights, a hill in Groton located directly across the river from New London, later became a battle site between the British and the colonists in the Revolutionary War. The British Navy sailed up the Thames River on September 6, 1781, and attacked the colonists less than one mile from where Winthrop had landed. Despite being positioned inside Fort Griswold atop Groton Heights, the colonists were soundly defeated by the British. The fort's commander, Colonel William Ledyard, was killed in the attack, and after independence was secured, the legislature honored Colonel Ledyard by carving out a small thirteen-square-mile area of Groton and creating a new town in his name. Ledyard was incorporated as a town in 1836.

Sitting at his dining-room table with a glass of orange juice and a yellow notepad, Holdridge jotted down notes for the night's lesson. Suddenly he was interrupted by a loud knock at the front door. He put down his pen and drank the last bit of orange juice in his glass. "I wonder who that could be?" he thought as he got up from the table and headed toward the door. It was midmorning, and he was not expecting any visitors. His wife, Sara, had taken their three-month-old baby and two-year-old daughter out to run errands.

On his front door stoop he found a stern-faced, large black man wearing a dark suit with a white shirt and dark-colored tie. The tight fit of his suit jacket displayed his muscular chest and massive arms. His shirt collar fit awkwardly around his thick neck. A pair of sunglasses was visible in his front pocket.

Before Holdridge said a word, the man unfolded a black leather wallet. Inside was a badge and a photo identification card that read "U.S. MARSHAL."

Holdridge had never been in trouble with the law before. Questions immediately began flashing through his mind. "Was someone in trouble? Are my kids OK? My wife? Have I done something wrong?"

"Are you David Holdridge?" the imposing marshal asked in a low voice.

"Yes," Holdridge replied hesitantly.

The marshal handed him a summons and a short stack of papers. Then he produced a receipt and pen. "Would you please sign here," he said as he pointed to a line with the word "defendant" next to it.

"What's this all about?" Holdridge asked.

"This is a legal summons and documents having to do with Indian claims," the marshal responded matter-of-factly.

Unclear of what was going on, Holdridge signed the receipt acknowledging that he had been served with court papers. Holdridge squinted as he looked the marshal directly in the eyes. "A summons?" he asked.

"You should probably consult an attorney," the marshal said flatly as he turned and walked toward his car, leaving Holdridge standing alone with the stack of legal documents. Holdridge noticed a gold insignia on the driver's-side door of the marshal's black sedan. The only words he could read were the big capital letters across the top that read U.S. GOVERNMENT. Standing motionless, he watched as the sedan pulled out of his dirt driveway, leaving behind it a cloud of dust that floated slowly across the front lawn.

Once the car was out of sight, Holdridge looked more closely at the papers he had just been handed. The first page read "United States District Court, District of Connecticut" across the top. Underneath that, on the right-hand side of the page were the words "Civil Action No. 76–193. COMPLAINT." The left side of the page identified Richard Hayward and the Western Pequot tribe of Indians as the plaintiffs.

"Skip Hayward?" Holdridge whispered under his breath. Holdridge was roughly the same age as Hayward and had known him since childhood. "I never considered him an Indian."

Under the heading "DEFENDANTS" was a list of twenty-seven names. On the top of that list was Holdridge Enterprises, Incorporated, a landowning corporation that David and his brother had formed to bring their father's land holdings under one entity. During the years that their father had been a first selectman, he had made a habit of buying up land in Ledyard that was sold at foreclosure. Most of the lots were undeveloped tracts of forestland. David's father had asked him to serve as president of the family corporation.

"Why is Skip suing us?" Holdridge asked out loud as he walked back inside and read further. "This is a civil action to restore the Western Pequot Tribe of Indians to possession of certain aboriginal and reservation lands in the town of Ledyard," the complaint read. According to the complaint, Holdridge Enterprises was illegally in possession of three wooded lots, amounting to nearly eighty acres. All three lots were about one mile from Holdridge's home and were adjacent to the existing reservation.

So perplexed by the absurdity of the lawsuit's claim, Holdridge did not know whether to get angry or laugh. He immediately called up his sixty-four-year-old father, told him the news, and asked if he had any idea what this could be about. But Paul Holdridge Sr. was even more confused than his son. He had purchased the three lots identified in the lawsuit back when he was the first selectman. All three property deeds and the titles to the land could be traced back to 1855 when the state owned the property. "There must be some kind of mistake," said Holdridge Sr.

When he served as first selectman, Holdridge Sr. had gotten to know Hayward's grandmother, Elizabeth George, quite well. He used to bring food and other items to her at the reservation, knowing that she lived alone and had no transportation off the reservation. David, then a young boy, usually tagged along. By his father's side, he acquired a great deal of respect for Ms. George and some familiarity with the reservation. But neither David nor his father had ever seen a tribe living there. And since Ms. George had died three years earlier, they knew the reservation had been abandoned altogether.

"Who are all these people calling themselves the Pequot tribe?" Holdridge Sr. asked his son.

"Well, I don't know," David responded as he looked over a list of defendants, names of neighbors and friends. "But we're not the only ones whose land they're after."

Sixty-two-year-old Wendell Comrie, the owner of a self-operated sawmill in town, was sued for 263 acres of pristine wooded land. As Holdridge would eventually discover, most of the land in question was vacant and adjacent to the reservation.

After he hung up the phone, Holdridge continued scanning the list. Sisters Eleanor Drake and Helen Curran, who had volunteered countless hours working for a Catholic charity that raised money for deprived Indian tribes in the Southwest, were sued for seventy-eight acres. Margaret Henkle, an elderly woman, was sued for fifty-two acres. Linda and Tod Frazer were sued for thirty-one acres.

Holdridge recognized that two of the defendants on the list did live on the property in question. Walter Domoracki, a poor, sixty-year-old farmer whose land bordered Comrie's land, had lived there for thirty-seven years. His ninety-year-old father had farmed the same land and still lived there with his son's family. The lawsuit accused Domoracki and his family of trespassing and threatened to take away their entire sixty-seven-acre farm.

Seventy-two-year-old George Burns and his elderly wife, Mildred, were also accused of trespassing and stood to lose their home. Their house was right next to the wooded lots owned by the Holdridges.

• • •

Before Holdridge realized it, the afternoon had passed. A good part of his was spent talking on the telephone to puzzled friends and family about the lawsuit. It was news to everyone who had been sued that an Indian tribe existed in their town. Yet none were more stunned than Holdridge's friend Lois Tefft. She and her husband Tom owned a large farm that bordered the reservation. The Teffts and Elizabeth George had been neighbors since 1958 when the Teffts bought the run-down farmhouse alongside the reservation and restored it. Lois, a rustic woman in her forties who loved the outdoors, did a great deal of the farmhouse restoration herself. After moving onto the farm, she made friends with Ms. George and the two of them often rode horses together. Lois owned a number of horses and enjoyed exploring the trails that weaved through her property and the reservation. She often brought produce from her farm to Ms. George's homestead. She also was well acquainted with Skip, having known him since he was a young teenager.

Of all the defendants, Tefft had the strongest friendship with Hayward and his family. The idea of opposing the Haywards in court sickened Tefft, who had even helped Skip and his wife during hard times.

Threatened with losing her farm, Tefft was the first defendant to call a lawyer. Within hours of being served papers by the same federal marshal who went to Holdridge's house, Tefft telephoned attorney Jackson King, a young lawyer at Brown, Jacobson, Jewett & Laudone, one of the most respected law firms in southeastern Connecticut. King lived in Ledyard and was one of Tefft's most trusted friends. The two met seven years earlier when Tefft was serving on the Conservation Commission, a local environment-conscious organization that worked to preserve land and natural habitat around Ledyard. In 1969 King joined the commission and began working closely with Tefft. In their joint effort to protect land from development, Tefft and King had hiked together and surveyed various wooded areas around Ledyard. One of King's favorite spots was the Pequot Indian reservation. Tefft and her husband had accompanied King and his wife on horseback through the reservation's trails on numerous occasions.

When Tefft reached King by telephone at his law office late in the afternoon on May 10 and told him that she had been sued, he immediately sensed the anxiety in her voice. "Why don't you and Tom come over to my house tonight," King told her over the phone. "This is important. Let's not wait."

That night, Lois and her husband sat at King's kitchen table with him as he read through the complaint. They waited anxiously as King, who specialized in real estate law and commercial business transactions, looked over each page. "This is ridiculous," King said after looking over the documents. "It's impossible."

"What do we do?" asked Lois.

"You have to respond," King said. "They're claiming primarily here, Lois, that your land belonged to them until it was illegally transferred back in the 1800s."

Tefft could not believe her farm was at risk.

"It can't be," said King. "The law protects people like you. You bought your farm in the fifties. There are all kinds of legal doctrines—'adverse possession,' 'laches.' On top of everything else, this is a ridiculous claim. Our system of laws can't allow this to happen to you."

No matter how sentimental Tefft felt toward the Haywards, King's assessment reinforced what she already realized. After being friendly neighbors for years, they were now legal adversaries. King knew that Lois respected the rights of Indians and the rights of the Pequots, but not at the expense of her own farm. There was no question when Lois went to him that they had to defeat the lawsuit.

It rained in Ledyard the day after Tefft met with King. The banner headline across the top of *The Day*, eastern Connecticut's largest newspaper, read, "Indians Sue to Obtain 800 Acres in Ledyard." Both Holdridge and Tefft were named in the article as codefendants. Hayward was identified as the tribe president and the plaintiff. The article went on to say, "The suit is similar to a court challenge in Maine, where Indians are claiming almost half the state was taken from them illegally."

Tefft called Holdridge and suggested that they talk to the other defendants and retain King's law firm to represent them. Holdridge, who also knew King, agreed. He was familiar with King's work on the Conservation Commission and his interest in local issues. Holdridge and Tefft split up the list of defendants and began telephoning them. Wendell Comrie did not know King but was eager to retain him when Holdridge called him. Comrie owned more than a quarter of the eight hundred acres involved in the suit. Approximately a dozen other defendants also agreed to have

King represent them. The rest of the defendants, claiming they could not afford to hire lawyers, chose not to join the group.

Although he had never handled a case involving Indian law, King seemed like the right guy for the job. He was a local, worked at a very reputable firm, and was particularly knowledgeable in property law. In addition to serving on Ledyard's zoning board, he frequently handled real estate transactions for clients. King grew up in New Haven and graduated from the University of Connecticut with a degree in history in 1965. Concerned about the Vietnam War, King applied to law school, partly out of hope that he would be skipped over in the draft. He entered the University of Connecticut Law School without any specific aspirations, but he immediately excelled and ended up graduating first in the class of 1968.

Still unsure of what particular type of law he wanted to specialize in, he was offered a coveted clerkship for the chief justice of the Connecticut Supreme Court, John Hamilton King (no relation). After clerking at the state supreme court for two years, he accepted a position with the law firm Brown, Jacobson, Jewett & Laudone and moved to Ledyard.

Academically, King was very bright. But his outward appearance was not nearly as polished. When he spoke, he used legal terms seldom understood by nonlawyers. He had a hard time maintaining eye contact. His shoulders had a slight hunch to them. And his white dress shirts looked too big, given his skinny build. Even in an expensive suit, he looked shabby. None of that mattered, however. He did not have to appear before juries. The firm assigned him to business-oriented work, representing small companies and individuals in real estate transactions. He also did some environmental litigation. In large part, King was a deal maker. Most of his work was done behind a desk or on the telephone, not in a courtroom.

At first blush, King was confident that he could defeat the complaint showed to him by Tefft. But since it involved an area of law he had no experience in whatsoever, he showed a copy of the complaint to his law partner Wayne Tillinghast, the firm's best trial lawyer. Like King, Tillinghast graduated from the University of Connecticut Law School and finished number one in his class. He was on law review and graduated with honors in 1960. He had been practicing for nine years longer than King.

Tillinghast, who had just turned forty and had a receding hairline, was one of the best medical-malpractice trial lawyers in the state. A conservative dresser who wore colored dress shirts and wide ties, he was in court almost every day. He knew every judge by name and knew his way around the courthouse better than any lawyer in the firm. There were few things he enjoyed more than a hard-fought trial, and he rarely lost. When King showed him the complaint, Tillinghast scoffed as he read that the Pequots were using a law written two hundred years ago to accuse the defendants of trespassing. "How could it possibly be?" asked Tillinghast. "This doesn't sound like much to me."

While standing around Tillinghast's desk, both lawyers discussed the various defenses they could raise to defeat the claim. "What about the statute of limitations?" Tillinghast asked. State law imposed a twenty-year time limit for filing trespassing claims. According to the complaint, the Indian land was unlawfully taken over in 1850. That was over 125 years ago.

"What about 'adverse possession'?" said King, referring to the property law that said even squatters established a legal right to possess someone else's land if the rightful titleholder to the property does not file a timely complaint with the court to remove them.

The defendants were by no means squatters—they all held legal titles to their property. But even if they were trespassing, they had been doing so for over one hundred years without any complaint from the Pequots. Under common law, the defendants would be recognized as the property owners. Possession is nine-tenths of the law.

"Forget all that," Tillinghast finally announced. "This statute, the Nonintercourse Act, was passed in *1790*. What are these plaintiffs talking about? These defendants have owned their land for years."

Both lawyers agreed the lawsuit filed by the Haywards was little more than nonsense. "This is going to be fun," said Tillinghast, who agreed to assist King in the case.

King scheduled a time for the clients to come to the law office for an initial meeting. Tillinghast, in the meantime, decided to research whether courts had decided any similar lawsuits. Since he studied history for a hobby and was well read on current legal affairs, he was not very optimistic that his search was going to turn up much. He was shocked at what he discovered.

The state of Maine was on the verge of losing half of its land base to two Indian tribes. Similar suits had been filed in New York, Rhode Island,

Louisiana, North Carolina, and Virginia. The lawyers in each case were Tom Tureen and his associates—the same ones whose names appeared on the papers filed against the Ledyard landowners. Tillinghast had never heard of Tureen. Nor had King. But in 1974 the *New York Times* had proclaimed Tureen's Maine office "a nationwide center for legal aid to Indians" and announced that his team was "taking up the cause of the Connecticut Indians."

Not only was the Haywards' lawsuit for real, but so were the lawyers who had filed it. And they had already taken legal action on behalf of another Connecticut tribe—the Golden Hill Paugussetts—located in Trumbull, about an hour and a half east of Ledyard. The case had received virtually no press in the Connecticut newspapers. Nobody took the case seriously.

Tillinghast knew nothing about Indian law, but he knew an ambush when he saw one. With almost no fanfare, the lawyers representing the Haywards had thrown the property titles of thousands of people around the Northeast into question. Now they were coming to Ledyard.

"To call Tureen and his staff experts isn't even accurate," said Robert Nicola, a Connecticut attorney who was appointed to the state's Indian Affairs Council in 1973. Hayward asked Nicola to assist Tureen's office in the case against the Ledyard landowners. Since Tureen's office was in Calais, over seven hours away, Nicola filled the role of filing all the legal documents in Connecticut. "Tureen and his team were the only ones [in the country] doing this kind of litigation, and they did nothing other than this," said Nicola. "Nobody had an iota of the knowledge, capacity, and legal expertise that they had. I was just flattered to be working with these guys. They were the only game in town and they knew the game very, very well."

Tureen's success alarmed Tillinghast. "What is going on out there with these cases?" he asked himself, knowing the defendants would be coming in to get advice from him and King in a few days. Most of the defenses he and King had discussed had already been raised in Maine and other places. In each instance, the courts had ruled Tureen's way. "What are we going to tell these poor people in Ledyard?" thought Tillinghast. "They are not going to believe this."

9

THE FIRM

DAVID HOLDRIDGE WALKED UP SHETUCKET STREET IN NORWICH UNTIL he reached building number 22. Large, Gothic pillars supported the front of the three-story structure. It had an intimidating stone facade and large plate-glass window. A small, rectangular gold sign imbedded in the stone surface by the front door read BROWN, JACOBSON, JEWETT & LAUDONE. When Allyn Brown and Milton Jacobson merged their respective law firms in 1966, they bought the building from the Hartford National Bank. The layout of an old bank was not ideal for setting up a law firm, but the location was perfect. The Norwich Superior Court building was directly across the street.

Holdridge pulled open the heavy door, walked up three short steps, and entered a second door that led into the office. A receptionist seated at an antique wooden desk greeted him. While waiting for the rest of the defendants to arrive, Holdridge observed the prints of old sea vessels decorating the lobby walls. Soon Wendell Comrie and his wife arrived, followed by Lois Tefft. The Frazer couple showed up. Helen Curran and Eleanor Drake came together. The elderly Margaret Henkle sent her daughter, Mary Barthelson, who stood to inherit her mother's land.

Although Holdridge was irritated by the lawsuit, he was not uncomfortable talking to lawyers. Having been around politics and business for ten years, he had any number of dealings with them. Most of the other defendants had not, however. And he sensed their fear at having to defend their land. Most of them were of very meager financial status and knew little about the procedure of fighting a lawsuit. Comrie and his wife were the only ones besides Holdridge who were not nervous. They were just angry—angry that they had to spend their hard-earned money to hold on to what was theirs.

King met the group and escorted them to the room where he and Tillinghast planned to meet with them. In stone silence, the group followed King through the law office and past an enormous vault once used to hold the bank's money. The thick iron door with a wheel-shaped combination lock was open, the shelves inside lined with letter-size yellow envelopes containing the wills of hundreds of the law firm's clients.

Past the vault, they arrived at an elevator, which took them up to the third floor. As Holdridge and the others stepped off the elevator, they walked through a doorway in a glass wall into the firm's law library. The two side walls and the back wall of the library were lined from floor to ceiling with books.

Sidestepping small brown stepladders that were situated near the tall shelves, the clients slowly filed in around the two brown, rectangular tables arranged end to end in the center of the library. Around it were roughly a dozen olive-colored chairs with wooden armrests. Holdridge sat down next to Wendell and his wife. The Frazer couple sat next to each other. Helen Curran and Eleanor Drake took seats at one end of the table. Lois Tefft sat facing Holdridge. Within a moment, all the seats were filled except the two at the head of the table nearest the glass wall. King and Tillinghast, with their notepads in hand, took those seats.

Through the glass behind the two lawyers, the clients had a direct view of the Quinnebaug River and the Via Duct Bridge. As King stood to introduce Tillinghast to the group, the only sound in the library was coming from the air vents in the ceiling.

Accustomed to representing wealthy doctors and big hospitals that could afford to defend against lawsuits, Tillinghast never had to worry about how his clients were going to pay for his services. Nor did he have to remind them that lawsuits could take years to resolve. Hospitals and insurance companies know all about the expensive, complex nature of litigation. As Tillinghast looked into the distraught faces of the Ledyard landowners, however, he knew they had no idea what they were in for. Wendell Comrie, dressed in blue-jeans overalls, rested his thick, rugged hands on the polished table. He was a lumberjack, not a sophisticated litigant. Lois Tefft worked on a farm and spent most of her time working to preserve conservation land. "Here you've got this group of people," he thought to himself. "And another group of people wants to take their land away. Here's litigation that could be massive. It's going to be a very long fight. They can't afford all this. I've got to think of a way to somehow make this less painful for them. But God, a few of these people may lose their houses."

This was the part of being a lawyer that Tillinghast did not like. Similar to a doctor explaining a grim diagnosis to a patient, lawyers sometimes have to be the messengers of bad news to their clients. Like illnesses, laws are sometimes unfair and often difficult to explain in laymen's terms. The consequences of being on the wrong side of the law can be harsh. And according to judges in other states, it appeared as though the law was against the landowners.

"This is more serious than we first thought it was," Tillinghast began. "Let us just tell you what we know so far. And then we will answer any of your questions. Then we will conclude by telling what we think is the way to proceed from here."

In very basic terms, Tillinghast and King explained the Nonintercourse Act and how the Haywards' lawyers had used it to file a number of other similar lawsuits to recover Indian land. But the landowners did not understand how an old law with such a strange name had anything to do with their land in Ledyard. As King tried to explain it, he was quickly interrupted. "How can it be?" asked Mrs. Comrie. "How can it be that these people can take our land away from us?"

"What right do they have to take our land?" her husband, Wendell, added indignantly.

"You know," interjected Tefft, "we can get along with Skip. I know him. Maybe we should go talk to him and try to work this out. We don't have to get all legal."

"No, no," shouted Mrs. Comrie. "What do they think they're doing trying to claim our land?"

"I know Skip too," said Wendell in disgust. "He's no Indian."

"That's right," a couple of other people chimed in.

"We know these people that are doing this," Helen Curran and her sister Eleanor Drake both said. "What right do they have?"

The anger in their voices was sharp, and Tillinghast felt control of the discussion about to slip away. "We're probably not going to be able to just talk to them," Tillinghast said, politely dismissing Tefft's suggestion. "Let us outline what we think should be the solutions to the problem. The first thing you think of is whether the Nonintercourse Act is still enforceable. And obviously it is. Other judges have enforced it. Next we consider whether the time thing is a problem. Obviously it is not. Other judges have said that the statute of limitations does not apply in Indian land-claim cases. So the third thing we need to look at is whether these people are a tribe."

"We know Skip Hayward is certainly not a full-blooded Indian," said Holdridge. "Even Elizabeth George was not."

"They don't have enough Indian blood," said Comrie.

"We're going to file an answer denying that they are a tribe and denying that they have any standing to sue," said King, while admitting that at this point he and Tillinghast had no basis for making such a claim. But the deadline for filing the answer was less than two weeks away. And researching the tribe's legitimacy was going to take months.

"How are we going to pay for this?" asked Holdridge. He and the others were not going to recover any money even if they won the suit. Only the Haywards stood to profit from the case. The best the defendants could hope for was to hold on to what they already had. They had nothing to gain.

King and Tillinghast fully understood the practical issue raised by Holdridge. From a financial standpoint, it made little sense to spend more money fighting to hold on to the land than the land was worth. And the longer the fight went on, the more costly it would get. Meanwhile, the Haywards were paying nothing for their lawyers. Their lawsuit was being financed by the Native American Rights Fund, which paid Tureen and his associates' salaries. Yet, if the defendants did not mount some sort of defense, they ran the risk of having the court simply award their land to the Haywards by default.

King recommended some cost-saving measures the group could take to minimize their legal fees. First, one of the defendants, someone who was a natural leader, should act as a liaison between the attorneys and the rest of the group. That would save King and Tillinghast from having to correspond with all the defendants individually. Holdridge, who had attended the University of Connecticut Law School for a couple of years before dropping out to obtain his graduate degree, was the natural choice. In addition to being the most educated in the group, Holdridge already had a leadership role in local politics.

Second, King encouraged the group to do their own research on the tribe. He and Tillinghast would research the legal questions about whether the Nonintercourse Act should apply in this case. But to prove the Haywards were not a tribe, the defendants were going to have to search census records, genealogy materials, and local Pequot history. It would be a lot cheaper, King told them, to divide into teams of two or three and do this work on their own rather than pay him and Tillinghast to do it.

"If we do the research, how much are we going to be paying for a retainer fee?" asked Holdridge.

"A couple thousand dollars," King said.

The figure surprised some of the defendants. But Holdridge, Tefft, and the Comries agreed to pay the entire fee, knowing that some of the codefendants could not afford to contribute.

"Are we going to lose our land?" asked Mrs. Comrie, bringing the boisterous discussion to an abrupt silence.

Tillinghast wanted to give them an assurance. "If we ever get this case before a jury, I don't think we are going to lose," he said. "Because the jury is going to try and find a way to prevent this from happening. But we may not get to a jury. Federal judges have decided most of these other cases, and the issues have been interpretations of laws. If we can get a jury issue, such as a factual question as to whether the Haywards are a tribe, we have a good shot." He did not sound optimistic.

From his home, Holdridge organized the codefendants into four research teams. Each team was assigned to different libraries, museums, and historical societies. They had two tasks. First they had to find documents to prove that the Western Pequot tribe had ceased to exist between the time the state auctioned off the eight hundred acres of reservation land in 1855 and the filing of the lawsuit in 1976. Tillinghast and King had suggested that the Haywards would be hard-pressed to establish themselves as the Western Pequot tribe if there were historical documents showing that the tribe had become extinct generations earlier. To some of the defendants, this seemed like an easy one. Even the *Webster's Dictionary* defined *tribe* as "a group . . . sharing a common ancestry, culture, language and name." After Elizabeth George's death, no one lived on the reservation. Before her death, she lived there alone. And an individual does not make a tribe.

The second task was related to the first—prove that the Haywards and the other plaintiffs calling themselves Western Pequot Indians were not active members of the tribe until it became a requirement for filing their lawsuit. The questions the lawyers suggested they pursue included: (1) Did any of these individuals identify themselves as Indians prior to the filing of the lawsuit? (2) Did all of these people participate in the tribal culture prior to the filing of the lawsuit? (3) Have these plaintiffs maintained a system of government like other Indian nations?

The task of doing historical research sounded more like fun than work to Holdridge. Local history was his hobby and he had plenty of experience. He had spent years doing academic research while earning his doctorate in political science and was well-versed in accessing card catalogs, indexes, microfiche, and archived records. Since the Comries had not attended college and had no experience doing research, Holdridge teamed up with them and headed to a one-room Indian museum in nearby Mystic. He quickly discovered that his years of studying in university libraries were of no help. The underfinanced Indian museum had no card catalog, no microfiche, and no archives. Sitting in a cramped cubicle with a badly worn file labeled "Pequots," Holdridge and the Comries stared at a stack of disarrayed documents ranging from old newspaper clippings to hardly legible records that were handwritten in the 1800s.

They were at a loss. Holdridge explained to the museum director that he and the Comries had been sued by the Western Pequots and were looking for tribal records from the 1900s and genealogy records on its members. To Holdridge's dismay, the museum director informed him that the state had kept scarce records on the tribe, while the tribe, apparently, had kept none at all. Their best hope was to search the state library in Hartford.

However, the museum director did bring out a collection of reports written by the overseers from the state's Indian Affairs Office that had been responsible for monitoring conditions on the reservation for the past 150 years. Scanning through the documents, Holdridge discovered some reports from the years 1850 to 1855—the period of time when the state sold off the eight hundred acres of reservation property. As he started to read, Holdridge immediately realized that the reports shed light on the reasons behind the state's decision to sell some of the reservation property.

When the Connecticut Indian agents visited the Western Pequot reservation in the early 1850s, they found only a few families consisting primarily of women and children. They had insufficient housing and were badly in need of food, clothing, and medical supplies. The agents were aware that the state had reserved the thousand acres of reservation land in Ledyard for the tribe's use. However, most of the land was either rock ledge or swamp, and therefore unsuitable for farming or other productive use. So the state agents proposed preserving a two-hundred-acre area that the tribe had been using for housing and other means and auctioning off the remaining eight hundred acres of less suitable land. The proceeds from the sale would go to the tribe and be put toward improving the living conditions on the scaled-back reservation.

The plan was taken to the Connecticut legislature and approved in 1855. With no opposition from the tribal members, Connecticut passed "An Act relating to the Ledyard Pequot Indians, and the Preservation of their Property." It authorized the sale of eight hundred acres of reservation land. "The money arising from [land] sales," read the law, "[shall be used] to erect . . . suitable houses for said tribe . . . and also to repair the houses now existing." The law also required the Indian agents to deposit the rest of the proceeds in bank accounts established for the tribe. The accounts were designated "for the use and benefit of said tribe . . . for the support and comfort of said tribe." In the decades that followed, the Pequots used the money for food, medical care, and housing and burial expenses.

In addition to being approved by the state supreme court, the law was in complete harmony with George Washington's intentions when he signed the Nonintercourse Act. "When you find it in your interest to sell any part of your lands," Washington told Indians of the Seneca Nation shortly after the Nonintercourse Act was passed, "the United States must be present, by their agent, and will be your security that you shall not be defrauded in the bargain you make." Washington intended to prevent greedy states from exploiting Indians and stealing their land. Connecticut kept none of the eight hundred acres sold at auction for itself, nor did it keep any of the profits. Acting in good faith, the Connecticut legislature's decision to sell land to raise funds for the women and children living on the reservation honored the spirit of Washington's law. Connecticut's only mistake was a technical one. It did not get preapproval from the federal government before conducting the land auction. But this technical violation was not carried out in bad faith and was not to the Indians' detriment.

Holdridge brought his discovery to Tillinghast, who was immediately encouraged. "This was not a case where some overseers were just selling off Indian land," said Tillinghast. "They actually went to the superior court and got permission from the state to do this. But according to the plaintiffs' interpretation of the statute, the overseers should have been going to the federal government. Well, didn't the state know that?"

The more Tillinghast thought about it, the more he became convinced that Tureen and the Haywards had a flaw in their case. Maybe there was a valid reason why Connecticut did not seek approval from the federal government. At the time, federal tribes—such as those on the western frontier—were considered wards of the federal government and entitled to its guardianship and protection. On the other hand, independent tribes—such as those throughout New England—were considered wards of the states and were under state custody. As a result their benefits came from the states and their reservations were established on state land, not federal land.

Scheduled to take a family vacation to Cape Cod, Tillinghast went out and purchased a bunch of Indian books in hopes of trying to find out what was going on back in the 1800s. He spent nearly his whole vacation immersed in history books. And on weekends he started driving to historical archives in Rhode Island and Connecticut. But his search for a paper trail to show that the federal government did not apply the Nonintercourse Act to state tribes in the 1800s proved fruitless. The history books were silent on that issue.

Sitting in his law office one afternoon in late August, Tillinghast had trouble concentrating on his other cases. His other cases were much more profitable to the firm than the Ledyard case, but all he could think about was proving that the Nonintercourse Act did not apply to the Pequots. "The whole thing just seems so wrong to me that this could happen," he thought. "That people could lose their homes over this. I have to figure out a way to prevent it." But he was spending a lot of time thinking about it. And that was a problem—time is money for lawyers. He had been thinking and researching all summer without billing the clients once.

It was nearly lunchtime. From behind his desk he faced a large, historical map of southeastern Connecticut covering his office wall. He had bought it for $100 back when the firm took over the bank building. Suddenly, his familiarity with local history gave him an idea. Tillinghast recalled that a local lawyer named Lafayette Foster used to practice law right down the street back in the mid-1800s. He was arguably the most famous lawyer of his day in southeastern Connecticut. He went on to be elected to the U.S. Senate. By 1863, when President Lincoln was assassinated, Foster was president of the Senate. He was next in line to Vice President Andrew Johnson to being appointed president. "Here's a guy who is in the Senate and he's on the Indian Affairs Committee," said Tillinghast. "He lives in Norwich, the next town over from Ledyard. He obviously knows about the Pequots. Wouldn't he know they were supposed to go to the federal government and not the state government before selling the tribe's land?"

Tillinghast got up from his chair, grabbed his briefcase, and left for Yale University, over an hour away. Foster had gone on to teach there after retiring from the Senate. Tillinghast's last hope was to look through Foster's personal papers at the Yale archives and see if he had written anything about the Connecticut Indians and the Nonintercourse Act.

Tillinghast spent the rest of his day at Yale and came up empty. Foster too was silent on the Indians and the Nonintercourse Act. Driving back to his law office, Tillinghast realized his time was being consumed searching for evidence that did not exist. There were no documents to prove or disprove the claims being made by the Pequots and their lawyers. Yet the burden had fallen to him and King alone to resist the tribe's efforts to seize twenty-seven landowners' private property.

But when he checked his messages late that afternoon, Tillinghast received his first indication that a more unified effort was being organized to fight the claims being filed by Tureen. A secretary from Hale & Dorr, the largest and most powerful law firm in Boston, had called to invite him to a meeting in Boston. The firm was sponsoring a strategy session for all defense attorneys around New England that were handling Indian land-claim cases. Hale & Dorr was prompted to set up the meeting due to a lawsuit that had just been filed on Cape Cod.

On August 26, Tureen's team sued the town of Mashpee, Massachusetts, and thousands of individual landowners on behalf of the Mashpee Indians. The lawsuit sought twenty thousand acres, which accounted for almost the entire town of Mashpee. Seeking to take back prime real estate at the gateway to Cape Cod's top vacation and resort area, the lawsuit sent an instant panic across the Cape. A Boston law firm refused to approve a bond issue for a new school to be built in Mashpee, which spurred local banks to refuse to lend money for home mortgages.

The town of Mashpee and its residents responded to the lawsuit by spending $350,000 to retain lawyers from around Boston. Hale & Dorr's James St. Clair, Richard Nixon's Watergate attorney, was chosen as the lead attorney to defeat Tureen and the Mashpee Indians.

"Mashpee was our Hiroshima," said Tureen. "That's where we dropped the bomb. We sued seventeen thousand defendants and showed what chaos could ensue if one of these cases was really litigated. We froze property transactions. We demonstrated in that case that people could not afford to fight us."

10

FRACTURED DIAMOND

AUGUST 1976

STRUGGLING TO KEEP HER COMPOSURE, ALINE SLID A CASSETTE TAPE INTO Skip's portable tape recorder. Rather than write him a "good-bye" note, she had decided to record one.

"I've left," she began, her quivering lips only inches from the tiny circular microphone. "And I ain't never coming back. I always thought that if I changed or did this or that differently, it would smooth things over. After seven years, I realize that nothing I can do will change anything."

She pulled the recorder back from her mouth and looked around the camper, which they were once again relying on for housing. The rat-infested house they had been renting in Stonington had been condemned. Since moving out months earlier, they had been living in campgrounds, state parks, and anywhere else they could find to park their pickup truck and camper. The previous day they had decided to park in Aline's mother's front yard.

"It has got to the point where I don't know where I'm going to wake up each morning," she said. "We live like vagabonds, worse than vagabonds. When you're not working, you're at the reservation. It used to be the same way when you were so involved with the church. It is just a different focus now. But the focus is never me. I come last in everything."

It was easier speaking into a tape recorder than to Skip's face. Free to say things she had always felt but did not dare say, she continued. "I'm just in your way. I was in your way in what you were trying to accomplish in the church. I'm in your way now with everything you're trying to do on the reservation. I was even in your way when you wanted to move to Montana. If you've said it once you've said it a million times: 'I'm the only thing stopping you from getting where you want to be.'"

She left the tape where Skip would find it and removed her last possession from the trailer—the sewing machine her father had given her.

Entering her mother's house, her clothing and other personal items already inside, Aline saw the puzzled look on her mother's face.

"Ma, I'm leaving. I just can't do it anymore."

"Well, you can stay here as long as you need to, Aline."

Aline dropped her things on her bed, the same one she had slept in for years as a child before marrying Skip. From now on, she would sleep in it again.

"Does Skip know you're leaving?" Betty asked.

"He'll know when he gets home from work."

Restless and sweaty, Aline rolled over and looked at the alarm clock on the nightstand beside her bed: 4:45 A.M. Skip should have discovered her tape by now, since he usually got off work from second shift at midnight. Hoping the tape would at least motivate him to come and try to talk her out of leaving, Aline slowly climbed out of bed. Disappointed, she walked into the living room and opened the blinds just far enough to create a peephole. The pickup truck was still parked in the front yard, the camper mounted to the back. No lights were on inside, and Skip's used car was not in the driveway. It appeared he had not returned home from work yet. Aline curled up on the couch, holding her hand in the blinds to see outside.

"He probably went drinking again," she thought. Since returning from Missouri, Skip, for the first time in his life, had begun drinking alcohol. Increasingly, he would frequent the bars when he got off work at midnight, drinking until they closed at two in the morning. His sporadic drunkenness only added to their already crumbling marriage.

The next time Aline looked at the living room clock it was 5:00 A.M. Suddenly she recognized the sound of Skip's car. Quickly, she shifted to her knees, watching in anticipation as he parked alongside the camper, then walked inside. The next ten minutes seemed like hours. Finally he emerged.

"Aline, what are you doing up so early?" Betty unexpectedly called out.

"Oh, Ma, you startled me."

"What are you doing?"

"Skip just got home. He just came out of the camper."

"Do you think he's going to try and get in the house?"

"I don't know. It looks like he's getting in the pickup truck."

The engine started up. Next the headlights came on.

Placing her hand on Aline's shoulder, Betty craned her neck to look out the window. She could feel Aline shaking ever so slightly.

Slowly, Skip drove the truck and camper out of the front yard onto the street. Never once looking back, he drove off, the taillights dimming as he went off out of sight. Sobbing, Aline clung to the shade. "That's it," she whispered. "He's gone."

"It is going to be all right, Aline. It is going to be all right."

THREE WEEKS LATER

After the first ring, Aline answered her mother's phone.

"Hello."

"Aline?"

"Yeah."

"It's Skip."

"Hi, Skip," she said, relieved at the sound of his voice. She had not seen or heard from him since the night he drove off.

"Well?"

"What?"

"Are you comin' back?" he asked.

"No, Skip," she replied, hardly surprised by his undiplomatic approach. "I ain't never comin' back."

"Well, can we at least meet? Can we talk?"

Aline paused. "OK," she said hesitantly.

"I'll come to your mother's house."

"That would be OK."

"I'll come this afternoon, before work."

"OK."

Despite the way he treated her, Skip had come to rely heavily on Aline. Her unexpected departure left him depressed and lonely. More than a lover, Aline had been his crutch. When he needed her support or help—to work at the restaurant when he was managing it, or to get a job and support them when he was engrossed in Bible study and church activities—he leaned on her. When she slowed him down, questioning his dreams or demanding his attention, he cast her aside. And whenever his plans failed, he took his frustrations out on her. But in every instance, she had been by his side—until now.

After sitting in front of her mother's house and talking to Skip for over an hour, Aline reiterated that she was not going back. She had decided to seek a divorce. Another phone call she had received earlier in the week, this one from Skip's mother, helped solidify her decision. Since marrying into the family as a seventeen-year-old, Aline had always enjoyed a close relationship with Mrs. Hayward. Her aspirations as Skip's fiancée were to be just like his mother.

Mrs. Hayward called to find out why Aline had left and if there was any way she would consider coming back and trying to work things out with her son. Aware of how deeply Mrs. Hayward loved Skip, Aline nonetheless decided it was time that she knew the truth about the violence in their relationship. She was not prepared for the response.

"I understand," Mrs. Hayward said with regret.

"I can't believe she believes me," Aline thought, appreciative of Mrs. Hayward's support.

In a strange way, Aline turned out to be a lot more like Skip's mother than she realized. Both had endured difficult marriages. But unlike Mrs. Hayward, who had nine children, Aline had nothing tying her to Skip. Children, Aline always feared, would have made it that much more difficult to walk out on Skip, which prompted her to stay on birth-control pills throughout the duration of their seven-year marriage.

In September of 1976, Aline filed for divorce. To pay for her lawyer, she determined to sell her wedding ring. To her dismay, it was worth far less than expected. "It is fractured," a jeweler informed her after examining it. "This diamond's virtually worthless."

11

STATE AID

ON SEPTEMBER 29, 1976, AT HAYWARD'S URGING, TUREEN FILED A MOTION dismissing family friend Lois Tefft from the suit.

The other defendants were told little about why Tefft was dismissed, only that the land survey the plaintiffs had relied on misidentified Tefft's property boundaries. King said only that an independent surveyor hired by Tefft revealed she should have never been involved in the lawsuit to begin with.

No explanation was given for how a piece of real estate as big as her farm could have been mistakenly identified on a survey. Nor were the other defendants told why surveys were not performed on their land as well to ensure that the tribe had properly identified the parcels in the suit. All the remaining defendants knew was that the codefendant most responsible for choosing King's law firm to represent them was no longer in need of a lawyer. "I have too many friends in the tribe, dear friends," Tefft said, expressing her desire to remain neutral in the feud. "I have a very close friendship with Skip Hayward and his family."

One defendant less, Tillinghast and King went to federal court in December and made their case for having the lawsuit dismissed. In his oral argument, Tillinghast chose not to challenge the Pequots' legitimacy. Hiring genealogists and historians as expert witnesses was too costly, particularly now that Tefft was removed from the case. So instead, Tillinghast relied on more established legal principles to persuade the judge to rule in favor of the landowners. Tillinghast reminded U.S. district judge Joseph Blumenfeld that the Pequots' claim was over a hundred years old; the landowners had marketable title to the property; and they had been in possession of the property for decades. Nonetheless, on March 4, 1977, Judge Blumenfeld rejected each of those arguments. "These defenses are insufficient as a matter of law in tribal actions to recover lands alienated in violation of the Nonintercourse Act," Blumenfeld wrote. He, like Judge Gignoux in Maine, had decided that the federal Nonintercourse Act trumped all the long-established state property laws.

"If the courts are willing to enforce this Nonintercourse statute, it is a political problem, not a legal problem," said Tillinghast. King agreed. "So let's go see our congressman," Tillinghast suggested.

Chris Dodd, a local lawyer from Norwich whom Tillinghast knew from court, had just been elected to his first term in Congress. His local congressional office at Thames Plaza in Norwich was just minutes from Tillinghast and King's law firm. He agreed to meet with Tillinghast on a Saturday morning.

"Something is wrong here," Tillinghast told Dodd, who was unfamiliar with the lawsuit and the legal theory behind it. "People are going to lose their land, and in some cases their houses, because of this claim. This is something that needs to be resolved politically." Dodd said little as Tillinghast briefed him on the history of the case and the potential problems it posed for Ledyard. The local angle interested Dodd. He had lived just a few miles from the reservation before his election to Congress.

The meeting with Dodd was Tillinghast's last formal work on the case. The dispute was rapidly moving from a legal forum to a political forum, and Tillinghast was a trial lawyer, not a deal maker. Just as important, the firm could not afford to keep two lawyers on a case that was earning the firm nothing. The responsibility of guiding the case through proper political channels in hopes of reaching an out-of-court settlement fell solely on King.

King and the defendants viewed Connecticut governor Ella Grasso as their most likely ally. The state, after all, was responsible for the predicament the landowners were in. It had auctioned off the Indians' land in 1855, giving rise to the lawsuit. Holdridge wrote to Grasso on behalf of the defendants, seeking her intervention. But Grasso rebuffed him, citing the Connecticut attorney general's opinion that the matter was "a private dispute."

Although he disagreed, Holdridge understood why the governor was not inclined to intervene. In her campaign to become Connecticut's first female governor, Grasso had prided herself on standing up for the underdog. And it was hard to imagine a greater underdog than a small, poor Indian tribe that had locked horns with established white landowners.

Grasso's response was indicative of a growing sympathy for the Pequots. For months Holdridge and his codefendants had been reading letters to the editor that implied he and the others were insensitive to the rights of Indians everywhere. One letter read, "Our American Blacks have gained most of the civil rights which are their due. Are the original inhabitants of our country to be relegated to poverty and prejudice because the majority of citizens are apathetic? I strongly believe that Indian people, who have been pushed around for years by the United States Government, should have the strong support of us all and that we can let these people have their heritage returned to them."

Holdridge noted that most of the letters in support of the Pequots had been written by individuals who lived in towns other than Ledyard and whose land was not impacted by the lawsuit. "There's a lot of public sympathy for their position and no one really thinks about the fact that now there's another set of people—us—who are being unjustly treated," Holdridge felt. "We're all alone, isolated. Neither local nor state government wants to help us."

Meanwhile, officials working in conjunction with the federal Indian Policy Review Commission contacted Grasso's office, explaining how desperately the Pequots needed funding, and asked for her support. Shortly after the lawsuit was filed, commission member George Tomer from the Penobscot tribe, along with his tribe's leader, Jim Sappier, set up a meeting between Grasso and Hayward in Hartford. Hayward thought Tomer and Sappier were kidding when they told him that Grasso had agreed to meet with him. "That's one of the funniest things I ever heard in my life," Hayward said.

In their meeting, Hayward, accompanied by Tomer and Sappier, asked Grasso for support in obtaining state grant money for housing and start-up businesses on the reservation. One of the ventures that Hayward was interested in pursuing was tapping maple trees on the reservation and producing syrup for sale.

Soon thereafter the state sent in its top forester, George Cloutier, to help Hayward and the tribe tap the trees. Cloutier had been with the state forest service since 1950 and knew the terrain on the Pequot reservation well. As district forester for eastern Connecticut, he was once in charge of policing the reservation's dense tree population for fire hazards.

Cloutier, a short man with a fragile build, found it odd that none of the Pequots could identify a maple tree, one of the most prominent species on the reservation for generations. His first visit to the reservation found Hayward struggling to distinguish one tree type from another. Cloutier cordoned off a section of woods and cut down everything in it except the beautiful red oaks and the sugar maple trees. Yet the Haywards still had trouble attempting to tap the oak trees.

With Cloutier's help and hours of practice, Hayward eventually became very efficient at producing and selling syrup. But his inability to get his family members to consistently work on the operation caused the venture to fail shortly after it began.

As time wore on, both the state and the federal government continued to allocate more funds to Hayward and his group. HUD loaned the tribe $1 million to build a housing development on the reservation. While his private life was collapsing around him, Hayward found himself the darling of groups wanting to donate money to his cause. The Connecticut Department of Economic Development awarded him a $20,000 historic preservation grant. The Catholic organization Campaign for Human Development gave him $45,000 to help his tribe with expenses on the reservation. And the American Revolution Bicentennial Committee devoted $1,500 to conduct genealogical research aimed at finding more Pequots.

Although the federal government did not officially recognize the Pequots as a tribe, Hayward's persistence and the support he was receiving from Tureen and other Indians in Maine were starting to pay dividends. Since Hayward took over the tribe in 1975, the Pequots had received more money per capita than any Indian tribe in the entire country.

Each time a new grant was awarded to his people, Skip found himself being interviewed by the press. Always the introvert, Skip suddenly found irresistible the allure of seeing his name in print. He watched the headlines closely: "Pequots Initiate Court Fight to Acquire Ledyard Property." "Pequots Have a Vision for Land." "Mashantuckets Move to Increase Their Tribal Membership."

Never before had his opinion mattered outside his closed circle of family and friends. Now he had his family clip out every article published about him and arrange them in large scrapbooks. In it, they had pasted articles from the *Hartford Courant*, the *Providence Journal*, the *New Haven Register*, the *New London Day*, and the *Norwich Bulletin*.

Meanwhile, the federal government rejected a written request by the Ledyard landowners to intervene in the lawsuit in hopes of finding a resolution. "There are apparently a great many cases of the same nature being processed both by the Division and the Department of Interior, putting a substantial strain on the manpower involved," wrote Justice Department attorney Peter Dorsey in a June 21, 1977, letter. "Both are unwilling to compromise their ability to handle the other cases to intervene in a case which is already pending in court where the parties have thus demonstrated their ability to proceed alone."

Tureen's team of lawyers had filed so many cases that the federal government did not have the resources to get involved in all of them. To Tureen, the Pequots' case was just one in a family of lawsuits he had filed. He was moving them along like a chess game. And Holdridge was starting to feel like a pawn. The federal government viewed the land dispute as a state problem. The state insisted it was a private dispute. The local town government remained neutral in the matter, but Ledyard continued to levy property taxes on the landowners, despite their inability to use the land or improve its value. Tureen made sure of that by attaching public notices to all the defendants' property titles at the time he filed the lawsuit. Under Connecticut's old *lis pendens* law, the notices essentially told all prospective buyers to beware: These property titles were being contested in a civil lawsuit.

"We can't sell our land," Holdridge told his wife. "Nobody will buy it, not even for a dollar. Nor can we borrow money to build or make improvements on it. No bank will lend to us. We can't do anything with our land except pay taxes on it."

12

THE PROMISE

A WOODEN, TRIANGULAR SIGN FASTENED TO A POST AND BEARING THE words "Comrie's Mill" hung over a stone wall that wrapped around the property at the corner of Gallup Hill Extension and Pumpkin Hill Road. Mounds of damp sawdust and stacks of neatly cut lumber lined the yard. Eight-foot-high stacks of uncut timbers waited outside a three-story brown barn converted to a sawmill. An extension to the barn contained a ten-foot-long mill saw supported by belts and pulleys. Flanking either side of the mill were two open-air warehouses that held the custom-ordered lumber for area builders and carpenters. An old flatbed pickup truck and a John Deere tractor sat idly on the circular dirt driveway.

Dressed in blue denim overalls and a worn flannel shirt, Wendell Comrie stood alone. The slight breeze ruffled his thinning gray hair. Resting his thick hands in his overall pockets, he was thinking about the lawsuit. It seemed to be all he thought about lately. Of all the defendants, he had the most land at stake. The 262 acres he owned were quite literally his livelihood, brimming with the trees that fed his mill. Losing it would hurt financially, but what ate at him more was the way in which he was losing it. People who had not previously resided in Ledyard, much less on the reservation, had moved to town, hired a fancy lawyer, and filed a lawsuit. It cost them nothing, yet they stood to gain everything. It was the exact opposite of his situation.

As a youth growing up in the Depression, Comrie was taught that he could not get something for nothing. But there were far fewer lawyers competing for work in those days, and as a result, much less litigation. As the 1980s fast approached, America was now home to two-thirds of the lawyers in the world. Americans spent more money litigating against each other than any other people in the world. As a result, old truisms were no longer as reliable. It was hard to accept, but at age sixty-three Comrie realized he was out of step with the times.

In 1918, when Comrie was two years old, his father unexpectedly died, leaving behind a wife and eight children under the age of twelve. Comrie's mother had no means to provide for her children and was forced to move out of their Ledyard home. Sympathetic Ledyard officials allowed the struggling family to move into the abandoned Johnson-Whipple School while Mrs. Comrie's older boys worked so the family could eat. When Wendell turned twelve, he found a job pumping gas at the only filling station that was within walking distance from their home. He received a nickel a day plus meals, and he worked hard for tips, offering to air up patron's tires and wash their windows. Comrie had put away every penny he had earned, even foregoing ice cream or going out with friends. By age sixteen, Comrie had saved $150, enough, he figured, to give his mother what she had always wanted.

"Mom, where would you like to live?" he asked her. "I want to buy a piece of land and build a house so we don't have to pay rent."

"Well, there's a piece of land in Ledyard that I always liked," she said, referring to a beautiful wooded lot at the corner of Pumpkin Hill Road and Gallup Hill Extension. As a child, she used to walk by the property every day on her way to school.

Comrie discovered that a man named Edward Spicer owned the land. It was not for sale, but Spicer, charmed by the boy's ambition, agreed to sell the fourteen-acre parcel for $500. After turning over his $150 for the down payment, Comrie turned to race home and tell his mother the news.

"Well, do you want a receipt, son?" Spicer asked him.

"I guess I can trust you, can't I?" Comrie responded.

Spicer grinned, appreciating Comrie's youthful inexperience. "What are you going to do if I die tonight?" Spicer asked.

Embarrassed, Comrie smiled. "Well, I guess you better give me a receipt."

Comrie spent the remainder of his high school days working after school and weekends to pay off the rest of the loan so he and his brothers could start building their mother a house. With his mother's health failing during his senior year, he was called to his mother's bedside, with two of his older brothers. Another brother was off frantically looking for a doctor. Their mother looked much older than her fifty-five years, and it was clear to Comrie that she would soon be joining his father.

As he leaned to comfort his mother, she weakly clutched his hand. He was her baby. "Wendell," she whispered.

"Yes, Mother, I'm here."

"Promise me," she began. "Promise me you'll always serve the Lord."

Choking back the tears, he leaned forward and kissed her on the forehead. "I promise, Mom," he cried softly. "I promise."

His mother never saw the house Comrie built. But in keeping with his promise to his mother, he invited his mother's sister, who was a widow, to come live in it with him and the other children. She gained a roof over her head, and the Comrie children gained a guardian. It was a good arrangement.

He eventually built his mill on the same property, right alongside the old house. He married and supported his children by making lumber. He never got rich, but he earned a reputation as the most honest businessman in town. Today, as Comrie looked around his mill, he sensed that the

Haywards were not being honest in their claim to be the Pequot Indian tribe, particularly after he read an opinion piece that appeared in the *New London Day,* entitled "The White Man Has Tried to Destroy Our Heritage." The author was Skip Hayward. In the closing paragraph to his article, Skip wrote, "Elizabeth George, one-time leader of the Mashantucket Pequots, has stated: 'They murdered and butchered our people, pushed us up into the rocks and ledges and kept the good land for themselves, and now they want the rocks and ledges.' How much will they take from us? Is there no end? They tried to take our name, destroy our heritage, our culture, our people. They take our land and they don't seem to want to stop until they have snuffed out our last breath. Then they will be freed of the troublesome Red Man."

What bothered Comrie was that no one was challenging Hayward's claims—not the media, the government, the public, or even his own attorney, Jackson King. Enduring months of frustration, Comrie and Holdridge had finally made some progress researching the Pequot tribe, only fueling their suspicions about the group that had sued them.

The Haywards had selected the 1910 census to establish whether one belonged to the tribe—anybody who could trace their genealogy to a person identified as a Pequot Indian on the census that year could join the present-day tribe. But according to the U.S. Census, there were only three full-blooded Pequots left in the entire United States in 1910—two males and one female. Further, the three full-blooded Pequots included both Western Pequots and Eastern Pequots, two distinct tribes. The census that year simply lumped both tribes together as Pequots. This raised the question, "If there were only three full-blooded Pequots (Eastern and Western) left in 1910, how many members of the Western Pequots could possibly remain nearly seventy years later?"

Comrie and Holdridge became even more skeptical when they looked at the state's Indian overseer records. In 1936, the state recorded that nine individuals lived on the Western Pequot reservation. However, none of them were among the three full-blooded Pequots who appeared on the U.S. Census in 1910. Rather they were three adult women (one of whom was Hayward's grandmother, Elizabeth George), two teenagers, and four children. State records identified these individuals as "resident members *of Indian blood,*" meaning they could be from any of Connecticut's five tribes, since the state did not bar members from other tribes intermingling on reservations. Two years later, in 1938, the reservation population dipped to six (two adult women, two teenagers, and two children). By 1956, there were only two women of Indian blood left on the Western Pequot reservation, George and her sister Martha Langevin. And by 1973, with the death of Hayward's grandmother, the reservation's Indian population reached zero.

Despite all of this information, King never raised concerns about the tribe's legitimacy when trying to get the judge to dismiss the case. Frustrated, Comrie decided to go see him.

"We *know* they can't be a real tribe," Comrie told King. "We have done the research and confirmed that the real Pequot tribe has been nonexistent for years. Why didn't you question their legitimacy as an Indian tribe?"

"We would have taken that approach—putting into issue whether the tribe met the standards of federal recognition," said King. "But that was going to require historians and other expert witnesses. We just didn't have a budget to do it."

Comrie knew they did not have a budget to afford a team of professional researchers, but he thought that was the very reason King had recommended at the outset that the defendants perform the research themselves. Yet after investing countless hours of personal time gathering the historical documents, those documents were somehow less credible in the eyes of the court because laypersons rather than history professors gathered them?

"I don't know much about the law," said Comrie in a frustrated tone. "But it seems to me the burden should be on them to prove they're Pequots, rather than on us to prove they're not. They should have to prove they are an Indian tribe before they can sue to take away our land."

Comrie, Holdridge, and the other defendants were unaware that U.S. district judge Walter Skinner in Massachusetts shared their view. Judge Skinner presided over the case brought by Tureen against the town of Mashpee and seventeen thousand landowners, the case Tureen referred to as "our Hiroshima." The defendants' lawyers' strategy was what Comrie was recommending to King: They challenged the plaintiffs' legitimacy as an Indian tribe, putting the burden on Tureen to establish that his clients were indeed a tribe and had standing to sue.

Under the U.S. Constitution, a plaintiff must be able to establish injury before it can seek to recover damages. The "standing to sue" doctrine permits the victim in an automobile accident to sue to recover medical costs. But it prohibits an uninjured pedestrian who witnessed the accident from suing to recover damages.

For groups of individuals to sue to recover Indian land, those groups must establish that they are indeed the same tribes that had land wrongly taken away. "The plaintiff must establish its status as an Indian tribe as of the date that the action was commenced in order to maintain this action in the form elected by the plaintiff," Judge Skinner ruled. On October 17, 1977—one year after the Mashpee lawsuit was filed—Skinner convened a trial solely to determine whether Tureen's clients were a bona fide tribe. The trial lasted forty-one days. The jury heard from expert witnesses—historians, sociologists, and anthropologists—from both sides. Then Judge Skinner gave the jury a list of yes-no questions—special interrogatories—designed to determine whether the Mashpee tribe that once inhabited Cape Cod had maintained its tribal existence without interruption up to the point the lawsuit was filed. Skinner instructed the jury to focus particularly on key dates ranging from 1790, when the Nonintercourse Act was passed, to 1976, when the lawsuit was filed. "I had instructed the jury that tribal status once abandoned could not be regained," said Judge Skinner.

On January 6, 1978, the jury returned its verdict: The plaintiffs were not an Indian tribe at the time the lawsuit was filed. Since the plaintiffs could not prove they were members of the old Mashpee Indian tribe, they had no grounds for recovering the tribe's old land. Case dismissed.

Tureen and his partner, Barry Margolin, appealed the decision. But on February 13, 1979, the U.S. Court of Appeals upheld the lower court's verdict. "It is undisputed that if plaintiff was not a tribe in 1976 it lacked standing to bring this suit," wrote U.S. Court of Appeals chief Judge Coffin, "and that if not a tribe at the critical times in the nineteenth century it was not protected by the [Nonintercourse] Act."

In upholding the lower court's ruling in the Mashpee case, the U.S. Court of Appeals spelled out in plain, clear terms what it would take under federal law to establish a right to recover Indian land under Tureen's Nonintercourse Act approach. "Plaintiff must prove that it meets the definition of 'tribe of Indians' as that phrase is used in the Nonintercourse Act," wrote Judge Coffin. "By a 'tribe' we understand a body of Indians (1) of the same or similar race, (2) united in a community (3) under one leadership or government, and (4) inhabiting a particular though sometimes ill-defined territory."

In addition to killing the lawsuit in Mashpee, Coffin's ruling called into question the Haywards' claim to being the Pequot tribe, given the manner in which they organized a new tribal government after years of dormancy. "A tribe must be something more than a private, voluntary organization," Coffin ruled. "You do have to find that it is something more than just a small coterie, a small band of enthusiasts who are supporting the Indian leadership. . . . There must be *continuous* leadership."

The only way for Tureen to overcome the devastating ruling handed down by the U.S. Court of Appeals was to appeal to the U.S. Supreme Court during the ninety days from the date the decision was issued. Otherwise, the appeals court ruling automatically became law. Tureen never filed an appeal, however.

"These land claims are something that we made up," said Tureen. "It was an utterly untested theory. If the Supreme Court ever tested the issue, it would say that the Nonintercourse Act did not apply to *any* of these tribes. So settlement was critically important to our strategy in all of these cases."

Unchallenged, Judge Coffin's decision became law in the federal court's First Circuit, which included the states of Massachusetts, Maine, Rhode Island, and New Hampshire. Although not binding on federal courts in Connecticut, the First Circuit decision would have certainly provided guidance to Judge Blumenfeld, who was presiding over the Ledyard case, had King requested a similar ruling. "If the jury found the group was a tribe at one date, but later had voluntarily become assimilated—had ceased to exist as a separate and distinct community—then the jury would have to find they were no longer a tribe," wrote Coffin.

The new law exposed the Achilles' heal in Hayward's case against the Ledyard landowners. In 1973, there was no tribal presence whatsoever on the Pequot reservation. And until Tureen came along, there was no tribal government. He wrote their constitution for them. And Hayward was not elected tribal chairman until 1975, just in time to file the lawsuit. At the time of Elizabeth George's death, none of the plaintiffs calling themselves Pequots were living together and functioning as a tribal entity. The critical conclusion of the Mashpee ruling was that a tribe, once dormant, could not be reactivated for purposes of filing a lawsuit to recover ancestral lands. If the Mashpee ruling were applied to the Pequots, Hayward's claim would stand no chance.

King had followed the Mashpee case closely. But Comrie and Holdridge had not. They were unaware that a trial had even taken place, or that the appeals court ruling offered new leverage to them in their case. As a result, when Holdridge went to see King at his law office sometime after the Mashpee ruling was announced, he went to inform King that some of the defendants were prepared to give away their land in order to make the legal dispute go away. They would ask nothing in return from the Haywards.

"Some of the defendants," Holdridge told King, "are asking, 'Shouldn't we just give up?' "

"You can't give up," King said adamantly.

King's answer puzzled Holdridge. Ever since the judge had denied King's motion to have the case dismissed, King had been warning that the chances of winning were slim. Yet he was encouraging Holdridge and the others to continue the time-consuming fight?

"Why can't we just forfeit the land?" Holdridge asked, thinking to himself, "Isn't that what the Haywards want? Our land."

"You could relinquish your land and the lawsuit would still go on," King insisted. "You might be found liable for having used the land unjustly all these years and have to pay damages for the illegal use of land. Who knows what could happen?"

For a moment Holdridge was speechless. Even if the defendants gave Hayward and his relatives their land at no cost, Hayward would still come after them for money damages?

Assuring Holdridge that he and Tureen were close to working out an acceptable solution to the lawsuit, King convinced Holdridge that he and the others could not simply give their property to the Haywards in hopes of making the lawsuit go away. Holdridge was never told about the Mashpee ruling and the leverage it could suddenly provide them. King concluded that the land belonging to his clients, excluding the two defendants whose homes were at risk, was not worth the expense of going to trial to protect. "Arguably, all of the defendants' land was not worth $200,000," thought King. "None of the land involved any houses or had any commercial value—for the most part." He felt the people did not have sentimental attachment to the rough land that seemed to have been purchased here and there by the defendants. From the firm's perspective, it was a question of "How can we afford to try a case for six months?" If they tried the case and won it, they might spend more money winning the case than the land was worth. The firm, he believed, was not a charity.

People who get sued tend to have one objective when they hire a lawyer: win the case. The same cannot always be said for the lawyers they hire. Attorneys must consider a range of factors in determining the preferred outcome in litigation, not the least of which is money. And in the civil litigation game, a lawyer can be more certain of receiving his fees when his clients settle. King was in such a position.

His clients were strapped financially and had not paid him since the original retainer fee three years earlier. Even if King took the case to court and prevailed, the landowners would be in no better position to pay him than if they lost the case. They were merely defending the right to keep what they already owned. To defeat Hayward and Tureen at this stage would secure the clients' land and restore peace to their lives after three years of uncertainty. It would not, however, generate any financial compensation and they would have to pay King's legal fees and expenses out of their own pockets.

An out-of-court settlement that gave something to the landowners and the Haywards, on the other hand, offered a way to offset some of the outstanding legal fees King had generated. Other defense lawyers who were opposing lawsuits filed by Tureen in Maine had agreed to such a settlement. The terms of the settlement were drafted by Tureen and patterned after the plan he had designed in his mind long before he ever filed the suits. He offered to drop the suits on two conditions: (1) the Maine Indian tribes had to be awarded federal recognition status, with all of its sovereign privileges, and (2) some of the Maine landowners had to sell their land at fair-market value to the tribes. To finance the purchase of the land, Tureen called on the federal government to appropriate nearly $100 million for the Indians, some of which would be used for economic development on the reservation. He framed his bold request by arguing that if Congress had done its job initially by monitoring the Maine tribes' land sales in the 1700s, there would have been no lawsuits. State officials in Maine became supportive of Tureen's settlement proposal because it transferred the financial burden from it to the federal government. And the government had agreed to join the negotiation rather than risk a trial that might award two-thirds of the state of Maine's land to the tribes outright. (Unlike in Mashpee, the Maine Indians had already been recognized as tribes by the state of Maine.)

King's desire to seek a similar deal in Ledyard fit perfectly into Tureen's plans to prevent each of his lawsuits from reaching the trial stage. Regardless of whether the Mashpee decision strengthened his clients' defense, King still wanted to avoid trial because it was costly and would gain him and his clients little; Tureen, on the other hand, wanted to avoid trial because he feared losing and the precedent that might set. King's eagerness to work out a settlement with Tureen patterned after the one being pursued in Maine gave the opposing lawyers a common goal: get the state of Connecticut and the federal government to go along with a plan that would allow the Haywards to purchase the defendants' land with money appropriated by Congress. The Pequot reservation would get returned to its original size, and the landowners would be compensated and have money to pay King for his fees and expenses.

The decision by King and Tureen to work together could not have joined two lawyers who were more opposite in their approach to law and in their objectives. Tureen had gone to law school to help impoverished Indians. King went in hopes of avoiding the draft. Tureen found law school boring, rarely attended classes, and achieved only mediocre grades. King loved law school, rarely missed class, and finished first in his class. Tureen spent his first two years out of law school in the outback of Maine working for clients who could not afford to pay him. King spent his first two years clerking for the chief justice of the Connecticut Supreme Court.

The biggest difference between the two men, however, was what made them tick. Money or privilege did not drive Tureen. He had his fill of those as a youngster. He got a charge out of using the law as a weapon to overturn the status quo. Filing Indian land-claim lawsuits that disrupted everyone from white landowners to government was more like pleasure than work.

King, on the other hand, was privileged enough to attend law school and had little firsthand experience with social injustice. As with many lawyers, he came to see the practice of law as a profession, not as a means to right society's wrongs. As such, he could advocate for his clients' interests, regardless of his personal views. That's a lawyer's job.

More than anyone, Tureen was most relieved by King's willingness to pursue settlement talks in the aftermath of the Mashpee ruling. "Mashpee was very scary," Tureen thought, "very scary. The case it most directly put at risk was Pequot. Pequot was really the only one left where tribal status was still in question." In Maine, the state and federal government had acknowledged that the Passamaquoddy and Penobscot were true tribes. Both had maintained a strong, uninterrupted tribal presence on their respective reservations stretching back to before the Revolutionary War. The Pequots had not. "I was afraid the whole house of cards would fall down as a result," said Tureen. "If we went down on one case, the momentum both legally and politically would stop. We would become vulnerable."

13

THE SECOND MRS. HAYWARD

SUMMER 1979

NINETEEN-YEAR-OLD CINDY FIGDORE HAD JUST FINISHED HER SECOND year of college at the University of Connecticut, where she was studying nursing. In need of a summer job, she moved back in with her parents in North Stonington, Connecticut, to work for Lenny LaCroix. He owned Mr. Pizza, a restaurant that was just a few miles down the road from Wheeler High School where Figdore had attended. Although the restaurant had a Ledyard address, its jukebox, cheap pizza, and free refills on soda made it a popular hangout for kids Figdore grew up with.

In high school, Figdore was a popular cheerleader and spent many Friday nights celebrating at Mr. Pizza with the varsity basketball team. Figdore's mother, who was a cheerleader adviser, often came along. After her freshman year of college, Figdore decided to waitress for LaCroix, who agreed to employ her each summer until she completed college.

On her first day in the summer of 1979, Figdore, dressed in her waitress outfit, pulled into the dusty driveway and parked in the narrow stretch of paved parking spaces under the sign MR. PIZZA. The place looked the same as always. The rustic building was painted dark brown and had a shingled roof. There were two small windows, each sporting a neon sign advertising alcoholic beverages. Five small lanternlike lights were evenly spaced across the front of the building. And a short porch with a brown wooden railing around it encased the entrance area, giving it the appearance of an old western-style saloon, where one might expect horses to be tied up outside. Even the surroundings looked like a scene out of the Old West. Located on an undeveloped stretch along Route 2 in Ledyard, it stood alone. Behind it, past a stretch of woods, lay the Pequot Indian reservation.

When she entered the restaurant, everything looked in place too. The wagon wheel hanging from the ceiling. The beaten hardwood floors. The booths with their high wooden backs and red Naugahyde cushions. The brick fireplace in the center of the restaurant with the stuffed deer head mounted to the brickwork. Shaded lamps hung from the ceiling. LaCroix was behind the counter, hustling to fill orders and cash customers out at the same time. "That was the beauty of a small town," Figdore thought. "Things always stayed the same."

Even the man sitting in the far back corner next to the jukebox was where he should be. His hair was pulled back in a ponytail. His skin was darkly tanned. The muscles in his arms looked like tight balls, with a big vein visible through his biceps. The shape of his thick chest was visible through his tight-fitting shirt. He looked like an actor.

She remembered him from the year before and found him attractive and charismatic. He was at Mr. Pizza every day that she worked the previous summer. He always sat in the same booth—all day long. He would stay there until the place closed after midnight. People were always coming to visit the man at his table. Most of them were from out of town—well-dressed lawyers, government workers, and even attractive women. Other times he would just sit there alone.

He had a name Figdore could not forget: Skip Hayward. But everyone referred to him as "the Chief." He was different from anyone else Figdore had ever seen. Out of curiosity, she could not help but watch him. Likewise, Hayward had watched her. He recognized her right away when she entered the restaurant to resume her summer job. She had a face that was hard to forget. Her figure was slender and well shaped. A discreet dresser, she was nonetheless used to getting looks from men and she knew that Hayward's eyes had been appraising her. Still, she was surprised when he approached her in May of 1979 and asked her out on a date. The invitation put her in an awkward position. He was thirty-one. She was nineteen. "He is a wild Indian," thought Figdore. "He has a wonderful heart. But he is so wild."

He would get drunk, then, with his friends, clear out all the tables in the center of the dining area so they could dance. Hayward would break out rolls of quarters to feed the jukebox as he danced to a range of music, from country standards by Johnny Cash and Willie Nelson to Devo's "Whip It," one of his favorites.

Despite Skip's persistence, Figdore never dated him during the summer of 1979. But when she returned to Mr. Pizza after her third year of college in May of 1980, she finally gave in. She accepted an invitation to go on the reservation with him one evening to meet his family. Away from the restaurant, the people Hayward hung around with there, and the alcohol, Figdore saw a different side of him. Charmed by his emphasis on family and hard work, revitalizing an entire reservation, and working to serve others, Figdore agreed to see him again.

Soon she introduced Hayward to her parents. They liked him but were very concerned about his age, his culture, and his reputation for being wild.

Over time, Figdore's relationship with Hayward deepened, and she developed passion for the tribe's attempts to restore their Indian culture and protect their lands. She became familiar with the lawsuit they were involved in against the Ledyard landowners. She met Tureen and other Indians from the Maine tribes. It fed her idealism.

After dating for three months in the summer of 1980, Figdore agreed to marry Hayward. Their marriage license illustrated the many differences between them. Under "AGE," he wrote "32," she, "20." Under "RACE," he "American Indian," she, "Caucasian." Under "OCCUPATION," he "Tribal Council Chairman," she, "Waitress." By agreeing to marry Hayward, Figdore was not only changing her name and address, she was changing her whole way of life. Despite having one year remaining until she graduated from college with a nursing degree, she agreed to drop out and move onto the reservation as the wife of the chief. Yet she knew as a non-Indian she would have no rights to participate in tribal meetings or vote in tribal elections.

The wedding was held on September 20, 1980, at the Second Baptist

Church in North Stonington. For Hayward, life's prospects seemed much brighter. He had a new wife, beautiful and young. They had a brand-new house under construction on the reservation that was being paid for by a $1.1 million grant from HUD. And money was being donated, appropriated, and loaned to the tribe in record amounts. Under Skip's leadership, the tribe's budget had multiplied 150 times since he organized his family members in 1975.

And he had a plan for things to get even better. He had been working with leaders of the Penobscot Indians in Maine that promised to bring more cash to the Pequots. In 1977, the Penobscots began offering high-stakes beano games (a form of bingo where beans are used as markers) on their reservation. Held primarily on Sundays, the games drew hundreds of people from Maine. Players paid up to $45 a person just to enter the game, which featured prizes as high as $25,000 in "Super Bingo." Almost immediately, the tribe started generating approximately $50,000 per month in gross revenues. It was a tremendous amount of money for people who were classified as the poorest in America when Tureen first arrived in Maine.

Skip had been to Maine and assessed the bingo operation. Convinced a similar operation could be even more lucrative in more densely populated Connecticut, he and George Tomer and other Penobscot leaders started discussing the potential to bring not only bingo but also other types of organized gambling to Ledyard. However, no plans could be carried out until a settlement was reached in the Ledyard lawsuit, for any disclosure of the plans would jeopardize the chances of a successful resolution for the Pequots. But Skip was prepared to wait.

14

BENEATH THE RADAR SCREEN

IN THE FALL OF 1979, TUREEN RECEIVED NOTICE FROM JUDGE BLUMENFELD saying he was on the verge of dismissing the Pequots' case against the landowners due to inactivity on the part of the plaintiffs. It had been over three years since Tureen filed the case and over a year since any effort had been made to resolve it. One of the court's so-called housekeeping rules, designed to prevent backlog on the courthouse docket, authorized Blumenfeld to dismiss cases that were inactive for more than a year. Tureen now needed to notify Blumenfeld what his intentions were, since it was the plaintiff's responsibility to move the case along.

Recognizing that his client's case was subject to dismissal, Tureen requested King's consent to an extension. King agreed, and Tureen wrote to Judge Blumenfeld.

"Plaintiff notifies the Court," replied Tureen in a letter to Blumenfeld, "that no action has been taken in this matter during the past year because settlement discussions are under way in this action." After receiving Tureen's memorandum, Blumenfeld agreed not to dismiss the case.

Tureen had let the Pequot case languish for three years because of other pressing priorities. In addition to handling eighteen lawsuits that were pending in six states (New York, Rhode Island, Massachusetts, Connecticut, Virginia, and Louisiana), he had reached a critical juncture in the Maine settlement talks. Maine's freshman senator, William Cohen, had been publicly campaigning against the Maine settlement. He disagreed with Tureen's whole premise for bringing the lawsuits. In Cohen's view, a ruling was needed from the U.S. Supreme Court to first determine whether the Nonintercourse Act entitled the eastern tribes to recover land. However, Cohen had softened his position, as public opinion in Maine shifted toward favoring an out-of-court settlement that would return some land to the tribe at the federal government's expense. The risks inherent in an all-or-nothing trial were too high; there was simply too much land in question.

Since the transfer of state land to an Indian tribe requires approval from the federal government, Cohen's support was critical. Ultimately, he and Maine's senior senator, George Mitchell, agreed to introduce the settlement plan in Congress as long as the state first passed a law approving the plan.

After months of negotiation between Tureen and the state, only one obstacle remained between them—gambling. The Maine legislature knew that the Penobscots had been illegally operating a high-stakes bingo operation on its reservation since 1977. State law prohibited high-stakes bingo games but allowed smaller-scale bingo games to be operated by individuals or corporations that were properly licensed by the state. But the tribe took the position that the state's regulatory laws pertaining to gambling did not apply on the reservation.

Before passing legislation to end the Maine tribes' land-claims suits, state lawmakers insisted that the tribes agree to language in the bill that would authorize the state to enforce its regulatory laws on the Maine reservations. It was a concession the tribes did not want to make. The Penobscots were badly in need of the revenue being generated by the bingo games. If it agreed to the state's terms, the Penobscots' bingo games—and the revenue they generated—would be shut down. More importantly, the tribe would be prevented from ever expanding its gambling business in the future. Once the state had regulatory authority on the reservation, any gambling operations would have to be approved by the state, which was highly unlikely in a state that forbids gambling as a matter of public policy.

Tureen understood the Penobscots' position. But he also knew that if he did not agree to the state's demand, the entire settlement might collapse. President Jimmy Carter, who had already agreed to sign the settlement into law once it made its way through the Congress, was trailing Ronald Reagan in the polls. And Reagan was on record opposing expensive settlements with Indian tribes that required the federal government to foot the bill. With the election fast approaching, Tureen figured he could not hold out in hopes of getting the state to soften its demand on the gambling issue at the risk of losing the entire settlement. "The tribes are getting all the other aspects of sovereignty," reasoned Tureen. "They are getting the right to have their own tribal courts, the rights to control their fishing and hunting, the right to control their internal affairs, and the right to exclude non-Indians from their political process. It is a compromise, no question about it. But they are getting a whole lot more than they had before." The tribes were also getting a tremendous amount of money and land that Tureen could help them use to invest in businesses other than gambling.

Tureen agreed to give the state authority to regulate gambling on the reservations. On April 3, 1980, Tureen's settlement plan passed both Houses in the Maine legislature and was signed into law. Later that summer, Cohen and Mitchell introduced the legislation in Congress. On September 22 Congress passed the Maine Indian Claims Settlement Act. President Carter signed the bill into law on October 10, and on December 12, $81.5 million was deposited in a U.S. Treasury account for the Maine tribes. The money was designated for the two tribes to purchase up to 300,000 acres of land they claimed in their lawsuits and to carry out economic development on their lands. It had taken him ten years, but Tureen had achieved the unthinkable. He had won millions of dollars in federal funds and secured 300,000 acres of land for two of the nation's poorest Indian tribes.

Despite Tureen's achievement, not all of his clients in Maine were satisfied. Penobscot George Tomer was furious. "We were screwed big-time," he complained to Tureen. "Neither tribe agreed to those terms. We've been locked out of gaming."

Disappointed in Tomer's reaction, Tureen shrugged off the criticism. The governing bodies of both Maine tribes had supported his concession, realizing the entire settlement would have collapsed had Tureen refused to compromise. John Stevens and many of the tribal members were far less interested in gaming than the right to practice their culture, protect their lands, and stimulate reliable forms of economic development.

Tomer, meanwhile, contacted Hayward, warning him not to let Tureen agree to a similar compromise over gambling when he negotiated the settlement with the Ledyard landowners. He advised him to be vigilant about not allowing the state to obtain jurisdiction over gambling on the reservation.

Tureen was already aware of Hayward's desire to bring gambling to Ledyard. He knew that the Penobscots had been talking with him about it since 1977. And after his experience in Maine and the criticism that came in the aftermath of the settlement, Tureen's primary concern in Ledyard was making sure that the state of Connecticut did not obtain regulatory control over the Pequot reservation. Unlike in Maine, where the Passamaquoddy and Penobscot were given $81 million and the right to purchase 300,000 acres of real estate, the Pequots stood only to get back 800 acres. Tureen knew the Pequots would be lucky to get $1 million in funds. This left them far fewer options to invest in compared to the Maine tribes.

"Gaming is the one best chance for the Pequots to really get something substantial out of this settlement," thought Tureen, who had seen Hayward's maple syrup business and numerous other attempts to make money on the reservation fail miserably.

The Penobscot Indians were drawing hundreds of players in a

remote area of Maine. In contrast, the Pequot reservation sits at the midway point between Boston and New York City, less than a two-hour drive to either city. "Compared to the Maine tribes, the Pequots' land claim involves very little land and very little money," Tureen thought. "But the Pequots have one thing the other tribes do not have—the proximity of a whole lot of non-Indians. The Pequots have more of these immigrants—Euro-Americans—within a tankful of gas than any other tribe in the country."

On September 17, 1981, Connecticut governor William O'Neill attended a ribbon-cutting ceremony at the Pequot reservation that marked the opening of fifteen new homes built on the reservation. The homes were built with the $1.1 million HUD grant secured by Hayward in 1979. "It's nice to come back to where it all began long before us white men were here," O'Neill said after the ceremony. "I hope it's here another three hundred years."

One month later, the local media began reporting that there had been a breakthrough in negotiations. Yet the terms of the settlement were nowhere near finalized. Interstate 95, the main highway that runs up the East Coast and connects Boston and New York, is less than ten miles from the Pequot reservation. A Connecticut State Highway—Route 2—intersects with I-95 and provides a direct route less than ten miles in length to the north side of the Pequot reservation. Approximately one thousand acres of undeveloped forest was all that stood between the existing reservation and Route 2. The thousand acres, however, were not the land at issue in the lawsuit. The defendants' land that was once part of the original reservation was located to the west of the existing reservation, making it less accessible. It was also poorly suited for new construction, given the steep rock ledges that covered parts of it. This was why the state gave it to the Indians to begin with—it was unsuitable for farming or development. If they were going to build gambling facilities, they needed better land that could be easily reached by potential customers, a consideration that had not been contemplated at the time the suit was filed.

Hayward wanted to incorporate into the settlement terms a provision that would permit the tribe to acquire the additional thousand acres of land between the reservation and the state highway. After arranging a meeting with King to discuss it, Tureen flew down to Ledyard and went with Hayward to King's law office. Neither David Holdridge nor any of the other defendants were told the meeting was taking place. Tureen was looking for large, contiguous areas and was counting on King's familiarity with Ledyard real estate to assist them in determining how many land parcels were included in the thousand acres and whether any of them were available for purchase.

At King's law office, King, Tureen, and Skip sketched out informal maps depicting the area that Hayward wanted to acquire. Most of the thousand acres Hayward was eyeing belonged to just two property owners, both of whom were likely to want to sell.

To the far north of the reservation was a three-hundred-plus-acre dairy farm owned by Sydney Hall, a man in his eighties whose health was on the decline. Since Hall and his wife had no children, there were no heirs in line to inherit the farm. "One might surmise that Sydney was a very old guy and at some point something was going to happen to the property," observed King. "You could call that available."

Just south of Hall's farm was an even bigger tract of land, a 550-acre parcel that extended all the way from the southern property line of Hall's farm to the northern border of the existing Pequot reservation. This parcel was so extensive that it not only abutted Route 2 but also extended to the other side of the state highway and stretched an additional eighty acres. "One might surmise that that is available too," King told them.

King told them the land was deeded to the George Henry Pratt Main estate, a name Tureen and Hayward both recognized. When they had filed the lawsuit, they included a claim against the estate, which included a small, obscure seven-acre parcel of land that was detached from the estate's primary landholding. This seven-acre tract was landlocked between Comrie's and Holdridge's land on the other side of the reservation. David Holdridge had never bothered contacting the overseers of the estate because he had never known George Main or even if he was still living. He assumed that Main had died many years ago, given that he had lived in town his entire life and never heard of the man.

King, however, knew that George Main was alive and lived in Putnam, Connecticut, approximately forty-five minutes north of Ledyard. King was also personally acquainted with Main's large estate. He had hiked the property numerous times and knew that in 1969, under the eminent domain law, the state of Connecticut cut a swath through the middle of the estate just wide enough for the new state highway, Route 2. The lawyer who helped Main get compensation from the state worked in King's law firm. King knew that ever since the state highway was put in, Main wished more than ever that he could sell the land, which he had let sit idle for over forty years. George, a fifty-year-old auto mechanic living in the other part of the state, had done nothing other than pay taxes on it every year. It was incredible to King that the land had remained undeveloped despite the fact that in the summer season Route 2 served as the main artery for people in southeastern Connecticut commuting to Rhode Island beaches.

Hayward and Tureen were encouraged that most of the thousand acres they wanted was in the hands of two individuals, an old farmer and an auto mechanic who appeared likely to sell. But Tureen realized that even if he came up with the money for Hayward to purchase Sydney Hall's farm and George Main's estate, an even bigger hurdle remained. A lucrative Indian gaming enterprise could be operated only on federal Indian land. Both Hall's and Main's properties were private landholdings subject to Ledyard zoning laws. Both properties were in a "rural residential" zone. Simply purchasing the land would not automatically convert the parcels' status to Indian country—even if the buyer were an Indian tribe. Only Congress had the power to change the designation of privately held land to federal Indian land. And there was no way Congress was going to simply take private land away from the state of Connecticut, remove it from the Ledyard tax rolls, and declare it federal Indian territory—especially if it suspected that the land was being eyed for a gambling operation.

Tureen and King's settlement agreement already called on Congress, with the state of Connecticut's consent, to reclassify the defendants' eight hundred acres of land as federal Indian territory once it was bought by the Pequots. The justification for reclassifying the defendants' land was based on the fact that it once was part of the original reservation. The land owned by Hall and Main, however, was not. Even maps that predated the American Revolution did not identify this additional real estate as Indian land. The first recorded survey of the area was taken in 1721. The map that resulted from that survey showed that the property now owned by Hall and Main was outside the earliest documented reservation boundary.

Beginning in 1761, the contours of the reservation boundary underwent a series of changes, but each alteration resulted in the reservation getting smaller, not bigger. The maps confirmed that there was no basis whatsoever for claiming that the coveted land between the existing reservation and Route 2 was once Indian land.

Without the thousand acres along Route 2 having any relationship to old Pequot land, Tureen needed another basis for asking Congress to declare it Indian territory with all the privileges that accompany sovereign land. With King's consent, an open-ended provision was added to the settlement legislation that said the new reservation would consist of "those lands conveyed to or acquired by said tribe as part of the settlement of its land claims in the town of Ledyard." This ambiguous language left the door open for the tribe to acquire land other than the defendants' eight hundred acres. But since the stated purpose of the settlement legislation was to end a protracted legal battle over the eight hundred acres, the question was: Would lawmakers read the bill carefully enough to recognize the loophole that had been added?

After Tureen and King drafted their settlement plan in the form of a proposed bill, they began meeting with Connecticut legislators. First, the state had to pass a law approving the settlement before the Congress could pass a federal law recognizing the transfer of state land to federal Indian land. During talks with the state legislature, Hayward's desire to obtain additional land for establishing a future gambling operation never came up. Tureen decoyed the state people away from the issue, purposely underplaying that aspect of the settlement. And the state never asked. The legislators were too concerned with making sure that the act included language that granted state courts jurisdiction over crimes and civil disputes that might arise within the newly created reservation boundary. Tureen completely disarmed them by offering to give the state authority to do both. Since states have no authority to do either on western reservations, Tureen's offer went a long way toward winning the support of many of the legislators. To them, Tureen's willingness to give the state the authority to prosecute felonies on the reservation and resolve civil disputes satisfied the legislators' chief concerns.

Hayward's chief fear was losing the right to set up gambling on the reservation. But Tureen calmed his concerns.

"To those who don't know the nuances and intricacies of Indian law, it sounds like I've made a huge concession," Tureen explained. "But in fact it wasn't because it doesn't matter whether a state court has jurisdiction to adjudicate criminal and civil matters. What's critical is whether the state has *regulatory* ability. And the legislation I proposed does not give the state regulatory authority. This is what holds open the possibility of gaming. In many ways, that is the most important thing in the Connecticut act."

In February of 1982 the state senate introduced a special act entitled "An Act to Implement the Settlement of the Mashantucket Pequot Indian Land Claims." In addition to giving the state no regulatory authority over businesses conducted on the reservation, the act stripped the state of authority to compel the tribe to comply with environmental regulations and pay taxes. And these privileges extended to the thousand acres east and north of the reservation—if the tribe succeeded in buying them. Tureen knew that there was not much awareness at the state level, particularly because the Pequots were so few in number.

Low visibility was just what Tureen wanted. The less people knew, the less opportunity for public opposition to mount.

On June 9, 1982, the act was approved. Connecticut lawmakers had paved the way for Hayward and his relatives to amass a contiguous stretch of real estate along a state highway while insulating them and the land from state regulations. "This act shall take effect upon the enactment of legislation by the United States," read the last sentence of the law.

The settlement's passage through the Connecticut legislature was far smoother than the one Tureen proposed in Maine. "Connecticut thinks it is getting this claim to go away and that the individual landowners will get something for their land," he thought. "And the state thinks it is getting a jurisdictional arrangement that won't create a lot of problems—one that is safe, where law and order will prevail. But nobody is looking at this closely."

Tureen could hardly believe how accommodating Connecticut appeared. "We never had to lie to anyone or mislead anybody," he thought. "We were never questioned about these other aspects."

15

THE MAPMAKERS

AS GENERAL COUNSEL FOR THE SENATE SELECT COMMITTEE ON INDIAN Affairs, Pete Taylor was the behind-the-scenes attorney most responsible for making sure that any federal legislation involving Indians was drafted properly. Senators trying to pass laws involving Indians relied on Taylor to guide their bills through a maze of congressional hearings, amendments, and votes in hopes that they would eventually reach the president's desk and be signed into law. Long before Senator Lowell Weicker told his colleagues in the senate that he was going to sponsor the Mashantucket Pequot Indian Claims Settlement Act, he brought it to Taylor to review in early 1982.

The bill came as no surprise to Taylor. He had been on the Senate's Select Committee on Indian Affairs since its formation in 1977. During that time he saw the Maine tribes and the Narragansett Indians from Rhode Island pass similar settlements with congressional approval. Taylor had known that the Ledyard settlement was in the works since 1980 when Hayward traveled to Washington to have lunch with him and discuss the lawsuit. Taylor, who first heard of the Western Pequot tribe while chairing one of the task forces for the government's Indian Policy Review Commission in the mid-1970s, was impressed with Hayward's attempts to revitalize the reservation. He knew that eventually Hayward's persistence, combined with Tureen's expertise, would result in the Pequots being recognized as a federal tribe with sovereign status.

But Weicker's primary objective in sponsoring the legislation was not to make the Pequots a sovereign Indian nation. He saw the legislation as the most practical way to end a property dispute between an Indian tribe and local residents of his state. "The Pequots are not seeking money," Weicker said in a written statement prepared for the Senate Select Committee on Indian Affairs. "They want a viable land base. This legislation would free them to devote time and funds to a continuation of the successful projects which they have begun. The settlement would also remove remaining clouds from titles held by present landowners."

However, the bill Tureen and King asked Weicker to sponsor did much more than merely resolve a land dispute. It had a much larger scheme, the details of which Weicker was never told. He had agreed to sponsor it after only a cursory explanation of the bill's intent. Weicker spent less than half an hour listening to Tureen, King, and Hayward explain the settlement before agreeing to help them.

Weicker's office asked Taylor to look the legislation over and make any recommendations that he saw fit. In doing so, Taylor noticed something Weicker and the Connecticut legislature had overlooked. The bill Weicker agreed to sponsor did not describe the specific properties that were to become part of the newly created Pequot reservation under the terms of the settlement. Instead, it merely said, "The term 'reservation' means the existing reservation of the Tribe . . . and any settlement lands taken in trust by the United States for the Tribe."

Taylor invited Tureen, King, and Hayward to Washington to meet with him at his office in the spring of 1982. Before the Senate committee conducted a hearing on the bill in July, Taylor wanted the three architects of the bill's language to make it more clear for the committee which Ledyard properties were going to become reservation land under the terms of the settlement.

"I think you guys need a map," Taylor told them. It was the first time anyone had asked for a map specifying what the reservation boundaries would look like.

"We don't have a map," said Tureen.

"You need a map to go with the bill," Taylor insisted.

"Maybe we can make a map," said King, who removed a town of Ledyard assessor's map from his briefcase.

The three were then ushered into an empty room with a table. As soon as Taylor left, they started creating the boundary. Using a red felt-tip marker, King started drawing a bright red boundary line that took in the existing reservation (two hundred acres) and the defendants' land (eight hundred acres). But King did not stop there. He, Tureen, and Hayward had been afforded a rare opportunity to design their own Indian reservation, with no one looking over their shoulders. They were making law that would alter indefinitely the lay of the land in Ledyard, Connecticut. And no one—Ledyard residents or the politicians they had elected to represent their interest—was there to watch or participate.

"We're in never-never land, uncharted waters," thought Tureen, watching King draw. "It's a question of understanding how big the envelope is and then how to position ourselves in the far corner of it, but not outside it."

With his red pen firmly applied to the map, King kept drawing the boundary line north, going away from the reservation. As he pushed the pen up Shewville Road, King suddenly made a jog to the left in order to take in a large section of land on nearby Fanning Road. The assessor's map reflected a large mass of undeveloped land between Shewville and Fanning Roads, and Hayward wanted it. King drew the red line around all of it, unaware that the outdated map he was drawing on did not reflect the fact that the land had since been subdivided into more than thirty house lots. Some of the lots already had new houses built on them. The boundary line King drew actually split some of the house lots right down the middle, leaving some of the homes half in and half out of the new reservation property.

King then took the line over to Sydney Hall's three-hundred-plus-acre farm, followed a defunct trolley line that used to run through the center of Hall's property, and brought the boundary line along to George Main's estate. He drew the line right along Route 2 to capture all of Main's estate property that sat between the old reservation and the state highway. King continued drawing the line straight down Route 2 until his pen reached Mr. Pizza, owned by Lenny LaCroix, one of King's clients. King chose to draw the line around his two-acre lot, excluding it from the new reservation boundary.

After avoiding LaCroix's pizza shop, King continued right down Route 2, then began drawing the line back toward the existing reservation. With Hall's farm and Main's estate now enclosed in the reservation boundary, only one more large parcel stood between Main's estate and the old reservation: Lois Tefft's farm. But King protected her land from the boundary too. The word TEFFT was written across the area where her farm sat, making it the only property on the entire map where the landowner was identified.

Finally back on Route 214—the road with the only entranceway onto the old reservation—King was set to link the end of the red border line with the point where he had begun drawing just moments ago. But first he took the pen and extended the boundary around a large tract on the opposite side of Route 214, across from the old reservation. Two sisters, Mary Barthelson of Ledyard and Patricia Crawford of California, owned the land. King had contacted them in advance, confirmed their interest in selling it, and agreed to represent them in a private land sale to the tribe.

Finally, King lifted the red felt-tip marker from the map. In a few minutes' time, he had created a new boundary that expanded the reservation area to over two thousand acres. In addition to all the defendants' land, Hayward would be entitled to purchase and have the federal government transform into sovereign Indian land over sixty privately owned land parcels, many of which had homes and farms on them. Included among them were some lots that were held in trust by the local land conservation group, on whose board of directors King sat. (See map on page 356.)

By including this land inside the new reservation boundary, King had effectively eliminated all other bidders on those huge pieces of real estate. While the owners were not obligated to sell to the tribe, and could sell to third parties, no other prospective buyer was going to pay for land that fell within an Indian reservation. As a result, if Sydney Hall or George Main ever decided they wanted to sell their land, they would have only one buyer—Skip Hayward.

And the boundary had an even more valuable meaning to Hayward from a development standpoint. "The significance of this boundary," Tureen explained, "is that anything acquired within that area automatically becomes federal trust land."

In an empty Senate committee room, two lawyers and the man who stood to benefit from their effort had created a tiny sovereign nation, complete with land that would become exempt from local, state, and federal taxation as well as environmental and zoning regulations. Elated, Hayward did not fully appreciate Tureen's deft negotiating skills. He had managed to secure for the Pequots far more than they anticipated when they filed the suit.

King, Tureen, and Hayward took the map to Taylor, who placed it with Weicker's bill. "We would like to make it part of the committee record," Taylor said. "We want to know, 'Where is this claim being extinguished?' And if it's creating a reservation land base, we want to know what it is we are creating. We want the record to reflect that Congress understands what it is doing."

Looking at the map King had drawn did nothing to alert the Senate that it was about to convert a great deal of privately owned land into Indian territory. Other than Tefft's farm, none of the other parcels were identified on the map. Nor did it distinguish between the eight hundred acres that were the subject of the lawsuit and the additional thousand-plus acres that Hayward wanted for development. Only someone very familiar with Ledyard geography would recognize that the map reflected two thousand acres of settlement land, while the only acres referred to in the bill were the defendants' eight hundred acres. Even Weicker did not realize it. When seeking the support of his colleagues in the Senate, Weicker explained that the bill "call[ed] for the establishment of a Federal trust fund of $900,000 to be used by the tribe to purchase 800 acres of land." He did not know that dozens of people, whose land had no relation to the lawsuit or the old Indian reservation, were being included in his bill. "If Weicker understood that level of detail," noted King, "I'd be amazed."

Since Holdridge had to agree to any changes in the bill before it went forward, King mailed him the revised language in Weicker's bill. But he did not include the map in the envelope.

When Holdridge read the ten-thousand-word draft of the law on his own, he read it the same way he read his first mortgage before signing on the dotted line. There were so many legal terms and complicated sentences that he left it up to his attorney to make sure his interests were protected in the documents. He was satisfied when he read the part of the bill that said, "The term 'reservation' means the existing reservation of the Tribe and any settlement lands taken in trust by the United States for the Tribe."

Holdridge noticed that under the heading "DEFINITIONS" the bill said: "The term 'private settlement lands' means (A) the eight hundred acres, more or less, of privately held land which are identified by a red outline on a map." He never thought to ask to see the map, because it sounded clear to him that the red outline encircled the eight hundred acres that he and the other defendants had been sued over. Not being a lawyer, Holdridge did not know the cardinal rule of statutory interpretation: when reading the "definitions" section of a bill, *read on*. Subsection (B) of the definition of "private settlement lands" included "the lands known as the Cedar Swamp which are adjacent to the Mashantucket Pequot Reservation."

The Cedar Swamp was a large section of real estate sitting in the middle of George Main's estate, a considerable distance from any of the land involved in the lawsuit.

But Holdridge had not noticed that.

On July 1, 1982, Senator Lowell Weicker introduced The Mashantucket Pequot Land Claims Settlement Act to the U.S. Senate.

16

A SMALL PRICE TO PAY

JULY 13, 1982
GROTON–NEW LONDON AIRPORT

FEAR. TUREEN SAW IT IN HAYWARD'S EYES THE MOMENT HE LOOKED AT him. Hayward feared flying, especially when it entailed sitting in the front seat of Tureen's plane. Privately amused by Hayward's phobia, Tureen could not wait to get airborne and resort to his habit of putting the plane on autopilot and doing legal work in the cockpit while flying at peak altitude. He relied on his passengers to alert him if they spotted any dangers.

Tureen was taking Hayward to Washington. Congress had scheduled two days of hearings on whether to pass the Pequot Settlement Act introduced by Weicker and Representative Sam Gejdenson. The White House had been demanding proof that Hayward and his people were a true tribe. The hearings were intended to answer that question. And committees from both the Senate and the House of Representatives had called Hayward to come and testify.

Since organizing his relatives into a tribe, Hayward had never had to defend his Indian status. Nor had he ever testified before the Congress. Now he found himself on his way to do both. His family was confident that he would convince the country's lawmakers. Yet Hayward was not so sure. He had not been to law school to study law, or even to college to study politics. His formal education consisted of a high school diploma.

Nor was he an expert in genealogy, which was likely to be the area of most concern to the committee members.

Hayward threw his bags into the back and climbed up in the copilot's seat. Tureen refrained from joking as Hayward fumbled with the seat belt in preparation for takeoff. During the flight, they had time to think about and discuss the importance of the next few days. If they succeeded and convinced Congress to pass the act into law, they would be on their way to more than they ever dreamed. The road had led them to this moment and they could not fail.

After arriving safely in D.C., Tureen and Hayward went directly to the Washington office of the Native American Rights Fund. Over and over they rehearsed what Hayward would say in his testimony the following day. Tureen had written a statement. All Hayward had to do was get up, read it like a speech, and sit down. Then Tureen would field all the sticky questions about genealogy.

It sounded like a great plan, but still Hayward was apprehensive. The destiny of Tureen and King's settlement plan—and any hopes of a Pequot gambling enterprise in Ledyard—was in the hands of the two congressional committees. On the Senate Select Committee on Indian Affairs—the first committee Hayward was scheduled to testify before—six of the seven members were from the West and well acquainted with Indian tribes and reservations. Barry Goldwater and Dennis DeConcini from Arizona, Mark Andrews from North Dakota, Slade Gorton from Washington, John Melcher from Montana, and Daniel Inouye from Hawaii. These were experienced and powerful men. If they were unconvinced that the Pequots were a legitimate tribe, the settlement would never even reach the Senate floor for a vote.

Tureen assured Hayward that everything was going to be just fine. Other than the chairman of the committee, none of the senators, Tureen predicted, would even show up for the hearing. And the chairman was not going to stand in the way of the settlement bill. He was Maine senator William Cohen, Tureen's old adversary-turned-friend who had worked with Tureen to settle the Maine cases. Cohen already supported the settlement formula that Tureen was proposing.

Where Hayward was likely to face some challenging questions was in the hearing before the Interior Committee and Insular Affairs in the House of Representatives, which was scheduled for the day after the Senate hearing. Those committee members were sure to attend the hearing and ask questions about the Pequots' tribal legitimacy. However, Connecticut representative Sam Gejdenson was presiding over the hearing. A friend and supporter of Hayward, Gejdenson had been lobbying his colleagues to support the settlement.

Also, the witness lists for both hearings were stacked with people who favored the bill. Besides Hayward, the other witnesses slated to testify were Tureen, Jackson King, Gejdenson, Weicker, and Dodd. The only person scheduled to testify who opposed the settlement was William Coldiron, President Reagan's solicitor from the Department of the Interior.

Coldiron was very suspicious about the settlement proposal, his doubts stemming from a curious petition Hayward had filed in 1979 with the Bureau of Indian Affairs, which asked the bureau to declare his people a tribe.

Hayward had filed the request right around the time that Tureen lost the Mashpee case because of his clients' inability to convince the court that they were truly a tribe. Tureen feared a similar court challenge from King and the Ledyard landowners. The Pequots' genealogy and history, which was far more suspect than the Mashpees', would not withstand the strict criteria for tribal status set up by the federal court. One way to avoid subjecting Hayward and his group to the same fate suffered by the Mashpee was to ward off a court challenge by asking the Bureau of Indian Affairs to declare that the Pequots were a tribe. With the rise in lawsuits being filed by groups claiming to be Indian tribes, Congress had authorized the BIA to establish procedures to judge the merits of such groups. As an alternative to going to court to prove tribal status, groups could subject themselves to a review process before the BIA. If the BIA found them worthy of being called a tribe, then the group did not need to litigate that issue before a judge or jury.

The requirements for proving tribal status established by the BIA included:

> Proof that the petitioner had been identified as a tribe from historic times to the present.
>
> Proof that a majority of the members of the tribe, as well as their ancestors, inhabited the area in or around the reservation.

Proof that the petitioners had been recognized as an Indian community distinct from other populations.

Evidence that the tribe had maintained political influence over its members.

The existence of a written governing document such as a constitution.

Current membership roles that established a genealogical link to a historically recognized tribe.

Jack Campisi, an anthropologist at Wellesley College in Massachusetts, was brought in by Tureen to help Hayward prepare his application. Campisi had testified as an expert witness for Tureen in the Mashpee case. And he was working as a consultant to numerous other Indian groups who were seeking to acquire land. When he and Hayward filed their application with the BIA on January 15, 1979, the Interior Department was staffed with President Carter appointees, and Tureen had established great relations with Carter and his administration.

Campisi and Hayward, however, did not send along any of the supporting documentation to support their application. Almost immediately after the application was filed, Tureen's strategy changed. First, King made it clear he was not going to go to court to challenge the Pequots' tribal status, as was done in Mashpee. With King's cooperation in the settlement plan, there was more to be lost than gained by having BIA researchers poke around in the Haywards' genealogy. Which was why Hayward, despite having anthropologists, historians, and the best team of Indian lawyers in the country at his disposal, did not submit the genealogical and anthropological evidence to go along with his petition.

Tureen felt the odds were better going through Congress than the BIA, particularly after Jimmy Carter was voted out of office and the Interior Department was restaffed with Ronald Reagan appointees. Unlike the court process, the BIA review process was a political one. And the Reagan administration, trying to rein in federal spending, made it clear to Tureen that it opposed awarding tribal status to groups seeking federal services and land through litigation.

Asking Congress to short-circuit the BIA process and simply declare the Pequots a federal tribe as part of the legislation to settle the lawsuit was an extraordinary step. Congress had designated the responsibility for reviewing Indian groups' tribal legitimacy to the more qualified researchers from the BIA. Since the BIA falls under the Department of Interior, William Coldiron was the government lawyer in the Reagan administration assigned to the office where Hayward's tribal petition had been filed. Nearly a hundred other applicants had petitions for tribal recognition on file in the same office. But Hayward's stood out. It was the one without any of the essential supporting materials the BIA needed to determine whether the Haywards were truly a tribe.

The empty file aroused Coldiron's curiosity. He planned to tell the Congress that the Reagan administration felt that it would be like putting the cart before the horse to award land, cash, and federal tribal status to a group that had yet to prove that it was an Indian tribe.

It was going to boil down to who could be more persuasive in the hearings: Coldiron or the supporters of the settlement.

With the start of the Senate hearing nine hours away, Tureen felt confident. As he fell asleep on a couch in a D.C. town house rented by the Native American Rights Fund, he knew the odds were in his favor.

Hayward, on the other hand, lay awake thinking about the speech Tureen had prepared for him. Their relationship had long since developed into much more than an attorney-client relationship. They were teacher and pupil. At Tureen's side, Hayward experienced things that law students only read about. Tureen had taken him along to appear in court proceedings, lobby powerful state and federal lawmakers, testify before state legislatures, and dine with politicians. And in a few hours, Tureen was going to take him to testify in front of a United States Senate committee.

JULY 14, 9:00 A.M.
DIRKSEN SENATE OFFICE BUILDING
ROOM 6226

"Good morning," Senator Bill Cohen said to everyone present. "The hearing will come to order."

Hayward looked around the room. Tureen was right. Not a single member of the committee was present other than Cohen. The seats to his left and right were empty.

"This morning," Cohen continued, "the committee will consider two pieces of legislation: S. 2294, a bill to settle claims of the Chitimacha tribe of Louisiana; and S. 2719, a bill to settle the claims of the Western Pequot tribe of Connecticut."

Tureen could not help but be amused at the irony. The man who had fought him so hard in Maine was now presiding over the hearing that would determine the fate of the Pequots' case. Only this time Cohen was chairing a hearing, and therefore in a more neutral posture.

"I note that I have had some experience with Indian claims based on the alleged violations of the Nonintercourse Act," Cohen continued, "and note for the record that in the audience today is counsel for the Passamaquoddy tribe (Tom Tureen), who was most extensively involved in the Passamaquoddy case—that is, the Passamaquoddy and Penobscot case. I am aware of how difficult it can be at times, and indeed divisive. I want to commend the parties who appear here today for their efforts to resolve disputes."

King, Tureen, and Hayward were so unified that it was hard to believe they were once adversaries. Together they sat as President Reagan's solicitor, Coldiron, prepared to step forward as the first witness. He wasted no time in expressing the Reagan administration's opposition to the settlement.

"We know very little about it or the basis of their claims," Coldiron said. "We do not have them [the Pequots] in our files. The Western Pequot group petitioned for federal acknowledgment on January 15, 1979. For some reason, there is presently little available information on file to indicate whether the group could meet the requirements for federal acknowledgment under the regulations."

Cohen listened politely as Coldiron argued that it was premature to finalize the settlement. There was simply too much at stake. The Pequots were about to get real estate, federally appropriated funds to pay for it, and—most importantly—sovereign status to do whatever they wanted on the land. "Enactment of S. 2719," Coldiron continued, "would establish a government-to-government relationship between the Western Pequots and the federal government and create a federal obligation to the group without the safeguard of detailed knowledge which would be available if the group's petition for acknowledgment were processed under the regulations."

Coldiron's testimony was hitting right at the weakest point of Tureen's strategy. But the committee members most likely to embrace the Reagan administration's view—such as conservative Republicans Barry Goldwater and Slade Gorton—were not present. Coldiron's arguments were falling on deaf ears. "Extending federal recognition to the Western Pequot tribe by legislation would bypass the administrative process established with congressional support for groups seeking federal acknowledgment," he reminded Cohen. "This process was established to provide consideration of petitions under a uniform standard based on systematic and detailed examination of historical evidence. Such a bypassing would set precedent which might encourage similar legislative requests from other groups with pending petitions."

Before concluding his testimony, Coldiron pointed out other concerns, as well. He complained about having insufficient information on the real estate involved in the settlement or its accessed value. "Consequently," he told Cohen, "we cannot determine whether the $900,000 is an appropriate settlement amount."

Connecticut senator Lowell Weicker, a Republican, was the perfect counter to Coldiron. "The Pequots are not seeking money," he told the committee. "They want a viable land base. The cost of this legislation to the federal government is not large, and is, in fact, smaller than the amounts involved in many other Indian land-claim settlements."

In Weicker's brief testimony, he never addressed the tribal status issues raised by Coldiron. Nor did Connecticut senator Chris Dodd, who focused on centuries of suffering endured by Indians. "A one-time appropriation of $900,000 is a small price to pay," Dodd insisted, "for more than a century of inaction by the federal government in meeting its statutory and constitutional obligations to the Mashantucket Pequot Indians."

Only Connecticut representative Sam Gejdenson tried to rebut Coldiron. "There is a tribe with 187 people who have lived on the 220 acres of the reservation for the last 250 years," Gejdenson told Cohen. "The Indians have lived on this land. They have a commitment to it. They are certainly a tribe.

"It is very easy for we in the majority to roll over a small group of Indians . . . and certainly a group of 187 Indians in eastern Connecticut,"

Gejdenson continued. "We are here to represent them and give them the same rights as any other individuals in this society has. I think this legislation does it."

Gejdenson's testimony was riddled with errors that worked in Skip's favor. He claimed that there were 187 Indians in the Pequot tribe, when in fact fewer than fifty-five names were on the tribe's official membership roles, less then half of whom actually lived on the reservation. Of those, none had lived there when Elizabeth George died in 1973.

Gejdenson's testimony also revealed just how little he knew about what the settlement actually entailed. Like Weicker and Dodd, Gejdenson was unaware that the bill he was supporting converted nearly two thousand acres—as opposed to eight hundred—into Indian land: "We are doing this with the least amount of disruption possible," he testified. "Not one homeowner is losing his home. We have put together an eight-hundred-acre tract of undeveloped land to give the Mashantucket Pequots a reservation." No questions were asked about the land that was going to be impacted by the creation of the new reservation boundary.

Meanwhile, Cohen was impressed with the nonpartisanship support for the plan from Connecticut state and federal officials in this case. Even the landowners and the tribe were unified.

After Gejdenson's testimony, Cohen called a brief recess. The downtime gave Hayward one last chance to review his written statement. Tureen informed him that when the hearing reconvened, he would be up next.

"Our next witness is Mr. Hayward, chairman of the Mashantucket Pequot tribe," said Cohen, as he brought the hearing back to order. "With him are Tom Tureen and Jackson T. King. Mr. Hayward."

"Good morning," said Hayward, dressed in a conservative blue suit, white shirt, and wide tie. "My name is Richard A. Hayward. I am chairman of the Mashantucket Pequot Tribal Council. I am here today to ask for your support for the passage of S. 2719. The bill, if enacted, would put to rest a problem which has existed for some time and outlived many generations of my people."

Instantly, Hayward found his rhythm, providing Cohen an impressive, step-by-step account of the Pequots' tribal history. He started with the Pequot War in 1637 and went up to 1855 when Connecticut auctioned off the eight hundred acres of the Pequot reservation that were the subject of the lawsuit. "In vain, we protested that the sales were contrary to federal law and violated our rights under [the] Constitution," Hayward testified. "My people have never consented to the forced sales of their land, nor has the passing of years diminished our sense of injustice."

By design, Hayward's speech made no mention of why Connecticut sold the land or what was done with the proceeds. "Were it not for the fact that our present tribal attorneys are representing us without charge, we could not maintain the pending federal court action," Hayward continued. "In May of 1976, the tribe entered federal court to regain eight hundred acres of reservation land which was deeded to the tribe in fee simple by the colony of Connecticut in 1761. Since that time we have worked with state officials, attorneys for the defendants, and our tribal attorneys and have reached an out-of-court settlement which will pay the current landowners for undeveloped property. Passage of S. 2719 will not only settle the tribe's land claims once and for all but will enable the tribe to plan for its overall land base and plan the tribe's overall economic development activity."

Before wrapping up his testimony, Hayward read a letter written by a Pequot tribal leader in the early 1700s. In the letter, the tribal leader had petitioned the colony of Connecticut to restore some of the tribe's original land.

As Hayward pulled back from the microphone, Tureen was proud. His prodigy was very persuasive. "Thank you very much," said Cohen. "It sounds as though he had a Harvard law education."

Hayward's swift exit from the witness chair was just what Tureen wanted. It was better that he, rather than Hayward, handle any questions about the tribe's incomplete application for federal recognition. To avert a debate on the merits of the Pequots' legitimacy, Tureen planned to distract Cohen at the outset by doing something very uncustomary—give no statement to the committee. Tureen would simply offer, at the outset, to take questions. It was a control device Tureen had thought up, since committee members usually rely on a witness's statement from which to draw their questions—similar to a lawyer conducting cross-examination on a witness. Tureen's decision to go right into the question stage would leave Cohen little to work with.

"We will next hear from Mr. Tureen," said Cohen.

"Senator, I am here primarily to answer questions," began Tureen. "I know that one question which will be asked will be in terms of the involvement of the [Reagan] administration. Let me say that . . . the Interior Department is aware of this claim. We discussed the Connecticut claim, not with the current administration but with the Carter administration when discussing the settlement of the Maine case."

"Do you have any correspondence in your files which you had with the prior administration?" Cohen asked.

"I would have to check, Senator," said Tureen. "I know that there were extensive conversations. We discussed what we thought would be the monetary size of the settlement in Connecticut."

"How did you arrive at the figure of $900,000?" asked Cohen.

The discussion was going right where Tureen wanted it to go—away from the Indian question and into the money question. Cohen had watched the federal government pay out $81 million to settle the Maine cases. The Pequots were merely asking for just under $1 million, a drop in the bucket, to end a six-year-old land dispute involving Native American land.

"The $900,000 figure is the result of an appraisal which we had done by the state of Connecticut," said Tureen. "We estimate that acquisition of the land in question will cost approximately $900,000. Hopefully there will be some leftover funds for economic development purposes.

"I wish that the committee could see what Skip Hayward has done in Mashantucket," Tureen continued. "It is truly a marvel. He has a hydroponic greenhouse, which is a marvel and a beauty to behold, and a model housing development there." Taking control of the hearing, Tureen went on to talk about a range of topics that had nothing to do with whether Hayward and the Pequots were actually a tribe. As he went along, however, he worked in subtle defenses to Coldiron's earlier testimony.

"It is my understanding that [the BIA] believe that they [the Pequots] could easily establish recognition status through that [review] process," insisted Tureen. "I feel that it would be a terrible waste of the federal government's resources and the tribe's very limited resources to have to go through that process. I think it is far more efficient all around, inasmuch as we all know that they will be recognized, to simply do it in the legislation."

Masterful, Tureen sat down, making way for Jackson King.

"Mr. King," said Senator Cohen, signaling King's turn to testify.

"I will be brief," said King. "We talked about the horrors which have happened to the Indians, but what about the horrors which have happened to the defendants in this case? They, like many other people in this country, have saved for their lifetimes to buy their homes and their lands. Now they find that they are confronted with extensive litigation wherein a possible outcome is a total loss of their homes and everything for which they have worked over the years."

The scene King described made perfect sense to Cohen. In Maine, the lawsuits Tureen had filed actually did threaten to take away homes.

"We have had the misfortune of having to advise our clients [that] this is a very solid claim," continued King. "It is a very solid, neat, specific claim from a legal point of view as far as the Indians are concerned. Our landowners are very anxious to have this resolved."

Before King finished, he gave the committee something else to consider. "There is one additional factor," King said. "There are other landowners who seem to have their properties clouded by the existence of the Indian claim, even though they are not within the original reservation's property. We feel that a resolution of this matter will take a bit of the cloud off those properties as well."

"Thank you," said Cohen. "Without objection, your written statement will be inserted in the record at this point."

Cohen brought the hearing to a close. Hayward and Tureen survived the first day of hearing without any serious challenge. They were halfway home.

JULY 15, 1982

The following day, William Coldiron was again the first witness to testify, and this time he was more determined to persuade the House committee. Connecticut representative Sam Gejdenson, however, was equally committed to defeating Coldiron's challenge.

"How long does the process take for the tribe to get recognition?" Gejdenson asked Coldiron.

"I think the Western Pequots [application] has been pending since 1979 and we have not received their submission [evidence] yet," said Coldiron. "After it is received I suppose it would take one year."

"Even though this tribe has been recognized in state law over the last two hundred years or more, you still think that we should go through the federal recognition process?" Gejdenson asked without giving Coldiron time to respond. "It seems that if we have a tribe in the state of Connecticut . . . that has lived on that land for all that period of time, it is a tribe. Why should we be forced to go through a long regulatory process if we are trying to simplify all that, and if we are given an opportunity to do it, let us do it quickly and cleanly. What is the advantage to the country or to the Interior Department if we find a very simple way to deal with something that otherwise would stretch out the inconvenience to landowners in the area, to the state, and to the tribe?"

As Coldiron sat poised to respond, Gejdenson continued. "If we can prove to the legislative bodies of this country, and the Congress, that by every definition used, these are tribes, why shouldn't we go ahead and do it?"

"If," Coldiron began, "you have a—"

"It may be a good precedent," Gejdenson said, cutting Coldiron off before he could complete his sentence. "If it is clearly the case, why should we spend a lot of time on it?"

"If all the material is available," Coldiron said, "I think it would be done very easily in this case because they have been a recognized tribe [in Connecticut]. However, they have not filed *any* materials with us to even look at. Their petition has been pending since 1979."

Committee member Dale Kildee, a Democrat from Michigan, asked Gejdenson for an opportunity to interrupt. "You say they have filed no data," Kildee said to Coldiron. "Are you not aware of *any* historical, genealogical, or anthropological data?"

"They have not filed with us in support of their petitions," answered Coldiron.

Rather than question why Hayward and Tureen had chosen not to file any evidence to the BIA, Kildee accused Coldiron of being at fault. "It seems the federal government has been derelict under the Nonintercourse Act," he began. "We let the state do what it did and you lost track of the genealogical, historical, and anthropological data. If the government is guilty of nonfeasance, perhaps we as the Congress should seek a remedy."

Coldiron hardly knew how to respond to the accusation. And before he could muster an answer, Kildee implied that to deny the Pequots was similar to the civil-rights violations suffered by blacks for decades in the United States. "We look at the 1890 Supreme Court decision of separate but equal with great dismay now," Kildee said. "Hopefully, we are more sensitive to people's civil rights now than we were a few years ago."

"I hope we are too," retorted Coldiron. "But we still have to have an administrative process to determine whether a group is in fact a legitimate group."

"My only point," said Kildee, "is that in trying to seek anthropological, historical, and genealogical data, the federal government might be helpful rather than just waiting for the tribe to turn data over, that they might be providing some assistance."

Kildee's suggestion, if followed, would have only spelled doom for the Pequots by revealing that the Pequot tribe had been dormant for decades and then started up again with four people sitting in Skip Hayward's sister's house listening to Tureen's lawsuit plans.

"Well, if we take that position," Coldiron said, "four people anyplace could get together and say, 'We are a tribe. We want the federal government to come in and prove that we are a tribe.'"

"I am not talking about four people," said Kildee. "I don't think this is just four people picked at random out of the phone book who want some recognition."

The debate between Coldiron and the committee members was starkly different from the testimony the previous day. It was clear to Tureen, Hayward, and King as they sat in on the hearing that Coldiron and the Reagan administration were not going to go away silently. Gejdenson, impatient with Coldiron's adamancy, briefly recessed the hearing and asked him to resume his testimony after the break. When the hearing reconvened, Minnesota representative Bruce Vento asked Coldiron if he was opposed to the Congress granting the Pequots federal recognition status.

"Yes, sir," Coldiron answered. "We think we ought to have evidence we can act on."

About to ask another question, Vento was interrupted by Gejdenson. "Excuse me," Gejdenson said. "If you would yield for a moment."

"I yield," Vento said.

"What you have heard here today and what you now know," Gejdenson said to Coldiron, "this is a tribe that has been recognized by the state of Connecticut for over two hundred years. They have lived on this land for all that period of time. Legally and in every other way in Connecticut they are recognized as a tribe. Wouldn't you say that that makes them a tribe?"

"Not necessarily," said Coldiron. "We would have to examine the evidence. There is a possibility they might not be. If it is so simple, why haven't they come in in the last three years? I don't understand."

The longer the argument between Gejdenson and Coldiron went on, the more apparent it became to other committee members that perhaps somebody should take a look at the Pequots' genealogy. "We just don't want any group to get one thousand acres of land," said Representative Vento. "There are consequences. It is not just the $900,000 here, which is substantial." Vento argued that it was only fair to let the BIA do its job and conduct the review. "If we take this tribe, what about the other seventy-two [that have petitions pending]?"

The momentum was starting to shift. Coldiron had been testifying for the entire hearing and had managed to keep the committee focused on the question of Pequot legitimacy. When Coldiron finished, Gejdenson called another brief recess. During the break, Tureen approached Coldiron in private and offered to turn over the proof that he was looking for. By the time Gejdenson reconvened the hearing, Tureen had agreed to meet directly with the representatives from the BIA.

Meanwhile, Gejdenson called the hearing back to order and invited Tureen, Hayward, and King to take a seat at the witness table. Hayward was back on center stage, only this time he could not rely on a written speech. The committee members wanted answers to questions.

"I guess the basic issue," Hayward began, "is the fact that the state of Connecticut . . . sold off eight hundred acres and the lands that we are suing to recover are the lands that were deeded in fee to the tribe. Also, as part of that, that also was part of the legislation, the tribe wishes to enter into a federal relationship." His opening was hardly smooth and made no attempt to answer Coldiron's charges.

"Maybe you would address the issue that we mentioned," Gejdenson prodded.

But before Hayward could respond, Tureen interjected. "Maybe I should do that, Mr. Chairman," said Tureen, who began by praising the BIA's review process. "But [the review process] is simply too cumbersome to use in this situation. I think we can provide them [BIA] with adequate information to satisfy them about the credibility of the claim of the Mashantucket Pequot tribe for federal recognition. It seems to me that that is the primary stumbling block to the settlement in this case."

"Has there been a tribal census or roll of tribal members compiled?" asked committee member Doug Bereuter, a Republican from Nebraska.

"Yes," Tureen answered. "Both the state and the tribe have maintained rolls consistently throughout history. Those rolls are available."

"What is the current membership," Bereuter asked.

"Forty-two on reservation," Hayward responded. "One hundred fifty-three off the reservation."

"It's a matter of record and it's been there," Tureen insisted. "I should mention the tribe also has a constitution."

Tureen finally told the committee that he had met privately with Coldiron during the recess. "We have spoken with the solicitor today," said Tureen, concerned by the opposition being thrown up by the Reagan administration. "We have arranged for a process by which we will provide them with the information that they want." With this announcement, committee members were satisfied, indicating they would fully support the settlement act.

17

RONALD REAGAN BLINKS

NO ONE WAS MORE SURPRISED BY THE TONE OF THE HEARINGS THAN Timothy Woodcock, the staff director for the Senate's Select Committee on Indian Affairs. Woodcock, a young and astute attorney, had served as Senator Cohen's staff director, where one of his chief responsibilities involved working intimately on the Maine land-claim settlement.

In Maine, the state fought tooth and nail over jurisdictional issues on the reservation, ultimately refusing to settle with Tureen if he did not agree to give the state regulatory power on the Passamaquoddy and Penobscot reservations.

Yet when Woodcock reviewed the language of Weicker's proposed bill after the hearings, he could not get over the fact that there was nothing in it that would give Connecticut the authority to regulate the Pequot reservation. Woodcock found this so odd that he called up Connecticut representative Sam Gejdenson's legislative aide Perry Pockrose. He wanted to make sure Pockrose understood how powerless this bill would leave the state of Connecticut once it was passed. "Is that intentional or by omission?" Woodcock asked Pockrose. "Where is the Connecticut delegation on this issue?"

Pockrose seemed puzzled by Woodcock's question and said that he would have to check with Gejdenson and get back to him.

Gejdenson, Weicker, and Dodd were sponsoring a bill that Tureen had drafted and that contained the provision: *Notwithstanding any other provision of law, Federal recognition is extended to the Tribe*. These thirteen words were the most crucial ones in the six-page bill. In the long run, bestowing sovereign status on Skip and his family was infinitely more valuable than the land—even the additional land—and the money they were receiving from the settlement. Without federal-recognition status, Hayward would be unable to have all the land exempted from local building and zoning regulations, state environmental laws, and property taxes. Those privileges were only afforded to federally recognized Indian tribes. Tureen had been able to get King—and as a result the Connecticut delegation—to agree to this without giving up anything in return. He had learned at a young age that salesmanship was a key to getting what he wanted.

Before his twelfth birthday, Tureen told his parents he wanted a bird he had seen at the local pet shop in his suburban St. Louis neighborhood. Instead of buying the bird for Tom, Tureen's father bought him dozens of one-pound bags of birdseed. Then he told Tom that if he wanted the bird he would have to earn the money to pay for it himself.

Tureen resented his father for not giving him the bird and determined to raise the money himself. Going door to door in his neighborhood, Tureen explained to his neighbors that he was selling birdseed to raise money to buy a pet. Virtually none of his neighbors owned birds, yet they bought every bag of birdseed he had. They sympathized with a young boy's desire to have a pet and admired his ingenuity and hard work to obtain it. For a few dollars each, they helped him achieve his dream.

In addition to getting his bird, Tureen learned a valuable lesson. *In order to get people to do something they don't really want or need to do—like buy birdseed when they don't own birds—convince them they are contributing to a good cause and make their contribution seem inexpensive.*

Weicker, Dodd, and Gejdenson wanted nothing more than to relieve the seven-year legal stalemate between the Pequots and the Ledyard landowners. Calling the Pequots a federal tribe rather than a state tribe seemed like a small price to pay to resolve the problem.

But Woodcock knew that the price was anything but small. "Any federal enclave where federal Indian law applies brings with it an enormous body of complex jurisdictional law," he thought. "The dynamic would change enormously if the state civil regulatory jurisdiction applied instead. That would mean that in order for the tribe to build a casino, it would first have to go to the state legislature and get them to authorize the land to be the site of a casino."

Woodcock and the other staff members on the Senate committee were well aware that the Pequots might look to build a casino on the Ledyard land if the bill passed. Small-scale gambling operations were already starting to crop up on Indian reservations, including some that offered casino games. For nearly a year, Woodcock's committee had been reviewing proposed legislation aimed at addressing gambling on Indian reservations.

A few days later Woodcock received a return phone call from Pockrose. "Well," Pockrose said, "I checked with Sam Gejdenson and the Connecticut attorney general's office and we don't care if there is federal jurisdiction there."

"Then that's what you're going to get," said Woodcock, chuckling to himself in amazement as he hung up the phone. He could hardly believe that a decision of such significance was being made so casually.

Nonetheless, Woodcock knew it was not his place to interfere with the settlement terms in Connecticut. "My job is to facilitate settlement that these entities had agreed upon," thought Woodcock. He assumed that Connecticut could figure out what its interests were. In his view, as long as federal interests were being protected and the settlement was an overall fair one, it was beyond him to inject his personal views as to what was appropriate.

• • •

By September, the House committee decided to support the settlement act. Similarly, Senator Cohen, on behalf of the Senate's Indian Affairs Committee, drafted a report in support of the bill's passage. Both Cohen and the House committee had received letters from the Department of Interior informing them that, despite Tureen's promise, Hayward had still not turned over the necessary evidence to establish that the Pequots were a tribe.

Nonetheless, both houses voted unanimously to pass the act on the basis of the strong bipartisan support from the Connecticut delegation. Tureen, with King's support, had convinced Weicker, Dodd, and Gejdenson to risk passing the legislation without first seeing any genealogical or anthropological evidence that the Haywards were actually the Pequot tribe. They had accepted Tureen and Hayward's assurances that the genealogy more than adequately established the Haywards' links to the Pequot tribe.

"It is all in the art of negotiating," felt Tureen, pleased that he had maneuvered his clients through the hearing process without subjecting their genealogy to scrutiny. "People think of entrepreneurs as people who get up in the morning and say, 'What risks can I take today?' They're not. Entrepreneurs are people who get up in the morning and say, 'What risk can I get somebody else to take today?'

"My job is to win, to make this crazy thing work. It is there to be had, so why not do it? Nobody is stopping us."

On April 5, 1983, though, someone did stop them: Ronald Reagan.

"I am returning, without my approval, S. 366, the 'Mashantucket Pequot Indian Claims Settlement Act,'" Reagan wrote in his stunning veto message to the Senate. "I agree that the most desirable approach to resolution and extinguishment of these claims is through agreements negotiated among the parties concerned. . . . However, this process must recognize certain principles if equity and fairness to all parties are to be achieved. Unfortunately, I find S. 366 violates several of these principles."

Reagan felt it premature to bestow tribal status on a group that had not satisfied the requirements for federal recognition, and he called on Congress not to bypass the established review procedures. Doing so in this instance, insisted Reagan, would bestow sovereign-nation status on a group whose background the government knew little about and invite other applicants to similarly expect to skirt the tribal recognition process set up by the Interior Department.

Reagan's veto thrust the Pequot case into the national spotlight. After the veto was announced, the *New York Times* put Hayward's picture on page one, alongside the headline "Indian Land Conflict Rekindled in Connecticut."

"When you think of all the money the government spends," Hayward told the *Times*, "I don't see why they can't settle with the tribe. Why not settle it already? The government's doing the same thing to Indians they did 200 years ago, only with politics instead of guns."

With the stroke of a pen, Hayward, his family, and their grand plans were left in the lurch. And nearly ten years of planning and preparation appeared scuttled. "It shows clearly the administration's lack of sensitivity for issues affecting minorities in this country," Gejdenson complained at a press conference in Hartford. "What happened here is political. The administration went after this because of a very narrow band of far right people."

While Hayward and Gejdenson were blasting the Reagan administration in the newspapers, Tureen went to work. He knew Congress had approved the bill unanimously, which signaled to him that it would not be too difficult to get the two-thirds vote required to override Reagan's veto. "What you do is get a senator on your side to support you," Tureen thought confidently. "Then you get him to get his buddies. They logroll and they trade."

And Tureen knew from the feedback he was getting out of Washington that Weicker was eager to get the settlement passed despite Reagan's opposition. The Senate committee's top lawyer, Pete Taylor, said Weicker went ballistic when he learned of Reagan's veto.

As the sponsor of the Pequot bill, Weicker was so angry at Reagan that he offered to let Tureen, Hayward, and a team of lobbyists use his Senate office as a makeshift headquarters to drum up support for overriding Reagan's veto.

"I don't think Weicker likes Reagan very much," Tureen thought, pleased by Weicker's support. "This is an opportunity to kick him in the shins, flex his muscles."

Only weeks after the veto was announced, Tureen picked up Hayward in Connecticut and flew him down to Washington in his private plane. Tribal adviser and anthropologist James Wherry also came along to help lead the lobbying effort.

When they arrived in Washington, they went directly to Senator Weicker's office. He gave them, along with a number of other lobbyists working for the Pequots, access to a large, open-air foyer area with couches and end tables. The room contained a row of five-foot-by-five-foot cubicles that were separated by five-foot-high dividers. Inside each cubicle were a telephone and a chair. When standing, Wherry could look over the tops of the dividers directly into Weicker's glass-enclosed office at one end of the room. At the other end of the room was a table that the group of lobbyists would meet around to strategize. They huddled closely at times, not wanting Weicker's staff to overhear certain conversations. At times they would whisper or go out of the room entirely.

Using phones supplied by Weicker, Wherry and a half dozen volunteers working under him contacted the office of every senator within a two-week period. At times, Weicker himself met with the group to get updates on the progress and lend his support. When there were certain senators who seemed more reluctant to go along with the override, Weicker would get personally involved. "I'm going to go talk to that son of a bitch," he would say to Wherry's group. Weicker knew his colleagues far better than the lobbyists did. With a tenure of over twenty years in the Senate, he was a powerful ally.

In less than two weeks, Tureen and Hayward's lobbying group nearly had the needed votes. One unexpected holdout, however, was Republican William Cohen from Maine. Weicker, upon hearing this, screamed out of his office, "Give that son of a bitch a lighthouse."

Wherry, who lived in Maine, understood immediately. At the time, the U.S. Coast Guard was automating lighthouses up and down the East Coast. Some of the lighthouses were being shut down altogether. Maine, in particular, was home to an abundance of lighthouses, many of which were historic and were featured on national postcards. There was great concern in Maine that the state was going to suddenly become financially responsible for maintaining a bunch of lighthouses that were no longer of use to the federal government. Any federal funding to maintain lighthouses in Maine had to be appropriated by the Senate's Appropriations Committee, of which Weicker was a member.

• • •

Responsible for guiding Weicker's vetoed bill back to the Senate floor for another vote, Senate committee staff director Timothy Woodcock did a preliminary head count and felt convinced enough votes existed to override Reagan's veto. He then telephoned James Watt, the Secretary of Interior in Reagan's cabinet, and informed him of the situation.

The news put Reagan in a potentially embarrassing and unprecedented predicament. He had never been overridden on a veto. Worse still, the Republicans in the Senate were leading the override push. In their view, the Pequot legislation was relatively insignificant in the federal scheme of things. Further, Connecticut was the only state impacted by the bill. And Connecticut senators Lowell Weicker and Chris Dodd strongly supported the legislation.

To avoid the public spectacle of an override from within Reagan's own party, Senate majority leader Howard Baker intervened. Woodcock and Pete Taylor were summoned to a meeting with Baker's staff, where they were introduced to Jamie Baker, who was the son of James Baker, Ronald Reagan's chief of staff. Jamie Baker would be the liaison between the White House and the Senate's Select Committee on Indian Affairs, where Weicker's bill originated.

"The Reagan administration is certainly interested in finding a way out of the cul-de-sac it is in," concluded Woodcock as he started working with Baker to produce a solution.

In a flurry of negotiations, the Reagan administration offered to drop its insistence that the Pequots produce documentation establishing their legitimacy as a tribe. In exchange, the administration asked the state of Connecticut to make a financial contribution of $200,000 to the $900,000 trust fund being set up by the federal government to finance the tribe's property acquisitions. Under the agreement the Pequots were assured that their genealogy would not come under review.

On July 19, with Reagan's support secured, Weicker, along with Gejdenson and Hayward, went back to the Senate's Select Committee on Indian Affairs to urge them to send the bill up for a vote a second time. "I am going to be brief," Weicker told the committee members. "I am delighted to be here with my good friend and colleague, Sam Gejdenson, and Richard Hayward, the tribal chairman, in order to hopefully start the process that will wrap up this difficulty of times past.

"At the urging of the majority leader," Weicker continued, "who wished to avoid an override situation, extensive discussions took place between Congress and the administration over this legislation. As a result of those discussions, the state of Connecticut has agreed to increase its contribution to the settlement by pledging $200,000 worth of road construction on the reservation."

"Well, Senator," said committee chairman Mark Andrews from North Carolina, "let me point out to those here what you already know, that the great work you did in forging a compromise has saved us from dropping the ball on this altogether. And I think once again it shows the fantastic capability that you have in making sure that when something like this comes up and gets vetoed, you can turn it around and come up with a product that represents a worthwhile compromise."

"Thank you, Mr. Chairman," Weicker responded.

Following Weicker, Reagan administration official John Fritz, the assistant secretary for Indian Affairs, assured the committee that the president would not object to the bill's passage. But he took the opportunity to warn other groups inclined to follow the Pequots' lead. "We wish to make it clear to any other tribes and states who desire legislative settlements of Indian land claims that we will not agree to such settlements unless we are included in the negotiations before the legislation is introduced," Fritz testified. "The department does not believe it can support any future legislation which would legislatively recognize a group of Indian descendants as a tribe unless it has had an adequate opportunity to review the historical and current factual bases for the group's claim to tribal status. . . ."

On October 4, 1983, Connecticut representative Sam Gejdenson stood in the House chambers and urged his colleagues to support Senator Weicker's bill. "There are no more controversial points regarding this settlement," Gejdenson assured them. "The bill provides eight hundred acres of land in Ledyard, Connecticut; establishes a $900,000 trust fund to purchase the lands . . . [and] grants the tribe federal recognition."

With unanimous consent Congress sent the bill back to President Reagan, who signed it into law on October 18, ending the Pequots' seven-year legal battle with the Ledyard landowners. Unbeknownst to Congress, the Settlement Act violated the federal law Congress had created to govern the recognition of Indian tribes. Under Section 83 of the United States

Code titled "Procedures for Establishing That an American Indian Group Exists as an Indian Tribe," Congress identified six "mandatory criteria" for petitioners. First among them is that "the petitioner has been identified as an American Indian entity on a substantially continuous basis since 1900." Had it checked, Congress would have discovered that Richard Hayward, the man representing himself as the chief of the Pequots, had never represented himself as an American Indian until it became expedient for filing a lawsuit.

Prior to meeting Tureen, Hayward consistently identified himself as "white" or "Caucasian" both on vital government documents and under oath. Only after recognizing the legal advantage to organizing a tribe did he start identifying his race as "American Indian" on vital documents.

The same scenario holds true for all seven of Hayward's siblings, as well as Hayward's mother, Theresa, and her sister Loretta. Theresa and Loretta, daughters of Elizabeth George, were the two adults primarily responsible for helping Hayward persuade other distant relatives to join them in forming a tribal organization. On their marriage licenses and on each of their children's birth certificates they always identified themselves and their children as "white." They too abandoned this practice, electing to call themselves American Indians after the lawsuit was filed.

It is conceivable that individuals identifying themselves as "white" could belong to an Indian tribe. Under Hayward, however, the Pequots had distinguished themselves as the only American Indian tribe without a single member whose professed racial origin is Native American.

The federal law's second mandatory requirement for establishing tribal status calls for proof that "a predominant portion of the petitioning group comprises a distinct community." And the community had to have an uninterrupted chain of existence going back through history. Yet address records confirm that in the decade 1965–1975, the Haywards and their relatives could not have lived together as a community; they did not even live in the same states. Mr. and Mrs. Hayward and their school-age children lived primarily in two states during the ten-year period: Rhode Island and Maryland. During that same time period, Skip Hayward lived in more than a dozen residences in five states: Massachusetts, Rhode Island, Maryland, Missouri, and Connecticut. Meanwhile, most of the Haywards' other relatives who joined his tribe lived in towns scattered throughout Connecticut, although some lived as far away as Florida.

None of these newly recognized Pequots lived on the reservation in 1973.

Elizabeth George did, however. And it was on her that Hayward and his family staked their claim to be Mashantucket Pequot Indians. Yet George's genealogy offers no proof that she descended from Mashantucket Pequot Indians. She was born on the reservation on March 19, 1895. Ledyard birth records indicate she had seven siblings: Mabel, born April 24, 1880; Amos, born December 25, 1882; an unnamed male, born November 25, 1884; Eunice, born November 12, 1888; Flora, born July 7, 1893; John, born February 20, 1896; and an unnamed child who was born April 5, 1898, and died minutes later.

Elizabeth George's parents were Cyrus George and Martha Hoxie, an interracial couple that married on November 2, 1879. Cyrus was one of the few blacks living in Ledyard in the late 1800s. His children's birth records show that his employment ranged from working as a farmhand, to cutting stone, to doing general labor. His wife, Martha, is the ancestor through whom the Haywards trace their Indian ancestry. When the Haywards organized their tribal organization, they relied on the U.S. Census conducted in 1910 and decided that anyone who could trace their genealogy to a person appearing on the Pequot reservation that year qualified for admission. Of the six adults listed on the Pequot reservation in 1910, Martha is the only one whom the Haywards descend from. The census identifies her as Martha Langevin, a forty-seven-year-old woman, who had given birth to fifteen children, eleven of who were still living at the time.

After her first husband, Cyrus, died on October 1, 1898, Martha married Napolean Langevin, a white man from Canada. Birth records identify Langevin's nationality as "French Canadian." Langevin, who became Elizabeth George's stepfather, lived with Martha and raised their children on the reservation. The abbreviation "In" (for Indian) appears beside his name on the 1910 census under the column labeled "color or race." The census, however, lists his "nativity" as "Canadian," as it does both his parents. This apparent discrepancy is explained by the "Instructions" to census takers.

In 1910, the federal government directed census takers to visit Indian reservations and to identify as Indian "detached whites or negroes living in Indian families." In other words, for the purpose of the census, whites and blacks who had moved onto Indian reservations and were living in Indian families were counted as Indians. Other than the 1910 census, Napolean Langevin is consistently identified as a white man of French Canadian descent. No genealogy exists linking him to the Pequot Indians. Nor was he Elizabeth George's blood father, which leaves only her mother, Martha Hoxie, as the Haywards' possible tie to the Pequot tribe.

Martha Hoxie was born in Ledyard in 1867. On some of her children's birth records, Martha's race is described as "black," on others "red," and on still others "white." The original documents have since been altered to read "Indian," yet neither a town clerk's initials nor any form of authoritative stamp of approval accompanies the change. Despite someone's attempt to revise Hoxie's identity, historical records offer no proof that her parents were Mashantucket Pequot Indians. The same records do, however, explain why Martha Hoxie's race is described as black, white, and red. On her birth record, Martha's father, John Hoxie, is identified as "black" under the column "color." (Although this too has been scratched out recently and replaced with the word "Indian.") Martha's birth record lists her mother as Jane Grant, an eighteen-year-old white woman from Ledyard.

The circumstances behind Martha's birth are a mystery. No marriage record exists for Jane Grant and John Hoxie. Nor did they have any other children together. And Jane used her maiden name on Martha's birth record at a time when it was customary for married women to take their husband's last name. These facts raise the question whether Jane Grant and John Hoxie were married at the time of Martha's birth. A marriage record from Ledyard dated May 7, 1859, casts further doubt on that prospect. It records that Mary Jane Grant, a seventeen-year-old white woman from Ledyard, married Dwight Burrows, a twenty-two-year-old white man from the neighboring town of Preston. No birth record exists in Ledyard for either Jane Grant or Mary Jane Grant. But it appears that Mary Jane Grant and Jane Grant are one in the same person.

Nonetheless, after giving birth to Martha Hoxie, Jane started going by the name of Jane Hoxie. Although there is no evidence that Jane and her daughter remained with John Hoxie, she nonetheless continued to use the last name Hoxie up until 1897 when, at the age of fifty-three, she married Fredrick B. Durfee, a forty-two-year-old white man from Danielsonville, Connecticut.

Contemporaries who knew Jane Grant described her as a woman

with "beautiful blue eyes." She died in 1933 at the age of eighty-nine. Her daughter Martha died six years before that in 1927. No genealogy records in Connecticut or Rhode Island establish that Jane Grant descended from Pequot Indians. If Martha possessed any Indian lineage, it came through her father, John Hoxie, who apparently abandoned her and her mother.

Apparently, only one document directly links John Hoxie to Indian ancestry. In 1900, at age seventy, John Hoxie identified himself as a member of the Narragansett tribe on a state Indian enumeration record. At the time, Hoxie was residing on the Eastern Pequot reservation in North Stonington, Connecticut. Hoxie's race on the census is reported as "black," which is consistent with how it was classified on other records.

While inadequate record keeping makes it virtually indeterminable just how much Indian blood John Hoxie possessed, historical records leave no doubt that the tribe he claimed association with was the Narragansetts of Rhode Island, not the Western Pequots of Connecticut. Similarly, John Hoxie's sister, Rachel Hoxie, is identified as "black" on vital records. The closest her name comes to association with Pequot Indians was her on-again, off-again residency on the Eastern Pequot reservation in North Stonington.

Also, John and Rachel's father, who was born in Charleston, Rhode Island, on Narragansett Indian territory, is identified as "black." But he too claimed membership in the Narragansett tribe. Historical records consistently connect the Hoxie family to the Narragansett tribe going as far back as 1770, prior to the American Revolution. Although the Hoxies appear to have descended predominantly from African American ancestry, it nonetheless remains apparent that they at one time were associated with the Narragansett Indians in Rhode Island.

All of this points to Elizabeth George having a faint connection to Indian ancestry. Yet the connection is not to the Western Pequot tribe but rather the Narragansett Indians—the very tribe responsible for aiding the English in destroying the Pequots.

So how did Elizabeth George end up living on the Western Pequot reservation if she was not a Pequot Indian?

At the time her parents, Cyrus George and Martha Hoxie, married in 1879, it was not uncommon for individuals other than tribal members to move onto Connecticut Indian reservations. Largely neglected by state overseers, the reservations attracted squatters and paupers alike, a practice that led the few remaining Native Americans to file complaints with the state.

Elizabeth apparently moved off the reservation sometime in her early adult years. She married Charles Clady, identified as a "Negro," and together they had five children: Charles Jr., Vera, Elizabeth, Donald, and Eva. After divorcing Clady, Elizabeth gave birth to a girl named Theresa on August 10, 1928. George was not married at the time of Theresa's birth. (Theresa is Skip Hayward's mother.) Two years after Theresa's birth, on August 28, 1930, Elizabeth married Theresa's father, Arthur Plouffe. He was a white man of French Canadian descent who worked as a truck driver. Elizabeth was thirty-five years old. She and Arthur had one more child together, Loretta Plouffe. Loretta and her sister, Theresa, were Skip's strongest supporters early on, and both of them signed the tribe's constitution and received leadership positions in the tribe.

In June of 1941, when Elizabeth George applied for her Social Security number, she identified herself as "white," "married," "unemployed," and "44" years of age. She and her husband lived on the reservation for the same reasons her father Cyrus did: affordability. As the years wore on, she either outlived or outlasted all of her family members, emerging as the vigilant caretaker and sole inhabitant of the reservation by 1973.

While Elizabeth lived alone all those years, her grown daughter, Theresa Plouffe, married Richard Hayward and moved with him around the country during his navy career. Loretta too moved off the reservation, marrying James Libby, a white man from Maine who worked as a welder.

In an attempt to compensate for these deficiencies in the genealogy and to legitimize their tribal claim, Hayward and his family formed a corporation called the Western Pequot Indians of Connecticut, Inc. The corporation's by-laws list the organization's objectives, establishes corporate membership rules, and spells out the voting rights of the shareholders. Even mandatory "meetings of the Association" are contained in the corporate by-laws. The properly drafted documents left no question that the Haywards satisfied the definition of a corporation—an artificial legal entity, created under state law for the purpose of granting a personality and existence distinct from that of its several members.

In the Pequots' corporation, the artificial legal identity was that of a Native American Indian tribe, while the several members were white Americans hoping to capitalize on the injustices inflicted on an extinct tribe. The corporation did not, however, transform them into the ancient Pequot tribe. As is in the case of families, there are generally only two ways to join a tribe: by birth or through marriage. Corporations, on the other hand, can be joined as long as the members approve, similar to joining a club. When Congress recognized the Pequots, it made joining an Indian tribe as easy as forming a corporation.

18

COMMENCEMENT

"PEQUOT INDIANS PREVAIL IN BATTLE BEGUN IN 1637," DECLARED THE *New York Times* two days after President Reagan signed the bill. Accompanying the article was a photograph of Hayward's sister Theresa standing in the old Pequot burial ground where her grandmother, Elizabeth George, was laid to rest. "There are grand opportunities coming up," Skip Hayward told the *Times*. "I see it happening."

Too, the Connecticut congressional delegation was pleased with the outcome.

"This legislation represents a precedent for other Indian land cases in Connecticut," said Senator Weicker, aware that other tribes in his state were contemplating land-recovery suits, "where a spirit of equitable compromise permits a settlement in a reasonable period of time at a reasonable cost to both the state and the federal government, while the interests of both property owners and Indians are adequately protected."

Senator Chris Dodd emphasized that both sides in the dispute got what they wanted. "All property owners reserve the right not to sell their property if they so choose," he said. "All have agreed to the settlement and none will be displaced from their homesteads."

And Representative Gejdenson assured his Ledyard constituents that the terms of the settlement ended the Pequots' lawsuit with the "least amount of social disruption."

The Connecticut congressmen did not refer to the sovereign-nation status that they had bestowed upon Hayward and his family. While they saw the whole case in terms of money and property, they did not realize how much property the tribe was actually going to obtain.

Their assessment amused Tureen. "They didn't understand this case at all," thought Tureen, who viewed the settlement as the beginning rather than the end of the Pequots' expansion in Ledyard. "It is a matter of what we can do with the status that we got, the money that we got, and the land that we got."

Even Tureen, however, did not understand that his clients had no apparent genealogical connection to the original Pequot tribe. Having never checked the genealogy records personally, he too assumed that Hayward's grandmother, Elizabeth George, was a Pequot.

12:00 NOON
OCTOBER 21, 1983
MASHANTUCKET PEQUOT INDIAN RESERVATION

Dining tables stood underneath a large canopy tent erected near the old Elizabeth George homestead. Foods described as traditional Pequot dishes were prepared by Hayward's sisters and covered the tabletops. A large fire was burning, as a medicine man stood by ready to perform a dance for a group made up of tribal members and specially invited guests who had gathered to hear Hayward offer a prayer to officially open the celebration. Days earlier, the guests had received a typewritten invitation that read, "The Mashantucket Pequot Tribe is celebrating the settlement of its Land Claims, Federal Recognition, [and] enactment of Senate Bill 1499." It was signed by Hayward and included a hand-drawn map with directions to "Elizabeth George Drive."

James Wherry was among the guests and listened respectfully as Hayward offered his Christian prayer. Hayward was now officially the chief of a federally recognized Indian tribe, and the festivities triumphantly marked a hard-fought achievement that had begun a decade earlier when Hayward met Tureen and vowed to breathe life back into a tribe long since extinct. Against remarkable odds, he had done it, securing privileges for his relatives that seemed unthinkable back in 1976.

But along with all the privileges came new legal obligations. Unlike before, Hayward and his family were now accountable to the Congress and the Department of Interior. The $900,000 that Congress appropriated for them to spend was held in a trust account that was overseen and managed by the secretary of interior. In the Settlement Act, Congress authorized the secretary to make $600,000 of the fund available immediately for the tribe to use, but specified that the money was only to be used for purchasing the land within the newly created reservation boundary. Congress gave the tribe until January 1, 1985, to complete the purchases.

After January 1, 1985, the secretary of interior was required to determine how much surplus remained in the Pequots' account and make it available to the tribe for "economic development" purposes. But before the secretary was authorized to release the surplus, the tribe had to document how it intended to spend the money. "The Tribe shall submit an economic development plan to the Secretary," read the law, "and the Secretary shall approve such plan . . . if he finds that it is reasonably related to the economic development of the Tribe."

Hayward had no experience drafting economic plans and wanted Wherry to take responsibility for the task. Wherry had already worked for two years on a part-time basis helping the tribe acquire money through loans and federal grants, and having helped Tureen draft that portion of the bill, he was very familiar with the clause in question.

Hayward offered Wherry an annual salary of $25,000 to come on board full-time as the tribe's economic development adviser. Eager to acquire real estate, Wherry accepted it and agreed to start on January 1, 1984.

When he assumed his duties, he learned that Hayward had already begun spending settlement funds, putting at risk Wherry's ability to design an economic plan that would be agreeable to the Department of Interior.

Right after the Settlement Act passed, Hayward had gone to see Lenny LaCroix about acquiring Mr. Pizza. Although King had purposely excluded LaCroix's property from the new reservation when he drew the settlement map, Hayward decided to make Mr. Pizza his first purchase. LaCroix had been talking about selling Mr. Pizza and getting out of the restaurant business, and had even discussed selling it to another Greek restaurant owner in the area. But Hayward was determined not to let go of the site that had so long served as his headquarters.

Once Congress appropriated funds in a trust account for the tribe, Hayward and LaCroix decided to make a deal. Standing outside behind the restaurant, Hayward initiated the bidding.

"How much do you want for the place?" Hayward asked.

"Five hundred and fifteen thousand," LaCroix responded.

"Is that enough?" asked Skip.

Caught off guard by the question, LaCroix paused. "Yeah," he answered.

To LaCroix's surprise, the price was agreed to within seconds.

As far back as his first marriage, Hayward's impulsive spending habits had landed him in financial difficulty and made him the target of dissatisfied creditors. But back then, he was earning slightly over $200 per week and spending it on consumer items like guitars, shotguns, and paintings. Now he had access to nearly $1 million in federal trust funds and he was buying land and a business.

Wherry knew all about Hayward's spending habits. Since Hayward had taken over the tribe, its budget had multiplied 150 times. Despite receiving government grants and private donations in amounts that exceeded anything experienced by other Indian tribes in the country, Hayward was still borrowing money. By the summer of 1983, he owed approximately $100,000 to the Connecticut National Bank. Hayward had established a friendly relationship with a loan officer there who agreed to advance him money on credit. One of the first items of business in Wherry's economic development plan was to pay off the debt in order to improve the tribe's creditworthiness.

He was beside himself when he learned of the agreement Hayward had struck with LaCroix, which threatened to plunge the tribe even deeper into debt. Wherry wanted to stop the deal, but it was too late. Hayward had already signed a purchase and sale agreement. The closing date was scheduled for February 14 at Jackson King's law office.

Angry at Hayward for agreeing to pay over a half million dollars without bothering to first have the business or the property appraised, Wherry went to see Hayward.

"Skip, the selling price is *grossly* inflated," Wherry complained.

Silent, Hayward's face hardly expressed concern.

"Restaurants are a bad idea to begin with, Skip," Wherry continued. "Rule of thumb number one is 'Don't invest in restaurants.' Rule of thumb number two is 'Don't invest in Greek restaurants unless you're Greek.'"

Hayward pointed out that he knew all about restaurants, having run the Sea Mist Haven in Mystic.

"But who are you going to have run this place?" Wherry asked.

"My sister is going to manage the place," Hayward said, referring to Theresa.

"What are her qualifications?" Wherry asked.

"She worked for me in Mystic and she worked at the cafeteria at Electric Boat," Hayward said.

"This is sounding worse by the minute," Wherry thought to himself. But when he indicated he wanted to renegotiate the price with LaCroix, he was put on notice that the price was firm. LaCroix was a friend, and both Tureen and King had already been notified of the sale price.

Frustrated, Wherry called and complained to Tureen, who admitted that he too saw some financial risk in the tribe taking over the restaurant. "They've failed miserably at every business venture they have tried up to this point," Tureen said.

But Tureen, realizing Hayward's mind was made up, pointed to the bright side. Hayward's previous failures were all start-up businesses. Mr. Pizza was an up-and-running business with cash flow of over $100,000 a year. All Hayward had to do was maintain it.

Wherry's job was to help find a way to pay for all of this. Under the terms of the Settlement Act, the tribe was given $900,000, of which Congress earmarked $600,000 for purchasing land inside the settlement area. LaCroix's property, however, was outside the settlement boundary. To use settlement funds toward the purchase price, Wherry would be limited to the remaining $300,000 in the trust account, which Congress had set aside for economic development purposes. Faced with the prospect of exhausting the entire $300,000 in reserves for economic development on a pizza shop—and still coming up short of the $515,000 purchase price—Wherry came up with an alternative solution.

First, he applied to the Bureau of Indian Affairs for an economic development grant. The BIA had a program to aid needy Indian tribes that were attempting to generate income to support tribal members. For tribes that qualified under the program, the government would pay up to 25 percent of the total purchase price in a business acquisition. In the Pequots' case, that amounted to over $125,000 (25 percent of $515,000).

Before awarding the grant, the BIA required a property appraisal verifying that Mr. Pizza was worth over a half million dollars.

Given the inflated price, Wherry had to consult with several appraisers until he found one who appraised it at the value he needed.

Wherry then got Hayward to enter into a private loan agreement with LaCroix, which required the tribe to pay less than $190,000 at the closing ($125,000 from the BIA and roughly $65,000 from the Settlement Act trust fund). LaCroix agreed to a private mortgage arrangement to finance the rest, allowing the tribe to pay the remaining balance, just over $325,000, through monthly payments at an interest rate of 12 percent. If the tribe defaulted, LaCroix reserved the right to repossess the property.

On February 13 LaCroix and Hayward went to Jackson King's law office for the closing. King, who represented LaCroix, drew up a mortgage deed that identified LaCroix as the "Lender" and the tribe as the "Borrower." Hayward brought along his cousin, Loretta Libby, who had been named president of the tribe's new corporation, M.P.T. Enterprises, Inc., an acronym for Mashantucket Pequot Tribe Enterprises.. Libby signed the documents on behalf of the tribal corporation. Since the loan was a private one, no banks or mortgage companies were present. King then recorded the deed at the Ledyard town hall and paid LaCroix's conveyance taxes.

Once the purchase of Mr. Pizza was complete, Wherry called a meeting with Hayward. Mr. Pizza had been bought on impulse. And there was too much at stake, both financially and legally, for Hayward to go off and make any more rash purchases of that nature. In this instance, Wherry had managed to bail Hayward out and preserve the settlement fund. But he wanted to ensure that Hayward understood the ramifications of rash spending.

"The settlement fund is a limited source," Wherry told Hayward. "Once it is gone, it is gone."

Wherry wanted to establish some ground rules and insisted that Hayward come up with a well-reasoned plan for how to spend the money set aside for the tribe by Congress. He asked him to put together a list of which parcels within the settlement boundary were top priority to the tribe.

Wherry gave Hayward a suggestion—forget about buying the defendants' land and focus on acquiring the prime parcels along Route 2 that were suited for development. Wherry had inspected the parcels owned by Holdridge and Comrie and determined their terrain and locations were ill suited for the kind of development plans Hayward was contemplating. Nor did Wherry want to spend fair-market value for Comrie's land when he discovered that Comrie, resigned to the fact that the tribe was going to get his land, had cleared all the valuable timber off his lot in the months prior to settlement. So Wherry advised Hayward to focus first on the George Main estate property.

"Screw that," Tureen angrily told Wherry and Hayward when he was informed of the suggestion. "We've negotiated with the defendants. We've *got* to buy from them first."

"I have looked at Comrie's land," Wherry argued to Tureen. "Comrie logged it. It ain't got shit on it. Besides, it is landlocked. You can't use it for development or anything else. It is forestland without forest. So let's let him keep it. Let's buy this land over near Route 2 [the Main estate]. It is far better. It is flat."

"You can't do that," said Tureen. "You can't just ignore Comrie. Besides, there's enough money that we don't have to think in terms of switching from buying the defendants' land to buying Main's land. We can do both."

Tureen fully realized the value of the Main estate property along Route 2 and wanted to acquire it as badly as Wherry did. There was no more suitable site within the reservation boundary to build a gambling facility. But Tureen first wanted to buy the defendants' land, particularly the land belonging to Holdridge and Comrie.

After talking with Tureen, Wherry visited Ledyard town hall to conduct research on the tax records and property records in preparation for determining appropriate prices for the defendants' land. While there, he also researched the records pertaining to George Main's 550-acre estate. When he came across the tax records on the estate, he spotted something that caused him to panic. In haste, he gathered up his papers and rushed back to his office to call Tureen in Maine.

19

WILLS, ESTATES, AND TRUSTS

FROM THE MOMENT HE PICKED UP THE PHONE, TUREEN COULD SENSE THE panic in Wherry's voice. "Main's property is in probate *right now,*" Wherry said. "Get on it!"

"How do you know that?" Tureen asked calmly.

"From looking at the tax records," Wherry said. "I could see that this is in probate. It could be actively being distributed as part of a will settlement."

Both men understood what this meant. Before focusing on the defendants' land, they would have to immediately determine how Main's property ended up in probate court and whether the tribe had any hope of acquiring it.

In 1982 Marcia White went to work as a real estate broker for Century 21 in their Ledyard-area office. New to the real estate business and eager to establish a list of clients, White went to the town hall and looked up the land records for properties along Route 2. A homeowner in a residential area along the state highway, she was aware that significant stretches of real estate along the highway were undeveloped woodlands. After determining who the owners were, she contacted them to see if they were interested in selling their property. George Main expressed interest.

Main had inherited all his landholdings in Ledyard from his father, Lafayette Main, a notorious land baron who was born in 1863 in a house located a few hundred yards from the Pequot Indian reservation. When George was eight years old, his mother died of cancer at age forty-one. Lafayette tried to raise George on his own, but he was nearly thirty years older than his wife and was in no condition to care for young George. So George was placed in a state orphanage, where he remained until age eighteen. By that time, his father had passed away too.

Raised in a state institution during the height of World War II, George had little when he was growing up. But in 1954, at age twenty-four, he discovered that his father had left behind a will that named him the beneficiary of roughly six hundred acres of land in Ledyard. Main needed money, so he went to see a lawyer about the possibility of selling the land. He chose Allyn Brown, who eventually founded King's law firm. Brown looked at the deed dated November 4, 1946, and discovered a problem. The deed transferred to Main "a life interest and use in and to the [land] for and during his life time and at his death to his children, if not children living then to his sisters in equal shares."

Brown explained to Main that he only had a lifetime use of the land. When he died, the land automatically transferred to his heirs. And if he did not have children, it was to go to his five sisters. Brown told him he could recommend another attorney who might help find a creative way to sell the land, but advised him not to. "George, that's going to be worth a lot of money someday," Brown told him in 1954. "Don't get rid of it." Main took Brown's advice. However, by the time White called offering to list the property, Main had done nothing but pay property taxes on the estate for thirty years. And there was no indication that its value was rising.

In the fall of 1982, White traveled to Putnam and met with Main and his attorney, Nick Longo. She brought with her a contract for Main to sign that established her as the exclusive listing agent for the property. The terms of the agreement provided Century 21 with a 10 percent commission regardless of whether White sold the property or Main found a buyer on his own.

During the meeting in Longo's law office he advised Main to sign the agreement. However, Longo took the opportunity to explain to White that this would not be the first time that Main had attempted to sell his land. But his past efforts had been hindered by a provision in his property deed, which he had inherited upon his father's death.

Under the terms of the deed, Main could not sell the land without the consent of the heirs (his children and his sisters) as well as the approval of the probate court. Any proceeds from the sale had to be placed in a trust fund until Main's death, at which time his heirs could withdraw the principal. Main was entitled only to the interest earned on the trust account during his lifetime.

White had no experience with wills, estates, and trusts. And she had never handled a property that had to go through probate court before the sale could be finalized. But she needed clients and figured she had nothing to lose by listing the property.

On January 17, 1983, White found a buyer. Irving Norman, a brick mason in Ledyard, offered to buy the land for $250,000. He handed White a check for $2,000 to go with his offer sheet. Main accepted the offer, and ten days later, on January 27, he and Norman entered into a purchase and sale agreement. At the signing of the contract, Norman wrote out a second check in the amount of $8,000, making his total deposit $10,000. No closing date was listed in the agreement. Norman and Main mutually agreed that the date would be determined after the sale had been reviewed by the probate court. In the meantime, Main gave Norman permission to start using the property.

Norman, a gray-haired man with a neatly trimmed flattop, was approaching retirement age. For most of his adult life he had worked six-day workweeks doing brick- and stonework on houses in Ledyard. During his thirty-year career he developed a reputation for superior craftsmanship and impeccable integrity. As a result, building contractors sent him an abundance of work, allowing him to earn a good deal of money. Norman invested it by purchasing undeveloped land around Ledyard, building residential homes on the land, then selling them for profit. But he had no interest in building houses on the 550-acre stretch that he had agreed to buy from Main. During numerous walks he took through the property while waiting for the sale to proceed through the probate court, Norman discovered that a large swamp—the "Cedar Swamp"—sat right in the middle of the estate. It was surrounded on all sides by rich forestland that was inhabited by a range of wildlife. While the land sale proceeded through probate court, he spent months building up by hand a walking path that stretched across a three-hundred-acre stretch of the swamp. Ultimately, he decided he would preserve the land as a natural wildlife refuge once he obtained the property deed.

In November of 1983, George Main's children filed a petition with the probate court indicating their desire to see the estate sold. And Main's siblings had indicated they would not oppose the sale. On December 13, Main petitioned the Connecticut Superior Court at Putnam to issue an order authorizing him to sell to Norman under a Connecticut law that permitted property owned by two or more persons to be sold if the sale would "better promote the interests of the owners." Nick Longo had been identified as the trustee of the trust fund to be established with the sale proceeds. The only remaining formality was for the probate court to process the paperwork.

• • •

The Pequot Settlement Act was carefully negotiated to give Hayward and his tribe the ability to take real estate along Route 2 that was unrelated to the lawsuit and have it become part of the Indian reservation. Main's estate was the prized piece of land that Hayward was after along the Route 2 corridor. Yet it appeared out of reach. Irving Norman had signed a contract to buy it. Main had accepted Norman's deposit and chosen Nick Longo to act as trustee over the trust fund to be established by the sale proceeds. Main's heirs had petitioned the probate court to approve the sale. And the court had no reason to do otherwise.

Hayward did not appreciate all the legal obstacles standing in his way. He and the tribe had the president of the United States reverse himself on a veto, so why not convince George Main and Nick Longo to accept their offer?

The issue was more complicated than that, however. Assuming Main would take a higher offer from the tribe, the first question was whether his attorney would go along with the idea, since it would require Main to disregard two good-faith contracts—one with Century 21 and one with Norman. Second, if Longo were willing to go along, how would Norman respond once he discovered he had been outbid? Would he counteroffer? Or would he sue to enforce his contract? And finally, how would Century 21 respond? It stood to lose $25,000 in commission if the land was sold privately to the tribe.

Tureen did not know Main, Longo, or Norman. And he was too far away to get the answers to all the questions on his own. So he telephoned King. "I know Norman some," said King. "He's a good old-time Yankee. Always had a very good reputation as a builder."

King also knew Longo and had talked to him casually about Main's property. "Nick said the poor guy [Main] has got this land and all he does is get a tax bill on it," King said.

"We're thinking about going and bidding a higher price for the property and seeing if we can get it," Tureen told King.

"Nick may feel funny about negotiating and talking to you when he's already got a good-faith contract with Irving Norman," said King. "Though technically it is a contract, that doesn't mean anything until it is approved by the probate court."

• • •

Spring 1984
Putnam, Connecticut

It was early in the evening when George Main, a short, stout auto mechanic in his fifties, turned on the porch light from inside his small, white, vinyl-sided duplex that he and his wife rented at 48 Mill Street. Then the telephone rang.

"Hello," said George.

"Hey, George, guess what?" said the voice on the other end.

Main recognized the voice right away. It was his attorney, Nick Longo.

"What?" asked George.

"I have some big news for you," Longo said.

"Oh, yeah," said Main. "What's that?"

"I understand the Indians are looking at your property."

"*What?*" Main shouted. "Which ones, the Eastern or the Western Pequots?"

"The ones on Indiantown Road," said Longo, unfamiliar with the fact that there were two splinter groups from the original Pequot tribe.

"That's the Haywards," said Main.

"Yes," said Longo. "That's the one. That was the name."

As George continued to talk to Longo, Claire sat nearby trying to figure out what her husband was talking about. When he hung up, George recounted what Longo had just told him. "Nick said, 'Don't sell to Irving Norman,'" George said. "Nick went to a meeting in Norwich and got a drift of the Indians having interest in our land. It was some lawyer meeting and they got talking about our land."

Longo never told Main who the lawyer from Norwich was who informed him that the Haywards wanted Main's land. But he concluded it had to be Jackson King. "Jackson King knows all about my land," thought Main. "He knows about the land because I had gone to Allyn Brown, the head lawyer in Jackson's law firm, years before for help with selling the property. Allyn always said my land would be worth a lot someday."

Main always hoped that Brown was right. But that was back in 1954 when Brown said that. Main hardly imagined it would be Indians who were in a position to pay lots of money for the property. As a child, George grew up amongst members of the Eastern Pequots, whose reservation bordered on his father's farm. They were destitute but friendly neighbors. The first bow and arrow George owned was custom-made for him by Old Bill Jackson, a member of the Eastern Pequot tribe who had befriended him.

George's father had a special fondness for Old Bill Jackson due to the kindness had he shown his son.

But Main's father hated the Western Pequots, whose reservation was farther away from the Main's family farm. The Mains and the Western Pequots had been locked in a bitter feud that stretched back to the mid-1800s when George's grandfather ran the family farm. After suffering repeated crop damage from roaming animals, George's grandfather killed a wild steer that had destroyed his crops and damaged some farm property. George's grandfather, unaware of who the steer belonged to, skinned it and hung the hide up in the yard to dry it out so he could make use out of it. A couple of days later, a man identifying himself as the chief of the Western Pequots showed up on Main's property with some braves. They said they had been feeding the steer and that it belonged to them. "You see how I cut that steer down the middle?" George's grandfather said. "You touch that steer, I'll put you up there and cut you the same way."

At the time, George's grandfather operated a country store out of his home, selling farm produce and supplies. The Eastern Pequots were welcome customers. But whenever Indians from the Western Pequots would come in, George's grandfather used to shoo his children into an earth cellar underneath the kitchen floor, where they remained until the Indians left. His run-ins with the Western Pequots were part of the family lore.

The feud continued when George's father, Lafayette, took over the farm. When George was ten years old, twenty of his father's sheep were mysteriously killed one night while the family slept. The next night, twenty more sheep were killed. On the third night, George's father purposely left some sheep unprotected in front of the barn and lay waiting with a shotgun in hopes of catching the culprit. Soon, a large, roaming dog showed up. It was from the Western Pequot reservation. "Some of the Indians had chows, German shepherds, and mixed breeds," George recalled. As soon as the dog went after the sheep, George's father sprang out of the barn and killed it. His father skinned the dog and made a rug out of it. George Main chuckled at the prospect of the Western Pequots suddenly taking possession of all of his family's land.

After Longo talked to Main, he called Tureen, who confirmed that the tribe wanted to buy the land and was prepared to make an offer substantially higher than Norman's. Longo then called two friends of his who were attorneys in Hartford, Tim McNamara and Bob Taylor. McNamara and Taylor represented George Main's daughters who stood to inherit the trust fund to be established from the sale proceeds. Unlike Longo, McNamara and Taylor were experienced negotiators and agreed to handle the negotiations with Tureen. A meeting was scheduled in Putnam for May 2, 1984, between George, his daughters, their respective attorneys, and Tureen.

As he rode with Longo to pick up Tureen at the airport and drive him to the meeting, Main did not understand all the technical legal aspects of what was about to take place. He knew only that the more the tribe paid, the more he and his daughters got. And he felt confident that McNamara, who was negotiating on behalf of Main's daughters, would get a lot more out of the tribe than Norman had offered to pay.

Longo and Main said nothing as McNamara and Taylor tried to get as much out of the tribe as they could. Tureen, meanwhile, knew he had to offer substantially more than Norman was offering, but not so much that he left Hayward with nothing to buy the land from the defendants. Ultimately, the sides agreed that the tribe would pay $375,000 for Main's land.

After the meeting, Tureen placed another phone call to King and informed him that Main had accepted the tribe's offer to buy his estate. "Would you be willing to search the title for us?" asked Tureen.

King agreed to.

"My guess," said King, "is that Irving would have gone up to two hundred sixty. Coming in at three hundred seventy-five knocks Norman right out of the picture. He's not going to bid against that. He's going to go home. It is not going to be a legal issue."

Norman, however, was never told that the tribe had offered to pay $375,000 for Main's property. When Norman called Main in the spring of 1984 to find out why the probate process had been stalled, he received no hint that anyone else was interested in the property. With vague assurances, he waited.

Meanwhile, Main's children petitioned the superior court for an order requiring a private sale to the tribe. Under Connecticut law, a superior court judge had to approve a request by a life tenant and his heirs for a court-ordered property sale. Taylor attached a memorandum to accompany the request. "The Main Estate is located in an area to which the Pequot Tribe claimed to have original title and was previously the subject of a lawsuit," wrote Taylor, who noted that the suit was settled by a congressional act. "Congress created a Land Acquisition Fund for the tribe. The proposed purchase of the Main Estate by the tribe would be paid for from the Land Acquisition Fund."

Taylor acknowledged in the memorandum that another offer had been made by Irving Norman, but pointed out that the heirs to the estate favored selling it to the tribe instead. "Because the Pequot Tribe has made a substantially higher offer," Taylor wrote, "these defendants asked the court to order that the sale be a private sale to the Mashantucket Western Pequot Tribe for the sum of Three Hundred Seventy-Five Thousand Dollars."

Taylor's memorandum ended up on the desk of superior court judge Sabino Tamborra at the district court in Putnam. Since the distribution of property through wills is generally done in probate court, Tamborra rarely had opportunity to issue rulings in will disputes. And he was not familiar with the history associated with Main's estate property. From reading the memorandum, he got the impression that Main's land was part of the original Pequot Indian reservation and had been included in the Settlement Act by Congress in an attempt to restore the tribe's land. He knew almost nothing about the tribe or its history.

Tamborra scheduled a hearing regarding the Main estate for June 7. He gave each side thirty minutes to present their case. First Tureen testified about the historical significance of the land to the tribe. Then both Main and his heirs confirmed that they wanted to sell to the tribe because they had offered substantially more money.

That afternoon he issued his ruling. "The court concludes that it is in the best interest of the parties to disapprove the offer made on January 17, 1983, by Irving Norman, Inc. and that the offer made by the Mashantucket Western Pequot Tribe to purchase the property for the sum of Three Hundred Seventy-Five Thousand Dollars should be accepted and approved."

• • •

The one property that Hayward could not wrestle away was the much coveted Spencer Hall farm—three hundred acres of open space adjacent to the Main estate along Route 2.

On March 7, 1895, Joseph Kellogg Hall moved to Ledyard and bought a 150-acre farm that straddled the Ledyard-Preston town line. Joseph's son Sydney was born in the farmhouse in 1899. While Sydney was growing up, Joseph expanded the farm to three hundred acres by purchasing various parcels adjacent to his land. He then turned it all over to his son during the height of the Great Depression. Since Sydney and his wife, Marion, were never able to have children, they were forced to hire outside help to work as farmhands. At the end of World War II, an eleven-year-old boy named Cliff Allyn, who lived just down the road in Preston, asked Hall for a job. Allyn soon became the son that Spencer never had, working long hours and eager to learn everything he could about farming. Even after he attended college and married, Allyn and his wife, Mary, continued to help Hall on his farm.

By 1977, Spencer was over eighty years old and no longer able to manage the farm. He had lived on it his whole life and wanted to ensure that it remain in good hands. He asked Allyn and his wife to take it over, an offer the Allyns humbly accepted, having always dreamed of owning their own farm.

On June 5, 1978, Hall sold them everything—the three hundred acres, the house, the barn, the livestock, and equipment—for $170,750. The terms and sale price were worked out without the use of any real estate agents or attorneys. At the closing, both sides agreed to use Hall's personal attorney. The Allyns paid their down payment with a personal check from their checkbook. "Is that going to be all right with you, Sydney?" Mr. Hall's attorney asked.

"If Mary wrote it out, it is good enough for us," Hall replied.

The Allyns took over the farm the next day. Yet by 1982, when Hayward was speculating on his chance of acquiring the Hall farm, he believed that Hall still owned the farm. Since Hall and his wife, then in their nineties, were still residing in the old farmhouse, Hayward's hunch was that they would soon die without any heirs and the farm would be sold. The tribe could then purchase it.

But when Allyn bought the farm in 1978, he agreed to let the Halls continue living in the farmhouse until their death. The Allyns, who already had a house within a few miles of the farm, agreed to continue using it as their residence while running the farm.

Spencer Hall died in 1984, just after Congress awarded the Haywards the money to start buying land. He went to his grave never realizing that the majority of his farm had been placed within the Pequot reservation. Nor were the Allyns aware of it, until they received a phone call in 1984 from a man identifying himself as a lawyer.

"I have a client who is interested in buying your land," the attorney said.

"What's he want it for?" asked Allyn.

"My client's interested in building a warehouse," he said. "They would have big trucks coming in and out. They need a place to build a truck terminal."

"Oh, really?" Allyn said.

"Yes. They are willing to pay about $250,000 for the property."

"Well, we're not interested," said Allyn, who then hung up abruptly, speculating that the client was the tribe. Allyn read the papers. He knew the tribe was buying up land. He had no idea, however, that his farm was now within the reservation.

20

OUT TO LUNCH

DAVID HOLDRIDGE WAS STARTING TO WONDER IF HE AND THE OTHER defendants were ever going to see the titles to their properties cleared. Nine months had gone by since Congress passed the Settlement Act. Yet he had heard nothing from Hayward, the tribe, or King about the properties. Finally, at the end of July, King called Holdridge and told him that Hayward had made an offer on the property. He was willing to pay $80,000 for the eighty acres Holdridge owned. Holdridge, not having appraised his land, thought $1,000 per acre was too low. "The land has road frontage," Holdridge complained. "My brother and I were planning to one day subdivide it into three building lots. This is more valuable than landlocked acreage. Ours meets the town zoning requirements for house lots. It is worth more than $80,000."

Adamant about receiving more before he would sell, Holdridge insisted on negotiating with Hayward directly. King agreed to set up a meeting at the tribal office on the reservation. Holdridge was both eager and apprehensive about standing face-to-face with Hayward, the man who had sued him and the others. Hayward was responsible for putting Holdridge and the others on an eight-year legal roller-coaster ride. Yet during the entire eight-year period, Holdridge had not once seen Hayward or met Tureen. Holdridge's only image of Hayward was from boyhood, when Hayward would spend his summers in town visiting his grandmother. Now Hayward was a tribal chief.

When Holdridge arrived at the reservation, he saw that King's car was already parked outside the tribe's construction trailer. Taking a deep breath, Holdridge approached the makeshift office and knocked on the door. Intrigued at what Hayward might look like, Holdridge tensed up as the door opened. Suddenly his eyes met King.

"Hi, David," King said, smiling and ushering him inside.

"Hi, Jackson."

"Come in and meet Skip."

Holdridge flashed an awkward smile as he made eye contact with Hayward, who stepped from behind his desk. Instinctively, Holdridge extended his hand, and Hayward took it while they politely exchanged superficial greetings.

Hayward sat down at his desk, and Holdridge sat down across from him. Holdridge noticed the top of the desk was covered with stacks of papers, and a large Rolodex was perched on a corner. A small bookcase abutted it. The top shelf held two telephones, one black and the other tan, while newspapers hung haphazardly out of the lower shelves.

Behind Hayward, a sliding-glass window offered a view to the woods behind the trailer. A faded ivory curtain with a limp drawstring framed the window, accenting the veneer-wood paneling on the walls. A carpenter's level stood in a corner of the room.

Holdridge's eyes settled onto an intriguing image on the desk's modesty panel. It was a laminated circular logo portraying a fox standing proudly under a tree, looking off into the woods. Newly adapted as the Mashantucket Pequot tribe's symbol, it represented two essential elements of the Pequots' turbulent history: Mashantucket means "much wooded land," and oral tradition held that they referred to themselves as "the Fox People."

Unsettled by the surroundings and meeting Hayward for the first time in years, Holdridge took a few minutes before he realized that Tureen was not there. "How are we going to negotiate a sale if Skip doesn't have a lawyer present?" Holdridge thought to himself.

After King made a few introductory remarks, Holdridge explained that he and his brother thought the land was worth at least $90,000. Hayward, who had lost interest in Holdridge's land, disagreed. Holdridge responded that he was willing to sell for $88,000, but no less.

"Well, Skip, this one you better take," interjected King.

"OK," Hayward responded, putting up no resistance to King's suggestion.

Relieved, Holdridge was pleasantly surprised that Hayward accepted the offer.

They would close the deal on August 29, the same day the tribe was scheduled to close on the George Main estate.

The next day, King called Comrie and notified him that the tribe was prepared to purchase his 268 acres for $220,000. Having already logged the land and eager to have the matter behind him, Comrie accepted the offer without argument. He too agreed to close the deal on August 29.

But the day after, Comrie had second thoughts. "Supposin' I decided to sell my land to someone else, or not sell it at all?" thought Comrie, who had never seen a copy of the Settlement Act. "What does the Settlement Act say about that?"

Comrie started to press against the glaring weakness in the Settlement Act. There was nothing in it that required any of the defendants to sell to the Haywards. Every one of the defendants could choose to hold on to their land.

Comrie wondered what would happen if none of the landowners decided to sell. But he knew that Holdridge was selling. And he, Comrie, had already given his word to sell, and he wanted to keep his word. Nor did he want any more legal wrangling. Like Holdridge, he just wanted this case to go away. It was time to get on with their lives.

• • •

August 28, 1984
Western Pequot Reservation

Small, puffy white clouds moved lazily across the azure blue sky overhead. Under the bright sunshine, eighty-five-degree temperatures blanketed the reservation. The humidity in the air was unusually low, ideal conditions for a hike in the woods. Bureau of Indian Affairs agent Billy Wakole, who had traveled up to Ledyard from Washington to inspect the reservation, was looking forward to a guided tour by Jim Wherry. Wakole, who is seven-eighths Indian, had spent eleven years in the air force before joining the BIA in 1977. A very tall man with a large chest and hair in a ponytail that stretched far down his back, Wakole was hired by the bureau and assigned to help tribes in land acquisition. By 1984, he had been named acting area director for the region of the country that took in Connecticut.

Under the terms of the Settlement Act, all the land *inside* the newly created reservation boundary automatically became eligible to be designated as "trust land" once the tribe purchased it. As such, the land was removed from state jurisdiction, exempt from state and local taxation, and exempt from state and local land-use regulations.

Wakole's authority arose from a 1934 law passed by Congress that authorized the secretary of Interior to act as trustee over Indian lands. Under the law, tribes that purchased land could transfer the property title to the secretary, who acts as an agent of the U.S. government. Congress established the trust relationship between the government and Indians to protect Indian land against further alienation. However, the trust relationship placed no fiduciary responsibility on the United States. The government kept the land titles, but tribes retained all ownership rights over the property. The ultimate purpose was to establish the government as the guardian over Indian lands while allowing individual tribes to retain complete authority to govern and use their lands as they chose.

With the Pequots scheduled to close on 1,200 acres the following day—including the Main estate, the Holdridge property, the Comrie property, and the land of a number of other defendants—Wakole had to inspect the properties and sign the deeds on behalf of the federal government.

Under the terms of the Pequot Settlement Act, all land purchased by the tribe within the newly created reservation boundary was automatically taken into trust by the United States. As trustee, the federal government serves as custodian over reservation property purchased and possessed by the tribe. The federal trust status extended to federal Indian land assures that the land will remain Indian country as long as the United States remains in existence. Once reservation land is taken into trust by the United States, it can neither be sold by tribal leaders nor seized by states. Nor can it be taxed or subjected to state and local laws, including building codes, zoning and wetland restrictions, and environmental regulations.

Before the government approved the Pequot land for trust acquisition, Wakole, who was acting as an agent of the government under the direction of the secretary of Interior, was required to review the property and make sure it conformed to the description of the land contained on the deeds. The Settlement Act did not authorize the Interior Department to take into trust Pequot land that was acquired outside the reservation boundary. The Pequots, like other Indian tribes, were free to purchase property outside its newly created reservation. But in such instances, that land was to remain subject to property taxes and local and state regulations.

Wearing dress shoes, slacks, a sports coat, and a shirt without a tie, Wakole followed Wherry onto a trail that was surrounded on both sides by parched brown leaves. The path led into the woods and eventually onto the first of three tracts of land owned by Holdridge. Rays of sunlight reflected off Wherry's shiny forehead, sparkling on the few gray hairs along his receding hairline. Wearing black, double-knit trousers, a tie, and a suit jacket, Wherry, who had conducted a personal study of the reservation's geography, pointed out the wide variety of trees and rocks along the way.

As Wakole surveyed the three lots that Holdridge had agreed to sell to the tribe, he bent over and picked up the rusted-out remains of an old metal can. He kept it in his hand as they moved on to the Comrie property, which abutted Holdridge's land. There he picked up more pieces of debris, scraps of aluminum, a frayed strand of rope, and pieces of plastic soft-drink containers. He made a necklace out of it by running the rope through the litter pieces, then wearing it around his neck.

Wherry, finding the necklace odd, led Wakole out of the defendants' land onto the additional properties that had been included in the new boundary. As they crossed Spencer Hall's three-hundred-plus-acre farm and proceeded toward Route 2, Wherry pointed out that the George

Main estate was something Skip really wanted but almost lost to Ledyard resident Irving Norman. "We got a steal on that land from the judge," said Wherry. "It was a steal. We had to argue that it was not in the best fiduciary interests of the trust to accept Norman's bid. Obviously, Main was very much in favor of the trust receiving more money."

Main's 550-acre estate was divided into a series of separate lots along Route 2. One of them, lot 110, consisted of eighty-two acres, all of which were *outside* the reservation boundary. Route 2 separated the eighty-two-acre tract from the rest of Main's estate and the reservation, making it ineligible for federal trust status. Since that land was not eligible to be taken into trust under the terms of the Settlement Act, Wakole was not required to sign the deed for it at the closings.

Walking along Route 2 on Main's property, Wherry and Wakole stopped in at Mr. Pizza for a break on their walk. It was the one property along Route 2 that was not within the reservation. "If you look at the settlement boundary," said Wherry, "there is a curious jog in it. It goes around that little property there. Why? It was owned by Lenny LaCroix. His attorney is Jackson. He told Jackson, 'I don't want my restaurant being in the settlement.' That was the only kind of ownership inquiry that had to be made prior to the settlement."

After leaving Mr. Pizza, Wherry led Wakole back onto the Main estate past the Cedar Swamp where Irving Norman had cleared a path. "Bill, right here we're going to build a bingo hall," said Wherry, pointing to a scenic portion of land adjacent to the swamp. Wakole observed a dense population of two-hundred-foot- high hemlock trees, the trunks of which were more than four feet in diameter. Skeptically, Wakole listened to Wherry's description of a large-scale, high-stakes bingo hall in the middle of a beautiful forest. "I told Skip," said Wherry, "'we got to figure out how to put in a big parking lot without cutting these trees down.'"

"Yeah, Jim," Wakole scoffed. "Let's go."

By the time the two men had completed the more than five-mile trek across all the land within the reservation boundary, their suits were wrinkled and sticky. Dust particles dotted Wherry's silver, wire-rim glasses. And perspiration dripped slowly down his face until it rested in the thick mustache that concealed his upper lip. Wakole's handmade necklace consisting of litter collected along the way was wrapped around his neck and dangled all the way to his chest.

While cleaning off his glasses, Wherry squinted and looked at Wakole. They were about to enter the tribal office, yet Wakole had not discarded the necklace. "Are you going to walk in the office like that?" he asked.

"Yeah," said Wakole, unembarrassed by his creation.

AUGUST 30

As was her routine when she arrived at her real estate office, Marcia White picked up the *New London Day* newspaper sitting on the coffee table. The top half of the front page carried stories about the space shuttle and Walter Mondale's campaign strategy to defeat Reagan. Uninterested in both stories and deciding she was too busy to read anyway, White dropped the paper back on the table. As she did, she noticed a small headline at the bottom of the page. "Tribe Regains Land in Ledyard as Claims Settlement Nears End." Curious, she bent over and picked up the paper again. Walking toward her desk, she began to read.

"The Mashantucket Pequot Indians took title Wednesday to about 650 acres here, signaling that the end is near in the tribe's eight-year struggle to regain reservation territory taken from it in the 1700s," read the opening sentence. Then White turned over to page two, where the article was continued. "The largest transaction Wednesday includes three tracts totaling more than 500 acres and extending back toward the Indiantown Road reservation from Route 2 belonging to George Henry Pratt Main. The land was purchased for $375,000."

"What?" White said out loud, attracting raised eyebrows from her colleagues. "What? This is a mistake."

Standing right next to her chair, White did not sit down. She reread the same sentence, then continued. "Richard Hayward, Mashantucket tribal chairman, declined comment on the tribe's plans for the property. 'We're developing a plan for it. It's not possible now to say what it will be,' he said. Much of the land, under federal jurisdiction, will not be subject to town regulations and will be off limits to town constables. However, noted Town Planner Linda Krause, the Mashantuckets have shown a great respect for the land, much of which abuts the Great Cedar Swamp. 'I think we can feel pleased that it will be preserved and properly reserved,' she said."

"I can't believe this," White said, her voice getting louder.

She immediately picked up her telephone and dialed Nick Longo's number.

"We had an exclusive listing agreement," she said angrily.

"That agreement was not valid," replied Longo, unfazed.

"What do you mean it is not valid?" said White, remembering they had signed it right in his law office.

"You neglected to get the signatures of remaindermen on the contract," Longo said.

White hesitated. Longo's big legal words had stumped her. She had never heard the word "remaindermen," a legal term referring to beneficiaries who stand to acquire property remaining in a deceased person's estate. Main's daughters' and sisters' interest in Main's estate remained after he died, according to the will. So, Longo explained, the daughters and sisters had to sign the contract for it to be valid.

All White knew was that she and Main had signed the contract right in front of Longo. They were sitting in his law office. And he never said anything about other people needing to sign the contract. Nor had the issue been raised since the contract was signed.

Flustered, White hung up the phone.

Then she picked the phone back up and called Irving Norman. When she told him that the property had been sold to the tribe, he thought she was joking.

"I can't believe it," Norman said. "How can that be?"

Since putting down $10,000 on the land, he had spent money having the land surveyed and many hours improving it. "I never even knew the tribe was looking at the land," Norman continued, "let alone that there was a court hearing scheduled to decide who should get it."

"I didn't know either," said White. "The first I heard of any of this was when I picked up the newspaper and read that it had been sold to the tribe."

White wanted to take legal action. But an attorney for the real estate agency concluded that it was not worth the cost. And Norman, although deeply disappointed, did not relish the thought of taking on an Indian tribe in a legal fight over property.

"I don't know how it ended up being awarded to the tribe," Norman thought. "I had a contract."

White returned Norman's two checks for $10,000. Since neither check had been placed in an interest-bearing account, Norman received nothing more. Later that day, he made arrangements to start removing his tools and equipment from the Main property.

Shortly after the closing, George Main and his children got a surprise of their own. They ended up seeing less than $250,000 of the $375,000 that the tribe paid for their land. The law firm that represented George's children billed the estate over $41,500 in legal fees. Longo's law firm billed Main an additional $25,000. And Main was charged over $58,000 in court costs, processing fees, and taxes—$51,000 of which was capital gains taxes. In the end, $124,500 went to lawyers, taxes, and processing fees.

David Holdridge read the same news article that Marcia White had read. He too was surprised to discover that the tribe had bought Main's estate. "They were given $900,000 by the government to buy up the land *in the suit*," Holdridge thought. "There were nearly nine hundred acres at stake in the suit. That comes out to about $1,000 per acre. Why aren't the landowners getting all of the money like we were told it was going to be?"

The part of the article that confused Holdridge the most was the reference to the tribe buying back its old reservation territory that it had lost in the 1700s. "George Main's land was not part of the reservation," Holdridge thought to himself. "Why are they being allowed to buy that land and have it converted to Indian territory? Jackson never told us anything about that."

Those questions were still on his mind when he went to his mailbox a couple of days later. While walking across his front lawn, thumbing through the day's mail, he came across an envelope with familiar stationery. The return address read LAW OFFICES OF BROWN, JACOBSON, JEWETT & LAUDONE, P.C. Standing in the same doorway where he had stood eight years earlier when the federal marshal served him papers, Holdridge opened the envelope. Inside was a bill in the amount of $8,800—10 percent of the amount he had received from the tribe for his land. "What is this?" Holdridge said to himself. King never said anything about taking 10 percent of the land-sale proceeds.

Holdridge put the mail down, picked up his car keys, and drove directly to King's law office. King had told the defendants that he would bill them very little up front and see how things turned out. As the lawsuit dragged on and received public exposure, King said the firm could underwrite some of the expenses due to the publicity being generated for the firm. "He never told any of us that we were going to be charged 10 percent," Holdridge thought.

From the moment Holdridge got in his car to begin driving to King's law firm, he tried to think of just what he would say when he confronted King. But by the time he found himself standing at the receptionist's desk, he still had no idea.

"My name is David Holdridge," he told the receptionist. "I want to talk to Jackson King."

"Is he expecting you, Mr. Holdridge?" she asked.

"Ah, no." He grinned. "No, he's not."

"Are you a client of his?"

"Yes."

"Let me call his secretary."

After the receptionist reached King's secretary, she told Holdridge to take the elevator to the second floor. When he got off, King's secretary was there to greet him.

"You're here to see Jackson?" she asked, recognizing Holdridge from his previous visits to the office.

"Yes. I'm here to speak to him about my bill," he replied.

"Well, Jackson is just out to lunch," she said with a smile. "He'll probably be back soon. You are welcome to wait for him."

Holdridge glanced at his watch. It was just after twelve. "All right, I'll wait for a while."

After taking a seat in the corner, he pulled out from his book bag a textbook and his lesson planner and began preparing some notes for his evening lecture. Each time someone came off the elevator, he looked up to see if it was King. The longer he sat, the harder it became to concentrate on his lesson plan. He started looking at his watch more frequently. When it reached one o'clock, he had waited long enough. He got up and approached King's secretary to find out why he was delayed.

"Jackson's still not back?" he asked.

A surprised expression came over the secretary's face. Suddenly, she had realized the irony of Holdridge sitting outside King's empty office. "They are celebrating," she said abruptly.

The announcement puzzled Holdridge. "Celebrating?"

"Yes, I thought you might be with them," she continued. "You are part of the case too."

Standing with a blank stare on his face, Holdridge cocked his head just slightly but said nothing.

"He's out with Skip Hayward," the secretary said matter-of-factly.

Seething, Holdridge paused before turning to get his bag. Silent, he thrust his textbook inside the bag and gathered up his loose papers.

Sensing she had said something wrong, the secretary stood awkwardly. "Should I tell him anything?" she asked.

"I'm just going to go along," Holdridge said, not bothering to look back at her as he walked toward the elevator. "I'll talk to him some other time."

Soon after returning to his home, Holdridge learned that he was not the only one who received a bill from King in the mail that day. Wendell Comrie's was for $22,000.

Convinced he had no choice but to pay the bill, Comrie wrote out a check for the entire amount and mailed it. "What Jackson did may be legal," Comrie told his wife. "But it wasn't proper."

"Ten of us hired him," he continued. "What he should have done was gotten a bill to Dave Holdridge for the ten of us and split it ten ways."

"That's not fair," Comrie's wife said.

"He's got our $22,000, so what does he care. That's the lawyer business for you."

21

INCORPORATED

SEPTEMBER 25, 1984
WATERFORD, CONNECTICUT

BY 9:30 A.M., A LINE OF CARS WAS BACKED UP AT EXIT 81 OFF INTERSTATE 95, six miles west of Ledyard. The traffic was headed toward the Crystal Mall, where more than one thousand shoppers stood eagerly outside awaiting the grand opening of the largest mall ever built in southeastern

Connecticut. Inside, a large red-and-blue foil ribbon hung in the food court, ready to be cut at a public ceremony being attended by public officials. Local business leaders and politicians were counting on the $70 million mall to create thousands of jobs and generate tax revenue. "This will attract people from all over New England," Connecticut governor William O'Neill told the crowd attending the ceremony, predicting the mall would change the complexion of southeastern Connecticut.

By late afternoon, page one of the *New London Day*'s afternoon edition was devoted to the mall's grand opening. The headline "Long-Awaited Crystal Mall Opens" appeared over a picture of government officials attending the ribbon-cutting ceremony. The opening-day crowds remained heavy until the mall closed its doors at 10:00 P.M. Three hours later, Connecticut state policeman Don Rich was driving his cruiser south along Route 12 in the Gales Ferry section of Ledyard. Just as he approached the intersection of Long Cove Road near the U.S. naval base, he observed a Kawasaki motorcycle approaching the intersection from the opposite direction. Its headlights were not on. As Rich got closer, the motorcyclist suddenly darted into a parking lot, slowed down long enough to flip his headlight on, then sped off on Long Cove Road toward Ledyard.

Rich immediately turned his blue lights on and gave chase down the dark, winding country road. But he could hardly keep up. For the first couple of miles, the bike raced furiously ahead until it came upon a vehicle traveling in the same direction. The vehicle in front of the bike was traveling the speed limit and approaching a blind curve. Rich began to gain ground on the bike when suddenly it veered into the oncoming lane and blew past the car while going into the blind curve.

Electing not to pass the car in front of him due to the curves and poor lighting, Rich radioed into his dispatcher. "I've withdrawn my pursuit," he reported. Rich cut off the chase because of the dangerous risks being taken by the motorcyclist. "The man was so out of control and so reckless in his desire to get away that the initial cause for starting the pursuit did not justify the type of actions that were going on," Rich said.

Within seconds, Rich lost sight of the bike's fading taillight altogether. Once he hit a straight stretch in the road, Rich passed the vehicle in front of him and continued down Long Cove Road. But as he rounded a corner moments later, he knew immediately that something was gravely wrong.

The motorcycle he had briefly pursued was lying on its side in the middle of the road. Rich slowed down, his eyes scanning the dark, wooded area as he pulled to the side of the road. There, to his right, was a body. The motorcyclist had misjudged the corner, hit a sand patch, and crashed into a telephone pole. A chill rushed over Rich's body as he got out of the cruiser to check whether the man was still alive. A twenty-year veteran less than one year away from retirement, Rich had never been involved in a high-speed chase that ended in a death. As he approached the rider, it was immediately clear that was no longer the case. Flesh was twisted in directions it is not meant to go, and blood loss was extensive. His vital signs were negative.

"He is DOA," said Rich, who radioed for medical help.

Inside the victim's wallet, Rich found a Connecticut driver's license. It read, "Rodney S. Hayward; Date of Birth—December 6, 1962; Address—9 Elizabeth George Drive, Ledyard."

Twenty-one-year old Rodney, Skip's youngest brother, had just completed his first day of work at a clothing store in the Crystal Mall.

At 2:00 A.M., the medical examiner performed an autopsy on Rodney. On the death certificate under the heading "Death Was Caused By," the examiner wrote, "Multiple fractures and internal injuries. Driver of motorcycle in single vehicle collision."

Shortly after the autopsy was complete, Rich drove to the reservation to notify Mr. and Mrs. Hayward that their son had been killed. After knocking on the door at their Elizabeth George Drive home, an outside light came on. Then the front door opened, and immediately Rich could see the fear in the Haywards' faces.

Calls quickly went out to Rodney's eight siblings, all of whom lived on the reservation with their respective spouses. When the phone rang at Skip's house, Cindy woke up and noticed it was after 2:30 A.M. She lifted the receiver and heard one of Skip's sisters crying on the other end.

"Born in Cherry Point, N.C., Dec. 6, 1962, he was the son of Richard H. and Theresa Plouffe Hayward of Ledyard," read his obituary. "He had just started working at the Crystal Mall and had previously worked for the American Cruise Line out of Haddam. He was a graduate of Ledyard High School in 1981, where he was involved in many sports, predominantly swimming." Funeral services were held three days later, and Rodney was buried in the Pequot burial ground on September 29.

• • •

The tragic loss of Rodney cast a sobering cloud over the small, close-knit group of family members who had migrated to the reservation. In September of 1984, fifty-four people belonged to the tribe, twenty-seven of whom lived on the reservation and twenty-seven of whom lived in nearby towns. The twenty-seven living on the reservation were joined there by forty-five of their relatives—parents, spouses, and children who professed no Pequot Indian heritage whatsoever. But they too were persuaded to follow Hayward on an odyssey toward financial independence. Even Skip's father, who always shunned visiting his mother-in-law, Elizabeth George, on the reservation, had moved into a newly constructed tribal home. Initially ridiculing the idea of organizing a tribe there, Skip's father no longer doubted his son's tireless legal maneuvering that had transformed this handful of lower- and middle-class American families into Mashantucket Pequot Tribal Enterprises. Skip's father, and others like him who made no attempt to portray themselves as Indians, viewed moving onto the reservation as more like joining a corporation than a tribe.

Incorporated as a landowning business entity, the group had acquired over 1,200 acres of real estate at no cost to them. And on their new land, the federal government built for them twenty single-family homes and ten multifamily dwellings, all of which were financed by HUD loans. The largest home was built for Skip and his wife, a two-story, five-bedroom house that dwarfed the Elizabeth George homestead on the land adjacent to the new housing development. Although the non-Pequot spouses taking advantage of this program, such as the husbands of Skip's six sisters, worked in the private sector, none of them were required to pay interest on their home mortgages. Under the HUD home-ownership program designed to aid poor people in acquiring affordable housing, Hayward's relatives were required only to make minimum monthly equity payments on the home loans, which amounted to no more than 25 percent of the tenant's adjusted gross income.

The group's designation as a federally protected Indian tribe entitled each individual member to live on the property under a different set of rules and laws than any of them had grown up under as everyday American citizens. Aside from the interest-free mortgages, the group also had been given a guarantee by the government that it could live indefinitely on the land without paying property taxes or abiding by local land-use regulations. After the frenzied year of property acquisition and new home construction that followed the 1983 Settlement Act, Hayward's followers were content to slow down and enjoy their newfound prosperity. They had little incentive to keep pressing for more privileges.

But Hayward was hardly satisfied, seeing the chance to acquire fabulous wealth. Without his family's input, he had been plotting with members of the Penobscot tribe in Maine to bring gambling to Ledyard. Throughout the late 1970s and early 1980s the Penobscots had offered bingo on their reservation, contrary to the state's wishes. On November 3, 1983—just weeks after President Reagan signed the Pequot Settlement Act—the U.S. Supreme Court ruled that the Penobscot Indians' gambling operation was illegal and gave the tribe three weeks to shut it down.

When a reporter from the Associated Press called the tribe seeking reaction to the news, Penobscot lieutenant governor Joseph Francis had some news of his own to report. "Connecticut is an extremely liberal state when it comes to gambling," Francis told the reporter.

"He [Francis] said the proposed Pequot hall would accommodate 3,500 people and should open by early next year," the Associated Press reported on November 4. "He said an estimated 25 million people live within a 100-mile radius of the Pequot reservation and that filling the hall should be no problem."

"If they [gamblers] drove to Indian Island [the site of the Penobscot bingo hall]," the article quoted Francis as saying, "I think they'll drive to that town [Ledyard]."

The Associated Press also quoted Penobscot tribal governor Timothy Love, who acknowledged that discussions over a jointly run bingo operation in Ledyard were at an advanced stage. Building design, revenue sharing, and how the operation would be managed were all things that Hayward had already privately agreed to. "If I was a bettin' man," Love said in reference to whether the bingo hall would be built in Ledyard, "I'd put my money on it."

Hayward's family disliked the idea, however. Their only image of gambling involved mobsters. They feared that bringing organized gambling to the reservation would disrupt their newly created paradise. When Hayward held a referendum on whether to build a five-thousand-seat bingo hall—the first step to achieving a full-scale casino—an overwhelming majority voted against it. His family members had followed his lead to the point of a financial comfort zone. They had no interest in continuing on to the point of tremendous wealth if it meant converting their private community in the New England woodlands to a host site for a tourist-attracting gambling business. They were happy just the way things were.

Cindy Hayward also disagreed with her husband's desire to pursue gambling. And she knew that a bingo hall was only the first step in his plan. He ultimately wanted to build a casino that rivaled the ones in Las Vegas. Although she was prohibited from voting in the tribe's referendum, she expressed her views to Hayward privately at home. "Sometimes when you get what you want it is not always the best thing," she warned, convinced that he would not be denied his goal.

Hayward dismissed her concerns, especially her notion that newfound wealth brought on by a gambling enterprise would change people for the worse. Hayward saw wealth as the ticket to a better lifestyle, one supported by an endless stream of money flowing from a bingo hall and eventually a casino. He viewed it as a just reward for the years of waiting it took to get federally recognized.

Impatient with his family's resistance, Hayward hastily scheduled a second vote on the bingo hall proposal and aggressively lobbied individual family members before the ballots were cast. Using a model that Tureen and the Penobscot Indians had shown him, Hayward calculated the millions of dollars that gambling would generate on his reservation. By plugging in a zip code, the model produced a formula that projected revenues if gambling were legalized in any given region of the country. The formula took in factors such as how many people lived within driving radius from the zip code entered; what their disposable income was; and what intervening opportunities to gamble existed. Its accuracy was uncanny, largely due to people's strong inclination to gamble. The propensity is as predictable as the propensity to eat or have sex.

On July 3, 1984, Hayward got his wish, getting his family to approve a bingo hall resolution the second time around. Nations, cultures, and religions are often a reflection of their leaders. The character and qualities of an individual leader, and the decisions they make, can shape the destiny of an entire people. Hayward's followers had agreed to make their land home to a gaming enterprise, hoping Hayward's personal desire to pursue wealth would make the entire group better off in the end as he had promised.

Tureen greeted the resolution with mixed feelings. He knew how bad Hayward wanted gambling and that it offered the one opportunity for him to generate real wealth for his people. With it, however, came the risk of organized crime. Hayward had already talked privately with some men from New York who offered to finance a high-stakes bingo hall in exchange for the right to manage it, an offer Tureen strongly admonished Hayward to reject. Instead, Tureen suggested a more traditional method of financing and relying on a management team consisting of individuals who were familiar to him and the tribe.

On July 25, 1986, Tureen got the United Arab Bank to loan the tribe $5 million to build the bingo hall. To secure the loan, Tureen convinced the BIA to advance $300,000 to the United Arab Bank as collateral. The Penobscots put up the rest of the collateral for the UAB loan in exchange for $250,000 a year in management fees and 20 percent of the net revenues. The Penobscots also promised to provide a management team to run the bingo hall during its first two years of operation.

Immediately after the tribe began construction on a thirty-four-thousand-square-foot bingo hall in the heart of the estate property it had bought from George Main, Connecticut attorney general Austin J. McGuigan threatened to bring criminal charges against the tribe for its failure to comply with state regulatory procedures. Under Connecticut law, bingo games were legal in the state and relied on by churches and charity groups to raise money. But only those groups that obtained a state permit and complied with strict bookkeeping and report-filing requirements were authorized to conduct the games. The state had never granted a permit for a group to build and operate a high-stakes bingo parlor.

Pointing to the Connecticut Indian Land Claims Settlement Act of 1982, Hayward and Tureen made it clear, however, that they had no intention of applying for a permit or complying with any of the state's regulations. It was now time for them to flex their muscles as a federally recognized tribe. It would soon become apparent to Connecticut that while it could enforce its criminal laws on the reservation, it did not have the ability to regulate affairs on the reservation. In Connecticut, bingo is governed by regulatory laws, not criminal laws.

While the bingo hall was being built, Tureen's firm went to court to head off the state's attempt to enforce its regulations. It asked U.S. district judge Peter Dorsey for an injunction that would forbid the state from enforcing its bingo regulations against the Pequots, citing language of the Connecticut Indian Land Claims Settlement Act.

The state argued that the tribe's refusal to comply with permit requirements and other regulations regarding bingo games amounted to a criminal offense. And the state maintained that it had the authority to enforce its criminal laws, even against a federal Indian tribe. Additionally, the state argued that a high-stakes bingo hall in full-time operation was drastically different from charitable bingo games held occasionally in church basements. And the presence of such an operation violated the state's public policy against gambling.

While Judge Dorsey considered the tribe's injunction request, Cindy walked out on Hayward after five years of marriage. She had lived with him through the final three years of the court battle against the Ledyard landowners. But she was unwilling to endure another legal fight, this one against the same state officials who had helped him convince the federal government to grant the family federal Indian tribe status in the first place. The more adamant he became about bringing gambling to the reservation, the more Hayward neglected Cindy.

The decision to end the marriage was an agonizing one for Cindy. She wanted only to spend her life raising a family with him. That was why she had dropped out of college and abandoned her promising career plans. It was why she tried to adapt her cultural upbringing as a New England Yankee to that of a Native American Indian. And it was the only reason she agreed to live as a second-class citizen from the moment she became Mrs. Hayward. Despite looking no different than her in-laws, the absence of any Pequot blood in her lineage stripped her of the choicest citizenship guarantee afforded to Americans—the right to vote. Unlike others who became Skip's friends in hopes of becoming rich, Cindy would have gladly remained middle class, or even poor, if only she could have his friendship. The day she moved off the reservation she had no job, no money, and nowhere to go but home to her parents.

While Cindy struggled to put together a new life, Hayward threw himself further into the affairs of the tribe. With the bingo hall under construction, he and his new business partner from Maine, Penobscot leader

Timothy Love, traveled to Washington on June 26, 1985. They both testified before the Senate's Select Committee on Indian Affairs regarding a bill called the Indian Gaming Regulatory Act (IGRA). Despite stiff opposition from states, some tribes around the country had started running small casino operations on their reservations. IGRA was a proposed federal law intended to regulate gaming activities on Indian reservations. Hayward, of course, had great interest in the final outcome of the bill. The ultimate language of the statute would determine whether he could fulfill his dream to build a casino.

Hayward and Love were presiding over two of the most prosperous Indian tribes in the entire United States. The Penobscots had received over $50 million in their settlement with Maine and massive tracts of valuable forestland. Yet both men decided to emphasize the financial needs of poor Indian tribes as their justification to Congress for passing a federal law that would allow them to bring casino-style gambling to Ledyard.

"All the revenues will be available to fund Mashantucket Pequot social and economic development projects like our Museum and Indian Research Center," Hayward told the committee.

Love also advanced the same theme. "While Indian gaming is not the answer to all the problems in Indian country," he said, "it has served to prevent some tribes from going into bankruptcy and it has enabled many tribes to continue to provide critically needed services and a source of development capital to begin diversifying their economies."

On January 9, 1986, Judge Dorsey ruled that Connecticut's bingo laws were not enforceable on the Pequot reservation. The tribe was free to run its bingo hall without interference from the state. "Connecticut has a scheme for dealing with bingo which is not part of the criminal code," ruled Dorsey, "but rather is part of the delegation of authority to municipalities. Bingo may be conducted in a municipality that affirmatively votes to permit it.

"The purpose of regulation," he continued, "is to permit the conduct or activity with limits or restrictions. In contrast, the purpose of a criminal statute . . . is to prohibit conduct or activity."

While recognizing that the state had authority to enforce its criminal laws on the Pequot reservation, Dorsey ruled the same authority did not extend to civil regulatory laws. "The grant to the states of jurisdiction over criminal laws is a grant of the authority to prohibit conduct," Dorsey said. "Such a grant is not the same as a grant of power to regulate conduct, otherwise permitted."

Dorsey also took the opportunity to criticize the state for applying a double standard. The state had argued that the Pequots' high-stakes bingo hall conflicted with the state's public policy against gambling. Yet the state was generating close to $1 billion annually in lottery receipts. "Bingo," wrote Dorsey, "can hardly be deemed to contravene a public policy against gambling in view of the state's daily encouragement and broad enticement of its citizens to participate in the state-run gambling which generates substantial revenue for the state as would plaintiff's bingo games for its governmental function."

Just as Tureen suspected, the ruling generated no local opposition. Both the town of Ledyard and its residents remained indifferent to the fact that they were getting the state's first high-stakes bingo hall in their backyard. Hayward, emerging more and more as Tureen's protégé, had developed a very disarming presence with people, especially those who had the potential to derail his plans. He had assured the public that the operation would remain small.

After opening on July 5, 1986, the bingo hall generated over $20 million for the tribe in its first year of business.

22

LAS VEGAS NIGHTS

ON JUNE 4, 1988, A SMALL GROUP OF HAYWARD'S RELATIVES GATHERED at his home for a private wedding ceremony at 4 Elizabeth George Drive. Three years after splitting up with Cindy Figdore, Hayward decided to marry again—this time to an American Indian. Forty-year-old Carol Carlson was from Minnesota and had previously been married. A former federal government employee, she and Hayward got acquainted during

Hayward's efforts to build up the tribe. She was Skip's age, and like him had not obtained a college degree.

But they were on the brink of wealth that rivaled that of some of America's most noted entrepreneurs. In three years the bingo hall had brought in over $60 million. It was small change, however, to what Hayward saw on the horizon. After four years of debate, Congress had finally approved the federal Indian Gaming Regulatory Act (IGRA). On October 17, 1988, it became law. With states and tribes increasingly clashing over unregulated gambling operations on reservations, Congress intended to end the dispute. The complex twenty-one-page law divided gaming into three classes: social games of chance that did not award cash prizes (Class I); bingo, whether played for cash or noncash prizes (Class II); and all other forms of gambling, including poker, slot machines, and all casino-style games (Class III). Under the new federal law, tribes were free to conduct Class I gaming without restriction. Class II gaming was also permitted by tribes whose land was located within states where such gaming was not forbidden by law. But for a tribe to set up casino gambling (Class III) on its reservation, certain criteria had to be satisfied. First, the tribe desiring a casino had to be "located in a State that permits such gaming." Second, the tribe had to enter into a compact with the state in which it resided. The "Tribal-State Compact" was intended to establish terms and conditions to govern the gaming activities. And third, the secretary of interior had to approve the compact and publish it in the *Federal Register*.

States remained confident that IGRA would do little to open the door for casino gambling on Indian reservations. Since Nevada and New Jersey were the only states that had casinos, and the federal law only allowed tribes "located in a State that permits such gaming" to open a casino, it was widely believed that only tribes in Nevada and New Jersey were eligible to seek casinos.

On March 30, 1989, Connecticut governor William O'Neill received a Federal Express package bearing a return receipt from Tureen's law firm in Portland, Maine. Inside O'Neill discovered a two-page letter signed by Robert L. Gips, a young lawyer who had joined Tureen's firm in 1983. With a combined degree in law and business from Yale, Gips was put in charge of creating a business plan for the Pequots. Mr. Pizza had already failed, going from profitable to out of business in just a few years under the Haywards' management.

"Dear Governor O'Neill," Gips's letter began. "I am writing on behalf of the Mashantucket Pequot Tribe to request that the State of Connecticut enter into negotiations with the Tribe for the purpose of entering into a Tribal-State compact governing the conduct of expanded gaming activities on the Tribe's reservation in Ledyard."

O'Neill read on but found no specifics on just what Gips meant by "expanding the tribe's gaming activities." Instead, the letter referred only to the tribe's desire "to establish a range of Class III gaming activities" under the federal Indian Gaming Regulatory Act. "We look forward to an early response to our request to begin actual negotiations," the letter concluded, "and stand ready and eager to meet with you . . . to develop a compact which will work well for the Tribe and the State."

O'Neill was the first governor in the country to receive a letter from an Indian tribe seeking to negotiate a tribe-state compact under the new federal law. Unfamiliar with the details of IGRA, O'Neill asked his acting attorney general, Clarine Nardi Riddle, to determine whether Connecticut was required to negotiate with the Pequots. Riddle examined the federal law and found that Class III gaming was essentially limited to casino-style gambling. Since state law prohibited casinos, and IGRA required Connecticut to negotiate with the Pequots only if the state offered Class III gaming, Riddle was puzzled by Gips's letter. The closest thing to casino gambling permitted was bingo, and the Pequots already had a bingo hall. Riddle asked Gips to explain just what games of chance the Pequots planned to add to their reservation.

Gips responded in a May 26 follow-up letter. "We suggest," wrote Gips, "that you assume that the expanded gaming to be conducted by the Tribe will consist of the identical types of gaming permitted by Connecticut's laws permitting operation of games of chance or 'Las Vegas nights.'" Riddle and others in the attorney general's office found it hard to take Gips's response seriously. For years Connecticut had carried a law on its books commonly referred to as the "Las Vegas Nights" statute. It allowed charitable organizations and nonprofit groups to sponsor fund-raising events once or twice a year that featured poker, blackjack, and other card games. Under the law, the winnings were limited to prizes other than cash. And only organizations that qualified as a bona fide charity or nonprofit could hold a Las Vegas Night.

"We have reached the following conclusion," Riddle told Gips in a July

19 letter. "The fact that Connecticut permits . . . 'Las Vegas Nights' to be conducted under license by charitable organizations for charitable purposes does not, under the provisions of the Indian Gaming Regulatory Act compel the State of Connecticut to enter into negotiations with the tribe for the ultimate purpose of the construction and operation of a casino on the reservation as you have proposed." On the other hand, Riddle pointed out to Gips, if the Pequots wished to hold Las Vegas Nights in a manner similar to a charitable organization, the state was prepared to negotiate.

Riddle's response angered Hayward and his attorneys. Gips and Tureen had carefully analyzed the IGRA statute and determined that Connecticut had no choice but to negotiate with the Pequots for a casino compact. Although Tureen knew that Congress intended the law to limit casino gambling on Indian reservations to those states that had legalized casino gambling, he saw a loophole in the language. The law said that Class III gaming activities were lawful on Indian lands "only if such activities are located in a State that permits such gaming for any purpose by any person, organization, or entity." To Tureen, whether a state permitted poker in a casino for profit or in a church basement for charity made no difference. The law said that if a state permitted the game for any purpose, it had to permit an Indian tribe to offer it.

Gips wrote back to Riddle on August 1. "We were naturally quite disappointed in the conclusion that you reached," he said. "Obviously, our own legal analysis . . . led us to the opposite conclusion." In his letter Gips persisted in asking Riddle for an explanation for why the state was resisting the Pequots' wishes.

In a final letter to Gips, Riddle hinted at the fear that Connecticut officials had over the Pequots' request. "In our opinion, 'Las Vegas Nights' . . . and commercial casino gambling . . . are not even remotely similar," she wrote. "Connecticut has no existing regulatory system which can even begin to police, monitor and control casino gambling. It has been estimated that the State of New Jersey in fiscal year 1987 spent some $47,000,000.00 to regulate the casinos which operate only in Atlantic City. If Connecticut must now create a casino regulating apparatus, the costs would be staggering."

Gips received Riddle's final letter on August 28, 1989. The next time Riddle's office received any correspondence from the tribe's lawyers, it came in the form of a "COMPLAINT" and was hand-delivered by a sheriff. The cover sheet read, "MASHANTUCKET PEQUOT TRIBE, Plaintiff, v. STATE OF CONNECTICUT, and WILLIAM A. O'NEILL, Governor of the State of Connecticut, Defendants."

The lawsuit asked the U.S. district court in Hartford to order the state to negotiate a compact with the tribe that would enable it to operate a casino in Ledyard. The suit did not surprise the state. But it was surprised to find that the tribe added another lawyer to its legal team in preparation for its case against the state. "Jackson T. King, Jr., Attorney for Plaintiff" signed the complaint along with Gips.

While representing the landowners who had been sued by the tribe, he had argued that it was in the best interest of the state to settle that lawsuit by agreeing to have the federal government recognize them as a tribe. The state agreed. Now the tribe was taking that status and asking a federal court to force the state to allow them to have a casino. And King was now representing the tribe. The last time state officials had seen his name in connection with the tribe, King was the lawyer for their adversaries.

Even with the addition of King, Hayward's expanding legal team still lacked one key component: a negotiator, someone who could represent them at the bargaining table once the court ordered Connecticut to negotiate a gaming compact under IGRA. Neither King nor anyone in Tureen's firm knew anything about setting up a casino or what it would take to regulate one. They needed an expert to advise the tribe, one who was superior to anyone the state could hire to represent the state's interests.

23

JERSEY BORN

MONDAY, MARCH 31, 1980

WITH A LONG TRENCH COAT COVERING HIS BRAWNY FIVE-FOOT, nine-inch frame, New Jersey assistant attorney general G. Michael Brown did not wake his wife and daughters to say good-bye before leaving their coastal home in Sea Girt. As the thirty-seven-year-old prosecutor, known by his colleagues as "Mickey," stepped outside, the salty sea breeze blowing in from the Atlantic Ocean whipped through his bushy, dark hair, ruining the part he had just neatly combed on the right side of his head. The predawn chill in the air offered a cold reminder that winter was lingering. His blue eyes detected nothing behind him as he looked into his rearview mirror, backed out of the driveway, and headed toward Freehold under the cover of darkness. At 9:00 A.M., just over three hours away, he was scheduled to deliver his opening argument in the most important criminal trial of his life.

In charge of the state's organized crime division, Brown had spent the previous three years heading up the state's investigation into the Mafia's presence in New Jersey. Working in concert with the FBI and the New Jersey State Police, Brown's team had bugged a small diner in Newark that was used by the upper echelon of New York's Genovese crime family. Hidden microphones and surveillance cameras allowed the authorities to listen in on the group's secret plans to divide Jersey into turf sections.

The undercover cops who sat up nights sipping cold coffee in unmarked cars while monitoring the mob through eavesdropping devices loved working with Brown. He knew the streets of Newark as well as they did. Before prosecuting mobsters, he had handled homicide cases for the Essex County District Attorney's office. He was at home on the streets or in a steak house after hours eating a juicy New York strip and drinking Budweiser beer. He would have been a great cop had he not turned out to be such a proficient trial lawyer.

Brown's investigation led to a twenty-four-count indictment of ten reputed mobsters, including Ruggerio Boiardo, the eighty-nine-year-old capo of the New Jersey segment of the Genovese crime family, and forty-nine-year-old Andrew Gerardo, Boiardo's immediate lieutenant. The indictment, which included charges of murder, extortion, conspiracy, robbery, loan sharking, and gambling, was the result of the biggest organized-crime investigation in New Jersey history. It prompted Attorney General John Degnan to boldly predict that his office was prepared to do something that had never been done before in an American courtroom: prove that the Mafia actually existed. "We are prepared," said Degnan, "to do just that—to demonstrate, in the course of proving other charges contained in the indictment, the existence of organized crime in the United States."

As he drove toward Freehold, Brown knew how much was riding on the trial. The *New York Times*, recognizing the historical nature of the case, did a preview of it, noting that despite America's thirty-year "war on organized crime," no state had successfully proven the existence of a nationally run crime syndicate. The mob's notorious "code of silence," or *omerta*, which was enforced by death against anyone who testified, had stymied countless prosecutors in the past. But Brown had an ace up his sleeve. His star witness was a member of the mob who offered to work as an informant. Patrick Pizuto, a convicted murderer who once served as the chauffeur to a crime boss in northern Jersey, agreed to wear a listening device to secret meetings where organized crime figures were present. In return, Pizuto received a reduced sentence, a new identity, and placement in a federal witness-protection program. Brown had videotapes of the Genovese crime family meeting at Kelly Ann's luncheonette on Roosevelt Avenue in Newark, as well as audiotapes of their discussions inside. The tapes had them splitting the state of New Jersey into turf areas.

As he parked his car outside the Monmouth County courthouse in Freehold, Brown approached the building with confidence. But win or lose, he had already decided privately this was going to be his last trial as a prosecutor.

Shortly before 9:00, a detective informed him that Pizuto had been delivered to the courthouse and was being held in a segregated holding cell. But he was having second thoughts about testifying. Brown asked the detective to take him downstairs to see him.

"Look," Brown said, "we're here. The jury's upstairs waiting. And as soon as the opening is over, I'm going to call you as my first witness. I anticipate you to testify truthfully and completely."

Pizuto said nothing as Brown turned and headed back upstairs swiftly. Pizuto's cold feet had accelerated Brown's adrenaline. "I don't know what the hell this guy is going to do on the stand," he thought to himself as Judge Michael Imbriani called the courtroom to order and invited Brown to make his opening statement. But what separated Brown from other prosecutors was his ability to improvise under extreme pressure. A talent that cannot be taught in law school, it is simply a natural part of one's character. And Brown's path to becoming a prosecutor was paved with experiences that made him a master when confronted by the unforeseen.

Raised an Irish Catholic in East Orange, New Jersey, Brown attended private Catholic schools from grammar school through college. In 1964 he entered Seton Hall Law School, where he supported himself by bartending at night and working summers as a lifeguard on the Jersey shore. In June of 1967 he graduated and joined the New Jersey National Guard. Four months after earning his law degree, he was sent to Fort Jackson, South Carolina, for basic training. He took leave to fly back to New Jersey to take the bar exam. After his return, he was made an E-2 corporal in the army and transferred to Fort McClellan, Alabama. There he put his law degree to use working as a courts and boards clerk in the staff judge advocate's office until his unit was deployed to Vietnam in March of 1969.

Brown's law school experience did not prepare him for what he saw when, after being airborne for twenty-seven hours, his military transfer plane dropped him at the Ben Wah Airbase. It was 110 degrees as Brown, then twenty-five, got off the plane at 4:00 in the morning. Bombs were going off all around the plane.

One of the first things Brown did was purchase from a street vendor a six-inch-high, smiling Buddha made out of mahogany. "This is going to get me through this experience," Brown thought to himself. There were no crucifixes for sale in Vietnam.

After sitting in the staging area on the base for two days, Brown was processed and received word from a lieutenant from Brooklyn, New York, that he had been assigned to drive a truck delivering military supplies to the troops.

"You gotta help me," Brown insisted. "I'm a lawyer, a licensed attorney in the state of New Jersey."

"So what are you doing here?" the lieutenant asked skeptically.

"I was in the National Guard and we got activated," Brown said. "That's fine. I did my year in the States and I got my year to do over here. But I'd like to work as a lawyer, not drive a truck."

After reviewing Brown's personnel file, the lieutenant called the military headquarters in Long Binh, South Vietnam. Brown was immediately reassigned to the staff judge advocate's office and given responsibility to handle special court-martial cases under the Uniform Code of Military Justice. The only personal item on Brown's military desk was the mahogany Buddha he had bought for good luck. Though he had no courtroom experience and had just recently passed the bar exam, Brown was assigned to handle high-priority cases involving military personnel charged with misconduct. One of his first cases required him to defend an army captain from New Jersey who had been charged with homicide in a case similar to the My Lai massacre. Brown met the captain, interviewed him for thirty minutes, then started the homicide trial all in the same day. It was a quick education in the practice of law.

For the months that followed, the courts and boards office would call Brown on a moment's notice and dispatch him to the site of a court-martial. Sometimes Brown was assigned to defend accused military personnel. Other times he prosecuted. He proved to be so effective that when the staff judge advocate in charge of his division completed his tour of duty, he asked Brown to take his place. But Brown was merely a corporal and the job could only be given to an officer. In exchange for his willingness to take the job, the army offered to make Brown a captain. Brown declined. "I don't mind doing it for a year," Brown told them. "I have this commitment because I'm an American. I'll do what everybody else has to do. But I'm not going to stay in Vietnam for five more years."

On December 22, 1969, Brown left Vietnam and was honorably discharged from the military. In 1970 he was hired as an assistant prosecutor in the Essex County prosecutor's office in New Jersey, where he started out earning $12,500 a year handling drug cases. Within six months he was promoted to handling primarily homicide cases until the state created a Division of Criminal Justice in the attorney general's office. The division had statewide jurisdiction to investigate and prosecute organized crime and political corruption cases. Brown was soon promoted to deputy attorney general. His first assignment was to prosecute thirty-eight inmates for their part in the 1971 Rahway Prison riot. The trials lasted eighteen months.

But no one was going to remember any of that if Pizuto failed to testify and Brown lost the most highly publicized trial of his career. He had promised to prove that a Mafia existed. And the New York media was waiting to see if he came through.

After completing his opening statement, he let the defendants see no sign of worry as he uttered the words, "The state calls as its first witness Patrick Pizuto." In silence, both sides waited. Then, court officers opened a side door to the courtroom. Pizuto walked in and took the oath. Then he testified as if he had never had any doubts. For the next three days he offered severely damaging testimony against the defendants. By the time he was done, skeptics were convinced that Brown might actually win.

Over the next eight weeks, the state meticulously made its case while the New Jersey newspapers devoted daily coverage to the trial. Then at the end of May, Brown received an unexpected telephone call from Attorney General John Degnan. Brown figured his boss was calling to get an update on the trial.

"The governor wants to see you," Degnan said.

"Right in the middle of trial?" Brown asked.

"Something has come up," said Degnan. "When you finish in court today, a state police helicopter will pick you up at 5:00 in Freehold and fly you down to the Seaview Country Club in Atlantic City. I'll meet you out front and take you inside to see the governor."

Although Governor Brendan Byrne was considerably older than Brown, the two had known each other for nearly twenty years. They had both grown up in East Orange. And when Byrne was a prosecutor, he hired Brown's older brother to work as an assistant prosecutor under him. Both Brown and his brother had worked on Byrne's election campaign. Brown figured that the urgent meeting with the governor had to have something to do with the case.

When he first arrived at the resort, Brown was met by Degnan and escorted to a private dining room where the governor was waiting.

"How's the trial going?" Byrne began.

Brown provided the governor with a detailed recap of events up to that point.

"So what are you going to do after this trial?" Byrne asked.

Brown suddenly felt he had not been whisked to Atlantic City to talk about the trial.

"I gotta get out of this business and make some money," said Brown. "I've been working as a state employee since I got out of the army. That's twelve years. I've had a great time. But I'm going to set up a law practice and try to make some money."

"Well, I got a problem," said Byrne. "And I need your help on it."

"Anything, Governor," Brown responded.

"I want you to take over the Division of Gaming Enforcement, the agency that licenses and regulates casinos."

Stunned, Brown straightened up in his chair. "I don't know anything about legalized gambling," said Brown. "I know bookmakers. I know loan sharks. But I don't know anything about legalized gambling. And that's an administrative agency. It is really not a prosecutor's job."

"Well, I want it handled like a prosecutor," insisted Byrne. "I'm worried about Atlantic City. I have serious concerns about the gambling industry and the effect it is going to have on the reputation of New Jersey."

New Jersey had recently legalized gambling in Atlantic City and was in the infant stages of casino development. Resorts International Hotel Casino was the only company that had been granted a permanent license. Caesars World Inc., Bally Corporation, and Playboy were among the few that were operating under temporary licenses. And a group of other Las Vegas companies hoping to access the East Coast's lucrative gaming market was in the application process. New Jersey's Casino Control Commission, which had among its responsibilities the screening of license applicants for links to organized crime, had become embroiled in a scandal. The FBI, as part of an undercover operation code-named "Abscam," had recently announced that it was looking into alleged bribes paid by prospective licensees to the state's casino licensing board. The FBI had videotape surveillance of its agents posing as businessmen willing to pay bribes. Money and influence were quickly moving into Atlantic City, and Byrne was searching for a way to restore public confidence in the state agency's ability to police the casinos.

"I'm dissatisfied with the way the division has been run," Byrne told Brown. "I want it run like a prosecutor's office, with that level of integrity and investigative know-how. And I'd like you to take it over."

"I don't think I want to do that," Brown said honestly. "I don't want to take over a casino industry that I know nothing about."

Under the table, Degnan kicked Brown in the shin, causing him to stop talking.

"Listen," said Byrne. "I'm only going to be in office another twenty-four months. If you do this, you will be the person who gets the experience regulating the gaming industry, casinos, New Jersey. It is going to be a highly visible job."

Byrne was a very intuitive politician. Casino gambling was taking off in New Jersey and many other regions of the world. If aggressively enforced, New Jersey's Casino Control Act had the potential to become a model for the world gaming market. It provided for a rigorous licensing process and imposed strict regulations on casinos in operation. As an expert on the industry, Brown would become a much wanted consultant when he retired from his post.

"Let me think about this," said Brown.

"I'll give you all the support you want," Byrne continued. "I will never interfere with anything you want to do. You will have a total free hand to enforce the Casino Control Act. No political intervention. It will be handled just like you are a prosecutor."

"Let me finish the trial," said Brown. "Can I get back to you in a week?"

"Sure," said Byrne.

During the helicopter ride back to Freehold, Degnan wasted no time chastising Brown. "Mick, are you out of your mind, telling the governor you don't want this job?"

"I *don't* want that job," said Brown. "I don't want to run an administrative agency."

"But you'll run it like a prosecutor's office," Degnan insisted.

"All right, John," said Brown impatiently. "All right. I'll do it. Let me get this trial under my belt. And give me some time off."

On May 30, with Brown still trying the case in Freehold, Byrne publicly announced that he had nominated him to be the new director of the Division of Gaming Enforcement.

During the first week of June, the telephone at Brown's Sea Girt residence rang one evening at roughly 8:00 P.M. Brown was working late at the office. His eight-year-old daughter ran to answer it.

"Hello," she said, holding the large receiver to her ear.

"If your father shows up tomorrow in Freehold," a deep male voice said, "you're gonna be a f----n' orphan and your mother is gonna be a widow."

Click.

The seemingly endless silence on the other end of the phone was finally interrupted by a dial tone. Trembling, the eight-year-old quickly called her father at work to tell him what had just happened. Brown immediately had some state troopers assigned to his house for his family's protection. It was the first time in his career that death threats had been made against his family.

The next morning, Brown, with his wife by his side, showed up in Freehold. He notified the judge of the previous night's events. The incident was brought to the defendants' attention before the jury entered the courtroom. Andrew Gerardo, the recognized leader among the defendants, asked the judge for permission to meet briefly with his codefendants and lawyer in the jury room. After they emerged, Gerardo walked directly over to Brown.

"We're not like that," said Gerardo, who had developed a respect for Brown's fearless approach to the case. "I apologize. It will never happen again."

Gerardo then approached Brown's wife, who was seated in the front row of the courtroom. "Mrs. Brown," he began. "I'm Andy Gerardo. I want to apologize. We're not like that. I really apologize."

Brown accepted the apology on behalf of his family. "This guy is classy," thought Brown, who had been dogging Gerardo for three years. "He's a true professional, a true 'Don.'"

Following Gerardo's apology, one of the codefendants asked the judge to revoke his bail, suddenly feeling insecure out on bail. He was ordered to jail and later sentenced to forty-four years in prison.

On June 20, the jury in Freehold voted to convict Gerardo and three codefendants. The Mafia is not "a figment of Hollywood's imagination," Brown told the *New York Times* after the guilty verdicts and prison terms were announced. With that he cleaned out his office and one week later took over at the state's Division of Gaming Enforcement. With a mandate from the governor to erase the stain on the division's public image, Brown investigated casino license applicants in the same aggressive manner he did the mob. Using an array of state police officers and special agents he had worked with for ten years as a prosecutor, Brown first looked into permanent license applications that were pending. In his first year on the job, Brown turned away from Atlantic City some of the world's most prominent names in the gambling industry. The investigation showed that Clifford and Stuart Perlman, the principal owners of Caesars World Inc., had ties to organized crime. Brown forced both men to step aside as a condition of the Boardwalk Regency Hotel receiving a permanent casino license.

Brown then put a similar demand on William O'Donnell, the chairman of Bally Manufacturing Corp., and Hugh Hefner, the owner of Playboy. Brown denied both men permanent operating licenses. And as promised, Governor Byrne did nothing to deter him. New Jersey quickly developed a reputation as a difficult place to acquire a casino operator's license.

On the Sunday before Lincoln's birthday in 1981, Brown received a telephone call at home from Degnan. "I'd like you to sit down and talk to some people from New York tomorrow," said Degnan. "They are considering coming into Atlantic City. They want to get a feel for what it is going to take."

Despite it being a holiday, Brown agreed to meet with them.

"Who are they?" he asked.

"Donald and Robert Trump, two builders in New York."

"Never heard of 'em."

"They are young guys, very aggressive, clean. The type of people we'd like to get into Atlantic City instead of all these Las Vegas gaming companies."

Brown took with him to the meeting his deputy assistant, Guy Michael, who had helped draft the state's Casino Control Act. He also made sure a New Jersey state trooper was present. To protect his reputation, Brown never met with a license applicant without a trooper present.

When Brown walked into the law office of Nick Ribas flanked by Guy Martin and an imposing state trooper, he was surprised at the youthful appearance of the Trumps. "Well dressed. Young guys. New York," Brown thought to himself as he quickly sized up the brothers before being formally introduced. "They look much different from anything we've encountered on other casino applications."

The Trumps explained that they were real estate developers in New York City and were in the process of building the Grand Hyatt Hotel in Manhattan. Their next objective was to develop a casino in Atlantic City. But they wanted to know more about the licensing and permit process. "How long is it going to take?" asked Robert.

"Well, with all the investigation and everything, about a year or two," said Brown, who sensed that the Trumps knew little about the gambling business.

"But it is only us," Trump said, pointing to his brother Donald. "We are not a big gaming company."

"We could streamline it," said Brown.

"Mickey, we're too young to have gotten into any trouble already," Trump said with a smile. "We've never been in trouble."

Brown did not return the smile. "Well, if that is true," he said sternly, "and there are no issues, we can get an investigation done in three to six months." He sat forward in his chair, looking the Trumps in the eyes. "But you gotta cooperate fully. And be available. We're gonna look up your ass. If you're clean, we'll get you licensed right away."

Six months later, Donald and Robert Trump were cleared to build Harrah's at Trump Plaza, the first in a series of resort casinos the Trumps went on to build in Atlantic City.

Shortly after Byrne left office in 1982, Brown resigned. And as the governor predicted, Brown was highly sought after for his expertise in the gaming industry. He and his deputy at the state agency, Guy Michael, opened a small law firm together in Atlantic City. Prohibited by law from working for clients involved with New Jersey gaming licenses for two years, Brown was hired by a number of corporations seeking to acquire casino permits overseas. And numerous foreign governments hired him to help draft licensing requirements and legislation for creating gaming regulatory agencies. By the mid-1980s, his list of clients included the Hilton Hotel Corporation, the president of Trump's Plaza, the British Gaming Board, and the Bahaman Gaming Board.

Another perk that Brown did not anticipate was the endless number of public-speaking requests he received. In 1989 he accepted an invitation to speak at the World Gaming Conference in Las Vegas. He and his wife boarded a plane at Newark Airport bound for Vegas. Even before they lifted off, Brown began reviewing his speech and practicing it on his wife. He noticed that the man sitting next to him in the aisle seat was looking over his shoulder and glancing at his papers.

"Are you going to the gaming conference?" the man asked.

"Yes," Brown responded.

"My name is Rob Gips," the man said. "I'm on my way there too."

"Hi, Rob. I'm Mickey Brown."

"What brings you to the conference?" Gips asked.

"I'm going there to give a speech," he said, hoping to avoid further conversation so he could continue writing.

"I work for the Pequot tribe," Gips said. "We're an Indian tribe in Connecticut and we're considering opening up a casino."

"OK," Brown said, hiding his skepticism.

"I must sound crazy to this guy," thought Gips. "He probably thinks

I'm on drugs. There are no *Indian* casinos to speak of in the United States."

After a brief pause, Gips asked Brown about his background. Brown handed him a business card.

"Do you mind if we give you a call?" Gips asked.

"Sure," Brown said, not wanting to insult Gips. As he returned to his speech preparation, he didn't give Gips or the Pequots a second thought.

24

A PROSECUTOR AND A PROPHET

APRIL 1990

READING THE INDIAN GAMING REGULATORY ACT (IGRA), CONNECTICUT attorney general Clarine Nardi Riddle was convinced that Connecticut had no obligation to negotiate with the Pequots over a casino. Congress, she thought, surely did not intend for IGRA to authorize tribes to build casinos merely on the basis that they were in a state that allowed churches to occasionally offer charity card games. But Riddle and her boss, Governor William O'Neill, also knew that they represented the first state to be sued under the new law. And there was no telling how federal judge Peter Dorsey would interpret it. He was expected to deliver his decision in mid-May of 1990 as to whether the state was required to negotiate a tribal-state compact with the Pequots.

While awaiting the ruling, Rob Gips placed a call to former New Jersey attorney general John Degnan. When Gips was a law student at Yale, he had spent a summer working for Degnan as his special assistant, writing speeches during the period that the attorney general's office was aggressively rooting organized crime out of the casinos in Atlantic City. He hoped Degnan could advise them on how best to prevent organized crime from establishing itself on the reservation in Ledyard.

"John," Gips said in a telephone call, "we are really getting serious about building a casino. We have a lot of legal issues to deal with. But we think we have a strategy for those. What I'm really concerned with is setting up a regulatory structure to police the operation. Are we crazy to think that we can do this?"

"Well," said Degnan, "it is a challenging issue. But you can probably do it. But I want you to talk to two people first. In terms of the management side, I want you to go talk to this guy Al Luciani. He helped write the Casino Control Act in New Jersey while I was attorney general. On the regulatory side, go talk to Mickey Brown. He had been head of the Division of Gaming Enforcement under me. Mickey was in charge of the licensing for the first six or seven casinos in Atlantic City."

Days later, Gips flew down to Atlantic City to meet with Brown at his law office. It had been a year since he had seen Brown, so when he walked into Brown's office, he was stunned.

"Oh, my God," he said as he started to laugh. "We've met before."

"Yes, we have, haven't we?" Brown said, laughing. "We actually met on an airplane. You're the guy who's going to build a casino in Connecticut on an Indian reservation."

As Brown realized whom he had agreed to meet with, he immediately thought he was wasting his time.

Gips spent most of the meeting educating Brown on the Indian Gaming Regulatory Act and the Pequots' plan to be the first tribe in the country to use the law to build a Las Vegas–style casino. The tribe wanted to hire Brown to help it set up the casino operation. The federal law contained a provision that required tribes and states to negotiate compacts designed to govern legalized gambling on Indian reservations. If Judge Dorsey ruled in the Pequots' favor, the tribe expected him to order the state to the negotiation table. The tribe also expected him to appoint a federal mediator who would ask both sides to submit a proposed version of a compact.

As Brown listened, he recognized all the things that the Pequots wanted. Increasingly, nations were turning to legalized gambling as a revenue source, and Gips was hoping Brown would draft the Pequots' compact, complete with provisions describing which games would be offered in the casino and how they would be run. The tribe wanted a series of regulations ensuring the integrity of the games and the safety of the tribe and its gambling patrons. Most importantly, the tribe wanted to establish a gaming regulatory operation that protected the casino from corruption and organized crime.

Little of this was new to Brown. He had been around the world helping various governments draft regulations to police legalized gambling operations. However, he had never worked for an Indian nation, nor did he have experience with the new federal Indian gaming law. These were the things that appealed to him. He liked new challenges, and the challenge of bringing the first casino to New England seemed too good to pass up.

Mickey Brown parked in front of a sign that read TRIBAL OFFICE. Turning the key, he killed the engine and radio simultaneously. Through the windshield he stared at the only building in sight, an aluminum-sided construction trailer with a set of wooden steps leading to a door. Brown straightened his sleek blue tie and white shirt collar before pulling on his blue suit jacket. He stepped out and took a deep breath. Noticing the sky was overcast, he retrieved his gray London Fog trench coat from the backseat. Black briefcase in hand, he approached the makeshift office.

A short, well-groomed woman with a pleasant smile sat at a desk just inside the door.

"Hi. I'm Mickey Brown from New Jersey. And I've got an appointment with Chairman Richard Hayward and the tribal council."

"They've been expecting you," said Hayward's secretary, Simone Harrett. "I'll tell Skip you're here. Can I get you anything first?"

"I could use a bathroom," Brown said. "I've been drivin' for three and half hours."

"Well, let me get you a cup of coffee and there's the bathroom," she said, pointing over Brown's shoulder.

Closing the flimsy wooden door behind him, Brown cupped his hands and splashed cool water on his face. He wondered how the meeting would go. Brown had represented some of the world's richest businessmen, as well as governors and heads of state. But he had never worked for an Indian chief.

Emerging from the bathroom, Brown saw steam rising from a white foam cup of coffee next to his briefcase. "Skip's off the phone now," Harrett said. "I'll take you in."

He followed her down a tight wood-paneled corridor, stopping outside a small office. Her arm extended, Harrett motioned for Brown to enter. As he did, a large man wearing khaki pants and a short-sleeve golf shirt that hugged his thick chest and biceps sprang to his feet. "Hey, I'm Skip Hayward. How are you?"

"I'm fine," Brown said. "How are you?"

"Thanks for comin' up," Hayward said. His casual attitude immediately put Brown at ease. "We're really happy you could make it."

"No problem at all," he said. Brown glanced around Hayward's tiny office. Indian artifacts cluttered the walls. Some feathers rested on a wooden shelf. Mountains of newspapers and files lined the walls along the floor. It was the most disorganized office Brown had ever seen.

"Well, I think everyone's here that's gonna be here. The tribal council is waiting in the conference room. Why don't I take you down and we can get started."

"OK."

In a rectangular room adjacent to Hayward's office, five tribal council members sat in metal chairs around a long folding table. Two brown ashtrays rested on its Formica top. Seated with the council was Rob Gips.

"Hi, Mickey," Gips said, extending his hand when Hayward escorted Brown in. "Let me introduce you to everyone."

Gips walked Brown around the table, giving him an opportunity to shake each council member's hand. "Mickey was in the Division of Gaming Enforcement in New Jersey when I worked for the state's chief justice," Gips told the council. "As you know, I've asked Mickey to come up and meet the tribe and talk about his involvement with gaming regulation and enforcement in the event that we go forward with a casino."

Hayward put down his coffee. "I'm sure you don't know much about Indians in Connecticut," he began. "But you have to understand, this is where we all lived, and all our ancestors lived. And then they all got killed off. Some got taken into slavery. Some got driven away. I've been around here since my grandmother's days, on the reservation. We've been very lucky, getting help from the state and federal recognition. With that came some money and some more land that we've been trying to build up and find ways to get people to come back to the reservation.

"And one way to get them back to the reservation is if we can offer them an opportunity," Hayward continued. "You know, a chance to be a part of something. We've raised lettuce, chopped wood, and raised pigs. Then we got into bingo in '86 and realized it's pretty lucrative. We run the bingo hall ourselves. And when we're done here, I'll take you down and show you what we have.

"But we've been talking as a tribe and we'd like to go ahead and expand this business into a casino. We wanna do it the right way and we wanna protect our reservation."

"Well, I'd certainly like to get involved up here," Brown said. "It sounds like a good project and I think I can help."

"I think the group would like to ask you some questions," said Hayward.

"I'll do my best to answer them," said Brown.

"Let's eat first," one of the tribal council members interjected, pointing out that it was nearly noon.

Everyone agreed, and soon one of the women of the council was taking orders. A half hour after the order was telephoned in to a nearby takeout deli, there was a knock at the door. A deliveryman entered carrying a cardboard box containing sandwiches wrapped in wax paper and cold cans of soda. Hayward's secretary took the order slip from his hand.

"What did you order?" she asked.

"Ham and cheese sandwich and a Coke," Brown said.

"That'll be $3.25," she said.

Brown handed a $5 bill for his sandwich as the six tribal leaders reached into their pockets and paid for their own lunch. Everyone contributed twenty-five cents toward the deliveryman's tip.

Brown couldn't help but grin to himself. This wasn't the usual catered business meeting.

Over the next two hours, Brown and the council discussed ways to insulate a casino from organized crime and how to set up regulations to protect the integrity of the operation. As they talked, Brown reflexively sized up the tribal leaders. They seemed genuine to him, without pretension. Their knowledge of gaming was limited to their experience with a successful but small bingo hall. They had no idea what they were getting into by building a casino. Still, there was Skip Hayward. In the little time he'd spent there, Brown saw clearly the authority he held and the unanimous willingness of the council to follow him wherever he would lead. The man had a vision.

Warming to them, Brown felt an obligation to provide a word of caution. "There are a lotta problems with casinos you gotta be ready to accept," he said to the group, while looking at Hayward. "It has its costs."

"Like what?" Hayward asked.

"Well, you're gonna increase business enormously," Brown said. "You're gonna draw large groups of people here, no question about it. But the glitz and the money of casinos sometimes have a corrupting influence on individuals. And there's another thing. Your neighbors aren't gonna like you. People are always going to try and find fault with what you're doing once you decide to put up a casino."

Satisfied with Brown's presentation, Hayward stood up. "C'mon with me," he said, waving his arm for Brown to follow him. "I wanna show you around."

Hearing raindrops on the metal roof, Brown grabbed his trench coat and followed Hayward outside to an old, brown Lincoln Town Car. Hayward drove it to a one-story rectangular building adjacent to a large empty parking lot.

"This is the bingo hall," Hayward said. "C'mon inside. Let me show you."

"These people are settin' up for a night session," Hayward said, pointing toward a small crew that was arranging chairs and tables that matched those in the tribal office. Brown looked around. The walls were cinderblock; the floors linoleum; the tables Formica. A snack bar in the corner had Coca-Cola signs hanging overhead. "Pretty spacious," he said.

"We get people comin' in on buses from all over," he said, walking Brown toward the rear of the hall. "Maybe we can start something here," Hayward continued, pointing in the direction of the wall farthest from the entrance to the bingo hall.

"You mean just put some gaming tables in at the back of the bingo hall?" Brown asked.

"Well, the only cleared land we have right now is the parking lot," Hayward said. "And we gotta keep bingo going. It's a very profitable business. So maybe we can build on to this and keep the bingo going at the same time."

"Well, what else do we got to build on here?" Brown asked.

"C'mon. I'll show you."

"Shouldn't we head back to the meeting?" Brown asked, noticing that the rain was picking up.

"No, c'mon."

Hesitating at the double glass doors leading outside, Brown looked at the rain. He was wearing dress shoes and his most expensive business suit.

"This guy's serious," Brown thought, staring at Hayward, who was holding the door open. "He really wants to go walk around the reservation in the pouring rain."

Not wanting to disappoint his prospective client, Brown buttoned his trench coat and pulled the collar up around his neck. Hayward led him across the parking lot toward the woods. "We could clear this all the way down to Lantern Hill Road," Hayward said. "It would give us a lot of space. And maybe we can open up the other side of the bingo hall and put a parking lot on that side of the hall. It is right next to Route 2, and we can make it wide open."

"Sounds good," Brown said. "It'd be nice to be right next to the highway."

"Here, come here," Hayward continued, sidestepping large rocks and tree stumps as he plodded into the woods.

Brown's feet sunk as he trailed Hayward into a swampy area, filling his leather shoes with mud up to his ankles. "I just wanna show you as far as we can go," Hayward said, oblivious to the weather.

Slipping as he tried to follow Hayward up a steep incline, Brown stopped. Goose bumps rose on his cold arms and legs. "Maybe we should head back," he suggested again.

"No, I gotta show you this," Hayward yelled over his shoulder as he pushed tree limbs from his path. "Let me walk you along the back property line."

His socks already soggy and his hair soaking wet, Brown trudged on, giving up on trying to stay dry.

"I think this is as far as we can go," Hayward said moments later. "If we get the casino going in the parking lot, then we can come back here and add a hotel and connect it both to the bingo hall and the casino."

Brown observed the enormous space between the two points Hayward was referring to. "What are we gonna put in the middle?" Brown asked.

"We're gonna put stores in the middle," Hayward said.

"*Stores?*" Brown asked.

"Yeah, like a shopping mall. Then everything would be all interconnected. And the people could come from bingo and park in back of the bingo hall. And the hotel would be on the other side. And the hotel guests would have a beautiful view into these woods."

"That'd be good," Brown said, impressed by Hayward's forethought.

"I wanna show you somethin' else," Hayward yelled over the sound of rain pelting the leaves.

Shivering, Brown felt the rain seeping through his suit to his undershirt. "You're gonna have to build garages," Brown said.

"Well, we're not gonna build garages up in the air," Hayward said. "If we're gonna build 'em, then they're gonna go down, underground. Because we're not gonna ruin the site."

"Where are you takin' me now?" Brown asked.

"You gotta see this view," Hayward said, climbing up on a rock. "Look, Mickey. Look. Look at the view from here." His wet, exposed arm fully extended, Hayward paused, looking like an explorer surveying newly discovered territory. "Isn't this beautiful?" he said. Tree-covered rolling hills stretched as far as the eye could see. "We just can't touch that. But here, right where we're standing, is where the casino is going to go, with this beautiful landscape as a backdrop."

Brown looked around. In every direction there was nothing but trees. There were no houses, no businesses, and not even a road. It struck Brown then that Hayward would build a casino in the middle of the woods on an Indian reservation. He saw it. The entire development plan was laid out in his mind. Hayward, coatless and drenched, with his hair matted down and mud up to his pant cuffs, was either a genius or a madman. "I've gotta work for this guy," Brown thought. "There's something about him. He's someone I wanna be with."

"And someday," Hayward said, repositioning himself on the rock and pointing back toward the direction where they had begun their trek, "I'm gonna build a museum there. It's gonna be a world-class Indian museum."

Brown nodded his head, forgetting how cold he was.

"Well, what do you think?" Hayward said. "What do you think of everything?"

Brown chuckled. "Skip, this is *amazing*," he said, shrugging his shoulders. "It's amazing. But don't you think we should just start by getting up a rectangular building comparable to the size of the bingo hall?"

"Well, we can, but here's where we're gonna wind up," Hayward said. "C'mon, let's head back."

"OK," said Brown. "I feel like a wet rat."

Hayward laughed. "So when can you start?" he asked.

"Well," Brown said, caught off guard by Hayward's directness, "does the tribal council need to meet and discuss whether they want me to work for the tribe?"

"Oh, they do," Hayward said. "We want you."

"Then I already started."

On May 15, 1990, just two weeks after Brown met Hayward, Judge Dorsey ruled in favor of the tribe and ordered the state to negotiate a compact. "Connecticut permits games of chance," wrote Judge Dorsey in his decision, "albeit in a highly regulated form. Thus such gaming is not totally repugnant to the State's public policy. Connecticut permits other forms of gambling, such as a state-operated lottery, bingo, jai alai, and other forms of pari-mutuel betting. Connecticut 'regulates, rather than prohibits, gambling in general and [games of chance] in particular.'"

At the end of his written decision, Judge Dorsey appointed a mediator and gave the state and the tribe sixty days to conclude a tribal-state compact.

The state appealed Dorsey's ruling to the U.S. Court of Appeals. While awaiting the appeals court ruling, Brown convinced Hayward to hire his friend Al Luciani to help Brown set up the casino operation. Luciani, who had previously worked with Brown in the New Jersey Attorney General's office, had just resigned as president of Golden Nugget Resorts in Atlantic City. Together, Brown and Luciani took Hayward and the tribal leadership on a tour of Atlantic City, introducing them to the mayor, the police department, and the Division of Gaming Enforcement. Then they met with a small group of casino executives who shared their thoughts and experiences about the business.

By the time the U.S. Court of Appeals issued its decision on September 4 affirming Judge Dorsey's ruling, a conceptual design of the casino in Ledyard had been formed. The casino would be called Foxwoods, and be bigger and better than anything in Atlantic City or Las Vegas.

When Connecticut filed the appeal, it ignored Judge Dorsey's original sixty-day time limit to reach a compact with the tribe. Missing the deadline, Connecticut forfeited its opportunity to negotiate the terms of the compact, triggering provisions in the Indian Gaming Regulatory Act that now required both the state and the tribe to submit to the court-appointed mediator a "last best offer" for a compact. The mediator's job was to choose the one that he felt was most consistent with the purpose of the Indian Gaming Regulatory Act. If the state did not consent to the mediator's choice, the matter was turned over to the secretary of Interior. IGRA authorized the secretary to approve the compact in its proposed form or to make amendments to it after soliciting input from the state and the tribe.

Governor O'Neill and Connecticut attorney general Clarine Riddle found themselves running up against a mountain of unfamiliar federal rules and procedures. Each appeal they made seemed to backfire, lessening the state's chances of stopping the Pequots. Meanwhile, Hayward sat back and watched his attorneys methodically secure for him the chance to fulfill his dream. Tureen had laid the groundwork for a casino back in 1982. In settling the tribe's land dispute with the Ledyard landowners, Tureen got the Connecticut legislature to agree not to enforce its regulatory laws on the Pequot reservation. Now Brown was creating for the tribe its own set of regulatory laws to police its gaming operation. And the federal government had put in place a law that left Connecticut no choice but to comply.

Brown submitted his proposed version of the tribal-state compact to the mediator first. Riddle and her deputy attorney general, Richard Sheridan, followed, turning over a massive 275-page document titled "Proposal of the State of Connecticut for a Tribal-State Compact between the Mashantucket Pequot Tribe and the State of Connecticut." In painstaking detail, the proposal defined hundreds of casino terms from "Handle" to "Pit." It also put in place procedures for the state to license casino employees and outlined a process that would enable the Connecticut State Police to enforce the state's criminal laws within any gaming facilities built on the reservation. Tribal police would have jurisdiction over the reservation proper. But the state police would retain jurisdiction within any gaming facilities. Finally, the compact called for an internal regulatory agency overseen by the tribe to protect against fraud and corruption. So once the state conducted background investigations and licensed a casino employee, it became the tribe's responsibility to ensure that employees complied with the law.

With both versions before him, the mediator began reviewing them in order to decide whose to select as the official governing document for the Pequots' gambling facilities: the tribe's or the state's. During the review period, Brown did his own appraisal of the state's version and recognized that it hardly differed from the one he had drafted for the Pequots. He then stunned Connecticut officials by withdrawing the tribe's compact, leaving the mediator no choice but to accept the state's version. He knew the tribe would be no worse off under the state's version, yet he had suddenly created the impression that the tribe was compromising to accommodate the state.

The tactical move produced just the affect that Brown wanted. Since the mediator's choice still had to be approved by the secretary of Interior, Brown figured he could virtually assure a favorable decision by demonstrating to the secretary that the tribe was willing to accept the state's version. Connecticut officials did not appreciate Brown's strategy. "To say that this is what the state wants is incorrect," complained Sheridan. "We do not want casino gambling." To demonstrate this point, Connecticut refused to sign its version of the compact after the mediator selected it. It had already appealed to the U.S. Supreme Court and was waiting to hear back from the court on whether it would hear the state's complaint about being forced to allow casino gambling within its borders.

With the Supreme Court not expected to make an announcement until May of 1991 as to whether it would add Connecticut's case to its docket, the mediator announced on October 22, 1990, that he was forwarding the state's unendorsed version to Secretary of Interior Manuel Lujan for final approval. The mediator's announcement was heralded as a victory for Native Americans. It put the Pequots on pace to become the first Indian tribe in America to build a full-scale casino. The *New York Times* announced the decision under the heading, "Indians in Connecticut Get Casino Gambling." The attention of the national press coincided with a conscious effort on the part of the tribe's lawyers to downplay its plans to build a Las Vegas–size casino in Ledyard. The plan called for Hayward not to make any public comments about the conceptual design. No one other than a tribal spokesperson was to answer questions from the press. It marked the beginning of a controlled effort on the part of Hayward's ever expanding team of legal advisers to screen media access to Hayward and his plans. Although accustomed to candidly discussing his future hopes with reporters, Hayward went along, fully understanding why candor about massive casino development would conjure up tremendous public opposition from neighboring towns.

The *New York Times* reported that a tribal spokesperson said "that no specific plans have been made about building a casino on the reservation." The spokesperson said only that the tribe had broken ground on an expansion of the bingo hall. "The tribe would not simply put up a tent and do some games," the *Times* was told.

The tribe's public relations strategy was intended primarily to protect its relationship with the town of Ledyard and its residents. Both had accepted the tribe's bingo hall as a relatively harmless operation that did little to increase traffic or crime in the community. "They've been good neighbors," said Ledyard town attorney Thomas B. Wilson. "It [the bingo hall] really hasn't impacted on the rest of the town." Residents who lived near the reservation even endorsed the bingo hall as an honest effort on the part of the tribe to be economically self-sufficient.

Weeks after the federal mediator forwarded the state's version of the compact to Secretary Lujan for final approval, Connecticut elected a new governor, former senator Lowell Weicker. He disdained gambling and vowed to continue the battle started by O'Neill to stop a casino from coming to Connecticut. But unless the Supreme Court ruled against the tribal-state compact, Weicker would be governor of a state with the biggest casino in the United States, to be built by a tribe he helped to create.

25

SECURED TRANSACTION

DECEMBER 27, 1990
LAW OFFICE OF BROWN & MICHAEL
ATLANTIC CITY, NEW JERSEY

BROWN KNEW THE STATISTICS. THE SUPREME COURT RECEIVES APPROXImately five thousand petitions a year from litigants seeking to have their cases reviewed. With only nine justices, the Court is equipped to handle less than 5 percent of those. The other 95 percent are turned away without a hearing, leaving the lower court decision to stand. The chances that Connecticut's case would be selected for review by the Supreme Court were no better than one in ninety-five. Brown liked those odds. And as an attorney in the gambling business, he had gotten used to relying on odds.

He also knew that Hayward had been riding one terrific spree of good luck, stretching all the way back to 1983 when Congress and the president decided to recognize him and his people as a federal Indian tribe. They had not lost a court case since. But good-luck streaks do not last forever. Brown feared that the same thing that started Hayward's lucky streak—his new status as chief of a federal Indian tribe—was about to end it.

For all the benefits of such status—and there were many—it was a liability when it came to borrowing money. And without money, Brown knew that Hayward's glorious dream to build a world-class casino and resort would never amount to more than a cheap fantasy.

The development that Hayward had in mind for his reservation was going to cost somewhere in the neighborhood of $250 million. Although he planned to build the casino in phases, the first phase alone had an estimated cost of $60 million. Gips had been out trying to find investors to finance the construction of the casino. But twenty-three different banks and brokerage firms from Wall Street to Boston had turned the Pequots down. Not one was interested in lending millions of dollars to an Indian tribe that planned to build a casino on a reservation.

Brown fully understood why. Hayward was asking banks to take a big risk but was unable to offer them the collateral to secure their investment. As Brown sat at his desk, he tried to put himself in a lender's position. "The borrower, in this case the Pequots, does not own the land they want to build the casino on," Brown thought. "The deed to the land says 'United States of America.' So if the tribe doesn't own the land, they can't mortgage it. You can't mortgage what you don't own. And if you can't issue a mortgage, how are you going to protect your investment? How would you collect if the tribe defaults on the loan for the casino building? You can't foreclose on the building. It is Indian land, owned by the United States in trust for the benefit of the tribe."

As the head of a new Indian tribe, Hayward was experiencing what old Indian tribes had known for generations. Tribes live in trailers for a reason: Banks will not take a home mortgage on land owned by the United

States. In the process of obtaining the legal rights entitling him to build an Indian gaming casino, Hayward had subjected himself to a system of Indian laws that caused American investors to shun him.

Brown got up from his chair and faced the window. He could see Atlantic City's famous Boardwalk. The casinos were open. It was two days after Christmas, yet they were busy. The holidays, especially the Christmas holidays, always meant good business for casinos. He understood why Hayward had worked so hard to get his family declared a tribe. But it was getting harder for Brown to envision holiday crowds filling up a casino in Ledyard.

As he sat back down at his desk, the telephone started to ring. Brown did not feel like answering it. Both the secretaries and his law partner were off for the holidays, and he was not in a talking mood. He thought about letting the answering machine pick up. Then he noticed the call was coming in on his private line.

"This is Mickey," he said, putting the receiver to his ear.

He recognized the voice on the other end immediately. It was coming all the way from Kuala Lumpur. It belonged to Colin Au, who worked for Brown's richest client. Au was a top executive for Genting Berhad, a Malaysian-based company that is publicly traded on the Hong Kong and Singapore Stock Exchanges. Au works directly under Lim Goh Tong, a Chinese national who is the chairman of Genting Berhad. *Forbes* magazine listed Lim as one of the richest billionaires in the world. His company's principal activities included hotels and resorts, plantations, property development, tour and travel-related services, utilities, manufacturing and trading in paper products, and supplying electric power. Lim also built the biggest resort casino in the world in 1978—Genting Highlands, the only casino in Malaysia.

Brown was always happy to hear from Au and Lim. They had hired him back in 1984 to help expand Genting Berhad's gaming industry in other parts of the world. In 1988, they appointed Brown as the director of Genting International Management Limited, a subsidiary of Genting Berhad. Brown was responsible for meeting with the company's representatives in London and New York four times a year to discuss gaming expansion in other parts of the world. Brown had also helped Genting develop a huge casino in Australia. Au and Lim were movers and shakers in the world of gaming. When they called and wanted Brown to go somewhere, he went.

"We're going to be in New York this week," Au told Brown. "Why don't you meet us for dinner and stay overnight in New York. We want to talk to you about some projects that we might want you to look at."

"Great," Brown replied, quickly forgetting about the depressing situation in Ledyard.

When Au and Lim arrived in New York two days later, they had brought with them Lim Kok Thay ("K. T."), Lim's son who served as the joint manager of the company. Brown met them at the Golden Dragon, a Chinese restaurant on East Broadway in Manhattan. By the time dinner was over, they had given Brown an assignment to look at a project they were considering in another country. Au then asked, "What else is going on? What else are you doing?"

"I'm working for an Indian tribe in Connecticut," Brown responded. "They've got the right to build a casino right off Interstate 95 in Ledyard, Connecticut. It's been approved by the federal court. *It's on appeal.* But we're confident we'll win. But we can't borrow the money to build it."

Au, Lim, and K. T. said nothing. But Brown could see from their faces that he had their attention. "We need financing," he continued. "We need about $60 million."

There was another pause.

"Tell us more," Au said.

Brown had a feeling Hayward's good-luck streak had just been revived. Genting had been expanding its gaming enterprise into countries far beyond the Asian rim. Brown had been helping Lim move his gaming empire into Australia, Europe, and South Africa. But Genting had not entered the most lucrative market in the world, America. Genting was eligible to apply for licensing in Atlantic City and Las Vegas. But Lim's style was to avoid areas that were saturated with gaming opportunities. His Malaysian casino thrived because it was the only one in the country. He preferred to enter a region that was heavily populated, build one world-class resort casino, and watch it thrive amidst no competition. Neither Vegas nor Atlantic City offered those conditions. And the rest of America was off limits, since casinos were illegal in every other state.

Au, Lim and K. T. listened intently as Brown laid out the whole history of how Hayward and his small tribe had secured the right to build a casino in Connecticut, free of government interference. He told them about the Indian gaming law and the trouble that the tribe had encountered trying to finance their plans.

"Let's go talk to them," Au said.

The next morning, Brown, Lim, Au, and K. T. filed into a stretch limousine and rode to Ledyard. Brown rarely traveled with the seventy-year-old Lim. And he knew that there was not much in Ledyard to show one of the richest and most well traveled men in the entire world. By Genting's standards, Hayward's little bingo operation was nothing. And the properties closest to it were nothing but farms and woods. It was rural New England, not the Las Vegas strip. There were no high-class restaurants. No luxurious hotels. Just woods and farms.

But even before he stepped out of the limousine, Lim was satisfied. He had timed the limousine ride from Manhattan to Ledyard. The biggest city in the United States was just a two-hour drive away.

Once outside the limousine, Lim immediately saw something else that no investor on Wall Street had envisioned. Twelve years earlier, when he built Genting Highlands, Lim chose a location known for its beautiful scenery. Lim built it in a heavily wooded area on top of a mountain.

As Brown nervously watched Lim look around the Ledyard woods, he knew from the expression on his face that he liked what he saw. "He sees Genting Highlands," Brown realized. "No competition, this would be the only legal casino in New England. It has a beautiful setting. And it is easily accessible by a major highway."

Lim and his associates then asked for a walking tour of the reservation. They were primarily interested in seeing the portion of the reservation that comprised the property previously owned by George Main. It offered the most scenic landscape, with its rich variety of trees and wildlife. And it directly abutted Route 2. Hayward, dressed in a business suit, proudly took the group on a walking tour.

By the end of the day, Lim and his associates had seen enough. At the conclusion of their visit, they called Steven Horowitz, their attorney who specialized in setting up large financial transactions for foreign companies looking to invest in the United States. Horowitz's law firm, Cleary, Gottlieb, Steen & Hamilton, is one of New York's biggest and most respected. Horowitz's firm was introduced to Lim and his Genting company a few years earlier by Solomon Brothers, a Wall Street firm that had done business with both parties.

By the time Horowitz talked with his Genting clients, they had already assessed both the risks and the upside benefits to financing a casino on the Pequot reservation. The risk was whether the gambling public would respond to a casino run by Indians, historically treated as outsiders both politically and in the business world.

But to Genting, the benefits far outweighed the risks. Expert in the casino business, Genting saw that the Northeast was a vastly underserved geographic area in a country that has a strong appetite for gambling. Ten percent of the American population lived within driving distance of Ledyard. New York and Boston were two hours away. Philadelphia, Baltimore, and Washington were less than seven hours away. And a host of smaller cities such as Hartford, New Haven, Providence, Worcester, Springfield, and Syracuse were only a few hours away. Even Toronto and Montreal were less than a day's drive.

And unlike a typical lender, Genting was qualified and eager to help the Pequots set up and run Foxwoods. Since there was no limit to how big the tribe could build its casino, the Genting group envisioned a casino that exceeded Genting Highlands, far beyond anything in Atlantic City or Las Vegas. And there was more than enough real estate to keep expanding the resort in the future.

Lim was well aware of the reasons American investors turned down the opportunity to finance the Pequots' casino, particularly the fact that the tribe could not mortgage their land because it was owned by the U.S. government. But Lim and his Genting associates had a creative method for protecting their interests that would not require a mortgage on the land. With Horowitz's help, they created a subsidiary company called Kien Huat Realty and appointed Lim's son, K. T. Lim as its director. The company's sole purpose was to finance the construction of the casino in Ledyard. Horowitz then negotiated a deal with Hayward's lawyers that allowed Kien Huat Realty to loan $60 million to the tribe to build the first phase of its casino. Together, the lawyers from both sides came up with a way to protect Kien Huat's investment without taking a mortgage. Horowitz recognized a provision in the federal Indian Gaming Regulatory Act that permitted non-Indians to manage casinos for up to seven years, as long as the BIA approved it.

As collateral, Lim and his associates wanted Hayward to agree to let the Genting group take over the management of the casino in Ledyard if the tribe defaulted on their loan payments.

The parties agreed to meet in Horowitz's Manhattan law office on February 25 to negotiate the other contingencies that Genting wanted in the contract. The deal they were contemplating posed some legal issues that had not been debated before Congress passed the Indian gaming law. In theory, Hayward was prepared to sign a contract that would give a foreign company owned by a Chinese nationalist the right to take over the operation of an American Indian casino built on land owned by the U.S. government but located within the state of Connecticut. Would the federal government recognize this complex financing agreement if the tribe actually defaulted on the loan? Lawyers on both sides knew the complicated question had likely not been considered by Congress.

FEBRUARY 25, 1991
NEWARK AIRPORT

"I'll take you . . . I'll take you where you want to be," sang Michael Hutchence, the lead singer of INXS, his Mick Jagger–like voice escaping from the windows of Mickey Brown's Cadillac Sedan DeVille. Brown did not go to law school to become a chauffeur. "Me, the wheelman, and five members of the tribal council and their luggage," he thought to himself, chuckling as he stood at the rear of his car holding a piece of rope in his hands. Hayward, dressed in a business suit, was helping his four tribal councilors load their luggage into the trunk. All four of them had come to watch Hayward sign the loan documents that were being drafted by their attorneys over at Horowitz's law firm. Their administration building was contained in a construction trailer, yet they were on their way to sign a loan for $60 million.

Brown stretched out the rope in his hands. The garment bags and suitcases were piled so high, he could not close the trunk. So he ran the rope through the trunk lid and tied it to the rear bumper. They exited the airport and headed toward Wall Street, where Brown thrived. The fast tempo, the big buildings, the intense atmosphere—all of it fit Brown's lifestyle. Hayward always preferred Montana. But he liked what New York had to offer: money. By the time Brown delivered him to his hotel at the World Trade Center, Hayward could not wait to go where no Indian tribe in history had gone before—to the top of the business world, where America's real power source lies.

Unable to check into their rooms until noon, Hayward and the others left their bags at the front desk and followed Brown across the street to the law offices of Cleary, Gottlieb. Gips and Horowitz were already inside trying to finalize their deal. The tribe had agreed to waive its sovereign immunity, giving Genting the right to sue them in a federal court if they failed to abide by the contract.

Genting also reserved the right to approve the president and CEO of the casino. Anyone the tribe wanted to appoint to that position was subject to Genting's approval. Genting warmly received Hayward's choice of Al Luciani, knowing he had learned the business under Steve Wynn.

The tribe had also agreed to pay Genting principal and interest as well as an incentive interest based on the success of the casino.

But both sides hit a snag in negotiations when it came to working out Genting's right in the contract to take over management of the casino if the tribe defaulted. Both sides needed the consent of the Bureau of Indian Affairs before it could move forward. Calls were made to the BIA's eastern area director, Billie Ott. If he did not go along, the deal was off.

While waiting for the deal to be finalized, Hayward and his four tribal council members passed a tribal resolution entitled "Mashantucket Pequot Tribal Gaming Ordinance: Regulating Certain Class II & Class III Gaming Activities." Barry Margolin and Gips prepared the twenty-three-page document, which authorized the establishment of a commission, overseen by the tribe, to regulate the casino. The commission had the power to conduct annual audits and investigate any aspect of the casino operation to ensure its integrity and lawfulness. The tribe chose Brown as chairman of the Mashantucket Pequot Gaming Commission. The ordinance also identified all the games the tribe would offer: blackjack, poker, dice, money wheels, roulette, baccarat, chuck-a-luck, pan game, over and under, horse race games, acey-deucey, beat the dealer, bouncing ball, and various lottery and horse and dog racing. Hayward signed the last page of the document, affirming that he and his tribal council had unanimously approved the ordinance.

Brown, Hayward, and the council members had been waiting the entire time in a large conference room across the hall. Their spouses, who had flown down separately after lunch, joined them there. Al Luciani was also present. All of them had been sipping soda and eating snacks for hours, waiting for the word that it was all right for Hayward to sign the deal. "Why don't we go take a walk," Brown suggested. "Let's get some fresh air." Everyone agreed that was a good idea and followed Brown across the street to walk around the Trade Center park. But the air was so cold, no one wanted to stay outside very long.

When they returned just before 5:00 P.M., Brown went into the room where the negotiations were taking place to see if there were any new developments. He returned to the conference room with news. "The loan gives the tribe $60 million," said Brown. "It gives Genting principal and interest. It gives them an incentive interest based on the success of the property. And in the event of default, the lender can apply to the Department of Interior's Bureau of Indian Affairs for the right to take over operation of the casino and run it, taking a portion of the profits until the loan is satisfied."

Billie Ott had agreed to go along with the proposal.

"We gotta have a dinner," Hayward announced. "We gotta have a celebration. And we need a lot of real good champagne."

"Where do you wanna go?" Brown asked.

"Can you call Windows on the World and see if I can have a dinner there?"

Brown liked Hayward's choice. The restaurant offered Rémy Martin Louis XIII cognac for $120 a bottle. An appetizer of caviar was $55. World-class chefs cooked duck, rack of lamb, and filet mignon. The tables were covered in fine white tablecloths; the seats softly cushioned, and admittance was restricted to those wearing a suit jacket. But Windows on the World was a landmark because of its spectacular views—the best in the world. Located atop the World Trade Center, its entire exterior is nothing but windows.

Brown walked over to a secretary at the law firm and had him dial up Windows on the World. The firm knew the people at the restaurant well and soon got a hostess on the line. "I represent an Indian tribe," Brown said. "We're just closing a loan next door and would like to have a dinner for about thirty people or more."

"I can put you in a private dining room," the hostess offered. "It's kind of a big room, but we can partition it."

"We'll take it," Brown said.

The hostess then suggested a menu with an entrée choice of fish or meat.

"That's fine," said Brown. "And plenty of champagne." Then he walked back over to Hayward, who was already celebrating with his wife and fellow tribal members. "Skip," said Brown, "we got a dinner."

Moments later, at 7:00 P.M., the lawyers were finally ready for Skip and K. T. Lim to sign the agreement. Long legal-size documents were placed in front of them. The top copy read "CONSTRUCTION MORTGAGE LEASE Between THE MASHANTUCKET PEQUOT TRIBE Lessor AND KIEN HUAT REALTY LIMITED Lessee." Hayward signed first, on a line that said "Richard A. Hayward, Chairman" underneath it. His signature was witnessed by two of his council members. Then K. T. Lim signed his name on a line that read "Lim Kok Thay, Director" underneath it. Colin Au and another member of the Genting group witnessed his signature.

Brown's adrenaline rushed as he watched the signing. "We got money. We got a casino. We're going to Windows on the World," he thought. He knew the whole deal was contingent on the Supreme Court declining to hear Connecticut's appeal—the Pequots had agreed not to draw on the loan until the court reached a decision. But the odds were one in ninety-five.

After the final signatures were applied, the attorneys took the documents and placed them in an envelope to be overnighted to Billie Ott in Washington for his signature.

Brown led Hayward and his group out of the law firm. Once they got outside, Brown leaped from the top step to the sidewalk. "We got us a casino," he shouted.

Across the street, the group lined up in the lobby of the World Trade Center and waited for an elevator. Two ushers dressed in dark jackets directed them toward the private elevator leading to Windows on the World. As Hayward entered, he saw buttons with numbers on them as high as 107. He was going all the way to the top, the 107th floor.

When the doors opened moments later, Hayward and the others were led down a carpeted hallway toward the restaurant. They passed an immaculately clean bathroom. Just inside the entryway, a black man wearing a white suit stood holding soft, white cotton hand towels. As restaurant patrons exited the bathroom after washing their hands, they extended their wet hands toward the man, who used his towel to gently dry them. Everything was done for the guests.

The dining area was dimly lit. Hayward had never seen such dazzling views. From so high above, the intimidating New York skyline was reduced to a carpet of lights. Looking down on the city, he knew that he had arrived. Everyone expected him to deliver a speech. He was, after all, their new ticket to fabulous wealth. Without him, there was no legal basis for building America's biggest casino in Ledyard, Connecticut. He held the key. He was treated as neither an American nor a foreigner, both of whom were barred from gaming in Connecticut. Hayward was the chief of a sovereign nation.

"Can I get everybody's attention," Brown said, standing next to Hayward. "Skip would like to propose a toast."

Smiling, Hayward raised his glass. "To our new partners, the Lim family, who are gonna help the tribe achieve its goals."

In response, K. T. Lim stood and raised his glass. "Today we celebrate the marriage of two families."

26

I WOULDN'T TAKE MY DOG TO ATLANTIC CITY

"I do not want casino gambling as a fact of life in our state. I don't want it laid at my door that Lowell Weicker did anything less than his best."

The announcement came at 9:30 A.M. on Tuesday, April 30, 1991. Governor Weicker was taking call-ins on Groton radio station WSUB. He made it clear that he was not ready to stop the legal fight against a casino coming to Groton's neighboring town. "I've left open the whole question," Weicker continued, "whether there are legal options the state should be pursuing."

Weicker's statements generated a front-page headline in the *New*

London Day: "Casino Plan Threatened by Weicker." The newspaper reported that Weicker had "launched a determined effort to block a planned gambling casino on the Mashantucket Pequot reservation in Ledyard." From the state's capital in Hartford Weicker said, "The Indians would be attracting organized crime, prostitution, and drunk driving." The governor also announced that he was calling on the Connecticut legislature to pass emergency legislation repealing the state's Las Vegas Night law. He wanted to outlaw the charitable practice to take away the tribe's justification for setting up a casino. "There's no question in my mind, nobody ever contemplated that Las Vegas Nights were an invitation to casino gambling," said Weicker.

Weicker's ploy shocked Hayward, Brown, and the tribe's attorneys. They knew he was unhappy with the Pequots' plans but didn't think he'd go to such lengths. Right after he was elected, Weicker had called them to his Hartford office to discuss their intentions and express his stance against gambling. He told them he was particularly concerned about organized crime coming into Connecticut. Hayward had both Luciani and Brown with him at that meeting, hoping their presence would ease Weicker's fears. "We've brought in Mickey Brown," Hayward said. "He was in charge of regulating Atlantic City."

"I know who Mickey Brown is," Weicker said indignantly, interrupting Hayward. "And I wouldn't take my dog to Atlantic City. That's what I think of Atlantic City and gambling."

Brown, angered by the remark, immediately stood up to walk out. But Hayward grabbed him by the arm. "Don't get up," he whispered in Brown's ear. "Sit back down."

Hayward then continued his presentation. He knew Weicker was furious, but he was confident Weicker could not stop them. Hayward's confidence, however, suffered a bit when Weicker vowed to make all forms of gambling illegal in the state.

"Indian people have faced a long and tragic history of broken treaties," Hayward told the media in response to Weicker's plan. "It would be very sad if Connecticut added another chapter to that history." Tribal lawyers insisted that Weicker was too late. Secretary of Interior Manuel Lujan had already issued a temporary decision approving the casino plan and was expected to issue a final ruling on May 14.

But on May 1, Weicker's attorney general, Richard Blumenthal, issued a formal opinion to Connecticut lawmakers backing Weicker's plan. His letter was addressed to the Senate president and the Senate majority leader. "We believe that eliminating the exception for Las Vegas Nights . . . would eliminate the legal basis for the District Court and Court of Appeals decisions that the Tribe was authorized under the Indian Gaming Regulatory Act to pursue casino gaming on its reservation," Blumenthal wrote. "The Secretary of the Interior has given notice that he intends to adopt the Compact submitted by but never agreed to by the State. The State has gone on record opposing the authorization, and interested parties have until May 17, 1991, to file comments."

Weicker's determination put him and Hayward at sharp odds. Less than a decade earlier, Weicker had been Hayward's biggest ally in Washington. Without his help, Skip would never have obtained the right to pursue a gambling enterprise in the first place. Suddenly, he had gone from the tribe's favorite politician to public enemy number one. The Pequots' spokesman issued a statement reminding the public that this was just another example of Indians getting shafted.

With Weicker pushing for a vote in the state Senate on his proposed emergency legislation in less than one week, the tribe did not sit back—it hired lobbyists from the Hartford law firm Robinson & Cole. The lobbyists' impact was immediate. First, every one of the state's thirty-five senators was contacted, many of whom came to the Pequots' defense. "I mean, how many treaties does the white man have to break?" asked state senator Lawrence Bettencourt, who said he had personally polled twelve of his sixteen Republican colleagues and that all but one of them were voting against Weicker's proposal. "I just don't think it's the proper way to go. It's a delaying tactic."

Second, Sam Gejdenson, who had cosponsored with Weicker the tribe's lawsuit settlement legislation, weighed in against his old friend. "If this was an American corporation that had worked out a deal with the state and the state tried to change it after the deal was done, I think there would be an uproar," Gejdenson said from Washington.

Third, the tribe released information to the press that downplayed the size of its casino plans. Al Luciani, who had been named to run the casino, called comparisons between the tribe's casino and the Taj Mahal in Atlantic City "ridiculous," saying the tribe's model would be "a conservative casino in a conservative environment."

"They have no intention of glitzing up or trashing the neighborhood," Luciani said.

Finally, the tribe unveiled a plan to pump $1 million into local tourism. The announcement was made in a letter from the tribe to state senator Steven Spellman, whose Stonington home was just minutes from the tribe's reservation. "It is the intention of the tribe to establish a budget of at least one million dollars annually, for the promotion of regional tourism in eastern Connecticut," Hayward wrote. "This promotional budget will be coordinated through the regional tourism district together with the area chambers of commerce and will, we hope, be supplemented by additional contributions of other members of the regional tourism industry." Hayward also promised to contribute funding to the local transportation and police departments from towns neighboring the casino. Spellman, who initially supported Weicker's plan, changed his mind and announced he would vote against Weicker's plan. "My reading is that a majority in both chambers is opposed to the amendment," he said.

Weicker responded to the tribe's aggressive lobbying campaign with a campaign of his own. On May 8, one day before the Senate planned to hold its vote, he issued a two-page flier to every state legislator outlining the dangers that accompany casino gambling. It contained a litany of threats to public safety, health, and the environment, including prostitution and drug use that he implied would increase the spread of AIDS, tuberculosis, hepatitis, and other diseases in the state. At an afternoon press conference, Weicker also pointed out that neither he nor the Indians could assure the public that organized crime would not come to Connecticut with the casino. "I'm not going to go ahead and make that statement," said Weicker. "I can do my best, but I don't think I'm going to be able to defy history."

Weicker told the press corps that if the legislature did not approve his emergency legislation it would be fully responsible for any problems that arose from the casino. "If the legislature does not cooperate—let's say they vote against it—then the advent of casino gambling in the state of Connecticut sits on their heads," said Weicker. "It's as simple as that. The question is whether or not the state of Connecticut is going to be stripped, by its own legislature, of its sovereignty."

Weicker's pressure tactics worked. On May 9, the state senate voted 18 to 17 in favor of Weicker's emergency legislation. His warnings against organized crime swayed the vote. Senator Fred Lovegrove, a Republican from Fairfield who had planned to vote against Weicker's plan, cast the deciding vote. He changed his mind after talking to Stanley Twardy, a former U.S. attorney working for Weicker. "Stan explained to me how money-laundering works," Lovegrove said. "As much as the Indians believe there will be no organized crime there, it's going to go in there."

The tribe's supporters in the Senate dismissed Weicker's warnings, however. "I can guarantee you that organized crime will never get an inch of a foothold into the Mashantucket tribe," said Senator Steven Spellman, disappointed in his colleagues' turnaround. "It will not happen, people. They have too many centuries of honor."

With the state House of Representatives scheduled to vote on the plan approved by the Senate, Weicker announced that he hoped Secretary Lujan would not approve the tribal-state compact if his bill passes. On the morning of May 16, however, Lujan's office announced that the secretary of the interior had already made up his mind. "He's going to sign it regardless of what the legislature in Connecticut does," said BIA spokesman Carl Shaw. By the evening of the 16th, it all became academic. The House defeated Weicker's plan in an 84-to-62 vote. Some state representatives ridiculed Weicker's warnings about the casino. "So this is Armageddon," said Representative Kevin Rennie from South Windsor, "where the world ends not with a bang, but with the spinning of a roulette wheel. Can anyone claim that one more addition [to gambling in the state] will mean an end to life as we know it?"

Publicly, Hayward was modest in victory, saying he held no bitterness toward Weicker. "I try to keep that feeling down," he said. "My grandmother told me when I was growing up as a child to never get involved in politics—that it's a dirty business."

One week later, Secretary Lujan published the tribal-state compact in the *Federal Register*, effectively making it a federal law. The following week the tribe broke ground on Foxwoods.

27

WHEEL OF FORTUNE

FOXWOODS OPENED ITS DOORS ON FEBRUARY 14, 1992. IT HAD TAKEN only 203 days from the groundbreaking to build the first phase, a sixty-thousand-square-foot structure that equaled the size of the smallest casino in Atlantic City. By 10:30 A.M., the casino's 1,700-space parking lot was filled to capacity. Eager gamblers entered the casino to find red and white poker chips neatly stacked in rows at the end of purple velvet tables. Comfortable chairs with high backs were arranged in a semicircle around them. The gold spindles on the wooden roulette wheels shone splendidly. The scent of newly laid carpet and fresh paint permeated the vast gaming area. And smiling, beautiful cocktail waitresses wearing imitation Indian costumes stood ready to serve.

By 12:30 in the afternoon, traffic was stalled to a standstill in both directions on Route 2 and state police were turning people away. By midnight, fifteen thousand people had entered the casino. All seventy-five table games were occupied. By 4:00 A.M., the scheduled closing time, two thousand people were still gambling. A decision was made on the spot to stay open round the clock. The second-shift workers were asked to stay on long enough to give the first shift time to get back to work early. For the next eight weeks, all employees worked long shifts until a third-shift staff could be hired and trained. Customer demand was so great that even Brown and Luciani's expectations were exceeded. Foxwoods was an instant gold mine.

To make room for Foxwoods, thousands of trees—white pines, hemlocks, and other species—had been clear-cut, reduced to mountains of wood chips and sawdust. Thousands of yards of concrete and tar had been poured in their place. Animals indigenous to the area, such as deer, partridge, raccoons, and birds, had undergone an overnight change in their habitat. With no local environmental laws to slow them down, the tribe had transformed the forest with an arsenal of excavators, backhoes, payloaders, concrete mixers, hydraulic drills, blasting equipment, and cranes. Yet the casino's instant success encouraged Hayward to push the building contractors to accelerate the casino's expansion.

Working closely with Brown and Luciani, Hayward asked the tribe's planning department to map out the long-term development plan for the future. On June 30, 1992, R. J. Birmingham, the tribe's director of planning and development, presented him with a memo that outlined the tribe's plans through 1995. It called for two enormous hotels, a ninety-thousand-square-foot community center for tribal members, a public safety facility, a forty-thousand-square-foot public-works building, and a monorail system to transport gamblers back and forth from Foxwoods. Birmingham's plan also reflected Hayward's dream to build a fifty-thousand-square-foot Indian museum.

But Skip was most interested in the last part of Birmingham's memo, entitled "Resort Development Projects for Near Future." It called for another casino with convention facilities and a showroom, all built on the other side of Route 2, directly across from the Foxwoods entrance. Birmingham's memo also reflected the tribe's plan to put in two eighteen-hole PGA golf courses; a camping area equipped to handle two hundred recreational vehicles; a fifty-thousand-square-foot shopping center; a 250-room resort lodge; a 100-room bed-and-breakfast; a skeet and hunting area; horse-riding stables; a baseball stadium; two restaurants; and a gas station and electric power plant to service this exclusive resort area.

Admiring Birmingham's skill at laying out development schemes, Hayward convinced him to abandon his job as a planner for the town of Stonington and come to work full-time for him and the tribe. The greatest skill Hayward had developed over the years was a deft ability to surround himself with capable people who possessed the practical knowledge to carry out his visions. He made it a habit of offering tremendous salaries to those most capable of getting in his way were they to work for the opposition. Birmingham was joined by the tribe's other new employee, attorney Jackson King.

After Foxwoods opened, King accepted Hayward's offer to come on board full-time as the tribe's general counsel. He was given an office on the reservation and put in charge of spearheading the tribe's push to go beyond the Settlement Area boundaries and obtain thousands of acres in Ledyard and the neighboring towns of North Stonington and Preston. Even before Foxwoods opened, Hayward and the tribe bought twenty-two properties in Ledyard that were outside the reservation. And in the six-month period following the opening of Foxwoods, the tribe bought seventeen more properties in Ledyard. Hayward viewed King as the natural choice to handle the tribe's real estate transactions. Not only was real estate law one of King's specialties, but King was someone Hayward could trust. After all, King had made possible all of Hayward's dreams by drawing the map that altered the reservation boundaries.

The tribe was so pleased with King that the tribal council voted to give him a substantial bonus on top of his new salary. King was called into council chambers and told of the bonus. He could hardly believe the amount. "Before we go any further," King said, interrupting the meeting, "I want to thank you for the bonus that you voted for me. I never expected anything like that. I never made that kind of money in my life. And I really appreciate you recognizing my efforts." With bonuses, King's annual salary was approximately $1 million.

"Those who labor in the earth are the chosen people of God," Thomas Jefferson once said. And Cliff Allyn believed it. That was why he bought the Spencer Hall farm in the first place—he simply loved farming. Working the land made him feel close to God and nature. It was also why it was easy for him to reject the tribe's offer to buy his three-hundred-acre farm for $250,000 in 1984. Some things are more important than money. Farming, Allyn believed, was one of them. He knew that America's small farms were in steep decline, and had been for decades. Ninety percent of the country's cropland was losing its topsoil to erosion faster than it could be replaced. Chemical-dependent conglomerates were buying out small farmers. And immigrant labor and produce imports were fast becoming the way of America's heartland. Cliff Allyn refused to let go of his three-hundred-acre farm.

But the tribe badly wanted that land for casino development. Their casino expansion was aimed directly at Allyn's farm. And they were sure they had the money to change his mind.

One fall day in 1991, Allyn saw a new Lincoln with New Jersey plates navigating down his long, dusty driveway. It stopped about twenty-five yards from where Allyn was leading a herd of dairy cows into the barn. A man in a designer suit stepped out and approached. A shiny watch was strapped to his wrist. Before the man said a word, Allyn had him figured out. He tucked his hands in the pockets of the blue apron that was tied over the top of his navy blue hooded sweatshirt. His black rubber boots, caked in manure, trudged slowly toward the man. When Allyn got close enough, he removed his right hand from his pocket and extended it toward the stranger. The man glanced at it. Dried mud stretched from Allyn's wrist to his fingertips. Reluctantly, he put his hand out and shook Allyn's hand. Then he introduced himself as a real estate agent working for the tribe. Allyn said nothing. The man then acknowledged that he was aware of the fact that Allyn had turned down an offer to sell the farm seven years earlier. But the tribe was prepared to make a new offer.

"How much," Allyn asked.

"Ten and a half million dollars," the man said.

Allyn could tell the man felt powerful just hearing himself say the words "ten and a half million dollars."

"Not interested," Allyn replied.

The tribe's real estate agent was incredulous. "You know what happened in Atlantic City, don't you?" he threatened. "There was a woman there like you. She owned a house and refused to sell to the casino companies when gambling was first legalized. Soon the casinos went up and just dwarfed her. Then she was forced to sell, and for much less money than she would have originally got. That's what's going to happen to you if you don't sell your farm."

Allyn did not know how big this lady's house was in Atlantic City. But he knew his farm encompassed three hundred acres. "If they're going to build over the top of me," he told the man, "they're going to have to be mighty big." And with that, he returned to his cows, leaving the man standing there in his fancy New York suit. "They think I'm just milking cows here," Allyn said under his breath. "But I know what's going on."

The man sped off, unable to believe that a small-time rural farmer so easily rejected a ten-and-a-half-million-dollar offer. By now Allyn had discovered that his farm was within the tribe's reservation boundary. As a result, he realized that if he ever did decide to sell, he essentially had only one prospective buyer—the tribe. No one else was going to purchase a farm located within an Indian reservation. It was irrelevant to him, though, since he never planned on selling it.

28

NEW IDENTITY

"CONGRATULATIONS."

Thirty-one-year-old Kenny Reels proudly accepted the praise for receiving more votes than any other candidate seeking election to the Mashantucket Pequot Tribal Council at the end of 1991. Reels had seldom experienced pride, praise, and popularity before joining the tribe in the mid-1980s. He had previously worked at an auto salvage yard. Now he was empowered to control and manage the affairs of the tribe alongside Hayward on the tribe's five-member governing body, which also acted as the board of directors for Foxwoods Casino. Reels's addition to the tribal council marked a change. When Hayward formed the tribal council and became its chairman, all the councilors were his relatives and his mother acted as vice-chairman. As such, they were well acquainted and understood their role: help Hayward build a community and a business enterprise to sustain it. However, Reels was not a blood relative of Hayward's, a point that concerned some of Hayward's family members. His qualifications for admittance to the tribe were largely a mystery. But the Haywards accepted him—albeit reluctantly—because Skip did. And Hayward had earned the kind of trust from his tribe that evangelists crave—purely blind faith. But even Hayward knew little about Reels's identity when he agreed to let him join the tribe.

Kenneth Mitchell Reels was born at 17 Hope Court, a twenty-by-twenty-four-foot box-shaped house with one bathroom and three bedrooms. The house in Wakefield, Rhode Island, a rural village in the town of South Kingston, had no heat or hot water and a dirt floor in the basement. Days later his mother received his birth certificate indicating his birth on April 18, 1960, and identifying his race as "Negro." The same classification was inscribed on the line calling for the race of his parents, Thomas Reels Sr., who worked at a railroad yard picking up cardboard, and Juanita Helen Sebastian, a homemaker.

Reels was born into a stormy household. His mother, a high school dropout from New York City, was fifteen when she became pregnant by seventeen-year-old Thomas Reels, who was also a high school dropout. On January 17, 1957, Juanita gave birth to Stewart Reels, their first child. On May 10, 1958, Juanita and Thomas married. Four days later, Juanita gave birth to their second child, Thomas Reels Jr. For each of the following six years, the couple had a child. Before Juanita's thirtieth birthday, they had eleven children. In all, they had fourteen children.

Kenny was the fourth-oldest child, experiencing more of the turmoil in his parents' marriage than some of his younger siblings did. In addition to being destitute and constantly pregnant, Juanita suffered violently at the hands of her husband. Eventually, she sought help from a clinic designed to provide legal aid to poor people. There, she confided that her husband had beaten her, knocked her teeth out, attacked her with a machete, and threatened to put a bullet in her head. He also threatened her children.

On January 26, 1973, when Kenny was twelve years old, his father was arrested for child abuse, though the victim in the case was not one of Kenny's siblings. The charges were filed in the neighboring town of Narragansett by Ruth Hay, an unmarried white woman Thomas Reels had been living with while he was still married to Juanita. Reels had fathered four children by Ms. Hay before being arrested for assaulting the youngest one, Bonnie Jean Hay, a sixteen-month-old baby girl.

Two days earlier, Bonnie Jean Hay had been rushed to the hospital in critical condition, having sustained massive head injuries. She was quickly transferred to the pediatric intensive-care unit at Rhode Island Hospital, where she died on January 28. Reels ultimately pleaded guilty to manslaughter and was sentenced to nine years in state prison. Five months later, Kenny started his freshman year at South Kingston High School, the same school his father had attended before dropping out.

The identity of Kenny's father was no secret in rural South Kingston. Homicides in the area were extremely rare, particularly ones involving children. But high school marked the beginning of Kenny's emergence from his father's shadow. He graduated in four years, never got in trouble with the law, and established a reputation among students and teachers as courteous, respectful, and hardworking. One of the most athletic kids in the school, Reels also excelled on the school's basketball team.

During his sophomore year he was approached by his biology teacher, Bill McEneaney, and invited to join the high school tennis team. Reels had never played tennis and viewed the game as one for rich white kids. But

McEneaney, who was the tennis coach and had a personal interest in helping Reels succeed, offered to teach him how to play. Within weeks, Reels could beat his coach and agreed to join the team. By his senior year, Reels led the team to the state championship.

While Kenny was a junior in high school and his father was incarcerated in state prison, Juanita Reels took steps aimed at giving her children a better life and a new identity. She decided to become a member of a tribe in North Stonington, Connecticut. North Stonington was home to the other reservation that surviving Pequots were assigned to in the aftermath of the Pequot War of 1637. The state of Connecticut had officially recognized the Indians on the two reservations as separate tribes—the Eastern Pequots of North Stonington and the Western Pequots of Ledyard. Both reservations were dormant when Hayward led the effort to revitalize the one in Ledyard, and his success inspired a group claiming to be descendants from the old Eastern Pequot Tribe. They began recruiting people who wanted to join the tribe to take advantage of the benefits Hayward had managed to secure in Ledyard.

Attempts by Reels and others to join the tribe prompted the state of Connecticut's Indian Affairs Council—a state agency comprising representatives from the state's five recognized tribes and three attorneys appointed by the governor—to hold hearings. The purpose was to resolve a growing controversy between those claiming to be true descendants of the Eastern Pequot Indians and the individuals they were denying tribal membership to, such as Juanita Reels and some of her siblings. On January 18, 1977, Juanita Reels was invited to Hartford to testify. She had no genealogical or cultural ties to the Eastern tribe. Nor did she know anything about the tribe's traditions or history. She did not even know the name of a single tribal member. But she knew that her father, Clifford Sebastian, had told her he was born on the tribe's reservation. And Juanita hoped to move her children back there if the tribe ever achieved the kind of prosperity Hayward was creating in Ledyard.

After taking an oath to tell the truth and introducing herself to the state's Indian Affairs Council, Juanita conceded that she knew almost nothing about the tribe she was attempting to join.

"Did you at any time during your childhood or adulthood go to the reservation?" the council asked.

"Yes, I think once he [Juanita's father] brought us back to the reservation," she said.

"And do you recall, who did you visit there?" the council asked.

"No, I was very young at the time."

"And that was the only time that you recall?"

"That I can recall."

After more questions designed to determine whether Juanita could establish evidence that she had participated in tribal activities, the council asked, "Are you a full-blooded Indian?"

"No," Juanita replied. "I wouldn't say completely full-blooded. I'm about even."

"OK," the council said, "When someone comes up to you and says for conversation or whatever, 'What are you, Irish or German or Yugoslav?' You say you are an Indian?"

"Yes," Juanita testified.

"Do you respond as to what particular tribe you are from?"

"Eastern Pequot," Juanita answered.

"Eastern Pequot?" the council asked skeptically.

"Yes," she affirmed.

"I have no further questions," the questioner stated.

Juanita's testimony did little to strengthen her case for joining the Eastern Pequot tribe. However, her appearance in Hartford introduced her to Skip Hayward. He too had been invited to provide testimony related to the sharp rise in membership applications to the tribes. The council believed that Hayward's grandmother, Elizabeth George, had passed on a great deal of oral history to him concerning both reservations. He had been asked to share what he knew with the council.

While waiting to testify, Hayward listened to Juanita and her sister Marjory's testimony. Both of them revealed that their grandfather, Jesse Sebastian, was married to Annie George, the sister of his grandmother, Elizabeth George. This relationship was known to members of the council and prompted them to ask Juanita's sister why she and Juanita did not consider themselves members of Hayward's tribe rather than the Eastern Pequot tribe.

"I feel that we should be recognized from both sides," said Marjory Pinson. "But the reason I declared the Eastern [tribe] is because it seems like the Western [tribe] doesn't want to recognize us." This response seized Hayward's full attention, since he was unaware of any attempt on the part of Juanita and her sister to join his tribe.

"Why do you make that statement, that they don't want to recognize you?" asked another council member.

"Well, not 'they' but one . . ." Pinson began before hesitating. "That we were niggers, can't get no plainer than that."

Her response stunned Hayward. The implication that he would prevent people from joining his tribe on the basis of skin color was hardly accurate. Race was the last thing on his mind when it came to applicants for tribal admission. At that point in the tribe's history, he was desperate to bolster the tribe's population. He had gone as far as to announce to a newspaper reporter that if the tribe could not find enough Pequots, "We will open the land up to Indians from other tribes." In 1977 he was still trying to build a big enough community on the reservation to convince Congress that his followers deserved to be recognized as a tribe. Hayward did not care what race the community consisted of. He had his share of character flaws, but prejudice was not among them.

When he was called to testify, Hayward, with his shaggy hair dwarfing his shirt collar, walked up and sat facing the council members, with his hands clasped together in front of him on the table. His shoulders hunched forward, Hayward pulled the small microphone to his mouth. "First of all," he began, "I would like to address myself to the two ladies that spoke previously about membership in the [Western] Pequot tribe. If they would have come to us we would have spoke to them and they would . . . you know . . . their grandmother is my grandmother's sister."

After implying that he would accept them as Western Pequots because their grandmothers were sisters, Hayward then went on to testify that he did not believe the Sebastians were true Pequot Indians. "My mother and I, we had quite a few conversations about the . . . about Indians. And her feeling was that the Sebastian side, that they weren't Indian." Hayward's ancestors, he testified, had told him that some of the early Sebastians lived on the Eastern reservation because they were poor and the Indian reservation was the only place they could afford to live.

At the conclusion of the hearings, the Eastern Pequot tribe did not accept Juanita Reels's petition for membership. But Hayward did. Hayward's family members were not as eager to have Reels and her Sebastian siblings—all of whom were black—join them on the Ledyard reservation. The prospect of outsiders with no familial or social relationship to the tight-knit tribe Hayward had formed gave rise to serious resistance by some of Hayward's family.

Before making his final decision, Hayward consulted with some of the Indian acquaintances from Maine whom he had met through Tom Tureen. The Maine Indian leadership sensed that Hayward's white family members were antagonistic toward his idea of allowing blacks to join the tribe. Instead, they wanted to remain an isolated group of less than one hundred people, with their own land. But the Maine Indian leadership reminded Hayward that his family shared a common ancestor, albeit a distant one, with the Reels and Sebastian family.

Unlike some of his relatives, Hayward did not view the decision to admit Juanita Reels and her Sebastian relatives through the lens of race. He viewed the decision in pragmatic terms. For the sake of expediency and achieving the larger goal of federal recognition, Skip agreed to adopt the Reels and their Sebastian relatives into his tribe. Yet genealogical and other historical records dating back to 1786 clearly indicated that Juanita Reels did not descend from Pequot Indians.

Reels's genealogy did not prevent Hayward from welcoming her and her thirteen children into the tribe, however. Her arrival in Ledyard was delayed after her husband's parole from prison. He moved back in with Juanita and the children and found a job, and he and Juanita tried to salvage their marriage. But in 1982, Juanita filed for divorce. At the time, Thomas still owed Juanita over $20,000 in child support. While the divorce case dragged through the Rhode Island court system, Kenny served in the army. He enlisted in 1979 and was honorably discharged in 1984. By then, his mother had obtained a restraining order against Kenny's father and joined the Mashantucket Pequot tribe in Ledyard.

Out of the army and looking for a job at age twenty-four, Reels was offered a position as the director of purchasing for the tribe. Reels accepted, moved to Ledyard, and was assigned to work under James Wherry, Hayward's economic adviser. Wherry treated Reels like his protégé, and within two years Reels became manager of the tribe's sand-and-gravel operation, a post he still held during the construction of Foxwoods. He gave that job up one month before the casino's grand opening, the day he was sworn in as tribal councilor.

The identity Kenneth Mitchell Reels inherited at birth did not promise he would be a millionaire before his thirty-fifth birthday; or that he would get elected to political office; or that he would receive a seat on the board of directors of a billion-dollar company. But Skip Hayward had granted him a new identity, complete with a new address, race, occupation, and economic status.

29

ACE IN THE HOLE

WEDNESDAY, OCTOBER 14, 1992
FOXWOODS EXECUTIVE OFFICES

"I'M FED UP!" AL LUCIANI YELLED, FURIOUS THAT HIS IMPATIENCE ONLY seemed to amuse Kenny Reels.

Despite Foxwoods's phenomenal success, Reels had been vocally criticizing Luciani for not paying proper respect to the tribal council. Luciani had fired the daughter of a tribal leader after she'd assaulted a fellow casino employee and a casino patron. Reels and the council demanded she be reinstated. It was just one in a litany of petty disputes about which the tribal council had summoned Luciani into tribal council chambers in order to lecture him. Luciani was so consumed by the tribe's political disputes, he had virtually lost all ability to operate the casino.

"You have no idea what it takes to run a casino," Luciani said. "I'm trying to run a multimillion-dollar facility with over three thousand employees. And you people keep coming down here and disrupting the operation."

"Look, I'm the owner," Reels said. "I can do whatever the hell I want."

"The tribe—and you particularly—have violated the provisions of my employment contract dealing with my ability to manage the property!" Luciani shouted. "There's been constant interference in terms of doing the day-to-day business. *Constant interference* in terms of undermining my management. And I've *had it.*"

"You don't know anything," Reels said. "You—"

"Kenny," interrupted Luciani, "if we don't reach an amicable resolution to my contract issues, I'm resigning effective this Friday."

Reels laughed. "Who needs you? We can run this place by ourselves. Besides, I've already talked to Deno about taking over."

Furious, Luciani ended the meeting. As soon as Reels left, Luciani instructed his secretary to get Deno Marino on the phone at once and schedule a meeting with him for the following afternoon.

THURSDAY, OCTOBER 15, 1992, 6:00 P.M.
FOXWOODS EXECUTIVE OFFICES

His conservative business suit hugging his stocky, five-foot-seven-inch frame, fifty-one-year-old Deno Marino stared at the closed door to Al Luciani's office. A certified public accountant who had previously worked as a casino regulator in Atlantic City, Marino had been a friend and business associate of Luciani's for ten years. He was one of the first people Luciani hired after being named CEO at Foxwoods.

Marino looked at his watch. Luciani had kept him waiting nearly two hours. He could not help but wonder if this sudden meeting had something to do with a conversation that he'd had with Reels and a fellow council member. "We want to ask you a couple simple things," Reels had begun. "Just listen, answer them, and don't ask questions."

"OK," Marino had told him.

"We know you came here with Al," Reels had said. "But if Al decided to quit tomorrow, for whatever reason, would you go, too?"

"Is there more to the question than that?" Marino had asked.

"No."

"Well, Al and I are very close friends. Al took me here. And I'm very happy here. Now if Al came and said there were things going on here that are illegal, then that's one thing. But if he came to me and said, 'I just had a fight with the council, I'm leaving,' then no, I wouldn't go. So if you're asking me would I jump out the window because Al does, the answer is no."

"Deno," Reels had said, "would you, if in fact Al left, sit in as acting CEO until we decide who to hire in his place, whether it be you or someone else?"

Thinking back to his response to that question, Marino suddenly heard Luciani's office door open. "Come in, Mr. Marino," Luciani's secretary said coldly.

Luciani remained seated, his elbows resting on his desk and his face buried in his hands.

Without saying a word to his longtime friend, Marino sat opposite Luciani.

"You and I can't go on like this anymore," Luciani said, looking up.

"What the hell are you talking about?" asked Marino.

"I can't believe that you would go behind my back and reach an agreement with Kenny Reels," Luciani said. "After the relationship we had? Deno, we've been friends. I brought you up here after you left the Casino Control Commission to basically give you an opportunity here."

The two men silently stared at each other. Finally, Marino shook his head. "If you actually believe what you just said . . ." Marino paused. Luciani continued to glare at him. "I—I don't know what to say," Marino continued. "Do you want to talk about this?"

"No, I don't," Luciani said, raising his voice. "You and I are done."

Marino rose from his chair. "Al, you don't have to fire me," he said. "Because I'm gonna quit. I thought you knew me better."

FRIDAY, OCTOBER 16, 1992
THIRTY MINUTES LATER
MYSTIC, CONNECTICUT

LIGHTS ILLUMINATED THE THREE FLAGS HOISTED HIGH ABOVE THE entrance to the Hilton Hotel. The American, Connecticut State, and blue-and-white Hilton company flags snapped in the chilly breeze. Their metal buckles clanged against the flagpoles. It was an otherwise quiet night.

Brown approached the lobby doors. Across the street "Olde Mystic Village" and the Mystic Aquarium were deserted. It was after 6:00 P.M., and the tourists had all retired for the day. Once inside the Hilton, Brown proceeded to the conference rooms, where the tribal council was meeting. When Brown first started working for the tribe, they held their meetings in construction trailers on the reservation. After Foxwoods opened, the council members felt they required a setting sophisticated enough for a governing body presiding over a multimillion-dollar business. Brown thought it was a waste of money to tie up conference rooms at the Hilton. But he understood his role. His job was to regulate Foxwoods and protect it against organized crime, not tell the tribal government how to spend the profits.

The meeting was already in session when Brown entered and stood inconspicuously in the back of the room. He was not really sure why tribal council member Kenny Reels had telephoned and asked him to attend. All that Reels said on the telephone was that something "urgent" had come up.

Driving from Foxwoods to the hotel, Brown thought about the changes he had observed in Reels since the day when he first met him two years before. He was very quiet and thoughtful when he first arrived in Ledyard. He had become more outspoken after getting elected to the tribal council. But Foxwoods had changed him dramatically, triggering a streak of arrogance and an obsession with meddling in the casino's management. The intoxicating sense of power that now came with governing a massive casino had given Reels a burgeoning sense of self-importance.

Brown could not imagine what was so urgent that his presence was needed at a tribal meeting. Foxwoods was doing fantastically. In less than eight months' time under Luciani's leadership, Foxwoods was on pace to take in roughly $300 million in its first year of operation. And Luciani was already overseeing massive expansion projects to increase the casino's size. Both Hayward and the Malaysian investors were very pleased with Luciani's performance as CEO.

Wishing he were somewhere else, Brown casually looked around the meeting. He spotted Reels and other members of council. Hayward was not around. Brown knew he wouldn't be. Reels had called this meeting. And Hayward, despite being the head of the council, rarely attended council meetings unless it was a meeting he called. Like Brown, he felt the council often wasted too much time in meetings debating things of insignificance.

Then Brown noticed some people whose names he did not know. They were employees from the casino. "What are they doing here?" he wondered. One of them, a poker dealer, was identified as a "witness" and asked to answer some questions.

"Witnesses?" Brown thought to himself. "What's going on here?" Suddenly a lump formed in his throat.

The poker dealer and other Foxwoods employees were testifying before the tribal council about alleged improprieties on the part of Al Luciani. And the council was behaving like both judge and jury, suggesting Luciani had been dishonest and secretive in his management style.

"What the f--- is going on here?" Brown thought.

Stewing, Brown listened in amazement.

Luciani was one of the most respected casino managers in the entire country, both for his integrity and his exceptional business sense. Only months earlier, tribal attorney Rob Gips, who was responsible for bringing Luciani to work for the tribe, had flown to Washington and testified before the Senate Committee on Indian Affairs, saying, "The tribe picked Mr. Luciani because of his impeccable reputation for integrity as well as his expertise." In contrast, Reels and the tribal council had no experience running a business, much less a casino taking in millions of dollars a day.

"They're accusing Al," Brown realized. Yet Luciani wasn't even present to defend himself.

Brown motioned for Reels to step outside the room where the two of them could be alone.

"Kenny, what's going on here?" Brown asked, looking up into the eyes of Reels, who was over six feet tall.

"We're gonna bring Al up on charges tomorrow," Reels replied.

"What do you mean 'charges'? What kind of charges?"

"He's not running the casino properly," Reels said.

"Kenny," Brown said, taking a deep breath. "Wait a minute. Let's think about this. Even if Al is responsible for whatever it is you say he did, this is not a big deal. You know Al's temperament. If you bring charges against him, he'll quit."

Reels said nothing. But the expression on his face said it all. Luciani's resignation was exactly what Reels wanted.

"Kenny," Brown said, pausing, "if he leaves . . . *who's* going to run the place?"

"Deno Marino's gonna step in," Reels announced. "He's been working with us for weeks."

Leaving Brown speechless, Reels returned to the meeting.

If the implications were not so serious, Reels's plan would have been comical. But the tribal council, the tribe's governing body, had decided, without input from Hayward, to get rid of the chief executive officer in charge of running Foxwoods. Reels was so smug, so cavalier, yet so ignorant. "No, stupid," Brown thought. He was jeopardizing the financial relationship the tribe had with the Genting investors in Malaysia. Hayward had signed a binding contract that reserved to them the right to approve the CEO of Foxwoods. Luciani was their man. He was the CEO they wanted to protect their $60 million investment. They would go ballistic if they found out that the tribe planned to replace Luciani with Marino.. "Marino," Brown thought, shaking his head in disbelief. "Al brought him here and gave him a job. Now he's conspiring to undermine him. He's aligned himself with Kenny."

Brown wanted to notify Hayward at once, but he was in the hotel's main dining room having dinner with some dignitaries. Brown was supposed to join them, but decided instead to return to the tribal council meeting and observe what else transpired. By 1:00 A.M., when the meeting broke up, Hayward had gone home to bed, unaware of his council's plans to remove Luciani. Neither Brown nor Reels and the council knew that Marino had quit after his meeting with Luciani and had headed back to New Jersey.

The next morning, Brown went to the casino early, aware that Hayward and the tribal council had a scheduled board of directors meeting in the conference room of the Foxwoods executive offices. Brown pulled Hayward aside before the meeting started. "Skip, listen," Brown said. "They're gonna bring up some allegations against Al at this meeting."

Puzzled, Hayward cocked his head and turned up the palms of his hands. "What do you mean?"

"Last night," Brown said. "I was . . . I couldn't get outta this discussion in the conference room at the Hilton. And Kenny is goin' to come after Al."

"Oh, no," Hayward said, shaking his head as he stared down at the ground. "What's this all about?"

"It's, you know, Kenny and company," Brown said, "tryin' to find fault with the way Al runs the business. And Deno Marino's involved."

"Marino?" Skip asked. "What's he got to do with this?"

"Kenny's already talked to him about taking over."

Hayward turned and entered the conference room, dismissing everyone except the tribal council and Luciani. They remained behind closed doors for the remainder of the morning. After lunch, Hayward appeared at Brown's office, looking as if he had not slept in days. "Al quit," he announced. "And we . . . we have to . . . we have to find a way to let the people under him know."

Brown paused, recognizing the anguish in Hayward's voice. "What do you wanna do?" he asked.

"You and I," Hayward began, "You and I have to talk to 'em. Get 'em all together."

Brown buzzed the secretary. "Pat, get all of the casino executives in the conference room right away." Hayward paced Brown's office in silence, waiting for everyone to assemble. Leaving him alone, Brown went into the conference room and waited with the twelve executives. Minutes later, Hayward entered. His lips and fleshy cheeks quivering, he made eye contact with no one. "I . . . I don't know how this happened," he said, "but Al quit."

A collective gasp echoed from around the table.

Tears started streaming down Hayward's face.

Brown buried his face in his hand.

"We're gonna have to get through this," Hayward said. "And Mickey's gonna help us. And I want Mickey to . . ."

Silence engulfed the room as Hayward hesitated.

"I want Mickey to help me get through this," Hayward said, turning and walking out of the room.

Foxwoods was only eight months old and it was without a CEO. And the casino's top auditor had walked out.

As Brown expected, the Genting lenders were not pleased. On the heels of Luciani's resignation, Brown was called to another emergency tribal council meeting. This time Hayward called the meeting. And when Brown arrived, Deno Marino was nowhere to be found, his resignation having been formally accepted. And Hayward had reasserted his control over the tribal government. Reels and the rest of the tribal council said nothing as Hayward addressed Brown. "You have to take over until we find a replacement for Al."

Bitter, but unwilling to challenge Hayward in the meeting, Reels sulked in silence.

That afternoon Brown resigned as chairman of the gaming board and took over as acting president and CEO of Foxwoods.

30

THE SKIP AND MICKEY SHOW

HIGH ROLLERS, SPORTING TUXEDOS AND RICH SUNTANS, FILED OUT FROM a train of stretch limousines that lined the curb outside Foxwoods. Their blond and brunette escorts were draped in gold, diamonds, and mink. Never before had an Indian reservation been so drenched in decadence.

Yet Brown believed the tribe needed something in addition to real estate to expand their resort: slot machines. Brown knew they were the primary attraction in casinos everywhere around the world. He had hundreds of them lined up along the walls at Foxwoods. Yet he could not turn them on. Slot machines were the one form of gambling that was not permitted under Connecticut's Las Vegas Nights statute for charitable organizations, and, in turn, prohibited at Foxwoods.

"We're not a full-service casino without slots," Brown thought. "We're doing great on table games. But there's an untapped amount of money that's mind-boggling that we're not getting." Brown estimated that in its first year of operation, Foxwoods generated close to $300 million—not nearly enough to pay for their massive development plans. Brown projected Foxwoods could surpass $1 billion annually if they installed thousands of slot machines. And he had a plan to make it happen.

When Congress wrote the Indian gaming law, it envisioned states and tribes entering into compacts (agreements or contracts between nations or states) that would govern gaming on Indian land. But in instances where states refused, as did Connecticut when it declined to sign the compact with the Pequots, Congress included a backup provision in the gaming law. It authorized the secretary of Interior to issue an administrative order in place of a mutually agreed-to compact. The order, referred to in the law as "procedures," carried the full force and effect of a federal law. And it proscribed the terms and conditions under which the Pequots could conduct gaming. So where states like Connecticut refused to sign a gaming compact with a tribe, Congress empowered the secretary of interior to take the unsigned version of the compact, make revisions to it, and then implement it as a federal procedure. As is typically the case when administrative agencies implement procedures, Congress also required the Department of Interior to first solicit "public comment" from interested parties, giving them an opportunity to express concerns and offer suggestions. But ultimately, the secretary is not required to incorporate any of these comments into the order.

The week before Lujan enacted procedures to govern the Pequots' gaming enterprise, he received over thirty pages of public comment from Governor Weicker and Attorney General Blumenthal. Some of their suggestions were incorporated into the final rules governing the Pequots' gaming operation. Others were rejected. But Lujan made one primary compromise. The tribe desperately wanted slot machines in 1991. The state fought this vehemently. Lujan chose a middle-ground position. He imposed a "moratorium" on slot machines on the Pequot reservation. The moratorium was a political compromise that pleased both sides. Weicker was happy because it prevented the tribe from getting slot machines.

The tribe's lawyers were even happier. Lujan's moratorium provided a way for the tribe to get slot machines in the future, something that was expressly forbidden by state law. Immediately following the clause that said the tribe had "no authority" to operate slot machines, Lujan included the word "unless." Lawyers love the word "unless." It signals the exception to a rule. Brown read Lujan's exception very closely. It said that the tribe could not have slot machines "unless it is determined by agreement between the Tribe and the State that by virtue of the existing laws and regulations of the State the operation of [slot machines] would not be unlawful on the ground that the Tribe is not located in a State that permits such gaming for any purpose. . . ." Lujan left the door open for the moratorium on slots to be lifted if the state agreed to it. Weicker, however, had fought the casino tooth and nail, particularly the slot machines. But the quickest way to unite two adversaries is to find them a common enemy.

Steve Wynn, the Las Vegas gambling tycoon, was lobbying Connecticut legislators hard for the right to build a casino in Bridgeport. Weicker opposed Wynn because he did not want any more casinos in Connecticut. The Pequots opposed Wynn because they didn't want him eating into their profits. Both had an interest in stopping Wynn or anyone else from building a casino in Connecticut. And the tribe's lobbyists in Hartford caught wind of something that just might persuade Weicker to enter a pact with the Pequots that would accomplish the tribe's designs: give the tribe the right to offer slots and shut everyone else out from doing the same. Brown was informed that Weicker was profoundly short of funds for his state budget—over $100 million short.

Phone calls were placed to an attorney on Weicker's staff and to Bob Werner from the state's Department of Special Revenue. A private meeting was scheduled with them at a steak house in Hartford. Brown took tribal attorney Rob Gips and one other lawyer with him. Over dinner, Brown made his pitch. "There is a lot of legislation pending for legalized casinos," Brown said. "Steve Wynn's group is trying to build a casino in Bridgeport. You may have slot machines someday in Connecticut. But we want slot machines now.

"You have no right to tax us," Brown continued. "We will enter into an agreement with you where if you amend the compact to give us slot machines, we will give you 25 percent of our slot win for as long as slot machines are not allowed in the state of Connecticut. If and when you pass legislation authorizing casino gaming, including slot machines, we'll terminate our pact."

"You've been in government," Weicker's counsel said. "We can't plan a state budget on some possible theoretical income from a gaming machine. You have to guarantee a minimum."

"I'm prepared to guarantee a minimum," Brown said in between bites.

"How much will you guarantee?" Weicker's counsel asked as he pushed his fork into his steak and cut it with his knife.

"One hundred million dollars a year, minimum," Brown said, trying not to talk with his mouth full. "Or 25 percent of our winnings. Whatever is greater."

Brown loved the stunned expression that suddenly appeared on the face of Weicker's lawyer who slowly put down his knife and fork, wiped his lips with his napkin, and stood up from the table. "I have to make a phone call," he said. He did not return to the table for more than twenty minutes. When he did, he wore a bright smile. "The governor will see you tomorrow morning at eight o'clock at his home," he said.

The following morning, Brown and Gips had breakfast with Weicker at the governor's mansion. They were treated to a wonderful meal. Weicker could hardly believe that the Pequots could come up with the kind of money Brown was promising. If Brown was offering $100 million a year to Weicker—and that was just 25 percent of the revenue—that meant the Pequots were going to pull in at least $400 million annually from little machines that had handles on the side and cost $1 to $10 to play.

"I can demonstrate that we can make that kind of money," Brown assured Weicker. He then displayed a series of charts. They showed the revenue amounts generated by the slot machines in Atlantic City, where there were many casinos in competition with each other. The charts also projected the enormous slot revenues that could be generated by Foxwoods, particularly if the state did not allow anyone else to compete with the Pequots for slot machine revenues. Brown's plan called for something similar to selecting one automaker in Detroit and giving it exclusive rights to manufacture sport-utility vehicles. By taking exclusive control of the most lucrative product in the auto industry, that company would be guaranteed to see its revenues skyrocket. In the casino business, there was no more coveted product than slot machines. For $100 million a year, Brown was asking Weicker to give the Pequots the corner on the market.

"You're gonna give the state of Connecticut $100 million a year and it's not going to cost us *anything*?" Weicker asked.

"It is not going to cost you a dime, Governor," Brown said. "We pay for regulating. We pay for state police. We pay for special revenue. We pay for the slot machines."

Not only did Brown's offer promise to fund the $100 million gap in the state budget, it gave Weicker power that the state otherwise was denied. Since the state had no authority to tax the tribe, Brown was offering a way for the state to fund its budget with proceeds from the tribe's casino.

However, there was a problem. In 1951, long before passing the Indian Gaming Regulatory Act, Congress passed the Johnson Act, a federal law that outlawed slot machines on federal lands, including Indian reservations. The law's purpose was to support states—states like Connecticut—that outlaw slot machines. It made it a federal offense to "transport" or "possess" slot machines on Indian land contained within states that forbade slot machines elsewhere within its borders. When Congress passed IGRA in 1988, it did not repeal the Johnson Act. Under IGRA, the only way for the Pequots to get around the Johnson Act was for Connecticut to legalize slot machines—a step the Connecticut legislature had not taken.

Planning to circumvent the Johnson Act, Weicker and Brown knew that their pact would cause an uproar in the state legislature. The governor was agreeing to do by contract what the Johnson Act said was illegal: allow the Pequots to operate slot machines without first passing a law to legalize slot machines. If Weicker's intentions became public before he went through with signing a memorandum of understanding with the tribe, the legislature would surely block it.

After convincing Weicker that he should clear the way for the Pequots to have exclusive rights to slot machines, Brown was called into a meeting at the tribal council chambers. Since Luciani had left, Brown had arranged for various candidates from Las Vegas and Atlantic City to interview with the council about the Foxwoods CEO job. Brown figured the council wanted to get his thoughts on which man they should hire. But that was not exactly what the council had in mind.

"We don't want any of them," Hayward said bluntly.

Brown said nothing. He really did not have complete confidence in any of the guys he had flown in either.

"We want you to stay on full-time in the job," Hayward continued.

Brown was not completely surprised by Hayward's announcement. He knew the Malaysians had serious reservations about turning the management of Foxwoods over to someone they were unfamiliar with. The casino was taking in enormous sums of money, which was in turn being spent on massive development and casino expansion projects. The Malaysians feared that hiring a CEO from the outside during such a volatile time was unwise.

The decision to make Brown the permanent CEO of Foxwoods was Hayward's, however. He didn't wait for his tribal council or his Malaysian investors to make a recommendation. He wanted Brown. Prior to Brown's arrival, Hayward's closest confidant was Tureen. But Tureen was more like a father figure and was often referred to by Hayward as "Father Tom." Brown, on the other hand, was more like the new kid in town who promised to show Hayward a thrilling side of life that he had never experienced.

Brown shared little in common with Tureen. He was conservative, a Vietnam War veteran, and a career law-enforcement agent. Tureen was a liberal, a war protester, and an anti-establishment type. Brown's friends were rich businessmen and well-connected politicians. Tureen preferred poets, Indians, and philosophers. As lawyers, both were exceptionally good at getting their opponents to comply with their wishes. But their approaches were starkly different. Tureen could convince a gun-toting bank robber that it was in his best interest to remove his mask and then talk him into smiling for the surveillance camera before leaving with the loot. Brown would simply take out a bigger gun and shoot the robber.

Tureen flew Hayward to Washington in a private plane and deftly maneuvered him and the tribe through the halls of Congress to make the Pequots a tribe. Brown drove them to Wall Street in a black Cadillac and made them a rich corporation. Tureen got Senator Weicker to feel sympathetic toward the Pequots and convinced him to take on President Reagan in order to secure sovereign rights for the Haywards. Brown infuriated Governor Weicker by helping the tribe secure the right to build a huge casino in Connecticut. Then he bowled Weicker over with so much money that the governor agreed to let the tribe have slot machines.

But Hayward's loyalty to Brown had nothing to do with money. He and Brown shared similar traits and hobbies. Both were raised in blue-collar families in the fifties and sixties. Although Brown became a powerful lawyer and Hayward a powerful Indian chief, both never forgot their humble roots. And both were more comfortable in blue jeans on a fishing boat with a cooler of beer than in business suits. Their favorite saying was: "I've been rich and I've been poor. And it's a whole lot more fun being rich."

When not running the casino, they fished together, played pool together, and partied together—all things that Hayward did not do with Tureen. And Brown and Hayward had an insatiable thirst for development. They both enjoyed building things. Hayward came up with the visionary schemes, and Brown found a practical way to achieve them. Together, they hoped to make southeastern Connecticut the casino capital of the world.

On January 13 Hayward and Brown drove to Hartford to meet Weicker, the man who was going to make them infinitely richer. When they arrived at Weicker's office, a seven-page Memorandum of Understanding was awaiting Hayward's and Weicker's signatures. The memorandum began by declaring that the "moratorium imposed on the operation by the Tribe of [slot machines] shall be suspended." It went on to say that it was illegal for anyone but the Pequots to offer slot machines, and that the state would receive 25 percent of the gross revenues from the machines.

A signing ceremony was scheduled for early afternoon in the governor's chambers. Both Weicker and Hayward were surprised to find that despite being invited, not a single representative from the media showed up to cover the event. They were so effective in keeping the deal private that Weicker's office had to delay the signing and renotify the media, emphasizing that this signing was pretty significant.

Once the reporters finally showed up, Weicker and Hayward signed the pact. Weicker then handed one of his pens to Brown as a memento. "I never thought I'd see this day," Brown quipped, recalling Weicker's statement one year earlier that he would not take his dog to Atlantic City.

The next day, members of the Connecticut legislature were furious. Attorney General Richard Blumenthal received a letter from Thomas Ritter, the speaker of Connecticut's House of Representatives. He wanted to know if the governor had exceeded his constitutional and statutory authority by signing a pact with the Pequots without first seeking legislative approval. Blumenthal sent a letter back saying that Weicker had not abridged the powers of the legislature. While conceding "there is no statute specifically authorizing the Governor to sign this agreement," Blumenthal argued that Weicker was acting within his authority. "In executing the Memorandum of Understanding," he wrote, "the Governor is acting as the chief executive, in effect, interpreting, implementing and executing the law—namely, the federal Procedures, a federal statute (IGRA), federal court rulings on the subject and state law."

On January 17, Brown turned on the first slot machines at Foxwoods.

31

MR. LOZIER GOES TO WASHINGTON

JANUARY 1993
LEDYARD, CONNECTICUT

JOE LOZIER OPENED THE BACK DOOR TO HIS HOUSE, AND A GUST OF COLD morning air whipped up against his face, which was shielded by a thick black beard. Behind him, the family dog, Wags, a beige cocker spaniel, stared up at him from his resting spot on the kitchen floor.

"See you later, boy," Lozier said, as the white screen door slammed behind him.

Frost covered the one-acre brown field next to his home, an eighteenth-century farmhouse with white clapboard siding and a stone foundation.

After climbing into his oversized pickup truck equipped with a cellular phone and two-way hand radio, Lozier eased it down his short dirt driveway and through the narrow opening in the granite stone wall. His house number, 204, was painted in white on the wall's corner stone. Careful not to hit the metal milk can propped up against the wall, Lozier looked both ways and pulled out onto Gallup Hill Road, which was named after the builders and original owners of Lozier's house in the 1700s.

Ten minutes later, at 8:50 A.M., Lozier walked to the kitchen at the rear of the Ledyard town hall and made a cup of coffee, just as he did every morning when he got to work. At 9:00 he walked past the receptionist desk outside his office and retrieved the morning newspaper. Glancing at the headlines, he sipped his coffee and walked slowly toward his chair. The sleeve on his dark suit jacket brushed against the American flag hanging from the flag stand beside his desk. His six-foot two-inch frame filled his leather chair. His broad shoulders hunched forward, and his large forearms rested sturdily on his desktop calendar.

He turned directly to the "Region" section. He always read the local news first, then the "Business" section followed by the letters to the editor. He rarely bothered with the national news or sports section, unless it was football season. He was an avid fan of Ledyard's high school football team. Steam rose from his white foam coffee cup as he started to read, ignoring a stack of correspondence on his desk that awaited his signature. The letters were dwarfed by stacks of manila files that seemed to mount the longer he was in office, increasingly eating up desk space. Scrolled up town maps were pushed up against photographs of his wife, children, and granddaughter positioned on one corner of the desk. Two phones and a Rolodex occupied the other corner. A wooden nameplate with a marble-smooth black face surrounded by a gold border teetered on the desk's front edge. The top of the nameplate read JOSEPH LOZIER. Beneath his name, two perfectly aligned gold screws fastened the nameplate's glass front to its wooden backing. The word MAYOR appeared boldly between the screws. It was the closest thing to vanity Joe Lozier possessed.

Lozier spotted a small article reporting that the Bureau of Indian Affairs had taken a twenty-seven-acre lot owned by the tribe into trust. Lozier scratched his beard. He was aware that the BIA had started taking land into trust for the Pequots back in 1984 after Congress expanded the reservation borders. He knew that once the tribe bought the privately held land within its reservation, it automatically was taken into trust by the government and converted into federal Indian land, a process that removed it from the Ledyard tax rolls and the jurisdiction of town land-use regulations.

"This must be some piece of land inside the reservation that the tribe has just recently bought," Lozier thought to himself. "Wait a minute," he said out loud. "This article says that the twenty-seven acres has been serving as a parking lot for Foxwoods."

Lozier reached across his desk and removed the elastic from the Ledyard zoning map that was scrolled up beside his coffee cup. Using a paperweight and a stack of files to weight down its edges, he located the reservation on the map. He put his long, thick index finger in the upper right-hand corner of the map and began moving it slowly along the inside of the orange, disjointed border entitled "Mashantucket Pequot Tribal Settlement Boundary." The twenty-seven-acre parcel was nowhere to be found. "It's not here," he thought. Then as he lifted his finger from the map, he spotted it. Unsure of himself, he lowered his reading glasses farther down his nose.

"How can this be?" he whispered. "This twenty-seven-acre lot is *outside* the reservation boundary. The BIA must have made some kind of mistake."

Pushing his reading glasses back up, Lozier looked at the news article again. It only confirmed his fears.

Clutching the newspaper in one hand and the map in the other, Lozier walked down the hall to the office of Anna Reiners, the town tax assessor. "I was never notified of this," he complained to Reiners, waving the newspaper in front of him.

Reiners, a quiet, timid woman in her fifties, tried reading the article while Lozier continued talking at her in a tone loud enough for everyone else in the office to hear. "I don't think the previous mayor was ever notified," he said. "What's going on here? Do you have any paperwork on this?"

Reiners vaguely remembered getting something from the federal government referring to trust land. But she received lots of correspondence from the BIA, most of which was filled with confusing language from federal Indian laws that are completely foreign to tax assessors in rural New England communities. Nervously, Reiners pulled open the top drawer to her metal filing cabinet and removed a thick file on which she had handwritten the words "Mashantucket Pequots." With Lozier peering over her shoulder, she shuffled through it until she found a letter from the Trust Services Realty Branch of the BIA in Arlington, Virginia. Billie Ott, the BIA's area director, had signed it. Reiners handed the letter to Lozier to read.

"Dear Ms. Reiners," the letter began. "This Agency has under consideration an application for acquisition of real property by the United States to be held in trust for the benefit of the Mashantucket Pequot Tribe of Connecticut." The letter then referred to an attachment that described the twenty-seven-acre parcel mentioned in the newspaper. "The determination of whether to acquire these parcels in trust will be made pursuant to the exercise of discretionary authority vested in the Secretary of interior," wrote Ott, who asked Reiners to provide tax and zoning information about the land to his office.

"I can't believe what I'm reading," Lozier said. "The secretary of interior has the power to increase the size of the Pequots' reservation? Congress had already done that in 1983. Now the Interior secretary, upon recommendation from the BIA, can make it bigger? What is going on here?"

He looked back at the letter and kept reading. "We invite your comments on the proposed acquisition," the letter said. "Any comments received within thirty days of the date of this letter will be considered."

Lozier looked at the date of the letter—August 4, 1992. Reiners had been in possession of the letter since August. "That was five months ago," he said. "Why wasn't I ever shown this letter?" he asked Reiners indignantly.

Reiners was speechless. For the past few years she had been inundated with letters from the government indicating that land within the reservation was being removed from the tax rolls and placed into trust. All of it up to this point involved land within the reservation. She had no reason to suspect that this was anything other than routine. The letter did not specify that the twenty-seven-acre parcel was outside the settlement boundary.

Lozier fumed out of Reiners's office, slamming the door behind him. The town's tax base had been diminished, and he never received the notification. It infuriated him that the letter had been sitting in the tax assessor's file cabinet. The true target of Lozier's anger was the BIA, not Reiners. But he was having what his wife kindly referred to as "a Joe Lozier explosion." When he lost his temper, anybody close by tended to get blasted.

After returning to his office, he dictated a terse letter to the BIA. "Kindly be advised that future correspondence relevant to [trust acquisition for the Pequots] be forwarded to the Mayor's office," wrote Lozier. Shortly after sending the letter to the BIA, Lozier received an unexpected visitor at his office. Wendell Comrie came to see him.

"Hello, Wendell," said Lozier. "What brings you here?"

"Just passin' through and thought I'd say hello," said Comrie.

Wendell and his wife had acted as surrogate parents to Joe's wife, Nancy, when she was born. Shortly after giving birth, Nancy's mother sustained a prolonged illness that confined her to bed, and the Comries took care of Nancy until her mother fully recovered. Lozier never forgot that. And he remembered that Wendell had agreed to sell his land to the Pequots in order to settle the lawsuit in 1983.

"Come here, Wendell, I have something I want to show you," said Lozier.

Comrie put his glasses on. On the table, Lozier unrolled a map.

"What is that?" Comrie asked.

"A map of the settlement area," Lozier said.

"This the first time I've ever seen this," Comrie said in amazement. His finger followed the boundary stretching all the way up to Route 2 where Foxwoods sat. "Nobody ever showed us this."

"Wendell, you've never seen this map before?" Lozier asked.

"Absolutely not," he responded. "It doesn't seem proper that Congress would do this without even telling us. We never agreed to anything like *that*."

"Well, this is the map that was created as part of the settlement to the lawsuit filed against you by the tribe," Lozier said.

"The question I have is does the federal government have a right to do what they did," Comrie said.

"Jackson King must have showed you this map," Lozier said.

"He had every opportunity to tell us about the map," Comrie said. "And he didn't even tell us about it. We never saw the thing." Comrie paused before continuing. "I don't think Jackson King is a very honest man. This is the first time I've ever seen that map of the settlement area."

"Wendell, I'm sorry," Lozier said.

"How can Congress have the authority to draw that map and do this? You can see how well kept the secret was. They put that map in without us knowing a thing about it."

"Why did you settle with the tribe?" Lozier asked.

"We were told that by settling with the tribe we would put an end to land disputes involving the Indians once and for all."

Lozier respected Comrie like a grandfather and trusted him like a priest. He sat behind Comrie and his wife every Sunday in church. And he knew that Comrie had received $260,000 for his land, a number that had been widely publicized in the local papers. But Lozier knew something about the money that was not public knowledge. Comrie donated all of it to finance the construction of a new chapel in their church. He also knew that Comrie felt Jackson King had taken advantage of him and the other defendants in the suit, an opinion Lozier shared.

"Do you have any papers from your case?" Lozier asked.

"Jackson King has them all," said Comrie, who complained that King was now working full-time for the tribe. The more Comrie said about King switching sides after representing the landowners, the angrier Lozier became.

"I'm no lawyer," Lozier said. "But I think you would have a tremendous lawsuit against Jackson King."

Comrie shrugged it off. He was too old for another lawsuit. He just wanted to make sure that the original agreement was honored. And he had been promised that by settling with the tribe, there would be no more attempts on their part to acquire land and extend their borders. "Dave Holdridge might have some papers," Comrie offered. "He was the lead person for our group. He worked with Jackson on it."

As soon as Comrie left, Lozier picked up the phone and called Holdridge.

"Hi, David, this is Joe Lozier."

"Hi, Joe," said Holdridge.

"Was it your understanding that the Settlement Act put an end to land claims and acquisition by the tribe?" Lozier asked.

"Yes," Holdridge responded.

"Do you have any papers to that effect?"

"I don't have any. But I'm sure there are papers available. But they would be with the law firm."

Holdridge paused, waiting for Lozier's response. But Lozier said nothing.

"The law firm is Jackson King, of course," Holdridge continued.

Laughing at Holdridge's dry humor, Lozier forgot to ask him whether he had ever seen the map of the Settlement area. He was too preoccupied with his anger toward King. He knew Holdridge was too nice a man to openly criticize King. But Lozier was not interested in niceties. He had had an unfavorable opinion of King ever since he represented a man who sued Lozier over a business disagreement. When the case went to trial, Lozier ended up testifying in his own defense and King cross-examined him. Ever since then, Lozier never cared for him.

Holdridge, like Comrie, was amazed at what had taken place since the Settlement Act's passage in 1983.

"I could request the file from King's law firm," Holdridge continued. "We were his clients, after all."

"Ah, don't bother," Lozier replied.

"It is time for this town to start looking out for its interests," Lozier said to himself after hanging up the phone. He stared at the white walls in his office. They offered no hint that he was capable of standing up to a politically powerful Indian tribe that was home to the world's largest casino. The walls were completely bare. No pictures of famous Americans. No letters of commendation. No framed diplomas from prestigious colleges or law schools. Joe Lozier's journey to the mayor's office was unlike that of most aspiring politicians, as was his purpose for being one.

Growing up as a teenager in the 1960s, Lozier's hero was Bobby Kennedy. His parents were Republicans, active Christians, and conservative. Lozier revered his parents, but figured his devotion to Kennedy would cause him to break tradition and register as a Democrat. That was OK with him, however. He prided himself on being different. In 1968, Lozier, at the age of twenty-three, graduated with a bachelor's degree in religious education from a private school owned by the Assembly of God church. That same year, his idol was assassinated. Lozier read every book written about Kennedy after his death. But he ended up registering as a Republican, and instead of pursuing his passion for politics, he went into business for himself as a builder.

For the next twenty-three years he built houses in southeastern Connecticut and managed rental properties while raising four children with his wife, Nancy. Lozier worked and managed the family's financial affairs. His wife stayed home and raised the kids. They attended the Nazarene Church as a family every Sunday and ate dinner together every evening. In 1989 Joe decided to get involved in local government and ran for a seat on the Ledyard town council, a seven-member body that works in conjunction with the mayor to govern the town. Lozier's mother advised against the move, saying, "Politics is a dirty business and you don't want to do it." She had watched her son go through the sixties without getting involved in the counterculture or political activism. Mrs. Lozier feared he would not hold up well under the pressures and unforgiving nature of politics. His wife, however, knew he would thrive in the political arena. Lozier repelled pressure like rain on an oil-stained deck. Right after getting elected to the town council, Lozier told his wife, "Someday, I'm gonna be mayor of this town."

Two years later, he announced his candidacy. At the time, Connecticut's economy was free-falling. Cuts in the Pentagon's defense budget caused General Dynamics, southeastern Connecticut's biggest employer at the time, to downsize dramatically. And the naval base in Groton reduced its size as well. Both the housing and job markets in towns like Ledyard were crippled as a result. Lozier's campaign centered on his strengths as a businessman with years of experience overseeing local development projects. He had virtually no political experience and was hardly diplomatic in his approach. He said what he thought with little fear of how it would be perceived or whom he might offend. His objective was to restore economic security to his town.

During his campaign in 1991, the subject of Foxwoods was seldom raised. People couldn't afford to buy a house. You couldn't even *give* a building lot away. People were more concerned about whether they would keep their jobs and hold on to their homes than whether or not Foxwoods was going to be a success. Most people were saying, "The Pequots are not going to get people to come into the woods to gamble. In this economy? Never."

But one day while out campaigning, a man asked Lozier, "Joe, what do you think?"

Lozier paused before answering. He had watched the first phase of

Foxwoods, sixty thousand square feet in size, go up at an unprecedented pace in a town that often made builders wait six months for a permit to build a second-story addition. "I think they are going to make more money than anybody can ever imagine," Lozier responded.

On November 5, 1991, Lozier received 2,148 votes for mayor—213 votes more than the incumbent mayor. Just like that, there was a new mayor in town—impetuous, unpolished, bold, and proud of it. His allegiance was to the traditions that he believed had made America great: industry, hard work, faith in God, and family.

Lozier's victory forced his wife to become a working mom, a role she had never before experienced. The mayor's job paid just $50,000 a year, well short of what was needed to support four children (one of whom was in college), pay a mortgage, and meet other family debts. So rather than sell his business, Lozier turned it over to his wife. She oversaw fifty rental properties, dealt with lawyers, and managed the finances for the business. Previously, she did not even manage the family checkbook.

The other major change in Nancy's life came from the requirement to attend public functions. Private by nature, she preferred to remain out of the spotlight. When she attended her first Memorial Day town parade in 1992, she inconspicuously sat down with her children in the VIP section of bleachers. A town worker came over and politely told her, "I'm sorry, ma'am. But you and your children are going to have to move. These seats are reserved for the mayor and his family." Without saying anything, Nancy started to get up and move before a woman behind her told the town employee, "She's the mayor's wife."

Going from "Joe and Nancy" to "the mayor and the mayor's wife" was tough getting used to. But as much as she disliked the new public exposure of her family, she convinced herself it was worth it. Foxwoods was causing Ledyard to undergo rapid and drastic changes. And she was sure Joe's fearless attitude and bedrock convictions toward protecting Ledyard's interests would best serve the town.

On January 27, days after talking to Comrie and Holdridge, Lozier made his regular report at the biweekly town council meeting at the town hall. He complained about the BIA taking the twenty-seven-acre parking lot into trust for the tribe. His report was followed by a presentation from his town planner, William Haase, who stunned the town council by explaining that the Pequots could buy land outside the reservation and have it converted to trust land by signing the title over to the BIA.

This fell under the purview of the Indian Reorganization Act (IRA) passed in 1934 by Congress to protect Indian lands against alienation. It authorized the Interior secretary to take title to Indian tribal lands and serve as trustee over them. The Indians maintained possession and control over the use of their lands, while the government became the owner of record, with the words "United States of America" appearing on the deeds.

In contemporary times, few tribes could afford to buy real estate outside their reservations with hopes of annexing it to an existing reservation by having the government take it into trust. The Pequots, however, were taking in hundreds of millions of dollars through Foxwoods. And the land records at the Ledyard town hall indicated the tribe was using the profits to buy up substantial amounts of real estate outside its reservation. Haase unveiled a color-coded map, which Lozier had asked him to prepare, displaying all the land that the tribe had purchased since the casino opened. In theory, there was nothing stopping the tribe from eventually asking the BIA or the Interior secretary to take possession of the titles to all the newly purchased Pequot properties, converting them to trust properties, and removing the real estate from Ledyard's zoning and tax laws. Haase predicted that the twenty-seven-acre parking lot was just the beginning of a wave of properties within the town that would become converted to federal Indian lands.

Haase's presentation locked the town council room in silence. Few members fully comprehended what Haase and Lozier were suggesting. By passing the 1983 Settlement Act, Congress had cleared the way for the Pequots to forever expand its land base. Lozier told the group that he had already scheduled a meeting in Hartford with Governor Weicker. But a couple of weeks later, Lozier again appeared before the town council and reported on what Weicker said about annexation. "I told Governor Weicker that the BIA took land into trust for the tribe that's outside their reservation," Lozier said. "Weicker said 'No, they can only take land into trust that's within the settlement boundary.'" Lozier told the council that he tried in vain to convince Weicker that the tribe has already done it and will surely ask for more land to be annexed in the future. "Weicker still didn't have that picture in his head," Lozier said.

Days after Lozier reported on his meeting with Weicker, Anna Reiners received another letter from the Trust Services Realty Branch of the BIA. It was dated February 24, 1993. This time she immediately took it to Lozier. It began just like the previous one, notifying Reiners that the bureau was considering an application from the tribe to have additional lands outside their reservation taken into trust by the federal government. As Lozier read further, he became alarmed. This time the tribe was seeking to have six separate parcels on the opposite side of Route 2 annexed to their reservation, significant acreage with commercial potential. To add a new wrinkle, the land they were after extended beyond Ledyard's borders into the neighboring towns of North Stonington and Preston.

When Reiners left his office, Lozier sat down in his chair and rested his back against his leather cushion. He stared across his desk toward the double-hung windows at the opposite end of the room. When he took office, the first thing he did was turn his desk around to face those windows so he could enjoy the view of the tall oak tree outside his office and the site of the town's schoolchildren playing across the street during recess.

But in February, the tree was bare and it was too cold for kids to play outside. He looked back down at the letter on his desk from the BIA. "Ledyard is not going to be Ledyard anymore," Lozier thought to himself. "If indeed the BIA and Pequots are able to do what they want without some checks and balances, then Ledyard is in some serious trouble."

Lozier knew that the town council was scheduled to meet later that evening, and he would have to recommend how they were going to try and stop the Pequots. "We need a lawyer," Lozier thought. "Someone who has a background in Native American issues, someone who is familiar with the workings of the federal government and the BIA. But how do I find somebody like that?"

Lozier knew a lot of attorneys, but none who worked in the areas he needed. As he usually did when he felt duress, Lozier bowed his head. "God," he whispered, "help me find somebody who is honest and will get the job done. Because I know we need someone."

Later that night when he went to the town council meeting, Lozier brought along a copy of the letter he had been handed earlier in the day by Anna Reiners. He read it out loud to the council and said the town of Ledyard could no longer sit back and let the government take land into trust that was outside the reservation. "The impact of this action is serious," Lozier told the council, holding up the letter. "And I intend to go to Washington, D.C., to meet with prospective attorneys for the town." At Lozier's request, the council introduced a motion to appropriate and transfer $1,000 to the mayor's personal expense account to pay for his airfare and hotel accommodations. All nine members voted in favor of the motion.

When Lozier arrived home that evening, Nancy was still awake.

"Hey, Nance," he said, "Do you want to go to Washington with me? The town is sending me down there to speak with Sam Gejdenson and a representative from the BIA, this guy Billie Ott. I'm also going to meet with some lawyers. We would have to pay for your ticket ourselves. But I thought we could go see the Smithsonian and get a couple days together alone."

"Sure," Nancy said. "I'll go."

After nearly missing their flight due to the bad weather, the Loziers arrived at National Airport in D.C. twenty minutes before they were due in Representative Sam Gejdenson's office. Dressed in a suit and carrying mismatched suitcases in either hand, Lozier hailed a cab. "What am I going to say to this guy?" Lozier said, looking for encouragement from his wife as he stood in the waiting area outside Gejdenson's office. Just then, the door opened and Gejdenson started walking toward him. "Joe, just keep your cool," she whispered under her breath.

Gejdenson shook Nancy's hand first, then escorted Lozier inside. As soon as they were out of sight, Nancy sat down on a waiting-room chair and pulled out a paperback book she had brought along. "He wasn't very impressive," she thought after standing face-to-face with a U.S. congressman for the first time in her life. "He looked more like a salesman."

Thirty minutes later Nancy saw Joe coming toward her. His face was cherry red. "Oh, boy," she thought as she quickly closed her book and threw it into her handbag without bothering to mark her place. "If we do not get out of here right away, there is going to be a Joe Lozier explosion right here in the congressman's office."

Without saying a word, Joe grabbed their suitcases and headed for the lobby door. Struggling to keep up with him, Nancy scampered behind him. Before she knew it, they had walked twelve blocks in cold Washington drizzle and Joe had still not said a word.

"What happened?" Nancy asked, laboring to catch her breath.

In front of a McDonald's, Joe stopped and put his suitcases down on the sidewalk.

"He told me, 'Your ancestors killed a lot of Indians,'" Joe shouted over the traffic.

"Well, what did you say?" Nancy asked. Joe was so worked up he did not even realize that his clothes were soaked clear through.

"I told him, 'I'm French Canadian. Most likely we were on the Indians' side,'" Joe responded.

Nancy burst out laughing.

"That about sums up my meeting with our congressman," he continued.

"Well, now what?" Nancy asked.

"Let's step inside and get a soda," he said.

Standing in line at McDonald's waiting to order, he continued to vent. "I come down here to get his support to work with the town, to get his help with the fact that Ledyard now is home to the largest casino in the world and that the Pequots have so many rights," Joe complained. "His response was that 'your forefathers or people killed them and they deserve all these things.' It was not what I expected him to say." Lozier could hardly believe that someone who held the dignified office of U.S. congressman would resort to an argument so foolish as "Your people killed the Indians, so the Indians deserve special privileges." The English killed Indians in New England in the 1600s. Many of the inhabitants of southeastern Connecticut today were Italian, Irish, German, Polish, and many other European nationalities other than English. They were no more to blame for the Indians' destruction than was Gejdenson, who was born in Germany in 1948 and listed his occupation as a New England dairy farmer before getting elected to Congress. "Gejdenson never milked a cow in his life," Lozier snapped.

After finishing their sodas, Joe and Nancy walked the remaining eight blocks to their hotel. After checking in, Joe showered, changed his clothes, and left for his meeting with Billie Ott at the BIA office. When he returned to the hotel nearly two hours later, he had a big grin on his face. "Billie Ott," Lozier said as he entered the room. "Oh, Mr. Billie Ott."

"I take it that meeting didn't go so well either," Nancy said.

"What a complete waste of airfare," Joe said. "Meeting with him was even more of a waste of time than Gejdenson. I know one thing now more than I did before we left to come down here. Ledyard has got to have legal representation if we are going to come out of this thing at all. We need someone qualified to take us through this because I know this is going to be hell.

"And another thing," Joe continued. "The taxi fares in this town are outrageous."

At 2:00 that afternoon, Joe entered the law offices of Perkins Coie on Fourteenth Street NW. Perkins Coie's expertise ranged from computer and high-technology law to international business transactions to lobbying to regulation of political activity.

Lozier met with attorney Guy Martin, one of the managing partners in the D.C. office. Lozier told him about the twenty-seven acres that had already gone into trust and complained about the additional 247 acres that the tribe was asking the Interior Department to take into trust. He also complained about the lack of notice provided by the federal government in both instances, as well as the ease with which the government could take land off the Ledyard tax rolls for the tribe.

Martin was quite familiar with the situation Lozier was describing. He worked in the Interior Department during the Carter administration as assistant secretary of the interior in charge of land and water resources. He knew how the Interior Department went about taking land into trust for tribes.

"Joe," Martin said, "it doesn't seem at all beyond the range of possibilities that Interior is going to go directly ahead on the tribe's 247-acre petition and do exactly what it had done in the instance of the 27 acres. You're in a very difficult situation, mainly because of timing. You have only two weeks until you're supposed to respond to Interior about this latest request. And I can't tell you how difficult of a position you're in with respect to the substance of your problem. I just haven't looked at it enough."

"What are our options?" Lozier asked.

"Well, here are my immediate instincts," Martin said. "Your best opportunity is to try to get a delay while we can assess your situation. My instincts are to immediately appeal at however high a policy level we need to to simply get a delay based on your status as a local government and the apparent haste at which this is being done. We need time to assess your situation and be able to make a meaningful response to this notice from the BIA. We need at least thirty days."

Martin's partner Don Baur had worked as an attorney in the Interior Department's solicitor's office for five years prior to joining Perkins Coie. Together, Martin and Baur had over twenty-five years experience on Capitol Hill. They were the type of lawyers Ledyard needed, but Lozier worried about how to afford them. He had his work cut out for him.

32

COWBOYS AND INDIANS

The Village of North Stonington

The black sign above the entrance read "Old Town Hall." But the white A-frame building with a red door looked more like a church than a municipal building. In rural New England it is sometimes hard to tell the difference, especially in North Stonington. Its first public meeting house was built in 1720 by the North Religious Society of Stonington. A historical marker alongside the town hall pointed out that the village grew out of a settlement formed in the 1660s that later became home to farms, sawmills, and grist mills, thus producing the nickname "Milltown" that locals still preferred to use in reference to their village.

Inside, fifty-five-year-old First Selectman Nick Mullane sat at a conference-room table that he used as his desk. A loaf of zucchini bread contained in a clear plastic bag sealed by a white twister tie sat on top of Mullane's microwave oven in the corner. Beside it stood a box containing packets of apple and cranberry tea. Other than mountain-size stacks of papers and maps, the only other items in his office were a grossly underused paper shredder, a fax machine, and a telephone, which Mullane always answered himself. Many residents in town knew the number to his direct line.

When Joe Lozier telephoned days after returning from Washington, Mullane took off his black-framed glasses with wide lenses and sat down in his wooden chair. His hair was neatly parted to one side, and his eyebrows sported more gray than his head. Mullane was alarmed by the news that the Pequots had applied to the BIA to have 247 acres of land—79 of which were in North Stonington—taken into trust and annexed to their reservation.

But Lozier had a plan. "Ledyard is going to retain a law firm in Washington to help us fight this," he said. "They're going to help us secure a thirty-day extension on the deadline for responding to the Interior Department. I think this is something that we ought to get together on."

"Wow," said Mullane. "How do we go about this?"

Lozier told Mullane that the first step was to seek a thirty-day extension for filing a formal opposition petition to the Department of Interior. In addition, a letter had to be written to the secretary of interior to outline the towns' opposition to the federal government expanding the reservation. Lozier told Mullane that the lawyers he had met with in Washington were preparing a legal argument.

After talking to Lozier for nearly an hour, Mullane agreed to join forces with Lozier. Next, Lozier placed a call to Preston's first selectman, Parke Spicer, a stocky man under six feet tall whose once muscular chest and arms had stubbornly given way to a pudgy stomach. A film of stubble on his cheeks and a blend of gray and black hair that he wore slicked back combined to make his fifty-five-year-old face look ruggedly handsome. Lozier and Spicer knew each other from Republican fund-raisers and cocktail parties.

Spicer was intrigued by what Lozier was proposing. He hated Foxwoods and the fact that it was less than one mile from Preston. It was not gambling that Spicer was opposed to, it was the unfair competition. Since Foxwoods opened, he had refused to step foot on the reservation. "Not once," he told Lozier in his gruff voice. "I can't be opposed to what they are doing on the one hand and go break bread with them on the other."

Lozier soon realized that Spicer was even more militant toward what was going on in Ledyard than he was. If Spicer had his wish, the entire casino operation would be shut down. Lozier was merely trying to make sure it did not get any bigger than it already was. Spicer predicted, however, that casino gambling was only going to get bigger and bigger thanks to the slot deal that Weicker had struck with Skip. "Weicker OK'd the compact," Spicer complained. "Well, federal law says the governor can't do that alone. It takes the consent of the people of Connecticut to legalize slot machines. This tribe is in violation of federal law. But nobody wants to stand up and be counted on that issue.

"What good would it do at this stage?" Spicer continued. "They're here. You can't stop them. Imagine trying to shut that casino operation down? We'd have World War III on Route 2. You talk about cowboys and Indians!"

Lozier shared Spicer's cynical attitude toward the way that politicians in Hartford and Washington had dealt with the tribe and the growth of their casino business. He told Spicer what happened when he went to see Gejdenson in Washington and try to enlist his help. "You think Sam wants to hear about this stuff?" Spicer said. "The guy is worthless. He is. I'm not shitin' you."

The more Lozier talked to Spicer, the more eager he was for Spicer to join him and Mullane in their fight to stop the tribe from annexing more land to its reservation. Spicer was a contemporary Rooster Cogburn—ornery, cantankerous, stubborn, but patriotic and possessed of unsurpassed personal ethics and integrity. Rather than back down from a fight, Spicer would seek one if he believed the cause was just. He was the perfect counterpart to Mullane's Andy Griffith–like disposition. Soft-spoken, polite, and unpretentious, Mullane was a tireless worker with a pragmatic approach to problem solving. The three of them, Lozier believed, working in conjunction with the lawyers in Washington could lead their little communities in standing up to their new unwelcome neighbor and preventing them from turning the entire area into casino country.

Even though Preston had only a half acre at stake, on March 25, Spicer called Lozier to tell him Preston was on board. "The Pequots are fast becoming someone that we're going to have to deal with because they're getting very powerful," he explained to Lozier. "With the slot deal they struck with Weicker, they have the only game in town. It's not going to take them long to amass some real dough. We have to begin to do something. We can't wait till the barn door is open and all the horses have run out before we try and shut the door."

Spicer's call was preceded by some very alarming news he and other

Preston officials had received the day before. Back in 1958, the Mountain Lake Land Company transferred to the Boy Scouts of America 1,200 acres of land known as the Lake of Isles, a sprawling, undeveloped tract of forestland that overlapped the boundaries of Preston, North Stonington, and Ledyard. The parcel got its name from the large lake located in the center of the property. The lake and its surrounding forest offered a vast outdoor wildlife refuge with capacity for camping, hiking, boating, and fishing. The Boy Scouts maintained the Lake of Isles and sponsored scouting activities there from the late 1950s through the 1980s. But by the early 1990s, the Boy Scouts were looking to sell the property. On March 24, 1993, the tribe paid the Long Rivers Council of the Boy Scouts of America $5,500,000 and took possession of the deed.

Even more alarming to Spicer was that the Lake of Isles property was extremely close to the existing Pequot reservation. The only land separating the 2,000-acre reservation from the 1,200-acre Boy Scout property was the 247-acre strip of land that was under consideration by the BIA for being annexed to the reservation. Spicer knew that one of the BIA's prerequisites for annexing land to an Indian reservation is that the land to be annexed must be contiguous with the existing reservation. If the 247-acre annexation petition was approved and became part of the reservation, then the 1,200-acre Lake of Isles property would suddenly become contiguous to the reservation and therefore eligible to be annexed as well.

"All I know," said Spicer, "is that it is a good thing you decided to find lawyers and get us together. In the beginning, no one took this thing seriously. The land that was granted to the tribe in 1983 by the federal government was 2,300 acres. It was a done deal, a boundary, a settlement. At the time it seemed like a reasonable amount of land for fifty people or less. But people in my town are starting to ask, 'What the hell is this?' Something is wrong here and we've got to correct it. I mean, after all, what the hell do they need all this land for?"

It is known in the gambling business as "the Classic Product Cycle." The cycle begins when legalized gambling is first introduced to a new geographical area. The newness of the opportunity to gamble drives an initial period of high profits. But as the newness wears off and the market becomes more saturated with opportunities to gamble, profits drop off significantly. The challenge facing every gaming company is to find a way to avoid the cycle by continually enhancing the desirability of the gaming product. It is the same challenge facing executives in the cigarette industry, the pornography industry, and other businesses enterprises that are wholly reliant on people's addictive tendencies. There is a constant need to control and sustain the urge in consumers to keep coming back for more. Cigarette makers do it by manipulating nicotine levels. Pornographers are less discreet. They simply get more and more graphic. And gambling companies just keep changing the scenery in an effort to make routine betting always appear fresh and exciting. New attractions—restaurants, hotels, and entertainment theaters—are the key to holding on to gambling customers. Brown's philosophy was never to go more than six months without opening something new.

Hayward shared Brown's view. While most casinos expand by adding new gaming space or building a new restaurant, Skip and Brown had something a little more elaborate in mind. The Lake of Isles property was the key to the master plan.

On March 22, just days before the sale to the tribe was finalized, the Boy Scouts' attorney, Glenn Buggy, sent a letter to the Bureau of Indian Affairs. "The [Pequot tribe] has advised us it will accept the property in fee simple by quit claim deed in an 'as is' condition," Buggy wrote, "and will *not* be making an application for inclusion of the property in the Indian Trust or as a Tribal land." A copy of this letter was also sent to Jackson King.

Although the attorneys for the tribe assured the Boy Scouts that the tribe had no intention of asking the BIA to take the 1,200-acre island-resort property into trust, that was precisely what the tribe had in mind. Shortly after the property was bought, Skip and a small group consisting of tribal lawyers and planners flew to China. The trip was one of many that the Malaysian investors arranged for Hayward. He visited the Great Wall of China and went on a tour of Beijing. This was no tourism vacation, however. Hayward went to meet with officials from the Chinese government. The Malaysians were eager to show the tribe models of things that they wanted the tribe to incorporate into the resort. Hayward loved staying in four-star hotels in Hong Kong, visiting the Malaysians' Genting resort in the Highlands, and stopping in Singapore to see some of the amusement parks there.

Days after Hayward returned from China, a five-member delegation of

Chinese government officials arrived in Ledyard. The delegation consisted of members of the Ministry of Construction of the People's Republic of China as well as representatives from a government-owned company called China Construction International. They visited Foxwoods, but the primary purpose for their trip was to inspect the Lake of Isles property. Architects in China were designing preliminary plans for an enormous, state-of-the-art Chinese theme park to be constructed in the heart of the Lake of Isles. Both Hayward and the Chinese officials believed a theme park would greatly enhance tourism on the reservation. Hayward also liked the idea of replicating sections of the Great Wall of China near the casino.

But adding a Chinese theme to Ledyard was only part of Hayward's latest development idea. In addition to touring Beijing, he had traveled to Europe and Japan looking for ideas to make Ledyard a premier tourism attraction spot in the world. He returned and had a conceptual design created for a climate-controlled mass of hotels and outdoor activities and swimming pools. Hayward wanted to dome an entire area in order to create an enclosed environment similar to Bermuda. And he hoped to make all of it more accessible by building an airstrip with a heliport service that offered direct flights to Bradley International Airport in Hartford and JFK Airport in New York.

While immensely expensive, Hayward's grand plan was endorsed by Brown, who thought bigger is better, as did the Malaysians.

33

THE PLEDGE OF ALLEGIANCE

BY THE END OF APRIL, GUY MARTIN AND DON BAUR HAD STUDIED THE three towns' case enough to know that they needed a lot more than thirty days to sufficiently oppose the tribe's annexation plans. Martin and Baur held numerous meetings with officials from Interior and convinced Bruce Babbitt to further delay his decision on the land until August 2. "We have secured a little daylight between now and when the Department of Interior makes its decision," Martin told Lozier, Mullane, and Spicer during a conference call. "We did that because we not only need time to construct a legal response to this 247-acre petition, but we need time to educate a fairly broad audience about what is happening. And we need time to build some kind of political pressure on these decisions."

Martin advised the three leaders to meet with Hayward and explain to him their reasons for opposing his petition for taking land off the tax rolls. "The idea is to slow down the process, create a role for yourselves in this process, and have the towns' perspective heard and your legitimate interests addressed," Martin told them.

APRIL 15
PEQUOT TRIBAL OFFICE

Spicer and Mullane rode to the reservation with Lozier. En route, Lozier told them what to expect from Hayward. Lozier's mind drifted back to 1975 when he was a young and upcoming developer. One of his first housing developments was on Phillip Lane, just a few blocks from the Pequot reservation. Lozier's business partner, Steve Watrous, hired Hayward to clear the building lots on Phillip Lane in preparation for building houses on them. Watrous and Hayward had known each other as teenagers, back when Hayward was just resurrecting the tribe. Lozier paid Hayward less than $6 an hour. Hayward worked hard and talked a lot about Indians. "Back then, Skip always talked about building up the reservation, bringing people back," Lozier recalled. "I always listened to him to be polite. But I never really took him too seriously. None of us did."

Lozier assured Spicer and Mullane that Hayward was the driving force behind the development project. "Skip's a good businessman," Lozier said.

None of the town leaders, however, were prepared for the Pequots' vice chairman, Kenny Reels. None of them had met him before walking into the tribal offices, and it became immediately apparent that he was going to be difficult to deal with. Reels began by delivering a lecture on racism and rights. When Spicer tried to steer the discussion back toward taxes, Reels got angry.

"I told ya," Reels said, looking directly into Spicer's eyes, "We . . . don't . . . pay . . . taxes!"

Spicer resented the fact that Reels did not have to pay taxes. By boasting about it, Reels had struck a raw nerve. At home, Spicer had a very old black-and-white picture hanging on his dining-room wall. It was not particularly attractive—the borders were frayed, the picture was grainy, and the paint on the black frame was chipped. But Spicer kept it up nonetheless. It was a picture of two individuals—a man and a woman—both of whom were born in the Ledyard area just after the Civil War. In the picture, the man was dressed in wool pants and a blue, wool coat. The woman had long, straight, jet-black hair. Her name was Georgianna Ainley, born in 1867. She was a Pequot Indian. She was also Parke's beloved grandmother. The man next to her in the photograph was Gorton Spicer, Georgianna's husband and Parke's grandfather. The two were married on September 10, 1891. When they achieved their fiftieth wedding anniversary in 1941, the local newspaper took their picture. One of their sons was Clarence Spicer, Parke's father.

Yet Spicer had no intentions of trying to join a tribe for financial purposes. "This is the United States of America," Spicer thought. "One nation, under God, indivisible. Yet our laws provide for these people to do certain things that the rest of Americans don't have a right to do. We are trying to divide this United States of America by saying heritage entitles people to different rights."

In Spicer's view, Reels and Hayward and the rest of the tribe ought to pay taxes on any land it acquired outside the reservation, as well as on their automobiles and their income. It was enough that they were given exclusive rights to operate a casino and given an exemption from taxes and land-use regulations on the two thousand acres of property within the reservation boundary.

The confrontation between Spicer and Reels capped off the first face-to-face talks between the tribe and the three town leaders. Afterward, Spicer was still angry about Reels's attitude. "I think what he [Reels] really thought was, 'We're Pequot Indians, and we now have this God-given right to do this,'" said Spicer. "And 'How dare you try and stop us.'"

"They want special privileges," said Mullane. "They think they're different. And if we oppose them, we get a confrontation on a racial issue, or a lecture on what happened in the 1600s.

"Well, you wanna know something," Spicer said. "I'm an American citizen. I was born in this country. And I'm not going to be held responsible for what somebody did three hundred years ago."

"The three of us are traditional in our beliefs," said Mullane. "We believe in the Pledge of Allegiance—one nation, under God, indivisible, with liberty and justice for all. Period. We charge the people taxes and try to preserve our residents' rights."

Five days after the meeting, Mullane received an unexpected letter from Jackson King, who had attended the session. "I must tell you that personally I question the wisdom of the three towns challenging the Tribe in the way they are," King wrote. "When we deal with officials of the state and federal governments, we are generally greeted with respect and admiration. . . ." Mullane had not even finished the sentence and he was ready to call Spicer and Lozier. But he kept reading. "A few weeks ago," King's letter continued, "we were at a dinner whereby the region as a whole proclaimed Skip Hayward as the Man of the Year and the 'Savior of the Community,' primarily for the economic activity and the jobs that have been created.

"Despite all of this," King continued, "you, the mayor of Ledyard and apparently the first selectman of Preston, have chosen to institute legal proceedings to stop the Tribe from placing certain property that it owns in trust so they can expand their reservation."

Mullane removed his glasses and rubbed his eyes. He had known King for a few years and had grown to distrust him. He put his glasses back on and finished the letter, which rambled on for three single-spaced pages. "It is my belief," King concluded, "that when the dust is settled the Mashantucket Pequot Tribe will have expanded its reservation to a reasonable size, and they will own and operate one of the finest resorts in the east, if not in the country."

After writing to Mullane, King sent a letter to Billie Ott at the Bureau of Indian Affairs. Ott's recommendation to the secretary of interior would largely influence Babbitt's decision on whether to approve the Pequots' annexation petition. "We are happy to note," King wrote, ". . . that neither the Towns nor the State are opposed to development by the Tribe." King told Ott that the tribe's plans would pose no significant threat to the towns' tax base. "It seems completely appropriate for the Tribe to acquire through purchase wholly undeveloped property adjacent to its existing reservation to try to re-establish a reservation of reasonable size," King continued. "We would suggest that permitting this property to be brought into trust is not only consistent with federal policy, but that federal policy would dictate that the acquisition be permitted."

At the close of his letter, King assured Ott that the people in the region supported the tribe's petition. "The Tribe has the support and gratitude of the overwhelming majority of the residents and governmental officials of Southeastern Connecticut," wrote King.

APRIL 30, 1992

Some days are just bigger than others. For Skip Hayward, April 30 was one of those days. In the morning he met with his tribal council and passed a tribal resolution allowing the tribe to borrow more money from their Malaysian investors. After passing the resolution, he signed a contract with the Malaysians that had been prepared by their New York attorneys. In exchange for monthly principal and interest payments, the Malaysians agreed to advance Hayward and the tribe $175 million. Brown also signed the document, attesting to Hayward's signature. Brown's friend Colin Au signed the contract on behalf of the Genting investors. The Bureau of Indian Affairs' Billie Ott and Billy Wakole also signed the loan. The BIA had to approve the deal before it could take effect.

The loan went a long way toward forging a three-way partnership between Hayward, the Malaysians, and the Chinese. The theme park that Hayward hoped to construct on the Lake of Isles property had an estimated cost that topped out at $300 million, and the Malaysians were not averse to helping the Chinese finance the project. Any resort development was sure to draw more customers to Foxwoods, boosting the returns on the Malaysians' investment in the casino.

The same day that the tribe's $175 million loan from the Malaysians took effect, the BIA received another trust-acquisition application from the tribe, this one for the Lake of Isles property. Billie Ott's office was asked to recommend to Bruce Babbitt that he convert the Lake of Isles property to trust status, along with the 247-acre strip of land that the tribe had submitted for trust status in January.

By the afternoon of the 30th, Hayward was on his way to Hartford to meet with Governor Weicker. It had been three months since he and

Weicker signed their Memorandum of Understanding that gave the tribe slot machines. Already, Skip and Weicker had agreed to amend their deal. Earlier in the month of April, Mickey Brown received an unexpected phone call at his Foxwoods office.

"Mickey, I'm sitting here with the speaker of the House of Representatives and the president of the Senate," said a tribal lobbyist, whose firm was receiving $100,000 annually from the tribe. "And they have to pass a budget or close down the state of Connecticut by June 30th."

The lobbyist had Brown's undivided attention.

"They are $13 million short of passage," the lobbyist continued. "And if they have to go forward and carve out $13 million, it is all going to be in social services—health care, child services, needs of the elderly. We'd like you to consider increasing your minimum [payment to the state from your slot revenues] for just one year."

Brown had already promised Weicker $100 million in exchange for the exclusive right to offer slot machines. Now the state was asking for $13 million more.

"You give them an additional $13 million," the lobbyist continued, "and they'll close their budget and you'll get credit for it."

Brown hung up the phone and immediately went over to the tribal council chambers. He interrupted a meeting in progress and told Hayward and the others about the call he had just received from the tribal lobbyist.

"What's it going to cost us?" Hayward asked, not bothering to consult his council.

"Quick numbers," Brown answered, "instead of contributing 25 percent of slot winnings this year, you're going to contribute a little over 30 percent. The upside is you save social programs, needs for the elderly, and aid to dependent children."

Brown knew that there was another upside to this deal. And he knew that Hayward knew it too. But some of the other council members had to be clued in. "We're gonna pull their nuts out of a fire," Brown explained. "They are going to have a budget that will include all these social services that they were about to cut. And you did it.

"You will become *the* people—the tribe, the business entity—that saved the state budget and saved all these programs," Brown continued. "Everybody in that legislature is going to know that you came through to break the deadlock at the eleventh hour."

"OK," Hayward said.

The other council members eagerly went along. It was a done deal. In less than ten minutes the tribe decided to give $13 million to the state.

Brown could not wait to get back to his office. He loved working with Hayward because everything was streamlined. There was no democratic process, no bureaucracy. Hayward just made up his mind and everyone followed.

"You got a deal," Brown told the tribe's lobbyist over the phone. "I'll prepare a one-page amendment to the state compact. Skip will sign it. You got your $13 million."

The one-page amendment to the slot deal contained a space at the bottom for Weicker and Hayward to sign. This time there were no press releases sent out and no reporters present. When it was over, Hayward returned to Ledyard. He had $175 million on its way from Malaysia. He had a petition into the BIA to get the Lake of Isles converted to trust land. And for a cool $13 million, he had the state of Connecticut in his pocket.

Two weeks earlier, the towns of Ledyard, Preston, and North Stonington had finally passed resolutions appropriating funds to retain Guy Martin and Don Baur as their attorneys. Combined, the three towns came up with just under $50,000 to launch a legal battle aimed at ending the tribe's massive development plans.

34

THE MASTER PLAN

JULY 25, 1993

IT WAS LUNCHTIME WHEN NICK MULLANE LEFT HIS OFFICE AT GENERAL Dynamics to drive to the Mystic Hilton. When he turned the ignition on in his Dodge truck, the AM radio came on immediately. The station was tuned to WFAN in New York, home to the biggest sports-talk radio program in the country, but today Mullane was not in the mood. After rolling down the window, he leaned over and turned it off. He was edgy and had been since Guy Martin and Don Baur had telephoned from Washington to inform him that Bruce Babbitt's Interior counsel, John Duffy, had agreed to fly up from Washington to meet with him, Spicer, Lozier, and Hayward to discuss the dispute between them. Duffy was bringing Billie Ott along from the BIA.

Days earlier, Mullane had sat with Spicer and Lozier while Martin explained why he thought Duffy had called the meeting. "Over at the Department of Interior they know who I am," Martin said. "It is not that they fear me. But they know that Don and I can mount a formidable political and legal case. I think they are thinking if they meet with you they can solve the problem by meeting directly with three local guys." In Martin's view, this was an opportunity for the three leaders to demonstrate to Duffy how opposed they were to the Pequots' plan and how determined they were to fight it. "Your position is that you do not think *any* of this land should be taken into trust and removed from the tax rolls," Martin said.

But as Mullane drove toward the meeting, he realized he felt intimidated by it all. None of the towns' lawyers was going to be present. So they had given Mullane the assignment of taking notes. Mullane was the most organized of the three town leaders, with an uncanny knack for paying attention to detail and a near photographic memory. The idea of making a written record of Duffy's remarks was a lot more appealing than talking to him. He would leave that up to Lozier and Spicer.

When Mullane arrived at the Hilton, Lozier was waiting for him inside the lobby. Together they went to the front desk and were directed toward a large conference room. The first thing they saw when they entered the room was a large table with white linen on it. It was covered with an array of sandwiches—seafood salad, tuna fish, turkey, roast beef—and iced drinks. A bowl with individual bags of potato chips was in the center. Pickles, olives, and other hors d'oeuvres were laid out on trays that were decorated with salad greens. "Nice spread," Mullane said. "First class."

As soon as Spicer parked his 1982 green GMC pickup truck in the Hilton parking lot, he felt like throwing it into reverse, backing out, and returning home. Convinced the meeting was going to be a waste of time, Spicer angrily climbed out of his truck and put on his sports coat. It was ninety degrees outside, but Spicer never went to official functions in short sleeves. He had a tattoo on his left forearm that dated back to his navy days. He figured the appearance of a tattoo would automatically diminish his image in the eyes of his political peers. Politics was always appearance over substance. That was the part about it that Spicer hated. So he compromised by refusing to wear suits. He wore sports jackets and slacks instead. But he always covered his tattoo.

Inside, he found Mullane and Lozier. "Where the hell is everyone?" Spicer asked disrespectfully, looking around for Hayward, Duffy, and Ott.

Before Lozier could answer, a waiter approached, offered Spicer an hors d'oeuvre, and invited him to help himself to the lunch buffet. "Who's paying for this?" Spicer asked, making no effort to disguise his grumpy tone.

"The Mashantuckets," the waiter said politely.

"Then I don't want any," Spicer snapped. "Take it away."

Nearly an hour later, Hayward entered the room, with Duffy and Ott trailing behind him. Ott was wearing a white shirt with a dark tie. Stylish, dark suspenders held up his suit pants. He had two pens clipped to his shirt pocket. On his wrist he wore what appeared to be a piece of Indian jewelry.

Appearing haggard, Duffy had his shirt collar open and his tie hanging loosely from his neck. The six men went into a private room alone. Duffy and Ott sat beside each other on one side of the table. Lozier, Mullane, and Spicer sat across from them. Hayward sat alone at one end of the table.

"I'm tired," Duffy began. "I flew in here for the day. I don't have time for all this." Appearing bored, Duffy did most of the talking and not, it seemed, for too long. He asked the town leaders and Hayward to meet once more before the Interior Department's August 2 deadline for deciding if the Pequots' land could be taken into trust. "I recommend you people get together and work it out amongst yourselves," Duffy said. "You must understand that the Department of Interior and the BIA has a trust relationship with the Indian tribes. And we are going to look out for their interests. So I recommend you get together and work this out. Because you are not going to like any decision that is made in Washington." They all agreed to meet again.

Just as Duffy was finishing, Kenny Reels entered the room. Before anyone stood to exit, Reels lectured the town leaders on tribal rights and sovereignty. Looking uninterested, Hayward said nothing. And nobody listened.

On the way out of the hotel, Reels pulled Spicer aside. "You know," Reels said, "we could settle this if we just had a beer–ball game."

Spicer was so angry he had to grin. "This guy's not the sharpest knife in the drawer," he thought to himself.

"You know," Spicer said, clearly agitated. "We can't settle it by having a beer–ball game. I'd play ball with you, but we're certainly not going to resolve anything on this issue. It's too big."

Reels smiled. His expression reminded Spicer of something a pundit had once said about Jimmy Carter: "Jimmy Carter doesn't understand that he doesn't understand." Spicer was convinced Reels was too ignorant. "He's just not a leader."

As he walked outside to catch up with Mullane and Lozier, Spicer could not help but recognize the difference between Hayward and Reels. Hayward seemed withdrawn and uncomfortable dealing with the enormity of the conflict. Reels was eager to march ahead, failing to recognize the depth of the towns' opposition.

By the time Spicer caught up to the others in the parking lot, they were already venting. "What the hell was that all about?" said Mullane.

"We waited an hour for this jerk," Lozier said.

"This was just a waste of time," Spicer interjected. "Listening to Duffy was pointless. The tribe already has the Emerald Castle out in the middle of nowhere. We should just paint Route 2 gold and call it the Yellow Brick Road to the Emerald Castle."

When the three leaders called Martin to report what happened, he sensed the unmistakable anger and resentment in their voices. But Martin knew they had accomplished the objective: to present a unified front and a willingness to fight. "Look," Martin said to the three leaders, "the message from Duffy was essentially 'We're planning to go ahead here and going ahead is the right thing to do and you should recognize that.' He was basically trying to call you off as much as he could. And you showed him that you're not going away quietly."

JULY 28, THREE DAYS LATER

Lozier, Spicer, and Mullane arrived at the tribe's office building on the reservation to meet with Hayward, Reels, Jackson King, and Bob Birmingham for the final time before the August 2 deadline. In five days, Bruce Babbitt was due to hand down a decision on the tribe's 247-acre annexation application. Both the Interior Department and the towns' attorneys hoped the three leaders could strike some kind of deal with the tribe that would spare Babbitt from making the decision. Lozier, Mullane, and Spicer were not optimistic about reaching a deal. But they were confident they could fulfill one of the instructions Martin and Baur had given them: find out the tribe's master plan. "We need to know how far the Pequots would like to expand if there were no limits placed on them," Martin had said to Lozier.

As the three of them sat down across the table from the tribe in their council chambers, Lozier wasted little time. "How far are you planning on taking this thing?" he asked. "We're hearing from our townspeople and the newspapers that you're talking about going from the Thames River to the Rhode Island border. Just what are your plans?"

At first, King was reluctant to share those plans, but Lozier became insistent. "Look, people are afraid. People are afraid of losing their homes and their futures. They're concerned. Most of our people's livelihood is tied up in their single-family homes. We need to see what your master plan is. What is your game plan? We need to know what you would like to do in the next ten to fifteen years so that people in the community can at least be aware of what you are trying to do. Fear is a terrible thing. By answering some of these questions, you will help eliminate some of the fear."

"Everybody is asking you where we are going?" asked King. "All right. Our immediate interests would be something about like this." King directed the three leaders' attention to his left. It was the first moment that the three town leaders realized there was an easel set up in the room. On it, tribal planner Bob Birmingham placed an oversized three-foot-by-four-foot map that depicted the southeastern corner of Connecticut. "We'll just draw a line." Birmingham then took a thick, black Magic Marker and proceeded to draw lines on the map showing how far the tribe wanted to expand its borders. As he drew, all three men strained not to show their amazement. Birmingham's lines took in enormous amounts of real estate in all three towns, going far beyond the 247 acres and the Lake of Isles.

Lozier estimated that Birmingham's drawing was showing approximately fifteen thousand acres of land that the tribe wanted to add to what it already had.

Spicer discreetly glanced toward Mullane, trying not to let anyone notice that he was making eye contact with him. Mullane's eyebrows were raised, and the skin on his forehead was wrinkled up like a bulldog. They both rolled their eyes, then quickly looked back toward the map without saying a word. Lozier never looked at Spicer or Mullane. He simply gazed at the map as if he were looking into a giant abyss.

Birmingham continued to talk. He indicated that some of the tribe's development plans included an additional casino, hotels, a couple golf courses, and some parking garages. Lozier was well aware that the area the tribe was targeting was not zoned as commercial property. Rather, it was a combination of forestland, residential neighborhoods, and farmland, all of which would be wiped out if the tribe carried through on its plans. "This is ironic," thought Lozier. "Both Jackson and Birmingham were so antidevelopment before they went to work for the tribe. I don't think either of these guys care, now." Then Lozier glanced at Hayward, who silently watched with approval as King and Birmingham did his bidding.

Spicer did not particularly care for King either, and had never exchanged a word with him, despite being his next-door neighbor. Spicer owned the last house on Route 117 in Preston on the Preston–Ledyard line, while King owned the first house on Route 117 on the Ledyard side of the line. Spicer was not surprised when Lozier told him that King had once defended Ledyard landowners in the lawsuit brought by Hayward and the tribe. "He switched sides for the money," Spicer thought. "If he doesn't do a million and a half to two million a year, he's not making a nickel."

When Birmingham and King finished their presentation, all three town leaders tried not to appear shocked by what they had just seen. Before leaving, they asked King to put in writing the ideas that he and Birmingham had expressed during the meeting. As soon as they were out of earshot from the building, their true feelings spilled out.

"Holy shit!" said Mullane. "Do they really want to take *all* that land?"

"Holy shit is right," said Spicer. "They're going *way* beyond the settlement boundary.

"This is really getting serious," Spicer continued as he wiped the sweat away from his forehead. "*Really* serious! Where in the hell is this going to end? If this is what they want now, how much more are they going to take in the future? According to their master plan, it won't be long before they gobble up Preston. How far can they expand? At some point, isn't the federal government going to say, 'What the hell is going on here?'

"They are getting enough power to suck up an entire county," he continued. "And this isn't like the Midwest, where the next house is four hundred miles away. This is impacting a lot of people in a densely populated area."

Mickey Brown attended none of the private meetings between the tribal leaders and the town leaders. But Hayward kept him well informed of what was going on in them. It was clear to Brown that Lozier, Spicer, and Mullane were hardly enthused about the tribe's plans to expand its development. Brown understood their gripe. He lived in a rural town in New Jersey, to which he retreated on weekends to get away from the pace of Foxwoods. Sea Girt was everything he wanted—small, quiet, picturesque, and safe. Many times Brown had thought how angry he would be had he bought a farmhouse along Route 2 in the late 1980s only to have the world's largest casino crop up next door.

Yet Hayward did not understand why the locals were getting so angry about the tribe's desire to keep expanding its territory. Forgotten was the argument that he passionately delivered to Congress in 1983: *It is an injustice when powerless people continually have their lands encroached upon by greedy outsiders whose sole intent is to exploit the land for personal gain.* Now that he possessed the money and the political leverage, he saw things differently. "I know that I've got a sense that with some folks the town boundaries [are rigid] and they think they should be like that from now to eternity," Hayward thought, "and what folks would like to have jurisdiction over would never change. But the world is changing and evolving every day. It has been for thousands of years, and I don't think we should be so narrow-minded that we think that those boundaries will never change."

Hayward had embraced the same argument that white settlers used to shrink the Indians' land base in the 1800s. Two decades of apathy on the part of the towns toward Hayward's buildup in Ledyard conditioned him to expect that he could continually expand his reservation in their town without reproach. The three towns said nothing when the tribe sued

Ledyard-area residents in 1976 and accused them of trespassing; when Congress gave Hayward nearly a million dollars and increased the size of the Pequot reservation from two hundred acres to two thousand acres in 1983; and when the tribe built a massive bingo hall in the mid-1980s. Some local leaders even applauded the plan. Finally, the towns mounted no opposition to the tribe's construction of the largest casino in America in 1991. So Hayward could not understand why people were all of a sudden opposed to the tribe's attempt to add a few more thousand acres to what they already had.

While King worked to convince the Interior Department to approve the tribe's annexation petition, Brown made a suggestion to Hayward. Circumvent the Interior Department review process by offering the three towns money to drop their opposition to annexation. As always, Hayward liked Brown's idea and authorized King to draft a proposal.

JULY 29
LEDYARD TOWN HALL

A courier carrying an envelope addressed to "Mayor Joseph Lozier" arrived at the receptionist's desk late in the afternoon. When his secretary handed it to him, Lozier was curious. He was not expecting any hand deliveries.

Prone to reading things while walking toward his desk, Lozier opened the package and pulled out the contents before getting to his chair. It was a three-page document printed on stationery bearing the letterhead of the Mashantucket Pequot Tribal Council. The bold-print heading across the top of page one read, "PROPOSAL REGARDING THE PLACEMENT OF LAND OWNED BY THE MASHANTUCKET PEQUOT TRIBE OUTSIDE OF THE SETTLEMENT AREA INTO TRUST."

Lozier sat down. "The following is a proposal of the Mashantucket Pequot Tribe to provide certain benefits to the Towns of Ledyard, North Stonington and Preston in consideration of their agreement not to oppose the application of the Mashantucket Pequot Tribe to place certain properties in trust." Lozier noticed that there was a map with the document that showed the areas the tribe wanted to annex to its reservation. It was not the same map he had seen the night before. But it was similar.

He read further. "In consideration of the agreement described herein, the towns will officially withdraw their present objection to the placement of properties into Trust. The Towns agree not to oppose those properties designated on the map that may be subject to future trust applications." He had no legal background, but Lozier was a businessman. He knew what was coming next—a payoff.

"In addition," the offer continued, "the Mashantucket Pequot Tribe shall pay an additional one million dollars (annually) to each town until a total of five million dollars has been paid to each town." Lozier summed it up quickly. In exchange for his cooperation with the tribe's massive development plans, his town and the two neighboring towns would each receive $5 million.

Skip's signature appeared at the end of the proposal, above a line that said "Richard A. Hayward, Chairman."

Lozier did not know who to target his anger at, Hayward for signing the offer or King for crafting it. "This is a joke," he said in disgust. Lozier could hardly believe that less than twenty-four hours after King and Birmingham had unveiled the map, Hayward was offering the towns $15 million in exchange for a green light to develop thousands of acres without any say from the towns. "Even if I owned this property, I wouldn't buy this deal," Lozier said. "This is a *bad* deal. They make millions of dollars a week at Foxwoods. So they are offering us approximately one week's revenues."

Lozier called Spicer and Mullane to see if they had received the same offer. They had.

"In our discussions, we asked the tribe, 'What's your goal? How much development are you going to do?'" Lozier said to the both of them in a three-way conversation. "We never said to Skip or Kenny, 'How much are we going to get?' That never came up."

"This is an insult," Spicer griped.

"The arrogance," said Lozier as he stared at Hayward's signature at the bottom of the offer. "The arrogance has just built up. You can see it. They think they can just buy and sell a whole community."

As Lozier, Spicer, and Mullane consulted their attorneys as to how they should respond to Skip's offer, they were completely unaware that the tribe had also delivered a copy of the offer and the map to the *New London Day*.

35

DAMN YANKEES

SATURDAY, JULY 31
LEDYARD

THE TOWN HALL WAS NORMALLY CLOSED ON WEEKENDS, BUT JOE LOZIER had gone there to deal with the crisis mentality sweeping through his town on account of the morning headlines. He and thousands of residents woke to the sight of a giant color-coded map on page one of the newspaper. Titled "Mashantucket Pequots' $15 Million Proposal," the map depicted a small green patch in the center representing the reservation. A thin blue strip bordering the northeast corner of the reservation represented the 247-acre area that the tribe wanted the government to take into trust. Just east of that, a large purple-shaded area encompassing the Lake of Isles had the words "to be added to reservation trust" under it.

But the map's red zone was responsible for townspeople's widespread alarm. The reservation and the adjacent 247-acre parcel and Lake of Isles property were encircled by a massive red area that fanned out into Ledyard, North Stonington, and Preston. The key at the bottom of the map indicated the status of the land colored red. "Boundary of area in Pequot proposal to 3 towns," it read. "If Ledyard, North Stonington, and Preston agree to this as potential reservation boundary, tribe would pay each town $5 million, plus annual 'impact aid' to compensate for lost property taxes and town services." (See map on page 355.)

As distraught residents besieged the town hall with phone calls demanding an explanation, Lozier's eyes settled on a quote from Mickey Brown that appeared in an article under the map. "The tribe hopes that by the year 2000, Foxwoods will be to Connecticut what Disney World means to the state of Florida. This is becoming a very, very big business very quickly."

"Disney World in Ledyard, Connecticut. That's just beautiful," Lozier said to himself sarcastically.

His elbows resting on the map, Lozier called Spicer and Mullane.

They too had gone to their offices. "I'm under siege," Mullane said. "Everyone is saying 'Not one acre!'" Residents had been lining up outside the North Stonington town hall to view the copy of the map that Mullane had received from Hayward. Spicer's secretary had fielded over seventy-five telephone calls before noontime. Almost every caller was violently opposed to the towns' accepting the tribe's $15 million offer. "All hell is breaking loose over here," Spicer announced, a touch of glee in his gruff voice. "The map has really stirred things up. People are going bonkers."

The anxiety was erupting in thousands of homes across the three towns as area residents woke up to the frightening sight of a map that threatened to turn their world upside down. Unlike mere words in black print, the colorful map was a graphic illustration of what their communities would be like if the tribe had its way. It showed that the tribe wanted nearly 15 percent of North Stonington's land base, 12 percent of Ledyard's, and 5 percent of Preston's. Approximately seven hundred residential homes and farms were within the tribe's target area. In Ledyard alone, the tribe wanted 2,325 acres of private land that had a combined appraised value of $61.2 million and included 376 single-family dwellings and 541 total parcels of property.

SUNDAY, AUGUST 1

Interior Secretary Bruce Babbitt's schedulers could not have picked a worse time for him to visit southeastern Connecticut. Twenty-four hours after the map was published in the newspaper, Babbitt came to the area to tour a proposed heritage corridor in the eastern part of the state and to announce a plan to increase the salmon population in the Connecticut River. He quickly discovered, however, that reporters attending his press conference had other issues in mind. Babbitt's deadline for deciding on the tribe's 247-acre petition was less than twenty-four hours away. Now that the tribe had put the world on notice that its master plan was to increase its reservation by ten thousand acres, the press wanted to know how that would impact Babbitt's decision.

"We have no intention at this time of getting involved," Babbitt told the press. "My feeling, as a trustee of Indian tribes, is this thing can best be worked out as people talking as neighbors." The announcement was stunning. The secretary of interior was the only person authorized to decide on the tribe's petition. Yet Babbitt was saying he had no intention of doing so.

Another reporter then asked if he had seen the tribe's $15 million offer. Babbitt said he had not but revealed that Sam Gejdenson had described it to him the previous evening. "I think the development is very encouraging," Babbitt said. "What I'd like to see is for them to keep meeting to work it out."

Unwittingly, Babbitt had just thrown fuel onto the fire. The tribe's true motives were out in the open, and area residents fully expected Babbitt to denounce them and rule promptly and in their favor with regard to the tribe's annexation petition. Babbitt, after all, was recognized nationally as a strong proponent of the environment. President Clinton had appointed him with the promise that he would advance the pro-environment stance he had campaigned on in 1992. Yet the Pequots' development plans came with a host of potentially negative impacts on the environment. The tribe planned to develop an enormous resort community as a satellite to the biggest casino in the world. The ten thousand acres they hoped to purchase for their long-term development scheme was primarily a mix of land zoned as forest, residential homes, and farms.

"Bruce Babbitt is just hoping the problem will go away," Spicer said to the press the day after Babbitt's visit to the area. "But it won't go away. It's the secretary's duty to make a decision. We need some direction here so we won't be battling this same issue over and over again for the next twenty years. His office has the final decision, so it's pretty difficult to stay out of it when you have the final decision."

Weeks after Babbitt's visit, hundreds of white signs with red letters showed up all over the three towns. Nailed to trees, staked along roadsides and in residents' front yards, and taped to coffee shop windows, the signs read NO ANNEXATION: NOT ONE ACRE. A grassroots citizens group calling itself "Residents Against Annexation" had formed in the three towns. They packed school gymnasiums to hold forums. They met in residents' homes and made fliers encouraging people to organize, then stuffed them in every mailbox within the three towns. And by October, they had gained enough public support to force the three towns to hold a referendum. Residents Against Annexation wanted to pass an ordinance in each town that prevented the three town leaders from accepting any offer from the tribe that included annexation. The referendum question asked: "Shall the town of Ledyard, through the town council and the mayor, oppose acquisition in trust (e.g. annexation) by any governmental entity of any land in Ledyard for the benefit of an Indian tribe when such land is located outside the boundary of that tribe's federally recognized reservation?" The questions in Preston and North Stonington were essentially the same. If more voters checked "Yes" than "No," Lozier, Mullane, and Spicer would be barred from further talks with the tribe over annexation.

When Guy Martin and Don Baur heard that the towns were going to hold a referendum, they told the three leaders that they opposed the idea. Although Martin thought $15 million was absurdly low, he nonetheless wanted to keep negotiation channels open. Martin felt that as long as the tribe was willing to talk, the town leaders had a chance to shape some type of settlement. Then at least the townspeople could vote on the settlement and decide whether it was more acceptable to them than years of costly legal battles over land annexation.

Martin felt that Babbitt's announcement to put off his decision on the Pequots' 247-acre annexation was historic. Neither the BIA nor the Interior Department had ever ignored a decision deadline in order to allow non-Indians and Indians to conduct private talks in hopes of working out their own solution. It was the secretary's prerogative to rule on annexation petitions, and he routinely did so without trying to accommodate the non-Indian neighbors of tribes. Martin also knew that no municipality in America had ever mounted such vocal opposition to an Indian tribe's effort to have land taken into trust. He feared, however, that if the towns got their backs up too much and missed their opportunity to sit down at the negotiation table, Babbitt would lose patience and side with the tribe.

Lozier opposed the referendum idea for the same reasons and decided he would vote against it. He wanted to fight annexation, but he preferred to do it at the negotiation table rather than in the courtroom.

Mullane also feared that the referendum might create a backlash against the towns by the federal government. But he felt obligated to vote in favor, since he knew his community strongly supported it.

Only Spicer actively promoted the referendum, convinced it would pass with a large majority and unify the towns.

• • •

Tuesday, November 23
1:00 p.m.

Staring out his office window, Lozier saw one hundred miniature American flags stuck in the grass beside the sidewalk leading to the elementary school, where the voting booths were set up. They had been placed there by the group Residents Against Annexation, members of which stood outside the school holding signs that read NO ANNEXATION. VOTE YES NOV. 23RD. YES TO HOME/FAMILY. Lines of residents—senior citizens, middle-aged people, young fathers holding infants over their shoulders, housewives, police officers, construction workers, schoolteachers, firemen, and tellers from the bank down the street—had turned out to vote.

When the polls closed at 8:00, Lozier waited in his office for the results. Camped in the parking lot across the street, Residents Against Annexation also waited, sipping hot chocolate and coffee from thermoses and foam cups. Drivers passing between the town hall and the school honked to show their support for the residents. The referendum was taking on the appearance of a high school pep rally, complete with chants and clapping.

Finally, a moderator in charge of the voting machines determined that more Ledyard residents had turned out to vote on the referendum than had turned out to vote in the previous elections. And 92 percent of them said that town officials should oppose any attempts on the part of the tribe to annex land. As people began popping corks on champagne bottles in the parking lot, Lozier drew the blinds shut and turned off his light. He was among the 8 percent of Ledyard residents who had voted against the referendum, hardly a favorable position to be in for a man whose job stability relied on public support. "This referendum isn't going to solve anything," he said to himself, shaking his head. "We've still got to deal with the Pequots."

In North Stonington, 73 percent of the residents voted in favor of the referendum. Nick Mullane felt relief, assured that he had a clear signal from the town on which way he should lead.

In Preston, Parke Spicer stayed up celebrating until well past midnight. Seventy-eight percent of Preston's residents voted for the referendum. "We're not just doing this for our three little towns," Spicer announced from the town hall basement, standing beneath a painting of

George Washington. "We're doing it for America. Whatever happens here is going to determine how decisions like this are made in small towns all over this country with regard to the expansion of Indian gaming. If we're gonna do battle in this country over this issue, let it begin here."

The results of the three towns' referenda backed Bruce Babbitt into a corner. Babbitt wanted the town leaders to negotiate with the Pequots, but now municipal ordinances said Lozier, Spicer, and Mullane could not negotiate over annexation. As a result, Babbitt had two politically unpopular options. He could grant the tribe's wish to add an additional 247 acres to its reservation. But that would require him to ignore the voice of the overwhelming majority of residents in the towns who opposed annexation at the ballot box. Or he could reject the Pequots' annexation petition, drawing their wrath as well as that of other Indian tribes across the country that would criticize him for ignoring his trust responsibilities to Indians. Neither option was appealing.

In December of 1993, Babbitt teleconferenced with Senators Dodd and Lieberman, Congressman Gejdenson, Connecticut attorney general Richard Blumenthal, Don Baur and Guy Martin, and Hayward. Searching for a way to remove the controversial decision from the Interior Department's hands, the group agreed that the leaders from the towns and the tribe should sit down with a federal mediator and try to resolve the annexation problem through alternative dispute resolution. Babbitt agreed to delay any ruling on the tribe's annexation petition in the interim, convincing Martin and Baur that he was looking for a way around the referendum.

Martin and Baur also believed that if mediation failed, Babbitt would grant the tribe's annexation petition. And once a ruling was handed down by a federal agency—such as the Interior Department—it has less chance of being reversed on appeal than a court case brought up on appeal before the U.S. Supreme Court. So they advised the three leaders to try mediation.

Lozier did not need much convincing to go along. But Mullane and Spicer were less enthused. "I've got a town ordinance that requires me to 'oppose annexation of any land in North Stonington by a tribe or a governmental body,'" said Mullane. "How can I participate in mediation that is intended to reach a compromise on annexation? That would test the fundamental principles of a town government system."

Baur explained that the federal mediator was aware of the binding nature of the referendum. "Any agreement that emerges from the mediation process will still have to be put out to the broader community for approval by the voters in each of the three towns," Baur explained. "If the mediation process produces an acceptable result that is approved by the voters, then you will have achieved a solution based on consensus that will avoid the need for litigation."

Despite the assurance that townspeople would have a final say, Spicer balked. In Spicer's view, rearranging the boundaries of Indian reservations was not the job of a first selectman making $16,000 per year. It was the Interior Department's responsibility. And if Babbitt ruled against the towns, then Spicer was prepared to sue the Interior Department.

"Look," Martin told Spicer, "don't be silly. You should try and make the best deal you can and then judge that against the costs and implications of litigation. Litigation is not a sure thing. This is a tough case to win. Why not take advantage of this to try to negotiate something?"

Finally, Spicer relented. He agreed to mediation only so he could avoid disrupting the unity with Lozier and Mullane.

On April 19, 1994, the three leaders and Hayward signed a Memorandum of Understanding outlining the ground rules for the mediation. Paramount was the requirement that the talks be held in secrecy. Town residents, tribal members, and the media were barred from attending. If the two sides reached a preliminary agreement, it would then be put to the towns and the tribe for a vote of acceptance or rejection.

After a summer of sixty-hour weeks spent trying to hammer out an agreement, the three town leaders and the tribe were each asked by the mediator to produce a last best offer. But Spicer, overcome with physical fatigue and stress, lacked the strength to continue. "I just don't know how much longer I can do this," said Spicer, saggy dark circles under his eyes.

"This whole process is just overwhelming," Mullane agreed. "We're getting pressure from Washington lawyers, angry residents, senators. I've got Senator Dodd telephoning me at my office at General Dynamics in the middle of the day. He called me last week and said, 'How ya doing, Nick? Just thought I'd drop a call and talk to you about what's going on.' He talked to me for twenty minutes. I've got a senior senator calling me at work."

"We're being asked to decide the future for tens of thousands of residents," complained Spicer. "I can't do it alone anymore."

"Try and hang in there, Parke," Lozier said, noting that Spicer had lost considerable weight since the mediation process had begun.

"If my second and third selectmen don't join this process and start coming to these mediation sessions with me, I'm going to quit," Spicer said.

"Quit the negotiations?" Mullane asked.

"No," said Spicer. "Quit as first selectman."

"Huh?" Mullane said.

"I mean it," Spicer said. "This is bigger than me. And I'm not going to make these decisions alone anymore."

The tribe too had grown impatient with the protracted mediation process. So the mediator collected both sides' final offers and from them crafted a proposal, and then submitted it to both sides for their consideration. It called for the Pequots to annex approximately five thousand acres of land to its existing reservation (half of what the tribe wanted), yet it gave the towns authority to enforce its zoning laws on the annexed land.

On September 6, Lozier, Spicer, and Mullane reviewed the mediator's proposal with Guy Martin and decided to reject it. But they were willing to use it as a basis for one last round of talks with the tribe.

Across town at the reservation, tribal leaders reviewed the proposal with their attorney Jackson King. They too voted to reject it. Reels adamantly opposed any settlement that required the tribe to give up its sovereign status. Hayward, although not as militant as Reels when it came to sovereignty, was so confident that Babbitt would rule his way he had no fear of walking away from the mediation process. So the tribal council broke off talks, killing the mediation process altogether. The next day, Jackson King disclosed confidential aspects of the federal mediator's proposal to the press. "We don't want any secrets, because we have nothing to hide," King told the media. The move violated the confidentiality agreement Hayward had signed at the outset. Then on September 11, the tribe went further, publishing a full-page letter in the *New London Day* entitled "A Message to our Neighbors." It spelled out the tribe's last best offer for everyone to read in full.

King and the tribe's tactics caught everyone involved in the mediation process off guard. The town leaders and their attorneys were furious. "It's an extremely poor bit of professional behavior on the part of King," Martin complained. "By releasing these documents, the tribe has created a situation where a negotiated settlement will *never* be reached. So in that sense, Jackson King has become the best friend of the anti-annexation folks. Jackson has pointed the way toward litigation."

With the tribe's confidential last best offer out in public, Residents Against Annexation demanded that the three town leaders follow suit. Lozier, Spicer, and Mullane asked Martin for advice.

"The hardest thing to do as a public official is to do anything that is closed or refuse to release information," Martin told them. "That's sort of the bottom line of our government. But in this case, there's been an agreement to negotiate something behind closed doors and then put it to a vote. So pledges were signed not to release the negotiation documents. That's very common in negotiations, whether it's a contract or government action."

"But why can't we release it now that the process is over?" asked Mullane.

"If we come to litigation, that would be harmful to the three towns," explained Martin. "You don't want your negotiation positions aired out before going into litigation. It's a mistake legally and in terms of your political strategy to release these documents."

This time Spicer agreed with Martin fully. "Some of the things that we discussed during those negotiations," Spicer said, "clearly were *never, ever* going to happen! But we discussed them in the course of negotiations. And those are the kinds of things that really sound bad when the press gets ahold of it. It doesn't make any difference that we did not take those things seriously. The way it will be portrayed in the press is, 'You were negotiating to turn over ten thousand acres of land.' And I am really, really unhappy that the tribe has printed its documents in the newspaper."

As Lozier listened to Spicer, Mullane, and Martin talk on the conference call, he could not stop stewing over the stack of protest letters on his desk from Residents Against Annexation. The group's leader had sent a certified letter demanding Lozier turn over all documents pertaining to the mediation process. "Since you have failed to honor our oral requests [for documents], we are obliged to make this formal written request pursuant to the Connecticut Freedom of Information Act," the letter said. The group also promised to sue Lozier if he failed to comply.

"I'm not givin' them a thing," Lozier insisted. "I signed a document promising not to release papers. I intend to honor it."

36

RACE MATTERS

AT THE HEAD OF THE TRIBAL COUNCIL CHAMBERS, TWO GOLD NAMEPLATES rested less than two feet apart on the dais. One bore the inscription "Richard A. Hayward," and marked the chairman's seat; the other, "Kenneth Reels," marked the vice-chairman's seat. Despite appearances, Hayward and Reels rarely sat side by side, since they did not usually attend tribal meetings together. Seldom around the reservation, Hayward maintained a presidential-candidate-like schedule, traveling throughout the country and beyond to examine other world-class resorts and to drum up political support. Since Foxwoods opened, he kept company with the rich, the powerful, and the famous. He had gone on a cruise with the sultan of Brunei, slept in the Lincoln Bedroom while visiting President Clinton, and attended shows with Frank Sinatra.

Reels made it a point to stay close to home. He surrounded himself with an entourage of lawyers, business consultants, and personal assistants who were hired after he gained power and the tribe grew wealthy. And they kept him apprised of the growing unrest among tribal members. Complaints were coming from the newer, predominantly African American members who were dissatisfied with benefits being offered by the tribe. Some were content with their newfound wealth. Patricia Fletcher, for example, had been a single mother raising five children in Brooklyn, New York, when she ran into a distant aunt while attending a wedding in the late 1980s. Her aunt told Fletcher of the promise of financial prosperity on the horizon at the Pequot reservation. Fletcher moved to the reservation in March of 1989 and joined the tribe. She began drawing a salary of $45,000 as an administrative assistant for the tribe. After Foxwoods opened, Fletcher moved into a 3,500-foot home with two fireplaces, a sauna, a Jacuzzi, two staircases, and an in-ground pool surrounded by a rustic wooded yard.

Others, however, saw how much money Foxwoods was generating and felt entitled to much more. "They told us before we moved in you only have to pay $70 or so a month [for housing]," said Vincent Sebastian, who worked in construction before moving to Ledyard. "Then just before we moved in they went up on us. I have to pay $500 a month!" Sebastian joined the tribe figuring he would become an instant millionaire. "Right now I figure we all should have gotten five to seven million dollars," he said. "I haven't got my first million. My wife's got to work. People should be enjoying themselves. Why can't I have a BMW? They [tribal executives] got condominiums in New Hampshire. Only thing I got is that new house.

"Hey, I'm a Mashantucket," he said. "I want to feel like a Mashantucket. Don't make me feel low. Don't take millions and give me just a little."

Sebastian's son had previously been incarcerated on a drug conviction before joining the tribe. After his release, Sebastian's son expected the tribe to provide him with a generous stipend. The tribe offered him a small stipend and $50 per week in food vouchers. Under Hayward's philosophy, Sebastian's son would have qualified for a much larger amount if he enrolled in school and stayed out of trouble with the law. But Sebastian saw the requirements as unjust. "They took away my son's incentives," Sebastian complained. "They can't tell my son he has to go to class. Why should you be forced to go to class? It's like being in prison. If you give people money, you don't tell them how to spend it."

Hayward had long made it clear that he did not want the success of Foxwoods to turn the reservation into a welfare state, where tribal members lose their incentive to work and go to college. He believed it was enough to offer tribal members nice homes, generous stipends, and free education and health-insurance benefits. But as Foxwoods' profits steadily increased, discontent within the tribe spread.

Sebastian and others saw skin color as the motivation behind the policy that dispersed higher stipends to members based on longevity in the tribe. Most of the old-timers in the tribe were white, while the newcomers were primarily black. And word got around the reservation that Hayward's ancestors had historically disliked the presence of blacks on the reservation. "All of them are of Negro blood and are 'squatters,'" one of Elizabeth George's relatives complained in a 1950 letter to the Connecticut governor. "These people are getting the benefits from the reservation that should be for the Pequots."

Vincent Sebastian resented the tribe's white ancestors, who he believed looked upon blacks as inferior members of the tribe. "My mother used to sell her land in Rhode Island to feed these white niggers—Indians, if you want to say," Sebastian said.

Other members agreed, among them sixty-six-year-old Phyllis Waite. "I was the first tribal member of color to come back [to the reservation]," Waite said. "There were personal attacks on me because of the blacks I brought in [to the tribe]."

Reels paid particular attention to these complaints. He was also aware of the members who felt they were victims of racial discrimination at the casino, both in Foxwoods' hiring practices and in the way they were treated inside the facility. "The white Indians were more approachable to the powers that be," Waite said, referring to the hiring practices at Foxwoods. "Our people are so mistreated at the casino. I walked in one night. We were asked to leave from a table. I said, 'We're tribal members!' I looked up and who came in but a whole lot of white people. I wasted no time in hollering."

In Hayward's absence, Reels addressed the unrest by asserting his authority and solidifying his power. Under the tribal constitution, when the chairman is absent, the vice-chairman has the right to act as chairman and with the council's consent pass tribal resolutions—orders that carry the weight of a tribal law. Reels endorsed a resolution altering the structure of the tribal government by adding two seats to the tribal council to better reflect the tribe's changing racial diversity. He also helped form a grievance board that provided tribal members an opportunity to voice rising concerns over the distribution of jobs, housing, benefits, and incentives on the reservation. The tribe also struck the one-sixteenth blood requirement as a prerequisite for membership in the tribe.

These moves pleased African American tribal members, who quietly began encouraging Reels to run against Hayward in the annual tribal elections. To them, Reels listened and responded to their concerns, while Hayward listened only to Mickey Brown. And like his supporters, Reels disagreed sharply with Hayward's and Brown's views on what the tribe should do with its fortune. Hayward insisted on investing Foxwoods' profits in commercial development projects, real estate, and the acquisition of nongaming businesses off the reservation rather than into the pockets of tribal members, a strategy endorsed by Brown. Brown, who had Hayward's full trust in terms of his ability to manage the tribe's billion-dollar asset, felt that reinvesting Foxwoods' proceeds back into the business made much more sense than wasting it on excessive spending by tribal members.

In 1995, under Brown's leadership, Foxwoods made more money than any casino in U.S. history. The "handle" (or gross earnings) exceeded $1 billion, with net earnings, or EBIDA (earnings before interest, depreciation, and amortization), exceeding $300 million. Yet Brown was being forced to borrow money to pay for construction upgrades to the casino. The $300 million-plus in casino profits for 1995 was turned over to the tribal council, which had fallen largely under the control of Reels. In Hayward's frequent absence, the tribal council had approved budget measures that drained the casino revenues. The council took approximately $100 million off the top to pay for tribal government and other costs, including seven tribal council members' salaries, benefits, private expense accounts, travel expenses, and other operational costs that ate up roughly a third of the casino's profits. The tribal government's spending represented the highest expenditure per capita by any government in the world.

Of the remaining $200 million in casino profits, a significant portion was spent paying annual six-figure stipends to some adult members on the tribe's burgeoning membership rolls. In 1990, before construction of Foxwoods began, the tribe had 194 adult members. In 1993, after Reels was elected vice-chairman of the tribal council, he took over the tribe's enrollment committee. As such, he had oversight responsibility for who was admitted to the tribe. During his tenure, the percentage of African Americans in the tribe increased dramatically. Also, headhunters were secretly employed and specifically instructed to recruit only people of color to fill employee positions within tribal-run businesses. In 1993 alone, a hundred new members were allowed to join the tribe, a 36 percent increase that pushed the tribal population to 275 adult members. As a result, the tribal council also underwent a dramatic change in its racial makeup. By the start of 1994, Hayward was only one of two white members left on the council. Meanwhile, Reels's mother, Juanita, was among those elected to the council. And by August of 1995, the tribe listed 383 members on its rolls.

The influx of new members placed great strain on the casino's profits. In addition to paying generous stipends to adults, the tribe also paid smaller stipends to all the children, as well as housing costs, medical coverage, day care, college tuition, and other membership benefits. The spending left few proceeds for construction costs, forcing the tribe to borrow large sums of money to finance their development plans, which included golf courses, a theme park, more hotels, an airstrip, and camping and boating facilities. Despite a $200 million credit line made available to them by the Malaysians, the tribe was driven to issue approximately $300 million in bonds in an attempt to raise more capital for construction costs.

Its ability to borrow hundreds of millions of dollars through the bond market was fueled by the "A" rating the tribe's gaming enterprise received from Standard & Poor's in 1995. It marked the first time that a gaming company had received an "A" rating, which tells investors that the bond issuer's capacity to meet its financial commitments is strong. Along with the rating, Standard & Poor's also issued a credit-analysis report of the tribe's gaming company and a list of five essential keys for investors to evaluate in assessing the business risks associated with investing in a gaming company. Two of the five keys identified by Standard & Poor's were "access to the property and adequate parking facilities." Parking and access "drive a casino's profitability," according to a Standard & Poor's report entitled *Gambling on the Gaming Industry*. Parking determines how many bodies can enter a casino. The more convenient it is for patrons to drive their own car, park it inside a garage, and walk to an elevator and into the casino, the stronger the attraction. From day one, Foxwoods' capacity always exceeded its parking spaces.

The tribe now found itself suddenly beholden to the bond ratings system. If unable to maintain a preferred "A" rating, revenue for development would dry up. The push to get approval from the Interior Department to annex land for the purpose of building parking facilities took on paramount importance.

Despite their differences, Hayward's and Reels's personal ambitions were remarkably similar. The year after Foxwoods opened, Hayward and his wife moved off the reservation and out of Ledyard completely. They purchased a $770,000 home on Fischer's Island Sound in Morgan Point—an exclusive, predominantly white area of Groton—with very few homes and framed by the Atlantic Ocean. To expand their waterfront property, the Haywards also bought an adjacent strip of land beside their home for an additional $150,000. It contained a one-bedroom bungalow and more coastline access.

Like Hayward, Reels too moved off the reservation and out of Ledyard after the profits started rolling in from the casino. In 1995, Reels, a bachelor, paid $555,000 for a house with beachfront property in New London, the town with the highest African American population in southeastern Connecticut. His property contained a hundred feet of shore along the Thames River.

Although both had moved off the reservation, they maintained addresses there, taking full advantage of the tax-exempt status granted to automobiles owned by tribal members living on the reservation. Hayward owned a red four-door Lincoln, a gray four-door Lincoln Town Car, a black Ford Ranger, and a black Oldsmobile Bravada, all registered to his former address of 9 Elizabeth George Drive on the reservation. Reels owned a red Dodge pickup truck, a red Chevy Suburban, and a black Lexus registered to his address at 11 Ephraims Path on the reservation.

With Jackson King's assistance, Hayward and his wife also formed a limited liability company. Under the name Bannerstone, LLC, Hayward purchased valuable commercial and residential property around Ledyard, including parcels off the historic Gallup Hill Road. Similarly, Reels, with the help of his own financial advisers, formed KR Investments, under which he started buying up investment properties in Norwich. He bought a Laundromat, two apartment complexes, an office building, and a nine-hole golf course for $451,000.

Power was the only area in which Reels played second fiddle to Hayward. Presiding over the tribe from its start-up days in the mid-1970s to its achievement of fantastic wealth in the 1990s, Hayward had earned respect and name recognition among federal politicians, the press, and international businessmen. And as chairman of America's richest Indian tribe and chairman of the board of its monstrous casino, Hayward had political influence that transcended his tribe. His name had become synonymous with Pequots and Foxwoods. Outside the reservation, Reels remained a cipher.

The memorandum made Brown edgy. It was issued by the tribal council and announced the hiring of a new internal auditor for Foxwoods. Under other circumstances, Brown would have been relieved, as he had been searching for one since the previous auditor left the job months earlier. However, the memorandum on his desk informed him that the council had hired Deno Marino to fill the position. Brown shook his head. Reels had hired him back while Hayward was away on a business trip. The last time Brown had seen Marino was the week Luciani was ousted as CEO of Foxwoods in 1992. Brown never forgave Marino, convinced he had conspired with Reels and other council members to run Luciani out. Now the man Brown disdained was going to be in charge of auditing the books for Foxwoods.

37

DISCOVERY

WHEN MEDIATION TALKS BROKE DOWN, GUY MARTIN ASSURED JOE LOZIER that the towns would get their day in court. Martin had learned that the Interior Department would approve the tribe's 247-acre annexation application in light of negotiations breaking down. He also learned that he would get a chance to challenge the Interior Department's decision before it took effect. Bruce Babbitt's legal counsel, John Duffy, assured Martin that they would delay putting the ruling into effect in order to give Martin time to file a temporary restraining order in federal court.

Martin and Duffy had a relationship dating back to the early 1970s, when they were neighbors in Washington, D.C. They made extensive renovations on their homes at the same time, borrowing tools from each other and helping one another when possible. They became friends and gained great respect for each other, traveling in similar circles in their careers. When mediation talks broke down between the three towns and the tribe, private negotiations between Martin and Duffy heated up. Martin negotiated an agreement with Duffy whereby Duffy agreed to announce Babbitt's decision in a way that would give the towns time to go to court and seek a preliminary injunction before the land was taken into trust.

In anticipation of this, Martin's law partner, Benjamin Sharpe, was added to the towns' legal team. As one of the firm's best trial lawyers,

Sharpe assumed the primary responsibility for suing Babbitt once the decision was announced. He began preparing a request for a preliminary injunction.

Sharpe's addition to the case was coupled with the decision by Connecticut attorney general Richard Blumenthal to join the towns in suing Babbitt. Blumenthal's announcement united the three towns and the state against the tribe and the federal government. It also reunited Blumenthal and Sharpe. Back in 1973, Sharpe clerked for Supreme Court Justice Harry Blackmun, and he had recommended Blumenthal, then a young law school graduate, to succeed him.

On May 1, 1995, the Interior Department announced its decision in a press release. "The Interior never wanted to force opinions down anyone's throat," a spokesperson for Interior said. "Everybody wanted negotiations to work, and everybody knows this is going to be hard to live with. We just couldn't wait forever." The press release said the federal government would complete the procedures to officially transfer the land into trust within a week.

One week after the Interior Department's decision was announced, Sharpe and Blumenthal separately sued Bruce Babbitt and accused him of abusing his discretion as the Interior secretary by acting in an "arbitrary and capricious" manner when deciding to approve the tribe's trust application. Sharpe argued that the terms of the 1983 Settlement Act, which created the tribe and its reservation, also prohibited the federal government from taking any additional land outside its reservation into trust. Sharpe claimed that Babbitt knew the provision existed but ignored it and did what the tribe wanted regardless. And he asked the federal court to issue a preliminary injunction halting the Interior Department from taking the land into trust in order to review the administrative record to determine the motivation behind Babbitt's decision.

JUNE 27, 1995

Judge T. F. Gilroy Daly, whose six feet five inches and gray hair cut an imposing figure, invited Sharpe and lawyers from the Interior Department to meet in his chambers. Shortly after arriving, Sharpe realized that Judge Daly did not think a preliminary injunction was necessary. Instead, Daly wanted the Interior Department to give its word that it would delay taking the land into trust until he had enough time to look over the record in the case. When Sharpe countered that an order was necessary from the judge because the Interior Department's word could not be trusted despite whatever assurances the lawyer gave, Daly took exception.

"Mr. Sharpe," Daly said in a soft yet deliberate tone, "it has been my experience that lawyers are honorable. I just don't see any reason for an injunction. A lawyer's word is his bond.

"Wouldn't you agree, Mr. Armstrong?" Daly said, turning to the Interior Department's lawyer.

"Well, I'm not sure the secretary wants to do this," Armstrong replied. "We might hold off taking the land into trust for a week or so. But we are not prepared to do more than that."

"Mr. Armstrong," Daly said, "I have the power to hold your client in contempt. I just want to make sure you understand it is *my* schedule that counts, not your client's."

After listening to Sharpe and Armstrong continue to argue over the need for an injunction, Daly finally cut off the argument. "Mr. Armstrong, I'll tell you what," he said. "I'm going to sit here and talk nothing but baseball with Mr. Sharpe. And why don't you walk in the other room there and call your client and see if he won't agree that he's not going to take this land in trust until I decide this case."

Armstrong left the room and returned a few minutes later. "Well, Your Honor, I'm pleased to say that I've reached my client and they are prepared to say they won't take the land into trust for four weeks."

"Thank you, Mr. Armstrong," Daly said. "But I think you missed the point. The point is I wanted you to ask your client that he agree not to take the land into trust until *I decide* the case. I think you better go back in there and call him again."

Judge Daly and Sharpe talked baseball for a few more minutes until Armstrong returned a second time. "Your Honor, I'm pleased to report that my client says he will not take the land into trust until you decide the case," Armstrong began, "if Mr. Sharpe's clients will agree that the Indians can park on this land in the interim."

"Wrong answer, Mr. Armstrong," Daly said. "I want you to know I'm entering the order this afternoon enjoining the secretary of Interior from taking the land into trust."

Stunned, Sharpe listened as Armstrong silently endured Daly's order. Daly had just changed his mind from not issuing a preliminary injunction to issuing one without even holding a hearing. "Talk about seizing defeat from the jaws of victory," Sharpe thought to himself, realizing that the Interior Department had pushed Judge Daly right where Sharpe wanted him to go. That afternoon, Judge Daly issued a court order indefinitely blocking Babbitt from taking the Pequots' 247 acres into trust until the lawsuit was resolved.

Sharpe immediately returned to Washington to start preparing his case for trial. He had roughly six months to come up with the evidence to back up the allegations he had made when he filed the lawsuit, namely that Bruce Babbitt had ignored federal procedures and violated federal laws when he approved the Pequots' trust application. Normally, Sharpe would have the benefit of the discovery process, a pretrial device used by lawyers to force the other side to turn over potentially damaging information through depositions and document requests. But discovery is not permitted in lawsuits that challenge decisions made by federal agencies, such as the BIA or Interior Department. The only thing the Interior Department was required to turn over to Sharpe was a certified copy of its administrative record relating to the Pequot trust application.

For weeks, Sharpe, with the help of Don Baur, poured over thousands of pages of documents contained in six bound volumes turned over by the Interior Department. But he honed in on three internal memos from BIA officials to Babbitt's secretary over Indian affairs, Ada Deer. The memos outlined the justification for Babbitt's decision to convert the Pequots' 247 acres to federal trust property.

The first memo Sharpe reviewed was dated May 1, 1995, the same day that Babbitt's decision was announced. In it, the director of the BIA's Trust Responsibility office, George Farris, told the Interior Department that the Pequots planned to use the 247 acres as a buffer zone designed to limit development.

"*Buffer zone?*" thought Sharpe. "This is kind of confusing." Sharpe had a set of construction plans that the tribe had created for the 247-acre area back in 1992. The blueprints depicted a parking garage, parking lot, lodging, shops, a two-million-gallon water tank and supply system, and a portion of a golf course.

Sharpe also had a copy of a letter he had obtained from the Connecticut Traffic Commission. A consulting firm working for the tribe had written it, outlining the tribe's request to have Route 2 widened. Referring to the 247-acre parcel, the letter said that the tribe planned to perform "major earth work and rock ledge removal."

Sharpe turned back to the Farris memo. "The BIA knew damn well this land was not going to be a buffer zone," Sharpe said to himself.

Setting the Farris memo aside, Sharpe turned to the second memorandum, written by Franklin Keel, the BIA's area director. Keel's memo was dated January 27, 1995, four months before Farris's. Keel also addressed the question of how the tribe intended to use the land in question. "The Tribe plans to use this land to provide a buffer zone as a barrier for commercial development," Keel wrote.

Sharpe laughed. By asking to have the land taken into trust and converted to federal Indian land, the Pequots were attempting to remove the 247 acres from local and state land-use regulations and tax laws. But land-use regulations and tax laws do not prevent the tribe from preserving land in its natural state or designating the land as "green space." As the owners of the property, the tribe was perfectly capable of maintaining the land as green space without transferring the title over to the federal government. But in order to develop the land without paying taxes or complying with local zoning and environmental laws, the tribe needed the government to take possession of it and convert it to federal Indian land.

Finally, Sharpe turned to the third and final recommendation memo. It was dated October 28, 1994, and was signed by Keel's predecessor, Billie Ott, the former eastern area director for BIA. Ott began his memo by writing, "On January 1, 1993, the Mashantucket Pequot Tribe submitted an application to the BIA Eastern Area Office for the conversion of six parcels of land into trust for gaming purposes. This land consists of 247 acres which will be used for parking in support of their casino operation."

"Gotcha!" Sharpe whispered. Ott's memo was the earliest of the three fact-finding reports written to Babbitt's office on the Pequots' intended use for the land. And it verified that Ott knew they intended to use the land to support Foxwoods. Sharpe looked at the footnote Ott had typed at the bottom of his memo. It defined "gaming purposes." "Land is considered for use for gaming purposes if it is an 'enhancement of a recent gaming facility,'" Ott wrote. "In this context the subject parcels are to be used as a parking lot in support of the Mashantucket Pequot's Class III gaming operation, therefore, the land is considered to be used for 'gaming purposes.'"

Sharpe reveled in Ott's admission. "The BIA's guidance that Ott cites in this footnote could not be more explicit," Sharpe whispered to himself. "It is a description of when a trust acquisition involves gaming. Ott says that if the tribe is adding a parking lot to be used by gamblers parking, then it is clearly a gaming purpose."

The Indian Gaming Regulatory Act forbade taking Indian land into trust for gaming purposes unless it was contiguous with an existing reservation. Yet the Pequots' 247-acre parcel was separated from its reservation by Route 2.

Sharpe smiled as he carefully arranged the memos from Farris, Keel, and Ott side by side. "This is the best evidence that Babbitt's decision was arbitrary and capricious," Sharpe thought. "No one can tell us what the real intended use of the land was."

In the bottom right-hand corner of each document Sharpe attached a sticker bearing the word "Exhibit." He then presented the documents to Judge Daly as evidence that the Interior Department administrative record was flawed. He asked Judge Daly to grant him permission to conduct discovery and depose members of the BIA and Interior Department. The government protested Sharpe's request vehemently, arguing it was improper in an administrative record-review case to permit discovery. Ninety-nine times out of a hundred, judges agreed. Daly ruled Sharpe's way, however, permitting him to question a limited number of individuals who had worked on the Pequots' application. Depositions were scheduled to begin in the fall of 1995.

While Sharpe started compiling a list of people to depose, Don Baur sent a series of maps to Ledyard's town planner, Bill Haase. The maps were part of the administrative record and reflected the 247-acre settlement area. Baur asked Haase to locate the deeds and property titles to each of the parcels within the 247-acre area and then attach them to the corresponding lots shown on the map. When Baur received the map back from Haase, the six lots within the 247-acre area were tagged with a corresponding deed and title.

Baur noticed that the last lot within the area—Lot 110, an eighty-two-acre parcel that was the largest of the six lots—had a yellow sticky attached to it with a handwritten note from Haase. "Don," Haase had written, "this is odd. It seems like some money was used from the settlement fund to buy land outside the settlement boundary." Baur removed the note from the deed to Lot 110 and noticed that the deed showed the tribe had purchased it in 1984. "This particular parcel was purchased early in the tribe's history, when it had no money other than the settlement fund to buy land," Baur thought. "Settlement funds were most likely used to pay for Lot 110."

Baur immediately reviewed a letter he and Sharpe had seen in the administrative record. Roger Sumner Babb, an attorney in the solicitor's office, wrote it on January 28, 1988—more than three years before Foxwoods opened. It was addressed to the BIA's Billie Ott, who had previously written the solicitor's office seeking a legal opinion on whether the BIA had authority to take land into trust that was outside the Pequots' reservation. "In a letter from the tribe's attorney, dated December 17, 1987, a strong case is urged that lands acquired outside the 'settlement lands' must retain its fee status only when the tribe's settlement funds are used for the acquisition," Babb wrote to Ott. "This interpretation of the statute is at odds with its legislative history, and we cannot agree with it. The legislative history states 'that lands not falling within the definition of 'settlement lands' are to be held in fee by the Mashantucket Pequot Tribe and are not to be taken into trust by the United States.' The contours of the Act are immediately apparent. Lands acquired by any means *within* the 'settlement lands' may be taken in trust. Lands located *outside* the 'settlement lands' must be held in fee and are not subject to restrictions against alienation."

Baur saw that Ott responded to Babb's ruling with another memo that called Babb's opinion "rigid." Then, Babb sent a second memo to Ott on May 30, 1990, and changed his opinion. In the second memo, Babb concluded that the BIA could take land outside the Pequot reservation into trust as long as the land was not purchased with funds from the $900,000 Congress set aside for purchasing land within the settlement area.

Together, Baur and Sharpe looked at the deed to Lot 110 and recognized that it was part of the old George Main estate property. Most of the estate fell within the reservation and had already been taken into trust back when it was purchased in 1984. They noticed Billy Wakole from the BIA's realty office had signed the deed that transferred most of the estate over to the government. But Wakole did not sign the deed to Lot 110, an indication that the BIA knew that the Settlement Act forbade them from taking land into trust that was outside the settlement area.

Sharpe and Baur were stunned that Babb reversed his own ruling after Ott complained. He had gone from saying that land outside the reservation could not be taken into trust to saying that land outside the reservation could be taken into trust as long as the land was not purchased with settlement funds.

"Wait a minute," said Sharpe. "Let's start from the predicate here. Our view is that under the terms of the 1983 Settlement Act, *no* further lands can be taken in trust outside the settlement area. So in our interpretation of the act, the source of funds to buy land is totally irrelevant. But when Babb changed his opinion and proceeded down this path where the source of funds became important, I just don't think anyone at BIA thought about the consequences of this decision."

"Right," said Baur. "If Lot 110 was purchased with settlement funds, it was illegal for the secretary to take it into trust, under Babb's analysis."

"Better still," said Sharpe, "if the BIA knew Lot 110 was purchased with settlement funds and then approved it for trust acquisition anyway, then we really have something here.

"Let's find out what Mr. Wakole has to say about Lot 110 in deposition."

The moment that Kenny Reels hired him back as the tribe's internal auditor in January of 1995, Deno Marino knew he would be at odds with Hayward and Brown. Reels was at loggerheads with both men over the way Foxwoods was being run. And Reels made it clear to Marino that he wanted him to come back and scrupulously audit every aspect of the casino, going back to day one. He gave Marino carte blanche to investigate everyone, including Hayward and Brown, to see if he could detect any evidence of impropriety.

After expanding the audit staff from five to thirty people, Marino convinced the tribal council to form a separate independent audit committee, comprised of only three members: himself and two tribal council members. Without Hayward's knowledge, Marino led them on an investigation into Hayward's alleged private dealings with the building contractor who had built Foxwoods. But after months of investigation, Marino lacked evidence of any wrongdoing.

"What do you think we should do?" Reels asked Marino.

"I'd like to call a couple of CPAs whom I know from Atlantic City who specialize in construction contracts. You should have them take a look at this."

Both Reels and Marino immediately knew they had a problem. In order to hire CPAs as outside consultants, Hayward would have to give his approval. Yet he was the chief target of the investigation.

Without disclosing the motivation, Reels pushed the tribal council to endorse Marino's plan. When Hayward caught wind of it, he resisted, distrusting Marino.

With the investigation stalled, Marino met privately with Reels in his office about some unrelated matters. After the meeting Marino walked past Hayward's adjoining office and headed toward the elevator. While waiting, he saw Hayward, darkly tanned and dressed in a Hawaiian shirt and dungarees storming toward him. "Who the hell do you think you are?" shouted Hayward, who was darkly tanned from a recent vacation. Hayward was enraged by rumors that Marino was investigating allegations concerning him and the construction of Foxwoods.

Convinced Hayward would strike him, Marino retreated until his back was pressed up against the elevator doors. As the doors opened, a security guard stepped between Hayward and Marino, giving Marino a chance to move into the elevator. "Get the hell outta here!" Hayward shouted. "I don't wanna see you again!"

38

BIG BOYS DON'T CRY

NOVEMBER 6, 1995

"WHAT'S GOING TO HAPPEN IF DAD LOSES?" SIXTEEN-YEAR-OLD SCOTT Lozier asked his mother, Nancy, on the morning of the election.

Nancy Lozier dismissed the question with a joke, but privately, she too was convinced her husband was not going to win reelection. When Scott left the room, she stood alone, thinking about a crucial decision Joe had made months earlier that she believed would cost him his job as mayor.

Shortly after the towns sued Babbitt and the federal government, a local reporter uncovered evidence that Jackson King and the tribe had sent a confidential forty-page document from the mediation sessions to the BIA after the talks broke down in 1994. The documents King provided the BIA implied that the three town leaders were willing to permit the annexation of much more land than the mere 247 acres contained in the tribe's application. The Interior Department relied on those documents for part of its justification for allowing the tribe to annex the land. When news of the story surfaced, Jackson King readily admitted to sending the document to the BIA. "We sent it and we have no bones about it," said King.

"Unbelievable," fumed Spicer at the time, stunned by King's disregard for the confidentiality agreement. "Unbelievable. I don't know what to say. Signing things don't mean much anymore. The Memorandum of Understanding has been turned into a piece of garbage. I would think any credibility the tribe had is gone at this point."

Martin and Baur were also furious with King, viewing his actions as a blatant attempt to manipulate the mediation process to gain political advantage. But members of Residents Against Annexation, who were already after Lozier to release to the public the last best offer he and the other two leaders had made to the tribe, were more angry at Lozier than King. They had always distrusted King and the tribe, and had argued it was reckless for the towns to participate in any negotiations with them.

Nancy remembered how Joe felt tremendous pressure to release his documents from the mediation following King's admission. Since Spicer and Mullane had previously admitted to destroying their copies, Lozier was the only one left with a copy. And the longer he kept them secret, the more ammunition he provided his political opponents to use against him in the campaign. Lozier talked to Mullane about it and told him he felt justified by virtue of the confidentiality agreement in keeping the documents private. "You might be right," Mullane warned. "But you might be *dead* right."

Finally, Lozier called Guy Martin for advice. "How much would it hurt our legal case against the Interior Department if I release some of the things that were in that agreement?" asked Lozier. "The reason I'm asking is because it would benefit me big-time politically if I can release some information about the mediation agreement to the public."

"I understand it will help you politically," said Martin. "But it will hurt us legally."

"Well, I'd like to give them *something*," Lozier said.

"Joe, you do what you have to do," Martin said, careful not to offer political advice to Lozier. He was retained to represent the towns' legal interests, not advise Lozier on his political strategies. Lozier was on his own on this one.

When Joe hung up with Martin, Nancy asked him what he was going to do. He wasted little time responding. "First of all, I signed a piece of paper and gave my word that I would never release the documents," he said. "So what good would my word be as a politician if I broke my word and released them now in an attempt to get reelected. Second, Guy Martin said I would hurt the three towns' legal case against the government if I released them at this juncture."

Lozier never released the documents. And on October 22, 1995, the Freedom of Information Commission ruled that he did not have to. It rejected Residents Against Annexation's petition to force Lozier to disclose the documents. The commission's ruling vindicated Lozier against his critics. But Nancy feared the victory over RAA before the commission would cost him at the ballot box.

Suddenly, Nancy stopped thinking about all that. She was interrupted by the familiar sound of Joe pulling into the driveway with his new Lincoln.

"Nancy," he called moments later as he came through the back door, "how many votes do you think the new Lincoln will get me?"

She knew he was joking but couldn't bring herself to laugh.

"It doesn't matter," she said somberly, "because I don't think you're going to win anyway."

NOVEMBER 7

It was 8:45 A.M. when Joe arrived at the town hall. But he was unable to follow his typical routine. He was unsure he would still be Ledyard's mayor by day's end. After looking at his mail, he walked across the street and voted at the elementary school. At 9:00 A.M. he exited the voting booth. The polls had already been open for three hours. As he walked back to his office alone, he tried to convince himself that he still had a chance. He had given everything to the town. He was the first leader in any of the area towns to stand up to the tribe. He had found the Washington lawyers. And his opponent in the race was Wesley Johnson, a member of the town council—the same town council that authorized every move that Lozier made.

Nancy kept Scott and Amy home from school to help rally people to vote for Joe. For weeks they had been driving around town stuffing fliers in mailboxes, putting up signs, and talking to residents. But Election Day was spent making telephone calls, hundreds of them, to prospective voters. By 6:30 P.M., Nancy had rounded up all four of their children, including the two who no longer lived at home. "I started feeling like he was going to lose and I wanted all of his kids there when it was announced. That's how we do stuff here—as a family—whether it is good news or bad news."

At 7:30, Lozier joined his family at the Ledyard high school. At 8:00 the polls closed. Lozier's gray suit and his white shirt were remarkably straight, showing no signs of wrinkles or perspiration. He spotted his daughter Amy, her white wool sweater sporting a red ribbon around the neckline. Her soft brown hair dangled over her shoulders. "She's a beautiful girl," Lozier thought to himself before reaching for her tiny hand. At 8:05 a voice read the final tallies off as another woman simultaneously phoned them in to the local newspaper. Joe Lozier, 1,886 votes. Wes Johnson 2,042. Ledyard had a new mayor.

Lozier heard a familiar sniffle, then felt a teardrop on his hand. As a photographer approached, he wrapped his arms around Amy, shielding her face from the camera.

"He lost. He lost," said Nancy, her voice tailing off. It seemed like only yesterday that she had felt his lips against hers before he said, "I'll see you in four years." "Joe always kept his word," she thought to herself. It had been exactly four years, and now he was coming home. She glanced down and saw Amy crying in Joe's lap. Nancy knew that at school the children of Pequot tribal members had told her, "My parents hate your dad."

"It is ironic," Nancy thought. "The Ledyard residents, not the tribe, drove my husband out of office."

Relieved, in a sense, that he lost, Nancy knew how depressed Joe would get once the realization set in that he was not mayor anymore. But that was better than what she had endured for four years. No more fifteen-hour days. No more dinners with an empty chair at the head of the table. No more letters to the editor containing painful criticism of the man she loved. No longer would she have to secretly remove the nasty postcards from the mailbox that were addressed to her husband from town residents. "I'm just happy to have him back."

At 8:15, Joe took his family out for pizza. The following morning, he got up and went to work at his normal time. When Nancy picked up the newspaper, she saw him and their daughter on page one. The photograph was of Joe trying to console his crying daughter. "Of all the pictures in the whole world to print," said Nancy when she saw it. "That's terrible!"

In the days that followed, Lozier refused to show his true feelings in public. But the lack of support from the town tore him apart inside. Privately, he was devastated.

Nick Mullane was voted out of office the same day Lozier was. Despite having the best chance of getting reelected, Parke Spicer did not even bother running again. After twelve years in office, he decided to leave on his own terms.

NOVEMBER 9
WASHINGTON, D.C.
LAW OFFICE OF PERKINS COIE

When Ben Sharpe attended law school, one of his favorite classes was Evidence. Trials are often won based on what evidence is put before the jury, or more important, what evidence is excluded from the jury. Sharpe never ignored the rule he learned in law school. Nor did he forget the motto that accompanies it: preparation, preparation, and preparation. He relentlessly gathered facts through the discovery process so he could design questions that forced witnesses to either make devastating admissions or lie under oath. As he looked at the set of questions he had spent weeks preparing for BIA employee Billy Wakole, Sharpe could not wait until 9:30 to start questioning him. Sharpe and Baur had a strong suspicion from the documents that people in the BIA were aware that it was illegal for Lot 110 to be taken into trust by the Interior secretary. His mission was to find a way to get Wakole to admit that under oath.

At 8:55 Sharpe's telephone rang. There were three Justice Department attorneys on the speaker phone. He said nothing as he listened to them speak. A few minutes later he hung up and immediately dashed out of his office to find Baur.

"You're not going to believe this," Sharpe told him, a wide grin on his face. "Barry Brandon just called me from Justice. He had Ann Juliano and

Steve Carroll on the line with him. They had been preparing Billy Wakole for his deposition this morning, and discovered that Wakole *knew* that Lot 110 couldn't come into trust."

"Wakole *admitted* that?" Baur asked.

"It gets better," Sharpe said. "Wakole also told them that his boss knew it and he had basically instructed him to lie."

"And the Justice Department just told you all this?" Baur asked, puzzled.

"They felt they had an ethical obligation to disclose it," Sharpe said. "And with my permission, *they* would put it on the record when the deposition starts."

Twenty minutes later, the Justice Department lawyers showed up with Wakole at Sharpe's office. Wakole sat down next to the court reporter who planned to record the deposition. Four Justice Department lawyers sat next to Wakole: Barry Brandon, Ann Juliano, Steve Carroll, and Joel Armstrong. David Moran from the Interior Department solicitor's office was also with them. Sharpe sat across from Wakole and was flanked by Baur; their legal assistant, Patricia O'Toole; and Richard Blumenthal's assistant attorney general, David Wrinn.

All eyes were on Wakole as Brandon began the questioning before turning it over to Sharpe.

"Mr. Wakole, could you please state your name for the record?" Brandon asked.

"My full name is Billy Wakole."

"Mr. Wakole, where do you work?"

"I work for the Bureau of Indian Affairs at the Eastern Area Office in Arlington, Virginia."

"How long have you worked there?"

Sharpe was on edge as Brandon asked the preliminary questions, finally getting to the point where Wakole explained that he knew all along that Lot 110 had been purchased by the tribe from George Main with Settlement Act funds appropriated by Congress.

"Did you write this down or did you tell someone orally?" Brandon asked.

"I wrote it on a yellow pad," Wakole said. "I noticed in a couple of drafts later—typed drafts—that it was omitted. I don't know if it was inadvertently dropped by the secretary or whoever."

"Did you orally tell anyone of this fact?"

"I told my area director."

"And who was that?"

"Billie Ott."

"And what did Mr. Ott say?"

"At that point in time he didn't say anything. I pointed it out. I told him about it and pointed it out. Then later on I got the draft back that said, 'Don't add fuel to the fire.'"

"And that was written?"

"It was written on a yellow sticky."

"Other than writing it on the pad and telling Mr. Ott, did you make this fact known to anyone else?"

"No. I was never asked from that point on."

"I don't have any further questions."

Wakole's testimony supported all the suspicions that Sharpe and Baur had when they read the administrative record. Wakole admitted that Billie Ott, a senior official in the BIA, knew that Lot 110 was ineligible for trust acquisition and that efforts were made to hide this from Babbitt's office by removing references to it in the original draft memo that outlined the fact-finding process.

Sharpe proceeded to ask Wakole a different set of questions. He was particularly interested in the fact that the original draft report in which Wakole said he noted the problems with Lot 110 and delivered to Ott was not included among the documents turned over by the BIA during the discovery process. Sharpe knew it was illegal to suppress or destroy documents, particularly those that may be incriminating.

"You mentioned that you noted the fact that Lot number 110 was purchased with settlement funds in a document. I think you called it a draft memorandum."

"Yes," Wakole responded. "It's a draft memorandum that I prepared to make note of the case."

"To whom is that memorandum addressed?"

"That would go to two steps. First, to my immediate supervisor. Then it would go from there on to the area director."

"Do you know if that document still exists?"

"No. I don't know."

"Do you know whether your memorandum to the eastern area director is a part of the administrative record in this case?"

"I don't know. But I think it should be."

"I would agree with you on that," Sharpe said. "Let me have the reporter mark as Exhibit 3 a document entitled, 'Memorandum: To: Area Director, Eastern Area Office; From: Realty Officer, Eastern Area Office; Subject: Review of Trust Application, Mashantucket Pequots.'"

Sharpe paused briefly, shuffling through his notes. He had written down that Wakole claimed to have told only his supervisor, Billie Ott, about Lot 110.

"Did you speak to him in a conversation or was this through a memorandum or other written communication?" Sharpe asked.

"As I remember, I spoke to him orally and questioned the document in hand."

"At the time you were presenting him a draft?"

"One of the drafts. Yes. I think it was the second or third one. Somewhere along there, my original sentence was not included."

"And was it at that time that Mr. Ott said, 'Don't add fuel to the fire'?"

"Yes."

Sharpe shuffled his notes again. He had only one more area to probe.

"Have you ever had conversations with representatives of the Mashantucket Pequot tribe about this?" Sharpe asked.

"Yes," Wakole said.

"Can you recall with whom you might have had those conversations?"

"Mr. Jackson King was the representative of the tribe."

After Wakole said that he and King had discussed that Lot 110 was ineligible for trust acquisition, Sharpe pressed further.

"And what did Mr. King tell you?"

"He said he was aware of it and they were prepared to drop the parcel from the request."

"Did Mr. King disclose to you how he had become aware of this fact?"

"No."

"Did he indicate to you that he had been aware of it for some time?"

"No. But he should have. I mean, it is common knowledge."

"That 110 was the fee portion of the Main estate?"

"Yes."

By the time Wakole finished talking and left Sharpe's law office, Baur and Sharpe knew their case against the government had just taken a dramatic turn.

They asked the government to conduct an internal investigation looking into possible corruption at the BIA. Less than two weeks later, on November 28, the tribe withdrew their request to have Lot 110 taken into trust. After the tribe's announcement, the Justice Department determined that the Interior Department had no choice but to drop the eighty-two-acre parcel from the application because to do otherwise was illegal. The case was still a long way from going to trial, and the tribe's annexation petition had already been reduced by 82 acres to 165 acres.

For Lozier, Mullane, and Spicer, the developments in Washington were bittersweet. They each had only a few days left before they were scheduled to have their offices cleaned out in time for their replacements to be sworn in during the first week of December. "Hey, Joe," said Spicer. "All I can say is that it is a good thing you found these lawyers. Without them, our towns would never have come out of this thing alive."

When Lozier got home hours after Baur told him about the new developments in the case, he told Nancy, "Goliath suddenly looks vulnerable." Nancy sensed the tone of depression in his voice, however. This David would no longer be going to battle.

39

SOMEONE BROKE INTO YOUR OFFICES

THURSDAY, DECEMBER 7, 1995
FOXWOODS EXECUTIVE OFFICES

MICKEY BROWN WAS WORKING AT HIS DESK WHEN GEORGE HENNINGSEN, Foxwoods' senior vice president of operations, charged into his office. He seemed unsettled.

Before Brown asked, Henningsen said, "Somebody broke into the record room down at the Route 2 offices on Sunday afternoon."

"Who?" Brown asked.

"A state trooper and a tribal security guy," said Henningsen.

Brown scowled. "What's going on?"

"I don't know." Henningsen knew only that a locksmith record reported a break-in on November 12th, a Sunday afternoon.

Brown directed Henningsen to telephone the tribe's security director, Richard Sebastian, since he had apparently authorized the break-in. But when Henningsen reached Sebastian that afternoon, he denied involvement.

"I didn't authorize anything," Sebastian insisted. "They didn't break into anything."

"We got a locksmith bill," Henningsen said.

"I never authorized that," Sebastian said. "I'll investigate that for you."

Henningsen reported his conversation back to Brown, who then directed Henningsen to go forward with his own investigation. Even though Sebastian was a tribal member and in charge of the reservation's small tribal police force, Brown had disciplined him numerous times in the past and felt he was incompetent. Brown had so little trust in Sebastian's abilities that he had hired an outside security specialist to perform some of the duties that Sebastian was supposed to perform. Henningsen, on the other hand, was a former New Jersey state prosecutor and an experienced criminal investigator.

By the end of the day on the 7th, Henningsen received a report from Richard Sebastian. It was vague on details but indicated that the purpose of security officer Wilson's entry to the business records office on November 12 was to investigate "a foul odor that Wilson noticed when he was delivering food to the Security Office at the location" earlier that day. But Sebastian claimed that the foul odor was propane gas.

Brown had to laugh when he heard Sebastian's alibi. "The office is closed and is heated by electricity and they smelled *gas*?" Brown asked.

Henningsen shrugged his shoulders and grinned.

"So they broke in," Brown said. "They use a ruse that they smelled gas. And the first thing they do is put paper over the windows and then rifle through all these files? Find out what the hell is going on."

FRIDAY, DECEMBER 8

After arriving at the executive offices for Foxwoods, Henningsen and Foxwoods' general counsel, Robert Winter, had Michael Wilson brought in for questioning. When asked to explain what he was doing outside the business offices when he detected the foul odor on a Sunday afternoon, Wilson contradicted Sebastian's report. Wilson said that he had gone there to check on a security officer, not to deliver food. Wilson then said that he "preferred not to answer any questions" about the incident. He said that Sebastian had told him to direct all questions to him.

"Are you refusing to answer questions?" Henningsen asked.

Wilson hesitated, then agreed to continue. When asked what happened next, Wilson said that while outside the business offices, he smelled marijuana. As a result, he contacted locksmith Norman Vitale, filled out the necessary paperwork, and returned to the business office to investigate. He claimed he brought a state trooper "along for the ride." Wilson said that when he and the trooper got to the building, he still smelled "a burning substance which he felt to be marijuana." He admitted that he never invoked the company's emergency reporting procedures and had no explanation for why.

Henningsen asked him if his account was the truth.

"I wouldn't swear to it," Wilson replied.

After a few more pressing questions, Wilson finally admitted that his tale was a "lie" and refused to answer any further questions. Henningsen, who had already figured that out, had Wilson escorted into the waiting area in the Foxwoods' executive offices and instructed him not to leave the building under any circumstances. Henningsen then paged Richard Sebastian and directed him to come to the executive offices for questioning at once.

An hour later, Sebastian showed up. He told Henningsen that he had given Wilson "the 'okay'" to enter the building after Wilson called him at home on November 12 and reported the foul odor. Sebastian said that the state trooper who accompanied Wilson was Detective Richard Perron. Sebastian admitted to knowing Perron personally, having been introduced to him in the casino by another state trooper, Sergeant Jack Drumm.

As the questioning continued, Sebastian admitted that the report he had furnished Henningsen the day before was only "partially true," claiming he knew the "real" reason for the entry into the financial offices. Sebastian then went on to explain that two weeks prior to November 12, one of his assistants had received intelligence from "an elderly black female employee who worked in the finance department." She had alleged that someone in the finance department was secretly shredding documents and that someone had been blacking out information on documents. She suspected that some of the Foxwoods contractors were being billed twice. Sebastian insisted that the "real reason" for entering the finance room was to search for documents that could verify this employee's allegations.

Henningsen then asked Sebastian why he never notified Henningsen or Brown. Sebastian said it was because Wilson and the others had no "real evidence" of the alleged double-billing scheme.

By midafternoon, Henningsen and Winter reported their interviews with Wilson and Sebastian to Brown. He had heard enough. He picked up the telephone in his office and called over to the tribal chambers where the tribal council was in session. Aware that he was on speaker phone, Brown announced to the entire tribal council, "I'm suspending Richard Sebastian right now!"

There was a pause. "Why?" one of the council members finally asked.

The delay in the question gave Brown time to recover his breath before launching into one of his trademark tirades. "He allowed the state police to break into an office on a Sunday afternoon without any authority," Brown said, his voice quickly finding its staccato rhythm. "I don't know what they were looking for. I don't know what they took. I don't know what they planted. OK? No search warrants. It is a private building, located off the reservation. They broke into your office. Sebastian arranged it. He's suspended right now. I'm just telling you as a matter of notice!"

No one ever addressed the council in such a forceful manner. But Brown did not care. And not one tribal council member protested. Even Sebastian's father, Clifford, remained silent. "You do what you gotta do," Hayward finally interjected, giving Brown the go-ahead to suspend Sebastian. That afternoon, at 4:30 P.M., Richard Sebastian was suspended without pay.

Brown could not understand why the tribe's security division was secretly working with the state police to investigate its own employees in the Foxwoods financial office. And particularly why he, the CEO, had been left out of the loop.

While Brown and Henningsen vowed to continue their internal investigation over the weekend to better understand the motive and who was involved, Jackson King and tribal council chief of staff A. Searle Field huddled to work on damage control. They had become very skilled at suppressing its internal problems and preventing them from reaching the newspapers. In the event that Sebastian's suspension became public knowledge, they wanted to be ready.

The strategy that the tribe's advisers drew up over the weekend assured that the media would focus on the state police. A decision was made to have Hayward send a strongly worded letter to Governor John Rowland criticizing the actions of the state police. As chief executive officer of the state, Rowland presided over the state police force and was in a position to call for an internal investigation into the activities of the officer who entered the tribal office and the sergeant who approved it. Although the letter was to be signed by Hayward, the responsibility for writing it fell to A. Searle Field. Field, a lawyer with political aspirations of his own, was perfectly suited to craft language that would incite the governor to action favorable to the tribe.

Prior to becoming chief of staff to the tribal council, Field was Governor Lowell Weicker's chief of staff from 1993 to January of 1995. Once Weicker left office, Hayward hired Field to work for the tribe. Two months after taking the position with the tribe, Field attended a meeting with Governor-elect Rowland in Hartford to discuss their hope of building a casino in another part of the state. Shortly after the meeting, the Connecticut Ethics Commission accused Field of flagrantly violating the state law prohibiting former state employees from appearing in front of his former agency less than one year after leaving office. "Mr. Field is by far the most senior person who has been found in violation of this law," commission executive director Alan Plofsky said at the time. "He made a serious mistake." The commission called Field's conduct "exceedingly negligent" and fined him $2,000—the maximum penalty.

Weicker came to Field's defense by writing a letter to the commission. "We have a lot of regard for the [former] governor here in this office," Plofsky said in response to Weicker's letter. "But as Weicker himself said at the Watergate hearings, no one is above the law." Field ultimately signed a stipulation and paid a fine. "It never occurred to me that my attendance [at the March meeting with Rowland] would be in violation of [the revolving-door policy]," Field wrote.

He quickly established himself as the tribe's most powerful adviser.

MONDAY, DECEMBER 11

When Hayward arrived at his office in the morning, he had a number of documents on his desk pertaining to the break-in. Brown had sent him a two-paragraph memo notifying him that Henningsen and Winter were continuing their inquiry. "We will keep Council advised both orally and in writing as this inquiry continues and additional disciplinary action becomes necessary," Brown wrote. Brown had forwarded a copy of the memorandum to Jackson King.

Hayward also had Field's letter awaiting his signature. "Dear Governor Rowland," it began, "I am writing to enlist your immediate assistance in the investigation of an extremely serious situation which has just come to our attention. The enclosed investigative report would indicate that a member of the State Police has been involved in two illegal break-ins involving Mashantucket Pequot Tribal property.

"We cannot overemphasize the alarm and concern that we have for these activities," the letter continued. "I am sure you will agree that if these activities in fact took place it goes to the heart of the relationship between the Mashantucket Pequot Tribe and the State of Connecticut." Rowland, like Weicker, had come to rely on the tribe's more than $100 million in slot revenues annually. "We cannot imagine a more serious infringement upon our Tribe's rights of self-government, sovereignty, and privacy than to have police officers of the State of Connecticut engaged in what appears to us to be criminal activity involving Tribal businesses and properties," the letter continued. "In addition, in any society few activities are more dangerous or disconcerting than when police become involved in illegal or criminal conduct."

Hayward turned to the second page of the letter to read the closing paragraph that Field had written for him. "We would ask you to make this a matter of immediate urgency and that you provide the support of your office and the Connecticut State Police in bringing this matter to a conclusion as soon as possible. . . ." Hayward signed his name and the letter was sent out.

TUESDAY, DECEMBER 12
TRIBAL COUNCIL CHAMBERS

Brown could not wait to reveal the contents of the report in his hand. Henningsen and Winter had tracked down Nicole Adams, the security employee who had signed Norm Vitale's authorization to open the business records office. Under questioning, she admitted knowing that the stated reason for entry recorded on the locksmith request form was false. Adams said she signed it because she knew the entry was part of a two-month secret investigation being conducted jointly by Sebastian's tribal security staff and the state police. She also admitted attending meetings with a group of individuals, where alleged document destruction and alteration of records by Foxwoods employees in the finance department was discussed. Adams said that private records from the investigation had been stored in the desk of Gerry Maranda, one of Sebastian's subordinates. Adams said that Maranda had a "prior banking background" and was used for that purpose. She also said that the documents they had collected were turned over to "accountants" to review for evidence of criminal activity. She said an accountant had found no evidence of crime but confirmed the "documents were suspicious." She did not know the accountant's identity.

As the council meeting was called to order, Brown was asked to make his report. He told the council he had the results of the investigation and reiterated that Sebastian should be kept on suspension without pay. But Brown was quickly interrupted.

"This is a tribal member," Reels complained. "You have no right to suspend him without a hearing." Reels's sentiments were quickly supported by councilors Michael Thomas and Pedro Johnson.

"Shit," said Brown. "He broke into your office. It's your office. Do you want people breaking into your office without a search warrant?" Brown was incredulous. Reels, Thomas, and Johnson were more uptight at him for suspending Sebastian than they were at Sebastian for authorizing a secret break-in to the tribe's offices. Sebastian's suspension remained in effect, however. Hayward and the other three members of the council supported the suspension.

As the tribal council argued over what to do with Sebastian, Governor Rowland received Hayward's letter in Hartford. Less than twenty-four hours later he wrote a letter to the commissioner of the state's Department of Public Safety. "I am writing to you regarding a matter of the utmost importance," Rowland wrote. "I was contacted by Richard A. Hayward, Chairman of the Mashantucket Pequot Tribe. In his letter, he presented me with findings of an investigative report revealing that a member of the Connecticut State Police has been involved in two illegal break-ins involving Mashantucket Pequot Tribal property.

"We must take every step possible to determine whether the alleged wrongdoing occurred and, if so, to prosecute the individual(s) involved to the fullest extent of the law. I expect you to devote your attention and resources to addressing this matter."

The Public Safety commissioner immediately announced that the state police would be conducting an internal investigation into detective Perron's actions. The State Police Internal Affairs Unit agreed to probe whether Perron had committed "conduct unbecoming an officer and cowardice."

Similarly, Kevin Kane, the state's chief attorney, announced a separate investigation into potential criminal charges against Perron. Kane too had received a letter from Rowland. The actions taken by Rowland generated just the kind of public relations spin that the tribe had hoped for. Virtually all the focus shifted to Perron and alleged state police misconduct. "Break-ins at Casino to Be Investigated: Rowland Orders Probe into Charges Against Police Officers," read one headline on December 15.

The tribe also spent thousands of dollars in advertising, running a series of full-page advertisements criticizing Perron in Connecticut newspapers. "The sad thing about this whole matter is that if the state police officer now being investigated by his own department wanted information," the ad claimed, "all he had to do was ask, instead of sneaking around in the dark. There is such a thing as protocol, a right way to do things and a wrong way."

The tribe's efforts took the focus away from Sebastian's apparent involvement.

Christmas week, Brown and Henningsen's investigation moved on and continued to claim casualties. First, Henningsen learned that the "confidential source" in the finance department who was bringing allegations of "double billing" by Foxwoods employees was Geraldine Ramsey. She worked in the accounts payable department and insisted that vendors were being double billed. And the mystery accountant who was reviewing the documents that Ramsey was collecting was Gerald Maranda, a deputy under Sebastian. Maranda had some experience as a bank loan officer. In an interview with Henningsen, Maranda confirmed that he had been asked to review documents secured by Ramsey. When the documents failed to support the double-billing allegations Ramsey was making, Maranda got involved in a plot with Sebastian and Wilson to break into the business records office to look for more checks to Foxwoods vendors that might support Ramsey's claims. Henningsen also discovered that Sebastian had authorized a special investigation unit inside the security department. And they even had a code name for their break-in operation: "D-Day."

On December 26, Sebastian's temporary suspension was upgraded to a permanent termination. That same day, Maranda was also fired.

Brown and Henningsen's investigation came to a close shortly thereafter. Their authority to question witnesses extended only to employees of the Pequot Gaming Enterprise, so they had no jurisdiction to interview the state police officers regarding their role in the break-in. They had to wait for the State Police Internal Affairs Unit to complete its investigation. The results infuriated Brown.

Prior to the break-in, Sergeant Jack Drumm was contacted by Richard Sebastian and informed of a possible larceny in the Foxwoods accounts payable department. The employee bringing the allegation implied that Foxwoods management was involved in a billing scam and that she would face repercussions from them if they learned of her disclosure to the authorities. At Sebastian's request, Drumm and his commander, Bradley Beecher, went to Sebastian's home to discuss how best to handle the investigation. When they arrived, three members of the tribal council were present: Kenny Reels, Michael Thomas, and Pedro Johnson. They revealed that they were already secretly investigating a billing scam at Foxwoods and had asked the tribe's Independent Audit Committee to participate. Deno Marino was the head of the audit committee.

Days later, when the state police entered the tribe's billing office with a locksmith, it did so with full authority from the tribe. Sebastian assured Detective Perron, who actually searched through the files, that tribal vice-chairman Kenny Reels was informed of the investigation. A search warrant was unnecessary since the tribe presented itself to the police as the victim of a larceny. Search warrants are sought when court approval is required to search a suspect or suspect's premises.

Also, the police had been meeting with Deno Marino to discuss the investigation. When all this evidence came to light in the internal affairs investigation, the state police were exonerated. And in March of 1996, the state's attorney's office closed its investigation into criminal wrongdoing by Detective Perron, announcing no evidence of a crime existed.

Hayward and Brown met to discuss what to do about the embarrassing discoveries. "The tribal council went out and hired Deno Marino to try and 'get something on Mickey Brown,'" Brown said. "This is Deno Marino trying to catch us doing something wrong.

"He's gotta go," said Hayward. "He's a cancer in this overall business-governmental relationship and he's gotta go."

"I wanted that son of a bitch outta here five years ago," Brown reminded Hayward.

Hayward decided it was time for him to go again, this time for good.

April 1996

Deno Marino scoffed when he was notified that Jackson King wanted to question him about his involvement with the state police. But he agreed after Reels offered to sit in on the meeting and have no one else present. King had been lobbying the tribal council to let him probe Marino, insisting that his aggressive auditing style was exposing the tribe to unnecessary public relations nightmares. With Reels's assurance that he would be backed, Marino walked into Reels's office and sat across from King. Reels pulled up a chair beside him. Reels's secretary sat beside Reels, preparing to take notes in shorthand.

"So what is it you wanna know, Jackson?" asked Marino, who disdained King more than Hayward and Brown. With Hayward and Brown, Marino knew they were open in their opposition to Reels and other tribal council members. But Marino thought King was much subtler, willing to mask his true allegiance to Hayward and Brown in order to preserve his influence among the council.

"I want to know when you met with the state police."

"Jackson, have you ever read the casino compact? It says that the state police shall have a twenty-four-hour presence here. I work *daily* with the state police. If they call and ask to see me, I go. And I don't think twice about it. And I don't have to ask you for permission."

"Well, you let information out," King said.

"I didn't let information out. You're acting like the police are the enemy."

"Where did you meet with them?"

"At their barracks in Middletown."

"What did you talk about?"

"He asked me some questions about my background."

"Anything else?"

"You make it sound like the people I met with are the Mafia. Jackson, let's cut the bullshit. You don't like me. And I don't like you."

King leaned back in his chair as Marino raised his voice. "I don't have any respect for you!" Marino shouted, wishing King would argue back. But King remained composed, refusing to say a word once Marino lost his cool.

"You don't have any respect for me," Marino continued. "If you think you're gonna sit here and grill me in front of Kenny, you got another thing comin'. I'm not gonna take this shit from you or anyone else. This is over.

"I'm sorry, Kenny. But I just can't take this guy grilling me. I won't put up with this."

Satisfied, King left Reels's office without comment. Later that day, Marino submitted his resignation notice.

40

THE SHOWSTOPPER

BENJAMIN SHARPE WAS AMONG THE TINY MINORITY OF LAWYERS WHO actually enjoyed writing briefs. One of his private ambitions was to be a novelist. He had penned more than one unpublished dime novel and had a natural flair for storytelling. His style was to forget everything he had been taught about legal writing in law school and reduce his briefs to the simplest words and sentences so that any nonlawyer could understand them. He rarely quoted the law and never clogged his briefs with multiple references to prior cases. Justice Harry Blackmun recognized Sharpe's skill as a writer and assigned him to help write the "Facts" portion of the landmark opinion in *United States v. Nixon*, which outlined how the dispute over the Watergate tapes made its way to the Supreme Court. Blackmun taught Sharpe that good legal writing is clear, concise, and easily understood by the reader—just the facts.

In Sharpe's view, briefs are nothing more than a way for lawyers to communicate their thoughts to judges. And he knew from experience that judges are like any other readers. When they are bored they tend to skip over the pages. The key to holding a judge's attention is to make the brief provocative, so it stands out from the countless other briefs that judges have to read. Yet the most provocative thing Sharpe knew about the case against Bruce Babbitt was something he could not prove and dared not include in his brief.

Documents from the Federal Elections Commission confirmed that in a mere sixteen-month span between November of 1992 and February of 1994, the tribe had donated $450,000 to the Democratic National Committee in soft money. And in 1996 alone the tribe donated an additional $300,000 to the Democratic Party. Sharpe and his partners also knew that Hayward had been a White House guest of President Clinton's numerous times. The president invited Hayward to the White House on October 14, 1993, two days after the tribe contributed $100,000 to the Democratic Party's health-care initiative. One year later on October 18, 1994, the president telephoned Hayward from the White House seeking campaign contributions. In the weeks that followed that call, the tribe made two $50,000 donations to the DNC. Also, Hayward and his wife had attended a White House dinner in the East Room, been private guests at a function on the South Lawn, and been guests at the residence of Al and Tipper Gore. Hayward was present when Hillary Rodham Clinton and Tipper Gore were given a fourteen-foot Native American sculpture in a Washington hotel ballroom. Hayward escorted Al Gore to the event and introduced the vice president and his wife to the ballroom audience as "the people who will someday occupy the White House as first family." Later that same day, Hayward presented a smaller version of the same sculpture to President Clinton at the White House. And on November 1, 1995, Clinton invited Hayward back to the White House for coffee.

The tribe's political connections to the Democratic Party put Sharpe, Martin, and Baur in an awkward position. Their law firm served as general counsel to the House and Senate Democratic campaign committees. As a result, there were numerous discussions between the three lawyers on how to approach the tribe's contributions. Martin and Baur even assembled a timeline that correlated the tribe's donations with significant actions taken by the government on the tribe's behalf. It showed a remarkable sense of timing between the two. But it proved only that the tribe was pumping large sums of money to the Democrats.

"It just boils down to common sense," said Baur. "This is a very politically active tribe that has given a lot of money to the president and to the Democratic Party. That was no secret to the decision makers at the Department of Interior."

"Maybe I'm too cynical," said Sharpe, "but I think the whole system is so corrupt that it doesn't need to come top down. The BIA is controlled by Indians. The officials are themselves Indians. If they get a request from Indians to do something good for Indians, hell, they don't need campaign contributions to come out on that side."

Sharpe took issue with the BIA's disregard for its own policies and federal laws. And that was something he could put in his brief, since he could prove it. "We've got enough other evidence of clear impropriety here," said Sharpe. "The BIA was very, very sloppy. There was nothing in the record supporting their decision. I want a ruling that will affect the way they do business because I don't think they do business very well."

Sharpe used his brief to focus the judge's attention on a single sentence in the 1983 Pequot Settlement Act. As he typed the excerpt from the law into his brief, he was confident the judge's decision whether or not to grant his request for summary judgment would hinge on it. "The Settlement Act states, 'land or natural resources acquired under this subsection which are located outside the settlement lands shall be held in fee by the Mashantucket Pequot Tribe, and the United States shall have no further trust responsibility with respect to such land . . . and [the land] shall not be subject to any restriction against alienation under the laws of the United States.'"

"This one issue is a real showstopper," Sharpe thought. "This is the issue that we have to win for our clients." After typing in the excerpt from the law, Sharpe told the judge, "A literal reading of the section makes clear that the United States cannot take land in trust for the Tribe if the land lies outside the settlement area created by the Settlement Act."

As Sharpe finished his brief, he realized that one year of work on the case was going to come down to that single sentence. If the judge agreed with his argument, not only would Babbitt's decision on the 165 acres be reversed, but the Interior Department would be permanently barred from taking any lands outside the reservation into trust for the Pequots. Their plans for turning the 1,200-acre Lake of Isles property into a massive resort that included a Chinese theme park and more casinos would be history.

At 2:09 P.M. on July 1, 1996, Sharpe filed his brief in support of summary judgment with the U.S. District Court in Connecticut. One minute later, at 2:10 P.M., Connecticut attorney general Richard Blumenthal also filed a motion in support of summary judgment on behalf of the state. He too recognized that the ruling would likely turn on the judge's interpretation of the Settlement Act. Sharpe's and Blumenthal's staffs had been in close contact with each other while formulating the arguments for their briefs. In his brief, Blumenthal, in hopes of ensuring that the judge's decision was based on the 1983 Settlement Act, attacked the 1934 Indian Reorganization Act (IRA). The BIA had relied on it to justify taking land outside the Pequot reservation into trust.

The 1934 law authorized the Interior Department to take lands outside of reservation boundaries and place them into trust for Indians. But Blumenthal discovered that the Pequots did not satisfy the law's explicit definition for "Indian." "The term 'Indian,' as used in this title," the law read, "shall include all persons of Indian descent who are members of any recognized Indian tribe *now* under Federal jurisdiction. . . ."

Under the plain language of the definition, the Indian Reorganization Act applied only to tribes that were federally recognized in 1934. To support this conclusion, Blumenthal found court cases and transcripts from Congress that confirmed that Babbitt had no authority under the old law to take land into trust for the Pequots. A U.S. appeals court had previously ruled, "The language of [the law] positively dictates that tribal status is to be determined as of June, 1934, as indicated by the words 'any recognized Indian tribe now under Federal jurisdiction.'"

Finally, Blumenthal pointed out that the only way Babbitt could rely on the 1934 law to take land into trust for the Pequots was if the 1983 Settlement Act specifically gave him the authority. But the Settlement Act was silent on that score. It said nothing about the IRA. And as a general rule, if Congress doesn't state an intention to make a law retroactive in its reach, then it is not.

Together, Sharpe and Blumenthal were confident they would win their case against Babbitt on the strength of their briefs. But they quickly discovered that it was going to be a long time before they received an answer from the court. Judge Daly had died, which required the case to be transferred to another judge who was unfamiliar with its history. During the indefinite delay period, the temporary injunction against Babbitt's decision remained in effect.

Before summer was over, however, Sharpe learned that the Interior Department's Office of Inspector General had launched an investigation into charges of perjury and the making of false statements by Interior officials. Baur and his partner, Guy Martin, had met with Senator Joseph Lieberman and apprised him of the things they had turned up during discovery. Lieberman then asked the inspector general's office, which reports to the Congress and is responsible for preventing and detecting fraud, waste, abuse, and mismanagement within the Interior Department, to investigate the BIA officials. Any evidence of criminal wrongdoing would be then forwarded to the Justice Department for possible criminal prosecution.

41

SWIMMING WITH SHARKS

MICKEY BROWN WAS SURPRISED WHEN TWO MEMBERS OF THE TRIBE'S gaming commission showed up in his office and announced they were investigating one of his top administrators. "What's the nature of the investigation?" Brown asked.

"We're investigating the fact that an executive purchased stock in a company at an initial public offering (IPO) and that company did business with us," one of the gaming commissioners said. "The IWORKS company."

Brown was curious. The IWORKS company had created the entertainment center for Foxwoods shortly after the casino opened.

"There's nothing wrong with that," Brown said. "If they're doing business with us, then we know they're a good company. And they had an IPO that is handled by a brokerage house on Wall Street. We can invest in that company."

"Well, it has to be disclosed on their conflict-of-interest agreement," the investigator said.

"I think the conflict-of-interest agreement goes to ownership in a company doing business with the casino," Brown said. "Not owning stock in a publicly traded company. Before you start to make an issue of it, you better see a securities lawyer and make sure you understand it."

After the two men left his office, Brown shut the door. "*I* bought stock in that company," he thought to himself. "Three or four of us bought stock in it at the IPO. We signed up for stock. It went public. We got the stock. We kept it. We got rid of it."

Holding the palm of his left hand open, Brown used his right index finger to tick off the four fingers on his left hand as he counted the number of Foxwoods executives who bought stock with him at the IPO. "This is ridiculous," he said to himself. "This is allowed. We're investing in stock."

Brown never heard from the two members of the commission again. And the four individuals who the commission suspected had acted improperly were never questioned in the matter.

Shortly after that incident, Brown received another visit, this time from the tribal council's chief of staff, Searle Field. "Council wants you to pay for a tribal dance group to go to France in August and perform," Field said. "And we want to charge it to your marketing budget."

"I can't do that," Brown said. "That's not part of my marketing program. I have loan agreements where I have certified that we have kept our books in the ordinary course of business and in accordance with accepted accounting principals. I can't do that."

"Well, they want you to do it," Field insisted.

"Well, I'm not going to do it," Brown said. He was well aware that Field, a lawyer, must have understood the potential legal consequences of falsifying accounting figures on the casino's budget. "Does he do *whatever* Kenny wants?" Brown thought.

Days after his encounter with Field, Brown received a memo from the tribal council telling him to charge the tribal dance group's trip to the Foxwoods marketing account. That same day, Brown sent a memo back informing the council that he was unwilling to take the $70,000 from the marketing account because the trip was not for marketing purposes.

One day later he received a council resolution ordering him to do it. The order left Brown no choice. He decided to draw a line in the sand. "I have a resolution ordering me to do it from the board of directors," he responded to the tribal council. "I'll do it. But be on notice that on July 1 every year I have to file a certification with every lending institution that we owe money to for our line of credit. At which time, I have to certify that the books and records of the Mashantucket Pequot Gaming Enterprise are kept in accordance with accepted accounting principals. I am going to refuse to sign that this year because they are not kept in accordance with accepted accounting principals. We are charging money to a marketing budget when in fact it is a junket for tribal members who don't even work here."

Brown cut the check from his Foxwoods marketing account and sent it over to the tribal council chambers for the purpose of funding the dance group's trip.

JUNE 19, 1997

Once a quarter, all ten thousand Foxwoods employees met Mickey Brown in one of four meetings that were staggered over a twenty-four hour period to accommodate all three shifts.

As Brown wrapped up his second meeting, leaving him one more to go before the day ended, the tribal council convened in its chambers and directed its tribal police to find Al Luciani and escort him off the reservation. Luciani had been working as a consultant for the tribe since shortly after he was forced out as CEO of Foxwoods in 1992. Brown had brought him back to help oversee casino expansion and other development projects. The tribal police were told that Luciani and Brown had set up some fictitious companies and were submitting bills to Foxwoods payable to these companies. To protect their scheme, the police were told, Luciani and Brown were going to try and steal files from the business office before the truth was exposed. The police were instructed not to let anyone inside the business office to remove files.

Before Brown started his third staff meeting, Luciani was fired, locked out of his office, and taken off the reservation. His exit was so swift he had no time to call Brown and tell him what was happening.

At 4:00 P.M. Brown's phone rang in his Foxwoods office. It was Reels.

"Can you come up to council?" he asked.

"What's it about?" Brown asked.

"Well, we want to talk to you about somethin'," Reels said.

"Fine, Kenny," Brown responded. "But I got an employee meeting at 6:00. I call these meetings quarterly and there will be two thousand employees at this session. So I'll come up after the meeting."

"No, you gotta come up right now," Reels insisted.

Frustrated, Brown paused. "OK, Kenny," he said. "Should I bring anything?"

"Just come up yourself," Reels said.

"OK," said Brown as he hung up.

As Reels waited for Brown to arrive, he took his place at the head of the council chambers. Hayward was in Minnesota visiting his sick mother-in-law. In his absence, Reels had the full support of the remaining tribal council members and the encouragement from his personal advisers and assistants for the action he was about to take. One of his assistants was Anthony Beltran, a thirty-four-year-old black man from southern California. He disliked Hayward and Brown and had his sights set on running for a seat on the seven-member tribal council at the tribe's upcoming yearly elections in November. Reels supported Beltran's candidacy.

Anthony Beltran moved to Ledyard from California in 1992 and joined the tribe after being released from prison. In the 1980s he spent four years at San Quentin for stabbing a man outside Los Angeles.

One night in 1980, Beltran and a group of friends were driving down a street when they came upon a white teenager who was walking alone. According to testimony, Beltran announced that he wanted to "kill a white boy" before stabbing the teen in the back. The boy was left paralyzed for life from the chest down. The victim, who did not know Beltran, attended the trial in a wheelchair. After Beltran was convicted and sentenced to prison, he exited the courtroom and leaned over the victim's wheelchair and sneered, "You may be smiling, but at least I'm walking."

Beltran was paroled after serving four years of a seven-year sentence.

But in 1991 California authorities arrested him again, this time for aggravated assault with a rifle. The arresting officer reported that Beltran "kept challenging me to a fight. Beltran was also stating that all the officers were very racially prejudiced and the only reason he was arrested is because he is black." He was convicted of possession of a firearm by a felon and sentenced to 270 days in jail. After his release in 1992, Beltran was encouraged by his brother, who worked for the Pequot tribe, to move to Ledyard and take a job with the tribe's sand and gravel department. "When I got here," Beltran said, "somebody told me, 'We're in the process of rebuilding a nation.' It made a lot of sense to me."

Shortly after joining the tribe, Beltran was arrested in a town neighboring Ledyard. He was charged with intimidation based on bigotry or bias, among other things. Beltran had been stopped for a routine motor vehicle violation. "He called this officer 'a nigger selling out to the white man,'" Officer Patrick Mickens wrote in his report. "The accused also stated that he 'wasn't Rodney King and would kick the officer's ass.' The accused then exited his vehicle continuing to scream at the bystanders shouting, 'A nigger is about to get beat up,' causing the bystanders to leave the area in fear." Beltran later pleaded guilty to reduced charges.

Beltran's criminal record made him ineligible under state law to work at Foxwoods. But nothing prevented him from being in charge of the casino and overseeing its $1.3 billion annual intake if elected to the tribal council and given a seat on the Foxwoods board of directors. As a new member to the sovereign Pequot Indian tribe, Beltran was not subject to the state's strict gaming licensing laws. Once in the tribe, Beltran was beyond the reach of any state or federal gambling laws. "That is what self-determination and sovereignty are all about, us judging our own," tribal counselor Michael Thomas said. "Tony Beltran is emotional and forceful, and those traits are consistent with his horrible history. But he is putting them to good use now."

Thomas, who is from the suburbs of Providence, Rhode Island, is Beltran's cousin. He too moved to Ledyard and joined the tribe after it started taking in huge profits from its gaming enterprise. And like Beltran, Thomas was one of Reels's biggest supporters. Thomas was elected to the tribal council in 1994. "This entire place is about opportunity that could not otherwise be realized," said Thomas, who was on probation for drug dealing when he was elected. He had been arrested in 1987 after police found thirteen bags of cocaine under his driver's-side seat. He later served prison time in both Rhode Island and Connecticut before joining the tribe while out on probation. Under Connecticut law, Thomas was ineligible to vote in state or local elections, much less run for office. But like Beltran, there was nothing preventing him from running for government office in the tribe and gaining a seat on the Foxwoods board of directors.

Like Beltran and Reels, Thomas was outspoken in his racial views. "We are a people who by plan were divided by race," he said, "forced by isolation to intermarry with other people."

At 6:30 P.M. Brown arrived at the tribal council chambers. Jackson King and Searle Field were waiting for him outside.

"We got a real serious allegation by the commission here," said Field.

"What's the allegation?" Brown asked.

"You bought and sold stock in a company that does business with the tribe," Field said.

"The IWORKS stuff?" Brown said.

"Yes," both Field and King responded.

"Yeah, I did," Brown said. "So what?"

"Well," Field said, "that violates your contract not to have any outside business with someone that does business with the tribe directly, unless you disclose it."

"Well, I disclosed the ownership in my license application," Brown said. "So I didn't conceal it. But secondly, the conflict of interest says, 'If you receive income *other than in the ordinary course of business.*' This was the ordinary course of business. I bought and sold stock in a company like anybody else can do."

"Well, council thinks it's very serious," Field said. "And they want to talk to you about it."

"This is bullshit!" Brown said, as he turned and entered the council chambers.

All eyes were on Brown as he walked in and sat down. Brown quickly glanced around at the unfriendly faces flanking Reels. To Brown, it seemed like yesterday that he had walked into a tribal council meeting in a construction trailer and had cold deli sandwiches and sodas while being introduced to Hayward and his council for the first time. But no one was left from the tribe's 1990 tribal council except Hayward. His relatives had been voted out and replaced over the years.

Brown looked at Michael Thomas and remembered what Thomas had told him three months earlier: "The tribe is getting sick and tired of the Skip and Mickey show. It's our place. We own it. We're gonna control it." Knowing how Hayward hated discussing the tribe's racial feud, Brown never told him about Thomas's threat. It was one of many things that Hayward was in the dark about within his own council. He knew nothing about Anthony Beltran's lengthy criminal record or his plans to seek a seat on the council.

As Brown sat down and faced Reels, the wrenching feeling in his gut told him that both he and Hayward were living on borrowed time.

"There's an allegation against you by the commission that you own stock in a company that did business with the tribe and you didn't disclose it," Reels said.

Brown rose to his feet, just as he had done so many times as a prosecutor to address the jury. But now he was defending himself, and the jury viewed him as public enemy number one.

"Kenny, I'm familiar with this incident," Brown said, making no attempt to hide his disgust. He knew that Reels and Thomas and the others did not even know what an IPO was, much less understand the law governing disclosure statements on gaming license applications. None of them were subject to those laws. "I've talked to the commission about this in the past. This was an initial public offering that was bought on Wall Street and sold on Wall Street. Anybody has a right to do that. And that's not me owning a company that's doing business with the tribe. Secondly, I disclosed it on my license, so the commission was aware of it.

"Thirdly," Brown continued, hardly pausing for a breath, "the conflict of interest only applies if you receive income other than in the ordinary course of business, like a gift or a bribe or a kickback. I received income because I bought and sold public stock."

"Well, we want to be fair about this," said Reels. "We want to give you an opportunity to defend yourself."

"There's nothing to defend against," Brown insisted. "I bought and sold stock and it's in my application. I've been through this with the commission already. I don't think either they or you understand what an initial public offering is. It is buying stock in a public market."

"These things don't happen in *Fortune* 500 companies," interjected Jack Jones, one of Reels's advisers in the area of human resources.

"Well, this is very serious," Reels said. "And the commission is going to suspend your license tomorrow unless you resign."

"That's bullshit!" said Brown, seething.

"Well . . ." Reels began.

"You know what?" Brown said, cutting him off. "You people are tired of me. And I'm f----n' sick of you. I'll let you know tomorrow what I'm going to do. I may resign."

"Well, when are you going to resign?" Reels asked.

"If I resign, I'll resign tomorrow," Brown said as he headed toward the door.

King and Field trailed Brown into a private room adjacent to the council chambers.

"Mick, c'mon," King said. "We have to work this out."

"Jackson, this is ridiculous!" Brown said. "You're a lawyer. You know that. There's no conflict here. This is just a witch hunt to try and force me to do something. If they feel that strongly, maybe I should leave.

"Get an opinion from a lawyer at a securities firm," Brown continued. "Ask them whether or not you can own stock in a company that does business with an employer."

Suddenly the door to the room opened and Reels's adviser, Jack Jones, started to enter.

"You," Brown said, "you get the f--- outta here."

As Jones left, Brown turned to Field. "This is a setup, Searle," Brown said. "And damn it, I know you're part of it. I know you're involved with this. You of all people know what a fuckin' IPO is."

Expressionless, Field said nothing.

"Ice in his veins," thought Brown, glaring at Field. "Ice."

When Brown left the tribal office building, King followed him over to his Foxwoods office. "This isn't the way to resolve this," King pleaded as tears welled up in his eyes. "There's got to be a different way. You can't to that. What's gonna happen here?"

Brown was the one being run out of town, and King was coming apart emotionally. King was starting to realize what Brown had known for months—the power structure in the tribe had made a cataclysmic shift.

Hayward and Brown—the two who presided over the tribe and the casino when King came on board full-time, had lost control. The billion-dollar empire King had helped them build was changing hands.

King's tears caught Brown off guard. Brown's instinctive response to the council's actions was fury, not sadness. The moment highlighted the differences between Brown and King, two men who had spent the previous six years working together to serve Hayward and the tribe in different capacities as lawyers. Brown appreciated King's sentiments toward him, but thought that King, as legal counsel to the tribe, had a responsibility to stand up to them in this situation.

After driving home, Brown walked over to Anthony J's, an Italian restaurant across the street from his Mystic town house. There he met George Henningsen, the chief operating officer for the casino, and Bob Winter, Brown's general counsel. Brown had brought both of them to Foxwoods from New Jersey, and he wanted to warn them that their jobs were in jeopardy too.

Following dinner, Brown returned to his town house but could not sleep, despite having been up for nearly twenty hours straight. The billion-dollar business he and Hayward had built together was falling into the hands of men who despised them. Nor did they share Hayward's approach on how to spend the casino's proceeds. Reels's plan was to give more money to the tribal members. And Brown knew that Reels was finally going to get his wish, but not without paying a steep price.

The financing agreement to build Foxwoods gave the Malaysians the right to approve the CEO of the casino. To protect their investment, the Malaysians wanted Brown, who still retained a seat on the board of directors of some of their subsidiary companies. The Malaysians had tried previously on more than one occasion to discourage the tribal council from interfering in Brown's day-to-day management of Foxwoods. But Reels and his supporters on the council had brushed Genting's requests aside, telling them the council would not be told how to run its casino.

Brown could not get over the irony. By seizing control of Foxwoods, Reels and his backers were about to accomplish what the three towns and the state of Connecticut could never do on their own—slow down casino resort development plans in Ledyard, North Stonington, and Preston. By removing Brown, Reels was alienating Genting and severing the tribe's credit line to the Malaysians. Without their cooperation, there would be no Chinese theme park, no domed city, no airlink to JFK, and no PGA golf courses to go along with new casinos and hotels.

"It's arrogance," thought Brown, "ignorance bred on greed."

Early the following morning, Brown telephoned Hayward and told him everything that had transpired. "It's their attempt to force me out of office while you're out of town," Brown said. "And they're using the gaming commission to do it."

"They're at it again," Hayward said.

"Skip, unless you can resolve this, I'm leavin'," Brown said. "I'm not going to go through a public fight with the council over an issue like this."

"I'll see what I can do," said Hayward.

Within an hour, Hayward called Brown back. "I can't do anything now," Hayward said somberly. Reels and the council had resisted his long-distance plea to not go through with the firing. "I'm going to fly back immediately and try to resolve this."

"F--- it," Brown said. "I'm out of here. I'm so disgusted and disenchanted with them that I have had enough."

After hanging up with Hayward, Brown received a phone call from John Meskill, the director of the tribe's gaming commission. Meskill, the son of former Connecticut governor John Meskill, had resigned his post as executive director of the state's Division of Special Revenue to take the job for the tribe early in 1997. Like Searle Field, Meskill's transition from regulating gambling in the state to working for the state's biggest gaming company spurred conflict-of-interest complaints from state legislatures. Meskill had agreed to meet with Brown to review the documents in his licensing file.

"I don't think it is a good idea for you to come to the casino," Meskill told Brown. "I'll meet you at the Hilton." At the direction of the tribal council, tribal police had been stationed around Brown's office.

"Fine," said Brown, who arrived at the hotel at 10:00 A.M.

"Let me see this document that you and the council say I signed and failed to disclose on," Brown said when he walked into the meeting with Meskill.

"I'm told to tell you that they're going to fire you unless you resign," Meskill said.

"Let me see the document," Brown demanded.

Meskill handed Brown a photocopy of the disclosure statement from his license application. "The commission is going to vote to suspend your license," Meskill said. "And since it is a condition of your employment that you hold the license, then the tribe is going to fire you for not having a license."

Brown handed back the paper and walked out. He drove back to his apartment and telephoned his secretary at the casino. "I need you to type my resignation letter," he said. "We gotta do this right now!"

There was a long pause.

"What do you want it to say?" she asked, barely able to control her emotions.

"I resign my position as president and chief executive officer of Foxwoods Resort Casino, effective immediately."

After typing it, Brown's secretary drove to his apartment in Mystic. He signed it. At noon, she delivered it to the tribal council.

FIRST WEEK OF AUGUST
OCEAN CITY, MARYLAND

Brown and his brother Thomas, a New Jersey superior court judge, had fished in the White Marlin Open—the largest billfish tournament in the United States—for years dating back to the late 1970s. In 1996, they did so with Hayward from his boat. After Brown's departure from Foxwoods, he and Hayward agreed to meet at the tournament and fish together again. Brown's brother entered his brand-new forty-three-foot sport fishing boat and Hayward brought his. For a week they took no phone calls and did nothing but cast their lines.

One night, Hayward and Brown sat alone on the deck of Hayward's boat and reminisced over a couple of beers. Together they had forever changed the landscape of southeastern Connecticut. They had reigned supreme during the glory years of Foxwoods, glory years that were already ancient history. The lawsuit by the three towns had helped reduce the tribe's Standard & Poor's bond rating to a BBB, signaling to investors that adverse economic conditions and changing circumstances had weakened the tribe's capacity to meet its financial obligations. The Malaysians had also broken off relations with the tribe. The tribe was fast approaching the $1 billion mark in debt.

Brown knew the tribe's debt was a sore subject with Hayward. The casino was bringing in over a $1 billion a year, yet the tribe was forced to borrow money.

Only seven years earlier, Brown had followed Hayward on a rain-soaked walking tour through dense woods of George Main's estate property, pointing out where he planned to build a casino. "I looked like a wet rat," Brown joked, recalling the moment. Less than two years later they built the nation's biggest casino in 202 days. "Not to be glib," said Brown, "but the rest was history."

Together, they had stood side by side and met President Clinton during the campaign season.

They attended signing sessions at the governor's mansion when Weicker approved the slot deal.

They had joined Tom Clancy and tried to buy the New England Patriots. And when they lost to Bob Kraft, Brown purchased two luxury boxes at Foxborough Stadium, knocked the wall down between them, and created the biggest luxury box in the arena.

They attended concerts together, fished together, and drank together.

But while they were doing all those things, Kenny Reels was quietly altering the admission policies to the tribe, building his support base and supporting the election of his loyalists to the tribal council. They had conspired and plotted to remove Luciani and then Brown.

"Skip, they're gonna go after you next," Brown said in a quiet moment of candor.

Staring out at the still ocean, Hayward said nothing. He could not come to grips with the fact that people in the tribe wanted to destroy him and get rid of him. He was the reason they were all so wealthy. His vision and determination produced Foxwoods. And his willingness to let Reels and Sebastian join the tribe years earlier allowed them to reap the rewards.

Brown reached into the ice chest and removed two more cold beers, handing one to Hayward.

"He won't survive the next election," Brown thought.

42

YOU CAN'T TAKE IT WITH YOU

MASHANTUCKET PEQUOT RESERVATION
SATURDAY, OCTOBER 31, 1998

AT FIFTY, HAYWARD'S BLACK HAIR HAD RECEDED TO SOPHISTICATED GRAY. The early signs of aging were apparent in the faint creases in the skin around his enchanting dark eyes and the puffy bags tiredly sagging beneath them. The youthful muscle tone in his arms and chest had vanished, replaced by flesh, the result of fine wine, rich food, and new wealth. But no amount of money could hold back time. Only Hayward's clothes had improved with age. His tailored business suits and custom shoes were far more dapper than his adolescent corduroy pants, the frayed bottoms of which tickled his bare feet when he used to roam his grandmother's land as a child. Yet he was never as comfortable in his new skin.

Since the days when he longed to live in Montana, Hayward's appearance had changed as much as the Pequot reservation, which was once just a concept in his mind. But none made him more proud than the tribe's newest facility, a $193 million Indian museum and research center that opened in 1998. It was the largest Native American library in America. And Hayward had visualized all of it, including the 185-foot-high tower of steel and glass adjacent to the museum. The top of it contained an observatory from which tourists could get an aerial view of the vast kingdom Hayward had built. An abandoned two-hundred-acre Indian reservation transformed into a two-thousand-acre tourist attraction. It was home to the biggest casino in the world. And now it had the biggest Indian museum as well.

When, in 1973, Passamaquoddy Indian John Stevens had arrived at the Pequot reservation looking for Elizabeth George, the only structure he found was her run-down home. Hayward was so poor then he was sleeping in a camper mounted to his pickup truck. But Hayward slept in those days. Now he had so much money, so many possessions, and so much land that sleep—peaceful sleep—was hard to come by. He went to bed every night wondering how to secure it and haunted by the rumors: *Kenny Reels wants your job; he has enough backers to defeat you in the election. You're not going to be the chairman of the Pequots anymore.*

The implications of the rumors were maddening. Nothing Hayward had was his. It all belonged to the tribe he had created: the buildings, the land, the billions of dollars pouring into Foxwoods, even his grandmother's old homestead. He did not possess the title to a single building or the deed to a single acre of the reservation's land. His only control over all of it was in his capacity as tribal chairman. If voted out in the upcoming elections, everything he built would fall under the control of those who did not share his dream.

• • •

November 1

The Windsor knot in his blue-and-white-striped tie was snug under the collar of his starched white shirt. The tie matched his blue wool suit jacket. Hayward looked every bit the politician when he strode up the stairs at the tribal building, his family in tow, to cast his vote for himself as tribal chairman. Before he reached the top step, he knew the rumors were true. On the glass window in front of him was a picture of Kenny Reels. It was accompanied by a slogan asking tribal members to vote for him as chairman. Twenty-four hours earlier, Hayward had talked privately with Reels. In a gesture of intimacy, Reels assured him that he was not going to run against him. Reels gave his word. And Hayward took it at face value.

In silence, Hayward turned his eyes from Reels's picture and proceeded inside. There he voted and waited for the results. Reels showed up to vote, wearing a black turtleneck shirt that tightly hugged his massive stomach, chest, and shoulders. A hip black vest with a pattern of gray diamonds cloaked his shirt. A gold necklace hung from his thick neck. He also sported a Mohawk haircut for the occasion, along with a goatee.

Less than an hour after both men voted, the results were in. The Pequots had a new chief. By a margin of fewer than twenty votes, Reels defeated Hayward.

For nearly twenty-five years, Hayward, a loner by nature, had been alone at the top. Power was his only companion. Suddenly, alone felt very lonely.

Across the room, jubilant supporters surrounded Reels, hardly discreet in their victory.

Dejected, Hayward left the reservation and went home.

DECEMBER 15, 1998

The announcement was so overdue it was anticlimactic. U.S. District Judge Robert Chatigny granted Benjamin Sharpe's motion for summary judgment on behalf of the three towns. "The issue," Chatigny wrote in his decision, "is whether the area under the sovereignty of the Tribe can be expanded against the wishes of the State and the Towns without congressional approval." After accepting Sharpe's interpretation of the 1983 Settlement Act as outlined in his brief, Chatigny ruled, "The Secretary's decision to take the land into trust is 'unlawful,' and must be set aside. If the tribe and the defendants wish to proceed with the proposed transfer of title to lands outside the settlement lands, they must seek congressional approval. Plaintiff's motions for summary judgment are granted . . . and the Secretary is hereby permanently enjoined from taking those parcels into trust."

Ledyard, North Stonington, and Preston had finally won their court battle to stop the Pequots from annexing 165 acres to the reservation, or any other land outside the reservation.

The tribe's development plan was not the only casualty from the three towns' successful lawsuit against the Interior Department. The inspector general's office investigated the BIA's handling of the Pequots' petition. "The investigation disclosed that officials of the BIA and the Solicitor's Office, Department of Interior, were aware that parcels could not be taken into trust if purchased with settlement funds," the inspector general's report concluded. "However, only Billy Wakole, who was involved in processing the trust acquisition, was determined to have knowledge that lot 110 had been purchased with settlement funds, making the lot ineligible for trust acquisition."

After twenty-eight years as a government employee, Wakole was suspended and blamed for the BIA's impropriety in the Pequot case. No one else in the BIA or Interior Department was disciplined.

• • •

Late January 1999
Morgan Point, Groton, Connecticut

From inside his spacious seaside home, Hayward could see the cold blue-black ocean. Seagulls hovered aimlessly above the icy shore. Holed up in his house for more than two months since his defeat, he had sunk into depression, refusing to take phone calls or return messages. He had not stepped foot on the reservation in two months. It had become home to newcomers, strangers who cared nothing for Hayward's lifelong struggle to revitalize and build an Indian community.

Alone, he stared toward the horizon. What did he have left? Money. Stock holdings. Property. Cars. A boat. But his ambitions had cost him two wives. He had no children. And the thing he loved most—the thing he created—had been seized from him by those whom he had been willing to take in as tribal family members. Yet they never loved Hayward. They loved what he gave them—money, possessions, power, and unchecked freedom. And they were as loyal to him as thieves.

Hayward closed his eyes. He felt no peace.

EPILOGUE

BOCA RATON RESORT AND COUNTRY CLUB
BOCA RATON, FLORIDA
THURSDAY, JANUARY 28, 1998

WITH A STACK OF TICKETS TO SUNDAY'S SUPER BOWL AT MIAMI'S JOE ROBBIE Stadium in front of him, Kenny Reels punched in a number on his cellular phone. Waiting for the call to go through, Reels relished his position. Six days earlier he had been sworn in as tribal chairman of the Mashantucket Pequot Nation. The time had come to start acting like the man in charge.

"Hello," the familiar voice said over the phone.

"Deno," Reels said, laughing.

"Kenny? Where are you?"

"I'm down in Boca."

"What are you doing down there?"

"We brought a hundred and fifty high rollers to Boca to stay over for the Super Bowl. Deno, how'd you like to have dinner with me and the council tonight?"

"The council?"

"Yeah. We're all down here. C'mon down and bring your wife with you."

For the next three days, Marino and Reels golfed and dined together. Then on Sunday night, they attended the Super Bowl. When it was over, Reels cornered Marino back at the hotel. "By the way," Reels said. "We'd like you to come back."

"Based on the track record, as much as I'd like to, I don't think that's such a good idea," Marino said.

Reels flashed a grin. "Deno, I'm chairman now."

On February 8, 1999, Marino returned to Ledyard and was named a member of the Tribal Audit Authority, working in concert with the tribal council. This time Reels guaranteed him unfettered authority to investigate the operations of Foxwoods.

Reels wasted no time making other moves that Hayward never would have made.

After hiring Hayward's nemisis, Reels and the council slashed the budget for the Indian museum. Hayward had spared no expense to build the biggest Indian museum and research library in the country. And Reels, claiming the tribe lacked money, immediately reduced it to an extremely understaffed facility.

In March the tribe published an editorial criticizing federal judge Robert Chatigny's decision in the towns' lawsuit against Bruce Babbitt. Reels expressed the tribe's displeasure over the decision directly with the Department of Interior's assistant secretary for Indian Affairs, Kevin Gover, early in 1999. Weeks later, the Justice Department announced it would appeal Chatigny's ruling. Then Reels announced that the tribe would be holding a series of public forums and that he intended to invite the NAACP and Jesse Jackson's Rainbow Coalition to participate. Billed as an opportunity for residents to express their concerns about tribal development plans, the first forum held on April 22 was well attended by residents from Ledyard, North Stonington, and Preston.

With a wall-size video screen as a backdrop, Reels stood at the podium. "I'm just really grateful that people have come out of their homes to take the opportunity to hear the presentations of justice and federal law that we all have to follow," he began. "These are federal rights, *federal recognized rights*." Words flashed on the screen behind him as he spoke: "Sovereignty," "Self-Governance," "Self-Sufficiency," "Self-Determination."

"Lotta people don't wanna hear 'bout history," Reels continued. "But we always must remember what brought us to where we are today. We are not a selfish people. We get beat up by our citizens all the time. Now we got to speak up and ask for citizens to attempt to give pride and respect and recognize our sovereign rights."

As Reels gained momentum, shouts and claps of support rang out from tribal members seated in the VIP seats at the front of the theater. And residents from the three towns turned to each other in shock. They were handed white five-by-seven cards by ushers and asked to print their names, addresses, and comments. There would be no public forum, only a chance to submit remarks and other personal identification information to the tribe.

Disenchanted and feeling misled, townspeople filed out. Others left when Reels displayed his ignorance of Ledyard history when he tried to justify the tribe's purchase of large tracks of real estate in communities outside Ledyard. "It's not about greed, it's about need," he insisted. "Some people say we're buyin' up everywhere. They call it Ledyard because it's rock. It costs a lot of money to build and to blast rock."

Many missed the most telling thing Reels said all evening. "The federal government has a federal recognition process that was put in place by Congress," said Reels, straying far from the remarks his advisers wanted him to make. "You can go through the acknowledgment process or be acknowledged by Congress, as we did. What does the federal recognition process mean? The criteria is clear and it says you have to prove you existed as an Indian tribe and as a government forever." Not only was Reels unfamiliar with how Ledyard got its name, he did not know how his own tribe became recognized—without proving its existence forever.

Reels and his forum only further alienated the tribe from the three towns. Then at summer's end, he and the tribal council alienated themselves from rank-and-file members of the tribe. The council announced that tribal members' annual stipends were being cut in half. Despite Foxwoods taking in over $1 billion per year, the tribe was sinking further into debt and the council said it could no longer afford to pay its members such excessive amounts. The announcement produced the first public protest in the tribe's short history. On September 9, 1999, tribal members, carrying placards and shouting angry slogans at their leaders, lined the street leading to the tribal office building. Fists raised, the protesters demanded cuts in the tribal council's budget. "They can fly first class, take limos, and have corporate dinners that cost thousands of dollars but they're charging our kids $100 to ride the school bus," one member yelled.

Disputes on the reservation also escalated to violence in 1999. In November a man fired a gun into a group of people standing in front of a tribal home. The police reported that the shooting was provoked by an earlier argument on the reservation between tribal members. Weeks later, seven people were forced at gunpoint into a tribal home while three gunmen burglarized it.

Also in November, Roland Fahnbulleh, a resident on the reservation, was charged with kidnapping an individual at gunpoint from a home in Ledyard.

And Kenny Reels's nephew Ernest Reels was sent to prison after being convicted of sexually assaulting a fourteen-year-old girl on a wooded path behind Ledyard High School. While on probation, he failed six court-ordered drug tests before being transferred to a drug treatment facility, where he was later indicted for raping a fourteen-year-old patient there.

At the close of 1999, Skip Hayward tried to recapture control of the tribe. He challenged Reels in the annual elections, but was again defeated. While maintaining his seat as vice chairman, he had been essentially reduced to a figurehead. Indefinitely frozen out from the empire he built, Hayward nonetheless never has to worry about money again. Having presided over the tribe during the first seven years of Foxwoods' existence, he made enough money and obtained enough property to live comfortably through retirement.

Hayward's first wife, Aline Champoux, moved back to Rhode Island after her divorce from Hayward was finalized in the late 1970s. Today she lives alone in a low-income, two-room apartment, earning less than $15,000 per year working as a fisherman on a dragger.

Hayward's second wife, Cindy Figdore, remarried and is happily raising a family with her husband in Connecticut.

Wendel Comrie and David Holdridge still live in Ledyard. Comrie retired and spends his days taking care of his wife, whose health has declined. Holdridge continues to teach and has taken a renewed interest in the Pequots' land-expansion plans. In the fall of 1999, he learned for the first time that the 1983 Settlement Act that he consented to included a map. "This is the first time I've ever seen this," Holdridge said when presented with a certified copy of the map. "If I had seen this before the settlement, it would have caused an alarm. That *must* be more than eight hundred acres."

Wendel Comrie confirmed that King had never told them about the map, much less shown it to them.

Holdridge was stunned to discover that the map enlarged the reservation by more than a thousand acres and included the property where Foxwoods sits. "We were never told that was going to occur," Holdridge said. "We knew nothing about the settlement taking in all this other property."

Believing that perhaps a federal government official made the map, Comrie and Holdridge were speechless when they learned their lawyer, Jackson King, had drawn it. They were also unfamiliar with the decision handed down against the Mashpee Indians in the U.S. Federal Court in Boston, which said that before a group can sue to recover Indian tribal land it must establish that it is a tribe. Comrie and Holdridge had not heard about the Mashpee case. "Jackson never mentioned that to me,"

Holdridge said. "This is the first I've heard of it."

Curious to learn what else he had not been told by his lawyer, Holdridge called Jackson King's law firm and asked for a copy of his case file. He was told that King had given the file to the tribe's new Indian Museum and Research Center on the reservation. When approached, the tribe's research librarian confirmed that Holdridge's file was in the archives. But the librarian had been instructed to deny access to the file, claiming it had not been properly indexed and cataloged.

Jackson King, meanwhile, stayed on as legal counsel to Kenny Reels and the tribal council in the aftermath of Hayward's defeat. Ultimately, King has managed to hold on to his position longer than Tom Tureen and Mickey Brown.

Brown returned to private practice as a lawyer in New Jersey after stepping down as CEO of Foxwoods. Floyd M. Celey, formerly an executive with Hilton, succeeded Brown as CEO. Celey announced his resignation, however, in January of 2000. Brown, meanwhile, formed Manhattan Cruises, an offshore gambling boat servicing New York City. He received financial backing from Genting, which severed its ties to the Pequots after the tribe virtually paid off its construction loan for Foxwoods. Brown and Hayward maintain a close friendship.

Tom Tureen gave up the practice of law altogether. He is now an investment banker and venture capitalist, which has made him a millionaire. He never left Maine, where he still lives with his wife. His personal relationship with Hayward essentially ended after Foxwoods opened. Despite all the years he spent working to help Hayward and his family become recognized as a federal tribe, Tureen never asked for any financial compensation from the tribe after Foxwoods opened. Nor did Hayward or the tribe recognize Tureen's efforts when it built its massive museum. His name is absent from the displays depicting the tribe's rise under Hayward.

"I hate what Skip did to Tom," said Passamaquoddy tribal leader John Stevens. "When the Pequots got on their feet financially, they cut Tom off. Tom set the Pequots up when they had no money. He went through hell to do it."

Stevens and Tureen are still close. Like Tureen, Stevens does not hear from Hayward anymore. And his tribe did not prosper like the Pequots did. Most of the millions that Tureen secured for the Passamaquoddy was squandered and mismanaged. According to Stevens, more than $20 million of the money given them by Congress was misspent. "There was no preparation for this sudden transition to power," Stevens said. "It was crazy, all this money. It's something we never had before and when we got it we abused it."

Stevens and his wife, Susan MacCulloch, separated, yet they remain close friends. MacCulloch ultimately moved to an Indian reservation in New Mexico. "Susan is a good person, a true friend to Indians," said Stevens. "She's the reason we found the Pequot reservation. She's the one who did all the research. But Skip doesn't associate with us anymore. When he was poor, everybody helped him. He has never looked back and asked what he could do to help those same people."

Tureen too was hurt by the way Hayward abandoned him. "I miss Skip," Tureen said. "But people change, and people's needs change. And people behave differently when their needs change."

Tureen's legal expertise had transformed some obscure woods in southeastern Connecticut into the world's largest gambling mecca. Roughly forty thousand people a day pass through a resort that features 315,000 square feet of gaming space with over 6,000 slot machines and 350 table games; 1,400 hotel rooms; and 24 restaurants. Over six hundred individuals moved to Ledyard and joined the tribe, with thousands of others applying. "It's fascinating to look back at how this progressed from a tiny land claim involving eight hundred acres to a casino that employs thirteen thousand people," Tureen said. "This whole thing is just an interesting product of our legal system.

"There are Indian tribes that say the Pequots are a reconstructed tribe," Tureen continued. "And it is. It is a major phenomenon."

None of the dozens of tribes Tureen helped during his legal career prospered anywhere close to the extent that the Pequots did, and they did it without having to prove to the government that they were a legitimate Indian tribe. "The question of tribal existence was the thorniest issue—did they still constitute a tribe?" Tureen said. "If we had ever been put to the test on that issue, the facts would have been what they were. And we might or might not have won."

Asked to speculate on the possibility of what would happen if Congress exercised its power to revoke the Pequots' status as a federally recognized tribe, Tureen chuckled. "How bad could it be?" Tureen asked. "They can all go back where they were. A couple people living on the reservation in trailers and the other folks can go back where they were.

"The Pequots are really rich and politically powerful, for better or for worse," he continued. "But it is usually three generations from shirt to shirt. That is the story of most fortunes. The Rockefellers are a real exception. I know people that have made small fortunes by starting out with large ones."

•

After Joe Lozier and Parke Spicer left office in 1995, they went back to work in the private sector. Lozier returned to developing and built a successful Dunkin' Donuts alongside the casino property on Route 2. Spicer opened Parke's Place, a diner that serves breakfast and lunch in Preston.

Nick Mullane was voted back in as first selectman of North Stonington in 1997. Reunited with Washington attorneys Guy Martin, Don Baur, and Benjamin Sharpe, Mullane now spearheads the three towns' opposition to two other groups who have petitioned the Bureau of Indian of Affairs to become recognized as federal Indian tribes. Both groups claim to descend from Indians who once resided in North Stonington. If recognized, both groups plan to build a casino.

Mullane and the lawyers also continue to fight the Mashantucket Pequots' attempt to expand its Foxwoods resort by annexing land to the reservation. By the end of 1999, the three towns had spent and their lawyers contributed in excess of $1.25 million opposing annexation.

On January 6, 2000, the U.S. Court of Appeals in Manhattan heard oral arguments in *Connecticut v. Bruce Babbitt*. Justice Department lawyer Alice Thurston, arguing on behalf of the interior secretary, tried to persuade the three-judge panel that the lower court erred when it ruled that the 165-acre parcel outside the Pequot reservation could not be annexed to the existing reservation. Ben Sharpe, on behalf of the three towns, and Attorney General Richard Blumenthal countered that one of the purposes of the 1983 Settlement Act was to put an end to future expansion of the reservation boundary. Blumenthal pointed out that the Settlement Act already increased the tribe's reservation from 200 acres to 2,000 acres. "There is a very stark, irrefutable fact about the United States government's contention here," Blumenthal told the court. "And that is that there would be absolutely no outer limit on how much land could be placed into trust and removed—totally removed—from the state's jurisdiction."

The judges quickly identified that both sides were fighting over Congress's intent when it passed the 1983 Settlement Act. Ironically, Jackson King, one of the two men responsible for designing the settlement plan, sat silently beside Alice Thurston as she attempted to explain the Act. She suggested that the Act was intended to provide relief to the Ledyard landowners whose land titles had been thrown into question by the lawsuit filed by Tom Tureen on behalf of the Haywards. Sharpe and Blumenthal argued that the Act did much more than clear land titles. "The Act . . . established [the tribe's] sovereignty," Sharpe said. "It created a reservation where the tribe exercises that sovereignty. It dictated that that reservation was Indian country."

"This Act gave this tribe federal recognition," Blumenthal later echoed.

Seventeen years after the fact, the state of Connecticut had finally figured out what Tom Tureen was after when he negotiated on behalf of the Haywards: sovereignty and jurisdiction over land use.

"Connecticut expected this would settle things for all time because it really didn't think that the tribe would be able to come up with its own money to buy land outside the settlement area," one of the judges said. "So it thought that this was a good deal. But it turned out, unexpectedly, that this tribe has become immensely wealthy and could buy all of the state. The people who made the deal didn't think of that at the time. But that's not for us as a court to worry about. We have to interpret the deal that was made."

As the arguments wound down, one of the judges turned to Alice Thurston. "Might this tribe have gotten federal recognition without this law?" the judge asked.

"In the course of time, it might have," Thurston replied. "I do not know where their application was at the time."

After answering a few more questions about the tribal recognition process, Thurston added, "When the Department of Interior recognizes tribes, it is not saying, 'You are now a tribe.' It is saying, 'We recognize that your sovereignty exists.' We don't create tribes out of thin air."

As she turned to sit down, one of the judges stopped her. "I'm sorry," he said. "One more question. Suppose a law—a statute—recognizes a tribe that is not properly a tribe. Can anyone challenge that?"

"Um," Thurston hesitated, "I believe the Interior Department's decisions recognizing tribes are challengeable. Yes."

Thurston had misunderstood the question. The Interior Department did not recognize the Pequots. A federal law passed by Congress recognized them. And the judge was raising a hypothetical query: If Congress made a mistake in 1983 and granted federal recognition to people who weren't really the Pequot tribe, could the mistake be fixed?

Only the question is not hypothetical. Congress never investigated before declaring that the Haywards were the Pequot tribe. It didn't so much as ask to see a single birth certificate, not even from professed tribal chief Skip Hayward. Yet Congress is still empowered to ask for proof of legitimacy from those claiming to be Pequots. And if an investigation determined that the people operating Foxwoods are not really the Pequot tribe, then Congress has a remedy: Amend the 1983 law and revoke the group's federal recognition status.

MAPS

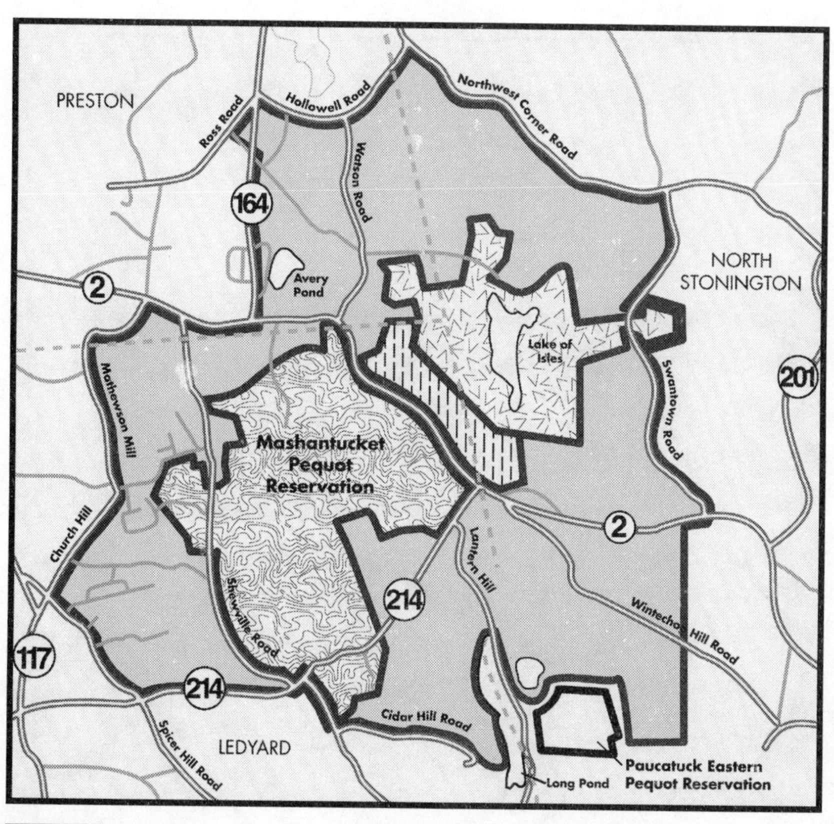

1,900-acre area approved for the Mashantucket reservation, exempt from town taxation and zoning when tribe-owned.

247-acre area in pending Mashantucket application to Bureau of Indian Affairs for addition to reservation trust.

1,200-acre former Scout camp Mashantuckets plan to add to reservation trust.

Area of lange-range reservation boundry in Mashantuckets' July proposal to Ledyard, North Stonington, and Preston.

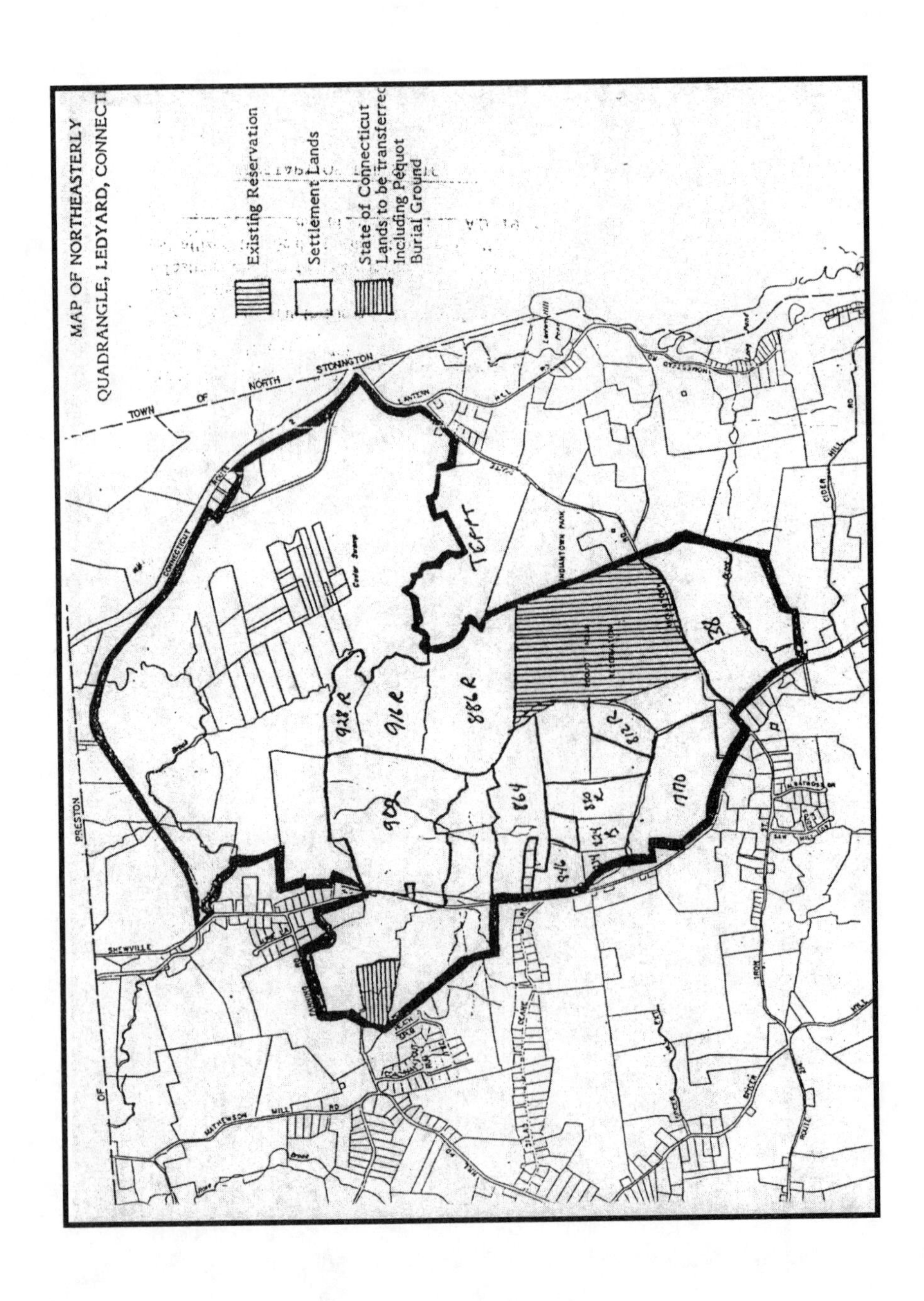
MAP OF NORTHEASTERLY
QUADRANGLE, LEDYARD, CONNECTI
Existing Reservation
Settlement Lands
State of Connecticut
Lands to be Transferrec
Including Pequot
Burial Ground
TOWN OF NORTH STONINGTON
PRESTON
SHEWVILLE
MATHEWSON MILL RD
INDIANTOWN PARK
CIDER HILL RD
928 R
916 R
886 R
864
1770
38

ACKNOWLEDGMENTS

"I won't be gone long."

That's what I told my wife Lydia on Saturday morning, June 6, 1998. We were supposed to spend the day relaxing at a beach in East Lyme, Connecticut. But I rushed off to the public library. Having finished writing my first commercial book only weeks earlier, I hoped to search for some reading material intended to stimulate ideas for my next book. At that point, I had never seen a picture of Foxwoods, much less visited it. I had only heard about it. I entered the words "Pequot Tribe" and "Foxwoods" on the library's reference computer. Six hours later I was buried in stacks of documents and reels of microfiche when a librarian tapped me on the shoulder and politely told me that the library was closing for the day.

Needless to say, I never met my wife at the beach. And for seventeen months I was consumed with researching the legal and political groundwork that led to the biggest casino in the world. Lydia supported me every step of the way. When people told me, "You'll never get to the truth," she always said, "Yes, you will." The influence of her confidence in me cannot be described in words. And on more than a hundred nights she went to sleep alone, while I worked deep into the night writing. If bylines were given to those who sacrificed the most during the writing of this book, Lydia's name would be on the cover, not mine. And my three-year-old son Tennyson's name would appear under hers.

Next, I owe thanks to the two men who guided me through this book: my agent, Basil Kane, and my editor, Mauro DiPreta. Every author should be so fortunate to collaborate with professionals of this caliber. I'm indebted to them for their work ethic, their integrity and their vision. Readers will never know Mauro's impact on this book. But it has not been lost to this young writer, who has found himself a mentor.

One of my fondest memories from working on this book involves my grandparents. Merle and Josephine saved every article pertaining to the tribe that was published in the *New London Day* between July of 1998 and February of 2000. Every week or two, an envelope containing clippings and handwritten notes would arrive at my Boston home via U.S. mail. And my grandmother Harriet, who used to live in Ledyard, compiled information from local libraries and regularly called to check on the status of the book.

My parents contributed to this book long ago, when I was a child. Their parenting instilled in me a love for hard work and a passion for truth, without which I would have never finished this project.

Toisan Craigg, Paul Osewlski, and Kyran Cassidy at HarperCollins were instrumental in making this a better book. I knew none of them before writing this book. Now I count them among my friends. And I am also grateful to publisher Cathy Hemming for giving me the opportunity to write.

My fellow students at the New England School of Law in Boston helped me get through my last two years of law school while writing this book. I am particularly grateful to my study group: Jeff Tomlinson, Bernie Walsh, Brian Lelio, Jack Connors, Dave Barry, and Lisa Reich.

The clerks at the Ledyard Town Hall—Elaine Henschel, Joyce Finn, and Calvin Brouwer—were a genuine pleasure to associate with while researching, as well as Ledyard Town Planner Bill Haase. I am also grateful to Mickey Brown's assistant, Carrie Donato. And without the expertise of law librarian Helen Litwack at the New England School of Law, I would have been at a loss on more than one occasion.

The excellent newspaper reporters in southeastern Connecticut and their years of covering the Pequots cannot go without mention. At the *New London Day,* Virginia Groark, Penelope Overton, Eileen McNamara, David Collins, Karen Kaplan, Stan DeCoster, and Julie Ladwig have filed hundreds of stories, most of which I read and relied on. Also, the works of *Norwich Bulletin* reporters David Rivera and Martha Cusick, as well as *Hartford Courant* reporter Lyn Bixby, were instrumental in my reporting. And *Boston Globe* reporter Wil Haygood's groundbreaking piece on tribal infighting was essential to this book.

Finally, I owe thanks to the countless individuals who agreed to be interviewed for this book. Thank you for welcoming me into your homes. Thank you for allowing me to search through your memories. Thank you for being so candid. Thank you for trusting me. Thank you.

BIBLIOGRAPHY

The author conducted approximately 650 personal interviews for this book. The primary sources were interviewed, in most instances, in excess of twenty times each. Many of the interviews were tape-recorded.

The author also filed dozens of public record requests under the Freedom of Information Act. As a result, federal and state government agencies turned over roughly 3,000 pages of documents pertaining to the Pequots. Additionally, 50,000 pages of documents were obtained from local town halls, local, state, and private libraries, the National Archives, and federal and state courthouses. The author was also given access to numerous private collections of papers and photographs.

The individuals who were interviewed, as well as the documents obtained and the places from which they were retrieved, are identified below.

AUTHOR'S INTERVIEWS

There are countless individuals who were interviewed off the record or on background in connection with this book. At their request, their names do not appear below.

Cliff Allyn, Preston, Connecticut • Mary Allyn, Preston, Connecticut • Don Baur, Washington, D.C. • Richard Blumenthal, Hartford, Connecticut • Mickey Brown, New York City • Russell Brown, Wakefield, Rhode Island • Ron Bryant, Mystic, Connecticut • Greg Buesing, Woodland Hills, California • Liz Cauliflower, Washington, D.C. • Aline Champoux, Narragansett, Rhode Island • Betty Champoux, West Warwick, Rhode Island • Jennifer Cinelli, Washington, D.C. • Wendell Comrie, Ledyard, Connecticut • Bob Congdon, Preston, Connecticut • Holly Cook, Washington, D.C. • George Cloutier, Windham, Connecticut • Nedra Darling, Washington, D.C. • Marylin Davis, Waterford, Connecticut • Alison Field, Washington, D.C. • Cindy Figdore, Plainfield, Connecticut • Lee Flemming, Washington, D.C. • Rob Gips, Portland, Maine • Melonie Glass, Washington, D.C. • Mark Goff, Milwaukee, Wisconsin • Larry Greene, Preston, Connecticut • David Guiher, Ledyard, Connecticut • Britta Hartwell, Mashantucket Pequot Reservation • Bill Haase, Ledyard, Connecticut • Tom Hartman, Washington, D.C. • John Herman, Meridan, Connecticut • David Holdridge, Ledyard, Connecticut • Steven Horowitz, New York City • Laura Larson-Jackson, Washington, D.C. • Franklin Keel, Arlington, Virginia • Pearl Kennedy, Washington, D.C. • Jackson King, Ledyard, Connecticut • Del Knight, Ledyard, Connecticut • Dan Kolkey, Sacramento, California • Linda Krause, Ledyard, Connecticut • Lenny LaCroix, North Conway, New Hampshire • Phoebe Lewis, Ledyard, Connecticut • Nick Longo, Putnam, Connecticut • Joe Lozier, Ledyard, Connecticut • Nancy Lozier, Ledyard, Connecticut • Al Luciani, Atlantic City, New Jersey • James Lynch, Waterbury, Connecticut • Susan MacCulloch, Rio Rancho, New Mexico • Deno Marino, Port St. Lucie, Florida • Guy Martin, Washington, D.C. • Mary McGratten, Ledyard, Connecticut • Jim Mackin, Washington, D.C. • George Main, Putnam, Connecticut • Clair Main, Putnam, Connecticut • Scott Martin, Montville, Connecticut • Tom Morozic, Los Angeles, California • Curtis Moussie, North Stonington, Connecticut • Nick Mullane, North Stonington, Connecticut • Ed Munster, East Haddam, Connecticut • Ann Nalwalk, North Stonington, Connecticut • Bob Nicola, Bridgeport, Connecticut • Irving Norman, Ledyard, Connecticut • Billie Ott, Arlington, Virginia • Steve Perskie, Atlantic City, New Jersey • Christina Pretto, New York City • Pamela Raposa, Newington, Connecticut • Don Rich, Noank, Connecticut • Rob

Ricigliano, Cambridge, Massashusetts • George Roth, Washington, D.C. • Jim Sappier, Boston, Massachusetts • Christine Schmidt, Preston, Connecticut • Jonathan Shapiro, Los Angeles, California • Benjamin Sharpe, Washington, D.C. • Debbie Sherwood, Nixa, Missouri • Sharon Snyder, Washington, D.C. • Parke Spicer, Preston, Connecticut • John Stevens, Passamaquoddy Reservation, Maine • Sherry Story, North Stonington, Connecticut • Sabino Tamborra, Norwich, Connecticut • John Taylor, Berlin, Maryland • Pete Taylor, Bangor, Maine • Susan Taylor, Berlin, Maryland • Lois Tefft, Stonington, Connecticut • Wayne Tillinghast, Norwich, Connecticut • George Tomer, Penobscot Reservation, Maine • Michael Tranchida, New London, Connecticut • Lee Treadway, Ledyard, Connecticut • Tom Tureen, Portland, Maine • Kari Vanderstoep, Washington, D.C. • Billy Wakole, Rosemary, Virginia • Sharon Wadecki, Ledyard, Connecticut • Tom Wadecki, Ledyard, Connecticut • Billy Wall, Narragansett, Rhode Island • Lucy Westfall, Branson, Missouri • James Wherry, Gales Ferry, Connecticut • Marcia White, North Stonington, Connecticut • Jennifer Williams, Sacramento, California • Timothy Woodcock, Washington, D.C.

PLACES WHERE RESEARCH WAS CONDUCTED

American Planning Association • Berlin, Maryland Chamber of Commerce • Berlin, Maryland Public Library • Boston College Law School Library • Boston Public Library • Brookline, Massachusetts Public Library • Brown, Williams & Jacobson in Norwich, Connecticut • Bureau of Indian Affairs in Washington, D.C. • Bureau of United States Census Bureau of Vital Statistics in New London, Connecticut • Century 21 Real Estate Office in Mystic, Connecticut • Charleston, Rhode Island Town Hall • Church of Jesus Christ of Latter Day Saints' Family History Center at Groton, Connecticut • Church of Jesus Christ of Latter Day Saints' Family History Center at Weston, Massachusetts • Conflict Management Group in Cambridge, Massachusetts • Connecticut Attorney General's Office • Connecticut Department of Special Revenue • Connecticut Historical Society Library in Hartford, Connecticut • Connecticut State Police Casino Unit at Foxwoods Casino • Connecticut State Police Internal Affairs Unit • Connecticut State Police in Montville, Connecticut • Corporations Division of the Secretary of State's Office in Hartford, Connecticut • Department of Interior • Department of Interior Inspector General's Office • Deuschenaux & Taylor in Washington, D.C. • East Lyme Public Library • Federal Election Commission • General Accounting Office in Washington, D.C. • Governor Pete Wilson's office in Sacramento, California • Groton, Connecticut Public Library • Groton Town Hall • Indian & Colonial Research Center in Mystic, Connecticut • Ledyard, Connecticut Police Department • Ledyard, Connecticut Town Hall • Mashantucket Pequot Indian Research Center • Mashantucket Pequot Tribal Police • Merrill Lynch, New York City • Missouri State Department of Motor Vehicles • Mitchell College Dean's Office in New London, Connecticut • Narragansett, Rhode Island Police Department • National Archives in Waltham, Massachusetts • New England School of Law Library • New London Public Library • New London, Connecticut Town Hall • Northeastern University Library • Northeastern University School of Law Library • North Kingston, Rhode Island High School • North Kingston, Rhode Island Public Library • North Kingston, Rhode Island Town Hall • North Stonington, Connecticut Town Hall • Office of White House Counsel • Perkins Coie in Washington, D.C. • Preston, Connecticut Town Hall • Probate Court at Putnam, Connecticut • Residents Against Annexation in Ledyard, Connecticut • Rhode Island Superior Court Judicial Records Building in Pawtucket • Secretary of State's Office in Hartford, Connecticut • Senator Slade Gorton's office in Washington, D.C. • Siedow & Associates in Los Angeles, California • Snow Hill, Maryland Public Library • Snow Hill, Maryland Town Hall • Social Security Administration, Baltimore, Maryland • South Kingston, Rhode Island High School • South Kingston, Rhode Island Town Hall • Standard & Poor's in New York City • Stonington, Connecticut Public Library • Stonington, Connecticut Town Hall • Superior Court at Norwich, Connecticut • Superior Court at Putnam, Connecticut • University of Rhode Island Library • U.S. Attorney's Office in Los Angeles, California • Wakefield, Rhode Island Public Library •U.S. District Court at Hartford, Connecticut • Wakefield, Rhode Island Town Hall • West

Warwick, Rhode Island Police Department • White House Public Affairs Office • Worcester County, Maryland Clerk's Office

UNPUBLISHED SOURCES

Papers of: Mickey Brown • Bureau of Indian Affairs (Mashantucket Pequot files) • Aline Champoux • Connecticut Department of Special Revenue • Connecticut Historical Society • Connecticut State Police, Internal Affairs • David Holdridge • Ledyard Mayor's Office • Ledyard Town Planner's Office • Ledyard Zoning and Wetlands Department • Joe Lozier • James Lynch • Susan MacCulloch • Nick Mullane • North Stonington First Selectman's Office • Office of Attorney General State of Connecticut • Office of Inspector General, Department of Interior • Perkins Coie • Preston First Selectman's Office • John Stevens • Sharon Wadecki

OTHER UNPUBLISHED MATERIALS

Babb, Roger Sumner. "Letter to Bill Ott," (re: reservation status for non-settlement lands of the Mashantucket Pequot tribe), June 1, 1992.

Birmingham, R.J. "Memorandum to Tribal Council and Project Development Team" (re: long-term development), June 30, 1992.

Birmingham, Robert J. "Report to Ledyard Zoning Commission," January 30, 1992.

Blumenthal, Richard. "Letter to Connecticut legislators," (re: tribal-state gaming compact and slot machines), May 18, 1994.

Bond, Thomas. "Letter to Richard Hayward," (re: finding of no significant impact), May 2, 1985.

"Briefing: Mashantucket Pequots," May 26, 1993.

Brewster, Cindy. "Letter to Joseph Lozier," (re: Freedom of Information Act request), September 16, 1994.

Brown, G. Michael. "Memorandum to Mashantucket Pequot Tribal Council and Jackson King," (re: break-in to tribal offices), January 11, 1996.

Buggy, Glenn. "Letter to Phillip Thompson, Bureau of Indian Affairs," March 22, 1983.

Campisi, Jack. "Historical Overview of the Mashantucket Pequot Tribe." (On file at the Bureau of Indian Affairs in Washington, D.C.)

Cloutier, George and John Olsen. "Forest Management Plan: Forest Lands of the Mashantucket Pequot Tribe," January 1986.

"Connecticut State Police Department of Public Safety Internal Affairs Investigation Executive Summary," February 26, 1996.

Conflict Management Group. "Memorandum to 'The Parties,'" July 18, 1994.

"Criminal Investigations Town of Ledyard and Casino, 1991 through 1995." (Prepared by a research analyst for the Connecticut State Police.)

"Criminal Statistics for Foxwoods." Prepared by the Connecticut State Police Casino Unit.

Department of Interior. "In Re Federal Acknowledgment of the Golden Hill Paugussett Tribe," Docket Nos. IBIA 97–59-A, April 25, 1997.

"Discrepancy in CT Department of Public Safety Crime Reports," memorandum from Ledyard Town Council member Cindy Brewster to the Counsel, April 10, 1997.

Dodd, Christopher and Joseph Lieberman. "Letter to Bruce Babbitt," April 6, 1993.

Duffy, Charles. "Letter to Speaker of the House Tom Ritter and Senate President Kevin Sullivan (re: tribal expansion), April 4, 1997.

"Fact Sheet," The World Trade Center in the Port of New York-New Jersey, January 1996.

Family Chronology Summary – Eastern Pequot Population by date and name. June 6, 1995.

Gejdenson, Sam. "Letter to B.D. Ott," April 2, 1993.

Haase, William. "Memorandum to Don Baur," (re: Jackson King), July 13, 1993.

———. "Impact of Foxwoods Resort & Casino on Local Host Communities Ledyard, Preston & North Stonington, Connecticut. (Available at Ledyard Town Planner's Office.)

———. "Memorandum to Joseph Lozier," (re: annexation), April 20, 1993.

———. "Memorandum to Joseph Lozier," (re: Pequot tribe's land acquisition), July 12, 1993.

Hayward, Richard. "Letter to Joe Lozier, Parke Spicer, and Nick Mullane," September 14, 1993.
———. "Letter to three town leaders," September 23, 1993.
———. "Letter to three town leaders," June 28, 1994.
———. "Proposal Regarding the Placement of Land Owned by the Mashantucket Pequot Tribe Outside the Settlement Area into Trust," July 29, 1993.
———. "Letter to Robert Ricigliano," September 7, 1994.
Henningsen, George and Robert Winter. "Memorandum to Mickey Brown," December 11, 1995.
"Index Crime Rate Per 1,000 Population – Ledyard & Foxwoods," Memorandum from the Connecticut Department of Public Safety to the Ledyard Resident Trooper," November 20, 1996.
"Invoice," Perkins Coie to Joseph Lozier and Town of Ledyard, May 17, 1993.
King, Jackson. "Memorandum to Phillip Thompson, Bureau of Indian Affairs," March 22, 1993.
———. "Letter to Billie Ott," January 26, 1993.
———. "Letter to Billie Ott," April 23, 1993.
———. "Letter to Guy Martin," April 27, 1993.
———. "Letter to Nicholas Mullane," April 20, 1983.
———. "Letter to Steven Burrington," November 7, 1994.
Larson, John and Cornelius O'Leary. "Letter to Attorney General Richard Blumenthal (re: opinion on Connecticut Las Vegas Nights statute), May 1, 1991.
Lieberman, Joe. "Letter to Bruce Babbitt," February 2, 1994.
———. "Letter to Bruce Babbitt," September 27, 1994.
Lozier, Joe. "Letter to Patricia Karns," March 29, 1994.
———. "Letter to Searle Fields," March 2, 1993.
———. "Letter to Kevin Quinn at Bureau of Indian Affairs," January 22, 1993.
———. "Letter to Representative Mary McGrattan," February 9, 1993.
———. "Letter to Richard Hayward," February 11, 1993.
Lynch, James. "A Report on the Lineage Ancestry of the Eastern and Pawkatuck Eastern Pequot Indians," December 1998.
Mashantucket Pequot PAC file contained on file at the Connecticut Secretary of State's Office.
Mashantucket Pequot tribal members "select list" and their campaign contributions, Federal Election Commission. Provided to the author on June 17, 1998.
"Mashantucket Pequot Tribal Nation Fact Sheet," distributed by tribal public relations.
"Memorandum of Understanding," (signed by Richard Hayward, the leaders of the three towns, and Conflict Management Group), April 15, 1994.
"Minutes," from Ledyard Town Council Meetings.
Mullane, Nicholas. Handwritten notes from meeting at Hilton Hotel with Interior Department officials and Skip Hayward, July 25, 1993.
———. "Letter to Christopher Dodd," March 2, 1993.
———. "Letter to Guy Martin," April 27, 1993.
———. "Letter to Governor Lowell Weicker," June 15, 1993.
Ott, Billie. "Letter to Anna Reiners, Tax Assessor," August 4, 1992.
———. "Letter to Associate Solicitor, Indian Affairs," October 27, 1989.
———. "Letter to Ledyard Tax Assessor," February 23, 1993.
Pequot Indian Papers; consisting of account book kept by William Williams and Enos Morgan, overseers to the Pequot Tribe of Indians in Groton, Connecticut, 1813–1820.
"Proposal of the State of Connecticut for a Tribal-State Compact between the Mashantucket Pequot Tribe and the State of Connecticut," submitted by Henry J. Naruk, mediator, (provided by State Attorney General's Office).
Reels, Kenneth. "Letter to Joe Lozier, Parke Spicer, and Nick Mullane," (re: negotiations), August 31, 1993.

———. "Letter to Joe Lozier," June 16, 1994.
"Report of Investigation, Mashantucket Pequot Trust Acquisition," Office of Inspector General. Case No.: 96VI–269, November 5, 1997.
Ritter, Thomas. "Letter to Attorney General Richard Blumenthal (re: memorandum of understanding signed by Governor Lowell Weicker and Skip Hayward), February 4, 1994.
Ritter, Thomas and Edward Krawiecki. "Letter to Attorney General Richard Blumenthal (re: legality of constitutional authority of governor to legalize slot machines on Pequot reservation), February 11, 1993.
Schweid, David. "Letter to Diana Urban, North Stonington Planning and Zoning Commission," August 11, 1994.
Seder, Michael. "Letter to Governor Lowell Weicker," August 16, 1993.
"The Pequot File," housed at the Church of Jesus Christ of Latter Day Saints' Family History Center at Groton, Connecticut.
Treadway, Lee. "Letter to Speaker of the House Thomas Ritter (re: concerns with tribal expansion), April 21, 1997.
Wakole, Bill. "Memorandum to Area Director, Eastern Area Office," (re: Pequots' trust application). Document not dated.
Weicker, Lowell. "Letter to Nicholas Mullane," September 8, 1993.
Wherry, James. *Environmental Assessment: Construction and Operation of a Bingo Hall Mashantucket Pequot Indian Reservation, Connecticut.* Document not dated.
———. "Letter to Keith Enders," March 7, 1985.
———. "Memorandum to Jackson King," January 20, 1999.

PUBLISHED SOURCES

ARTICLES

Abbott, Elizabeth. "Casino, Conn. police at odds," *Providence Journal-Bulletin*, January 21, 1996.
Adams, James Ring. "Clintonism in one state," *The American Spectator*, November 1983.
Allen, Mike. "Casino riches build an Indian museum with 'everything,'" *New York Times*, October 10, 1998.
Andrews, Bea. "Long-awaited Crystal Mall opens," *New London Day*, September 25, 1984.
Arditi, Lynn. "Casino: An old-fashioned banker learns to live with it," *Providence Journal Bulletin*, July 21, 1996.
Arellano, Christopher. "Annexation ruling a major victory for towns," *New London Day*, December 16, 1998.
———. "Bill ties Indian tax collection with land trusts," *New London Day*, February 25, 1998.
———. "Notice of appeal is forwarded in annexation case," *New London Day*, February 13, 1999.
———. "Pequots' lawyer questions town's $330,000 outlay," *New London Day*, September 21, 1999.
———. "Residents express concerns about tribe's gas project," *New London Day*, September 16, 1998.
———. "State DOT begins environmental study of proposals to solve casino traffic problems," *New London Day*, July 3, 1998.
———. "Tribe, town to discuss Lantern Hill truck traffic," *New London Day*, February 24, 1998.
Associated Press. "Indians look to Connecticut for beano," *Bangor Daily News*, November 4, 1983.
———. "Trial begins today in Jersey effort to prove crime syndicate exists," *New York Times*, March 31, 1980.
Bartholet, Jeff. "Indian land claims bound for out-of-court settlement," *Norwich Bulletin*, October 23, 1981.
Baumgold, Julie. "Frank and the Fox Pack," *Esquire*, March 1994.
Bishop, Gerald. "A progressive hand leads tribe," *New London Day*, February 16, 1986.

Bixby, Lyn. "Tribal shakeup remains mystery," *Hartford Courant*, November 3, 1998.

Brasher, Philip. "BIA is opposed to redistribution of tribal funding," *New London Day*, June 25, 1998.

———. "Indian tribes spend $5 million on federal lobbying," *New London Day*, July 20, 1998.

Carey, Kate. "Pequots bounce Hayward," *Norwich Bulletin*, November 2, 1998.

Carmichael, Barbara A., Donald Peppard, Jr., and Frances Boudreau. "Mega resort on my doorstep: local resident attitudes toward Foxwoods casino and casino gambling on nearby Indian reservation land," *Journal of Travel Research*, Winter 1996.

Carter, Kelly. "Report details casino's cost to N. Stonington," *New London Day*, March 2, 1997.

"Casino Lobbying Sets Records," *Business Times*, February 1996.

Chira, Susan. "Pequot Indians prevail in battle begun in 1637," *New York Times*, October 20, 1983.

Clancy, Mike. "Native Americans want land back," *Norwich Bulletin*, October 29, 1976.

Collins, Clare. "Indian tribe to get funds for ballfield," *New London Day*, September 26, 1984.

———. "Tribe regains land in Ledyard as claims settlement nears end," *New London Day*, August 30, 1984.

Collins, David. "Casino hits the jackpot," *New London Day*, February 16, 1992.

———. "Foxwoods VP is the latest to go in shakeup," *New London Day*, July 3, 1997.

———. "Luciani's resignation from casino surprised few," *New London Day*, October 20, 1992.

———. "Mashantuckets begin construction on $70 million Foxwoods expansion," *New London Day*, October 7, 1993.

Collins, David and Karen Florin. "Foxwoods attorney on job 4 years without permanent gaming license," *New London Day*, April 22, 1997.

Connor, Matt. "Life after Foxwoods," *Indian Gaming Business*, Winter 1998.

———. "The strength of ten," *Indian Gaming Business*, Spring 1998.

Connory, Tom. "Pequots have visions for land," *New London Day*, June 25, 1977.

Cooper, Michael. "Strife-torn Pequots re-elect chairman," *New York Times*, November 6, 1995.

Cusick, Martha. "Courtroom powwows," *Norwich Bulletin*, February 6, 1977.

———. "Dismissal of defense opposed in Mashantucket Indian suit," *Norwich Bulletin*, December 14, 1976.

———. "Indian affairs council hears claims for Pequot membership," *Norwich Bulletin*, January 19, 1977.

———. "Pequots initiate court fight to acquire Ledyard property," *Norwich Bulletin*, May 1976.

DeCoster, Stan. "Casino challenge endorsed," *New London Day*, May 2, 1991.

———. "Casino plan threatened by Weicker," *New London Day*, May 1, 1991.

———. "Casino wins House vote," *New London Day*, May 17, 1991.

———. "Indians gaining support," *New London Day*, May 8, 1991.

———. "Indians vow to help boost local tourism," *New London Day*, May 9, 1991.

———. "Interior will OK the casino," *New London Day*, May 16, 1991.

———. "Senate casts a cloud over casino plans," *New London Day*, May 10, 1991.

———. "Weicker raises stakes against Indian casino," *New London Day*, May 15, 1991.

———. "Weicker's plan to block casino hits snag," *New London Day*, May 3, 1991.

Diamond, John. "Pequot casino part of a trend sweeping across states," *New London Day*, May 26, 1991.

Duby, Christopher. "Pequots sweeten casino bid," *Fairfield County Business Journal*, October 16, 1995.

Economist, "How law is born," April 15, 1995.

Ellsworth, Karen. "The Indians vs. New England," *Providence Sunday Journal*, December 19, 1976.

Farragher, Thomas. "Veto of Mashantucket land bill draws ire," *New London Day*, April 6, 1983.

———. "Weicker to back Reagan re-election bid," *New London Day*, October 18, 1983.

Fenyvesi, Charles. "Why Connecticut tribe gave $100,000 to the Democrats," *U.S. News & World Report*, March 15, 1993.
Flinn, Jacky. "Pequot tribe fights for identity," *Hartford Courant*, November 12, 1978.
Freedman, Samuel. "Indian land conflict rekindled in Connecticut," *New York Times*, April 11, 1983.
———. "Old sales of Indian land declared final," *New York Times*, May 1, 1983.
Fromson, Brett. "The Pequot uprising," *Washington Post*, June 21, 1998.
Gattuso, Greg. "Tribe gives $10 million to museum," *Fund Raising Management*, December 1994.
Gibbins, Wendy. "Pequots want to involve Ledyard in economic development plans," *Norwich Bulletin*, June 20, 1998.
Groark, Virginia. "After 23 years of success, will Mashantucket chairman sit out election?" *New London Day*, September 2, 1998.
———. "After 23 years, Hayward urged by his family to retire," *New London Day*, November 2, 1998.
———. "BIA to wait on annexation," *New London Day*, August 2, 1993.
———. "Feb. 13 deadline for appeal of annexation case," *New London Day*, February 17, 1998.
———. "Five compete for two seats on tribal council," *New London Day*, October 16, 1998.
———. "Hayward ousted as Mashantucket chairman in upset," *New London Day*, November 2, 1998.
———. "Indian Affairs official supports Mashantuckets' annexation case," *New London Day*, April 7, 1999.
———. "Judge: State can rule in Pequot suit," *New London Day*, June 30, 1998.
———. "Mashantuckets are state's second largest congressional contributor," *New London Day*, October 22, 1998.
———. "Moore resigns job as Foxwoods marketing VP," *New London Day*, July 9, 1998.
———. "Police say loan-shark ring broken at Foxwoods," *New London Day*, July 14, 1998.
———. "Taking control of Mashantucket," *New London Day*, February 21, 1999.
Hanley, Robert. "Jersey wins right to play tapes as trial of reputed Mafia figures starts," *New York Times*, March 11, 1980.
———. "State sets out to prove there is a 'Mafia,'" *New York Times*, March 16, 1980.
Hays, Constance. "For fortunate few, tribal casino promises jobs," *New York Times*, December 13, 1991.
Hileman, Maria. "Senator questions Pequots' donations," *New London Day*, November 13, 1997.
———. "Sprawling toward the millennium," *New London Day*, (Special Series) May 18 through May 23, 1997.
Johnson, Kirk. "Anger measured by the acre as wealthy Pequots win the right to annex more land," *New York Times*, May 3, 1995.
———. "Indians in Connecticut get casino gambling," *New York Times*, October 26, 1990.
———. "New game for Pequots: party politics," *New York Times*, August 30, 1994.
———. "Pequot Indians' casino wealth extends the reach of tribal law," *New York Times*, May 22, 1994.
Johnson, Maria. "Governor assists at opening of new homes for Indians," *New London Day*, September 18, 1981.
Kaplan, Karen. "Mashantuckets reject annexation plan," *New London Day*, September 8, 1994.
Kemper, Steve. "This land is whose land," *Yankee Magazine*, September 1998.
King, Nick. "Native Americans may finally win one," *Boston Globe*, July 31, 1983.
Kohlberg, Jerome. "'Soft money is bad business," *New York Times*, July 5, 1998.
Ladwig, Julie. "Alive, well and resurgent," *New London Day*, November 27, 1975.
———. "Pequots in court to regain tribal lands," *New London Day*, February 12, 1976.
Larson, Kay. "Tribal windfall: a chance to reopen history," *New London Day*, July 26, 1998.

Liburd, Sondra. "CETA funds fan embers of hope for Ledyard's Indian reservation," *Norwich Bulletin*, December 21, 1978.
Mashantucket Pequot Tribal Nation, "A message to our neighbors," *New London Day*, September 11, 1994.
McCormick, Kathleen. "In the clutch of the casinos," *Planning*, June 1997.
McDonald, Maureen. "Indians to delay decision on games," *Norwich Bulletin*, November 9, 1983.
———. "Proud Indians plan their future after winning $900,000 claim," *Norwich Bulletin*, October 20, 1983.
McNamara, Eileen. "Loss of taxable tribal land has Ledyard pinching pennies," *New London Day*, July 1, 1998.
Middletown Press, "Munster doesn't give up easily," February 21, 1996.
Moore, Paula. "Indian gaming remains a gamble," *Denver Business Journal*, March 15, 1996.
Munster, Edward. "I'll stand up for Ledyard, Preston and N. Stonington," *Norwich Bulletin*, June 30, 1996.
Narragansett Times, "Hearing set for Tuesday in murder case," February 1, 1973.
Narragansett Times, "Bail denied murder suspect," February 8, 1973.
New London Day, "Drug center sued over rape incident," August 7, 1997.
New London Day, "Foxwoods dealer, patron arrested on drug charges," June 25, 1998.
New London Day, "Obituary: Elizabeth Plouffe," June 8, 1973.
New London Day, "Man killed in crash after chase by police," September 26, 1984.
New London Day, "Obituary: Rodney Hayward," September 27, 1984.
Overton, Penelope. "Major concessions were included in offer, Mashantuckets claim," *New London Day*, September 9, 1994.
———. "Pequots offer $15M land deal," *New London Day*, July 30, 1993.
———. "3 towns baffled by Babbitt's inaction," *New London Day*, August 3, 1993.
———. "Towns weigh Pequots' proposal," *New London Day*, July 31, 1993.
Peppard, Donald M., Jr. "In the shadow of Foxwoods: some effects of casino development in southeastern Connecticut," *Economic Development Review*, Fall 1995.
Pequot Times. "Chinese delegation visits southeastern Connecticut in connection with theme park planning," August 1993.
"Pequot tribe tops list of political donors," *New York Times*, June 29, 1997.
Peter, Jennifer. "Munster opposes annexation, would tax wealthy tribes," *New London Day*, June 19, 1996.
Powell, Chris. "Casino: misguided effort that may force state to compete," *New London Day*, May 27, 1991.
Providence Journal, "Baby girl dies after beating; man charged," January 29, 1973.
Providence Journal, "Bail is denied for man held in baby slaying," February 7, 1973.
Providence Journal, "Child's death suspect cited for nonsupport," February 1, 1973.
Providence Journal, "Infant girl badly beaten, man charged," January 26, 1973.
Providence Journal, "Man gets 9-year term in death of child," April 9, 1974.
Rabinovitz, Jonathan. "Connecticut's top gambling regulator quits to take a job with giant Indian casino," *New York Times*, January 16, 1997.
———. "For Pequots' point man, no task is too small," *New York Times*, November 17, 1995.
———. "Rowland tells legislature Bridgeport needs a casino," *New York Times*, October 26, 1995.
———. "Tribe sends early Christmas gift to Hartford ballet," *New York Times*, May 29, 1996.
Ravo, Nick. "Connecticut casino: eagerness and anxiety," *New York Times*, May 18, 1991.
Ridgeway, James. "Mister Softie," *Village Voice*, July 12, 1994.
Rivera, David. "Foxwoods fires two in wake of trailer break-in," *Norwich Bulletin*, January 11, 1996.
———. "Pequots renew Brown's contract," *Norwich Bulletin*, February 14, 1996.

Safire, William. "Pequots' casino venture will reflect badly on them," *New London Day*, May 31, 1991.
Sandberg, Jon. "Indians may rule on members," *Hartford Courant*, August 28, 1975.
Sheley, Matt. "Court denies Mashantucket land claim," *Norwich Bulletin*, December 16, 1998.
Sierman, Patricia. "Pequots approve own constitution, housing authority," *Hartford Courant*, February 22, 1977.
Silberman, Neil Asher. "Indian country," *Archaeology*, July/August 1991.
Sloan, Gene. "Gamble pays off with new Pequot museum," *USA Today*, August 7, 1998.
Spanier, David. "Home to a tribe of gamblers," *The Spectator*, February 3, 1996.
Stanley, William. "Her dying words were, 'Hold the land,'" *New London Day*, August 30, 1980.
Thorndike, Bill. "Indian leader downplays gambling parlor option," *New London Day*, November 22, 1983.
———. "Reagan signs bill settling land claim," *New London Day*, October 19, 1983.
Tuohy, Lynne and Mark Pazniokas. "Pequots lose annexation battle," *Hartford Courant*, December 16, 1998.
United Press International. "Byrne's choice for gaming chief," *New York Times*, June 1, 1980.
Vaughan, Kristi and Patricia Sierman. "Indians' quest: a matter of affirming identity," *Hartford Courant*, February 20, 1977.
Waldman, Hilary. "Maine parable: two tribes discover $80 million won't buy independence," *Hartford Courant*, May 27, 1994.
Waldron, Martin. "A 'hit man' derides quality of testimony," *New York Times*, June 29, 1980.
———. "Four are convicted of running criminal syndicate in Jersey," *New York Times*, June 21, 1980.
Walsh, Edward. "States try to rein in tribal gaming boom," *Washington Post*, April 12, 1998.
Weaver, Jacqueline. "The Ledyard – Mashantucket Pequots & C.R. Klewin," *Southern New England's Construction Journal*, Winter 1994.
———. "Foxwoods security state-of-the-art," *Southern New England's Construction Journal*, Winter 1994.
———. "The flash track dream team," *Southern New England's Construction Journal*, Winter 1994.
Weicker, Lowell P. "Congratulations to the Mashantucket Pequot tribe," *Southern New England's Construction Journal*, Winter 1994.
Winton, Ben. "Pequot museum," *Native Peoples*, Fall 1998.

BOOKS

Avery, John. *History of the Town of Ledyard 1650–1900*. Ledyard, Connecticut: Ledyard Historical Society, 1901.
Brodeur, Paul. *Restitution: The Land Claims of the Mashpee, Passamaquoddy, and Penobscot Indians of New England*. Boston, Massachusetts: Northeastern University Press, 1985.
Dunn, Richard S. and Laetitia Yeandle. *The Journal of John Winthrop 1630–1649*. Cambridge, Massachsuetts: Harvard University Press, 1996.
Harrison, Sandra. *A History of Worcester County Maryland*. Berlin, Maryland: Mayor & Council of Berlin, 1958.
Hauptman, Laurence M. and James D. Wherry. *The Pequots in Southern New England: The Fall and Rise of an American Indian Nation*. Norman, Oklahoma: University of Oklahoma Press, 1990.
O'Connell, Barry. *On Our Own Ground: The Complete Writings of William Apess, a Pequot*. Amherst, Massachusetts: University of Massachusetts Press, 1992.
Sheppeck, Ellen Mumford. *A History of Ocean City, Maryland*. Berlin, Maryland: Mayor & Council of Berlin, 1958.
Tecentenary Commission of the State of Connecticut. *The Indians of Connecticut*. New Haven, Connecticut: Yale University Press, 1933.

CASES

California v. Cabazon Band of Mission Indians, 480 U.S. 202 (1987).
Connecticut v. Bruce Babbitt, Civil 3:95cv00849 (Conn. 1995).
Mashantucket Pequot Tribe v. Connecticut, 737 F. Supp. 169 (D. Conn.)
Mashantucket Pequot Tribe v. McGuigan, 626 F. Supp. 245 (D.Conn. 1986).
Mashpee Tribe v. New Seabury Corp., 447 F. Supp. 940 (D. Mass. 1978).
Mashpee Tribe v. New Seabury Corp., 592 F.2d 575 (1979).
Mashpee Tribe v. Secretary of Interior, 820 F.2d 480 (1st Cir. 1987).
Mashpee Tribe v. Town of Mashpee, 447 F. Supp. 940 (1978).
Mashpee Tribe v. Watt, 542 F. Supp. 797 (1982).
Mashpee Wampanoag Indian Tribe v. Assessors of Mashpee, 398 N.E2d 724 (1980).
Montoya v. United States, 45 L.Ed. 521 (1901).
Montoya v. United States, 180 U.S. 261, 45 L.Ed. 521 (1901).
Morton v. Ruiz, 94 S.Ct. 1055 (1974).
Navajo Tribal Utility A. v. Ariz. Dept. of Rev., 608 F.2d. 1228 (1979).
Oneida Indian Nation v. County of Oneida, 39 L.Ed. 2d 73 (1974).
Passamaquoddy Tribe v. Morton, 528 F.2d 370 (1975).
Penobscot Nation v. Stilphen, 461 A.2d 478 (Me. 1983).
United States v. Maine, Civil No. 1966 N.D.
Western Pequot Tribe of Indians v. Holdridge Enterprises, Inc. Civil H–76–193, (1976).

CENSUS DOCUMENTS

"Indian Population in the United States and Alaska, 1910." Published by the Department of Commerce Bureau of the Census.
United States Census, 1810.
United States Census, 1820.
United States Census, 1830.
United States Census, 1840.
United States Census, 1860.
United States Census, 1870.
United States Census, 1900.
United States Census, 1910.

CORRESPONDENCE TO AUTHOR

Bryan, Ron (pastor of the Church of Christ in Mystic, Connecticut). Facsimile dated December 7, 1999.
Carnese, Dawn (legal advisor in the Department of Public Safety for the State of Connecticut), letter dated July 16, 1998.
Champoux, Aline. Letter dated December 2, 1999.
Champoux, Aline. Letter dated January 3, 2000.
Champoux, Aline. Electronic mail dated January 5, 2000.
Farrow, Cindy. Letter dated July 26, 1999.
Goff, Mark. Fascimile dated August 19, 1998.
NeVille, Karen (Worcester County Library, Snow Hill, Maryland). Fascimile dated December 7, 1999.
LaCroix, Lenny. Letter dated May 25, 1999.
Larson-Jackson, Laurie (attorney in the United States Department of Interior Office of Inspector General). Letter dated July 15, 1998.
MacCulloch, Susan. Facsimiles dated February 4, 1999, April 2, 1999.
Raposa, Pamela (Division of Special Revenue for the State of Connecticut). Letter dated July 13, 1998.
Raposa, Pamela. Letter dated July 17, 1998.
Taylor, Susan (Berlin, Maryland Chamber of Commerce). Letter dated December 1999.
White, Geoffrey (Federal Election Commission). Letter dated July 2, 1998.

COURT RECORDS

George Henry Pratt Main v. Susan Elsie Main Lucier, CV 830027923S, November 1983. Case file obtained from the Superior Court in Windham, Connecticut.

George H.P. Main v. Highway Commissioner, obtained from the Probate Court in Putnam, Connecticut.

Juanita Reels v. Thomas Reels P82–0160. Obtained from the Rhode Island Court Records Storage Facility in Pawtucket, Rhode Island.

Mashantucket Pequot Tribe v. State of Connecticut, Civil H–89–717 PCD. Obtained from the United States District Court in Hartford, Connecticut.

Mashantucket Pequot Tribe v. State of Connecticut and William A. O'Neill, 90–7508. Obtained from the Federal District Court in Hartford, Connecticut.

State of Connecticut v. Bruce Babbitt, Civil 3:95 CV 00849. Obtained from the Office of Attorney General in Hartford, Connecticut.

State of Rhode Island v. Thomas Reels, 73–9C. Obtained from the Rhode Island Records Storage Facility.

Western Pequot Tribe of Indians v. Holdridge Enterprises et. al. Civil Action No. 76/193. Obtained from the National Archives in Waltham, Massachusetts.

LAND RECORDS

Groton Town Hall

"Mortgage Deed, Richard A. and Carol J. Hayward," January 28, 1994, Vol. 582, page 749.

"Notes and Mortgage Modification Agreement, Richard J. Hayward," July 24, 1995, Vol. 610, page 410.

"Open-End Mortgage, Richard A. Hayward and Carol J. Hayward," November 29, 1993, Vol. 578, page 679.

"Warranty Deed-Statutory Form, Richard J. Smith to Richard A. Hayward and Carol J. Hayward," October 8, 1983, Vol. 575, page 823.

Ledyard Town Hall

The author received a computer printout sheet from the clerk's office at the Ledyard Town Hall listing every land transaction involving the tribe from 1984 through 1998. The author also received a computer printout sheet from the tax assessor's office at the Ledyard Town Hall listing the tax information on the properties obtained by the tribe. Other documents obtained from the Ledyard Town Hall include the following:

"Adjustable Rate Commercial Mortgage Note between Bannerstone, LLC and Chelsea Groton Savings Bank," December 28, 1994, vol. 248, page 164.

"Construction Mortgage Lease between THE MASHANTUCKET PEQUOT TRIBE and KIEN HUAT REALTY LIMITED," February 25, 1991, vol. 206, page 796.

"First Amendment to Construction Mortgage Lease," February 21, 1992. Vol. 216, page 514.

"Mortgage Lease between THE MASHANTUCKET PEQUOT TRIBE and KIEN HUAT REALTY II LIMITED," April 30, 1993, vol. 230, page 88.

"Mortgage between MASHANTUCKET PEQUOT TRIBE and UBAF ARAB AMERICAN BANK," July 25, 1986, vol. 155, page 359.

Warranty Deed vol. 246, page 290.

Quit Claim Deed, vol. 269, page 891.

UCC Financing Statement for Foxwoods Resort and Casino, Vol. 255, page 824.

UCC Financing Amendment, Mashantucket Pequot Gaming Enterprise, Vol. 276, page 1018.

UCC Financing Amendment, Mashantucket Pequot Gaming Enterprise, Vol. 259, page 330.

UCC Continuation, Mashantucket Pequot Gaming Enterprise, Vol. 257, page 290.

UCC Financing Statement, Mashantucket Pequot Gaming Enterprise, Vol. 206, page 878.

UCC Financing Statement, Mashantucket Pequot Gaming Enterprise, Vol. 231, page 312.

Warranty Deed, Mashantucket Pequot Tribal Nation, Vol. 263, page 375.

Warranty Deed, Mashantucket Pequot Tribal Nation, Vol. 269, page 700.

Warranty Deed, Mashantucket Pequot Tribal Nation, Vol. 270, page 668.
Warranty Deed, Mashantucket Pequot Tribal Nation, Vol. 271, page 43.
Warranty Deed, Mashantucket Pequot Tribal Nation, Vol. 271, page 526.
Quit Claim Deed, Mashantucket Pequot Tribal Nation, Vol. 272, page 269.
Quit Claim Deed, Mashantucket Pequot Tribal Nation, Vol. 274, page 835.
Warranty Deed, Mashantucket Pequot Tribal Nation, Vol. 281, page 351.
Warranty Deed, Mashantucket Pequot Tribal Nation, Vol. 281, page 441.
Administrative Deed, United States of America in Trust, Vol. 140, page 680.
Mortgage, United States of America Bureau of Indian Affairs, Vol. 155, page 359.
Warranty Deed, Bannerstone, LLC, Vol. 248, page 22.

South Kingston, Rhode Island

Assessment Summary for 17 Hope Court, Wakefield, Rhode Island.
Property Assessment Record for 17 Hope Court, Wakefield, Rhode Island.

OTHER LAND RECORDS

"Purchase Agreement between Mashantucket Pequot Tribe and Long Rivers Council, Inc., Boy Scouts of America," March 22, 1993. (Attached to letter from Glenn Buggy to Phillip Thompson.)

LAWS

Connecticut Indian Claim Settlement Act, Public Law 98–134, 97 Stat. 851.
Federal Administrative Procedure Act ("APA"), 5 U.S.C. s. 551.
Indian Gaming Regulatory Act ("IGRA"), 25 U.S.C. s. 2702 (1988).
Indian Nonintercourse Act, 25 U.S.C. s. 177.
Indian Reorganization Act ("IRA"), 25 U.S.C. s. 465.
The Johnson Act, 15, U.S.C. s. 1172. (enacted in 1951).
"Las Vegas Nights" Statute, s. 7–186a, p. 375 of chapter 98.
Maine Indians Claims Settlement Act of 1980, 25 U.S.C. s. 1721–1735.
Mashantucket Pequot Indian Land Claim Settlement Act of 1983 ("Settlement Act"), 25 U.S.C. s. 1751.
Mashantucket Pequot Tribal Gaming Ordinance, enacted February 25, 1991.
National Environmental Policy Act ("NEPA"), 42 U.S.C. s. 4321.
Procedures for Establishing that an American Indian Group Exists as an Indian Tribe, 5 U.S.C. 301.
The Snyder Act, 42 Stat. 208, 25 U.S.C. s. 13, (approved November 2, 1921).
Tribal Council Bingo Control Ordinance, enacted February 7, 1985.

MAPS

"Mashantucket Pequot Tribal Settlement Boundary and Lands for Potential Trust Annexation," W.R. Haase, Ledyard Planning Department, August 10, 1993.
"Master plan: Location Plan," by New England Design Incorporated, June 18, 1992.
"Master plan: Route 2 Corridor Mashantucket Pequot Resort," by New England Design Incorporated.
"Northeast corner of Ledyard," (Showing Lands of the Mashantucket Pequot Tribe), December 1984.
"Settlement Area: All Other Lands Are Land For Potential Trust Status," September 29, 1993.

PHOTOGRAPHS

Photographs were provided to the author by: Aline Champoux • Cindy Figdore • Lenny LaCroix • Susan MacCulloch.

Copies of photographs were also obtained from: North Kingston High School and South Kingston High School.

PRESS RELEASES

Dodd, Chris. "Dodd Asks Mediator to Help Resolve Dispute Over Land Claim," September 28, 1993.

Gorton, Slade. "Interior Appropriations FY 1999: Gorton Proposal Would Send More Dollars to Nation's Poorest Tribes," June 23, 1998.

Lieberman, Joe. "Lieberman Bill Would Limit Indian Annexation Power," June 21, 1995.

The White House. "Federalism," May 14, 1998.

REFERENCE SOURCES

Black's Law Dictionary. St. Paul, Minnesota: West Publishing, 1990.

Campaign Guide for Political Party Committees. Washington, D.C.: Federal Election Commission, August 1996.

Duncan, Philip D. and Christine C. Lawrence. *Politics in America 1998: The 105th Congress*. Washington, D.C.: Congressional Quarterly Press, 1997.

Fox, William F., Jr. *Understanding Administrative Law*. Washington, D.C.: Matthew Bender, 1983.

Funk, William and Sidney Shapiro and Russell Weaver. *Administrative Procedure and Practice*. St. Paul, Minnesota: West Publishing Company, 1997.

Madison, Michael and Robert Zinman. *Modern Real Estate Financing: A Transactional Approach*. Boston, Massachusetts: Aspen Publishers, Inc., 1991.

Merrill Lynch. "High Yield Gaming," April 15, 1999.

North Kingston, Rhode Island High School Yearbook, 1965.

Safire, William. *Safire's New Political Dictionary*. New York: Random House, 1993.

Scoles, Eugene and Edward Halbach, Jr. *Problems and Materials on Decedents' Estates and Trusts*. Boston, Massachusetts: Aspen Publishers, Inc., 1993.

Standard & Poor's. "State Review: Connecticut," October 13, 1997.

Standard & Poor's Creditweek Municipal. "Connecticut's Neighbors Eye Its Gaming Success Enviously," October 14, 1996.

Standard & Poor's Credit Analysis Reference Disc. "Gambling on the Gaming Industry," July 21, 1998.

Standard & Poor's. "Mashantucket Western Pequot Tribe, Connecticut," September 22, 1997. Standard & Poor's Public Finance Criteria 1998.

Standard & Poor's. "Revitalizaton Through Gaming: Detroit Now Rolls the Dice," May 11, 1998.

State of Connecticut, Register and Manual 1973. Secretary of State's Office.

State of Connecticut, Register and Manual 1974. Secretary of State's Office.

State of Connecticut, Register and Manual 1983. Secretary of State's Office.

"Supporting Federal Candidates: A Guide for Citizens," Federal Election Commission, 1996.

Webster's II New Riverside University Dictionary. Boston: Houghton Mifflin Company, 1998.

TAX RECORDS

Grand List for Town of Ledyard, October 1, 1997.

TRANSCRIPTS

Congressional Record – House, "Mashantucket Pequot Indian Land Claims Settlement Acts," October 4, 1983.

Congressional Record – Senate, "The Mashantucket Pequot Indian Claims Settlement Act," September 30, 1983.

Congressional Record – Senate, "Meetings of the American Indian Policy Review Commission," March 5, May 2, June 13, July 11, and September 12, 1975.
Congressional Record – Senate, "Meetings of the American Indian Policy Review Commission," February 20, 1976.
Connecticut Indian Affairs Council, Hearing on Membership in the Eastern Pequot Tribe of Connecticut, January 18, 1977.
Hearing before the Subcommittee on Indian Affairs of the Committee on Interior and Insular Affairs, United States Senate, September 12, 1972.
Hearing before the Committee on Interior and Insular Affairs, House of Representatives, July 15, 1982.
Hearing before the Select Committee on Indian Affairs, United States Senate, July 14, 1982.
Hearing before the Select Committee on Indian Affairs, United States Senate, July 19, 1983.
Hearing before the Select Committee on Indian Affairs, United States Senate, June 26, 1985.
Hearing before the Select Committee on Indian Affairs, United States Senate, February 5, 1992.
Hearing before the Select Committee on Indian Affairs United States Senate, March 18, 1992.
Indian Commission Meeting at Federal Building in Boston in April 1976.
King, Jackson. Speech delivered at Guard Theater in New London, Connecticut, May 14, 1999.
"Message to the Senate Returning Without Approval the Mashantucket Pequot Indian Claims Settlement Bill," *Administration of Ronald Reagan*, April 5, 1983.
Oral arguments before U.S. Appeals Court in *Connecticut v. Department of Interior*, January 6, 2000.
"Oversight Hearings, Committee On Interior and Insular Affairs, House of Representatives," January 9, 1992 and February 4, 1992.
Reels, Kenneth. Speech delivered at Guard Theater in New London, Connecticut, April 22, 1999.
Report: "Authorizing Funds for the Settlement of Indian Claims in the Town of Ledyard, Conn." Select Committee on Indian Affairs, September 29, 1982.
Report: "Authorizing Funds for the Settlement of Indian Claims in the Town of Ledyard, Conn." Select Committee on Indian Affairs, September 14, 1983.
Report: "Providing for the Settlement of Land Claims of the Mashantucket Pequot Indian Tribe of Connecticut, and for other Purposes," Committee on Interior and Insular Affairs, September 29, 1982.
Report: "Providing for the Settlement of Land Claims of the Mashantucket Pequot Indian Tribe of Connecticut, and for Other Purposes," Committee on Interior and Insular Affairs, March 21, 1983.
"Statement of Ada Deer before the Senate Committee on Indian Affairs," July 15, 1993.
"Testimony of Robert Congdon, Wesley Johnson and Nicholas Mullane before the Senate Committee on Indian Affairs," May 26, 1998.

Vital Records

Bell, Richard Robert. "Death Certificate," Ledyard Town Hall, March 25, 1974.
Bell, Tammy Lynn. "Marriage Certificate (to Randy James Weinberg)," New London Town Hall, June 1, 1992.
George, _______. "Birth Certificate," Ledyard Town Hall, November 25, 1884.
George, Amos. "Birth Certificate," Ledyard Town Hall, December 25, 1882.
George, Austin. "Certificate of Death," Ledyard Town Hall, April 5, 1898.
George, Cyrus. "Certificate of Death," Ledyard Town Hall, October 1, 1898.
George, Elizabeth Eva. "Belated Registration of Birth," Ledyard Town Hall, September 3, 1957.
George, Elizabeth Eva. "Marriage License," Ledyard Town Hall, August 20, 1930.
George, Eunice Bertha. "Birth Registration," Ledyard Town Hall, November 12, 1888.
George, Flora Elsie. "Belated Registration of Birth," Ledyard Town Hall, October 29, 1956.
George, John. "Birth Registration," Ledyard Town Hall, February 20, 1896.
George, Mabel. "Birth Certificate," Ledyard Town Hall, April 24, 1880.

Grant, Jane. "Birth Certificate (for her child born to Noyes Hoxie)," Ledyard Town Hall, 1862.
Grant, Mary Jane. "Marriage Certificate (to Dwight S. Burrows)," May 7, 1859.
Hayward, Belinda. "Marriage License (to Frederick Edward Enos, Jr.)," Ledyard Town Hall, December 3, 1983.
Hayward, Belinda. "Marriage License (to Gary Robert McKeon)," Ledyard Town Hall, May 7, 1988.
Hayward, Cynthia Lee. "Marriage License (to Charles William Shockley)," Groton Town Hall, October 16, 1976.
Hayward, Patricia Elaine. "Marriage License (to Lawrence James Byron, Jr.)," Ledyard Town Hall, March 23, 1984.
Hayward, Richard Arthur. "Marriage License (to Aline Champoux)," Groton Town Hall, June 21, 1969.
Hayward, Richard Arthur. "Marriage License (to Cindy Lee Figdore)," North Stonington Town Hall, September 20, 1980.
Hayward, Richard Arthur. "Marriage License (to Carol Jean Carlson)," Ledyard Town Hall, June 4, 1988.
Hayward, Richard Arthur. Membership Records from the Church of Christ, 1969–1974. (Obtained by the author.)
Hayward, Richard. "Trade Name Certificate (for Sea Mist Haven)," Stonington Town Hall, February 8, 1973.
Hayward, Robert Dale. "Marriage License (to Rebecca Ann Richerdson)," Ledyard Town Hall, August 3, 1985.
Hayward, Rodney. "Death Certificate," Ledyard Town Hall, September 29, 1984.
Hayward, Theresa Darnice. "Marriage License (to Richard T. Bell)," Ledyard Town Hall, August 9, 1970.
Hayward, Theresa Victoria. "Death Certificate," Ledyard Town Hall, March 7, 1996.
Hoxie, Lizzie Jane Wheeler. "Marriage Certificate (to Frederick B. Durfee)," Ledyard Town Hall, June 28, 1897.
Hoxie, Martha. "Marriage Certificate (to Cyrus George)," November 2, 1879.
Jackson, Rachel Hoxie. "Death Certificate," September 18, 1884.
Langevin, Alice Edna. "Birth Registration," Ledyard Town Hall, May 14, 1905.
Plouffe, Elizabeth George. "Application for Social Security Account Number," (obtained from the Social Security Administration office in Baltimore, Maryland), June 25, 1941.
Plouffe, Elizabeth George. "Death Certificate," Ledyard Town Hall, June 7, 1973.
Plouffe, Loretta Elaine. "Marriage License," Groton Town Hall, October 12, 1963.
Reels, Juanita. "Marriage Certificate (to Bruce Wayne Montey), South Kingston Town Hall, April 25, 1981.
Reels, Kenneth. "Certificate of Release or Discharge from Active Duty," South Kingston Rhode Island Town Hall, June 20, 1986.
Reels, William Henry. "Death Certificate," South Kingston Town Hall, October 18, 1985.
Sebastian, Juanita. "Marriage Certificate (to Thomas Reels)," South Kingston Town Hall, May 10, 1958.
Unnamed child (father Napolean Langeven, mother Martha Ann Hoxie), "Birth Certificate," Ledyard Town Hall, May 9, 1907.
Unnamed child (mother Loretta Elaine Plouffe), "Birth certificate," Ledyard Town Hall, March 23, 1954.
Watrous, Susan. "Marriage License (to Albert Whipple)," Ledyard Town Hall, April 22, 1973.

SOURCE NOTES

The quotes in this book are almost exclusively the result of interviews conducted by the author. Individual citations are not listed for each quote.

All of the primary documents quoted in the book are contained in the bibliography. Additionally, all laws, cases, property records and other documents referred to in the text are listed in the bibliography. The quotations appearing in the chapters pertaining to congressional hearings are contained in congressional transcripts, all of which are in the bibliography.

Individual sources are included only in instances where I relied on another writer's original reporting or where my reporting produced conflicting accounts.

CHAPTER 7: JOINING THE CLUB

The quotes attributed to Bruce Kirchner appear originally in Hilary Waldman's "New Life for a Forgotten People," *Hartford Courant*, May 22, 1994.

CHAPTER 10: FRACTURED DIAMOND

The divorce between Skip Hayward and Aline Hayward was finalized on June 13, 1978.

CHAPTER 19: WILLS, ESTATES, AND TRUSTS

In interviews with the author, attorneys Tom Tureen, Jackson King, and Nick Longo each gave conflicting accounts of how George Main learned that the tribe desired to buy his land. The account presented in the text results not only from the accounts of Tureen, King, and Longo, but also reflects the author's interviews with James Wherry, George Main, Judge Tamborra, Marcia White, and Irving Norman, as well as a comprehensive review of the legal documents and land records associated with this case.

The first time the author spoke with Nick Longo on November 11, 1998, Longo said that he initiated the discussions between his client and the Pequots. "I called Tom," Longo said. "I was aware of him because I do a lot of reading. I was aware of the litigation involving Indian tribes in Maine. Tureen had been written up in *Forbes* magazine as the pioneer lawyer in Indian land claims cases. We did not know at the time we called him that he was the Pequots' lawyer."

On November 16, when the author interviewed Longo's clients, George Main and his wife Claire, some conflicting information surfaced.

George Main told the author that he was set to sell his land to Irving Norman when he received a telephone call from his attorney Nick Longo, in which Longo said, "Hey, George, guess what? I got some big news for you. I understand the Indians are looking at your property." Main also said that Longo said he had learned of the Indians' interest through an attorney in Norwich. Main's wife corroborated this account. And according to the Mains, they understood the attorney in Norwich to be Jackson King.

In a follow-up interview with Nick Longo, the author asked him about Main's version of events. "I don't recollect," Longo said. "I'm not saying he is necessarily wrong. But I don't recollect that occurring. I probably read about it in the newspaper. I don't recall having found out the information indirectly and bringing it to his attention."

Jackson King told the author that after the Settlement Act passed he "got wind of [Irving] Norman's interest in the [Main] property." When asked how he found out that George Main was trying to sell his land, King responded: "I think it was Tom [Tureen] that told me. And it was well after the Settlement, '84 or so. It could have been Barry [Margolin—Tureen's law partner] or it could have been Tom. One of them called me and said that there was a developer named Irving Norman who had a contract and he was going to buy it. So he had a contract to buy it. I remember Tom saying something like, 'We're thinking about going and bidding a higher price for the property and seeing if we can get it.'"

King added, "I said to him [Tureen], 'I'm not involved with that. You take that up with Nick, because Nick may feel funny about negotiating and talking to you when he's already got a good faith contract with Irving Norman.'"

However, both Longo and Tureen agreed that Tureen did not place the initial phone call to Longo to start talks on the Main property. Rather, both men agree that Longo first called Tureen.

When the author informed Tureen of George Main's vivid recollection of being told by Longo not to sell his land to Irving Norman and instead sell it to the tribe, Tureen responded: "What would be wrong with that? Jackson certainly would have known that that land was with the settlement and that we would have liked to acquire it. And we were on very friendly terms with Jackson. He knew the details of it. And if he knew this guy [Longo], I can picture myself sitting around with another lawyer saying, 'Hey, you ought to call these guys up. They [the tribe] have money and they're looking for land.' Do the other lawyer a favor."

CHAPTER 20: OUT TO LUNCH

In an interview with the author, Jackson King confirmed that David Holdridge, Lois Tefft, and Wendell Comrie contributed to the initial retainer fee. King added that between six and ten defendants subsequently contributed sums ranging from $250 to $500 each toward the retainer fee.

King said that within a matter of months from when the retainer fees were collected, the firm was hopelessly behind in billing. "There was really no way that we expected these folks to be able to pay the bills," King said. He went on to say that he had several informal discussions with Holdridge throughout the ligitation in reference to the legal fees. Holdridge was emphatic that he never received a single billing invoice from King during the litigation. King confirmed that he may not have issued any invoices. King had hoped the federal government would pay his legal fees as part of the Settlement Act. "I discussed that with the head of the Senate Select Committee on Indian Affairs directly," said King. "And he said, 'Forget it. They would not pay legal fees.'"

When it became apparent that the Congress would not pay King's legal fees, King said that he spoke to his clients about charging them ten percent of the sale price of their lands to the tribe. "I remember telling my clients, 'What you have here is you're selling your land—if you want to, if you don't want to sell you don't have to—and you're going to end up paying a ten percent fee. Which is not unlike what you'd pay if you hired a broker.' I know we had those kinds of conversations."

When informed that Holdridge and Comrie insisted they were never told in advance that they would be billed ten percent of their land proceeds, King disagreed. "I remember talking to them in terms of doing it on a percentage basis," said King. "And I remember talking to them and analogizing it to a broker situation."

CHAPTER 26: I WOULDN'T TAKE MY DOG TO ATLANTIC CITY

The author relied on the original reporting of Wil Haygood of the *Boston Globe* for the quotes attributed to tribal members Phyllis Waite, Marjory Pinson, and Vincent Sebastian in this chapter. Haygood's article, "Tribe's riches create divisions among some," appeared on August 19, 1995.

The quotes attributed to Patricia Fletcher first appeared in Hilary Waldman's article, "New Life for a Forgotten People," *Hartford Courant*, May 22, 1994.

CHAPTER 27: WHEEL OF FORTUNE

In an interview with the author, Jackson King said that he began serving as in-house counsel to the tribe in March 1993.

CHAPTER 38: BIG BOYS DON'T CRY

Interviews conducted by the author with Billy Wakole, Billie Ott, and other members of the BIA's Realty office produced conflicting statements on whether Wakole notified Ott of problems associated with Lot 110 and what, if anything, Ott instructed Wakole to do about it.

Wakole is on the record, both in deposition testimony and in interviews with the author, saying that he notified Ott via written memorandum that Lot 110 was ineligible for trust acquisition due to it being purchased with settlement funds. Wakole is also on the record saying that his memorandum was returned to him with a handwritten sticky note from Ott that said, "Don't add fuel to the fire."

In an interview with the author, Billie Ott admitted writing the words "Don't add fuel to the fire" on a yellow sticky note. However, he disputed that the note was intended to influence Wakole to keep quiet about Lot 110's ineligibility. "Yes, I wrote such a note," Ott said. "And yes it had to do with a particular sentence. And as I recall, it was on the back of the write-up which I felt was a gratuitous remark. And I wouldn't know Lot 110 from Lot 1,000. The staff people that did the realty work would have to answer that question."

The author then reiterated Wakole's claim, that he made it clear to Ott that Lot 110 was a problem.

"The answer is no, I do not recall him telling me," Ott responded. "No, I don't believe he told me. In the presence of his boss, I specifically asked if any of the land had been purchased with settlement funds. And the answer was no. And I asked him later if there was anything in that report that could not be defended. And the answer was, 'No, we can defend everything.'"

CHAPTER 41: SWIMMING WITH SHARKS

For the quotes and case disposition information pertaining to Anthony Beltran and Michael Thomas, the author relied on the following sources.

Associated Press. "An ex-convict sits on Pequot Tribal Council," *New London Day*, October 26, 1998.

Bixby, Lyn. "Pequot official has record of violence," *Hartford Courant*, October 25, 1998.

Collins, David. "Thomas elected to tribal council while on probation for drug charges," *New London Day*, January 12, 1996.

In an interview with Lyn Bixby, Anthony Beltran denied saying that he was going to kill a white boy. "I said I was going to stab someone. That was it," Beltran told the *Courant*. "I was angry at the world, about my upbringing and poverty." The *Courant* also reported, "He further insisted he did not say anything to his victim as he left the courthouse." Both newspaper reporters, contacted this month, reiterated that he did.